Court House.   City Hall.   Birdseye View from Crescent Park   Michigan Trust Building   Post Office   Central High School St. Marks Church.
Grand Rapids.   Michigan.

GRAND RAPIDS, Mich.   River Front, East Side,

MONROE STREET, GRAND RAPIDS, MICH.   OTTAWA STREET, GRAND RAPIDS, MICH.

CAMPAU SQUARE, GRAND RAPIDS, MICH.   CAMPAU SQUARE, GRAND RAPIDS, MICH.

Heart&Soul

The Story of Grand Rapids Neighborhoods

Heart&Soul

The Story of Grand Rapids Neighborhoods

Linda Samuelson, Andrew Schrier, et al.

Foreword by
Arend D. Lubbers

Grand Rapids Area Council for the Humanities at the Grand Rapids Public Library
William B. Eerdmans Publishing Company

Heart & soul : the story of Grand Rapids neighborhoods / Linda Samuelson, Andrew Schrier, et al. ;
foreword by Arend D. Lubbers.
p. cm.
Includes bibliographical references and index.
ISBN 0-8028-3901-0 (alk. paper)
1. Grand Rapids (Mich.)--History. 2. Grand Rapids Region (Mich.)--History, Local. 3. Neighborhood—
Michigan—Grand Rapids—History. I. Title: Heart and soul. II. Samuelson, Linda. III. Schrier, Andrew. IV.
Grand Rapids Area Council for the Humanities.
F574.G7H4 2003
977.4'55--dc21
00-045325
Revised

Printed in the United States of America.

Printed by Gilson Graphics in Grand Rapids, Michigan.

For all neighbors in Grand Rapids,
past, present, and future.

Contents

SECTION I   **ORIGINAL NEIGHBORHOODS AND AMERICAN EXPANSION**

Time: Circa 100 B.C. to A.D. 1880
Topic: Archeology has shown that the history of Grand Rapids neighborhoods begins much earlier than the 19ᵗʰ century. Evidence suggests that people inhabited the area as early as the end of the Roman Empire. Indians, the Odawa in particular, lived along the Grand, undisturbed by Europeans until the beginning of the 19ᵗʰ century. After the War of 1812, however, missionaries and traders began to move into the Odawa villages. The missionaries and traders disagreed on how to deal with the Indians but one thing was for certain: Western expansion could not be halted and the days of the Indian were numbered. This expansion resulted in the creation of Grand Rapids and new neighborhoods.

SECTION II   WALKING NEIGHBORHOODS

Time: Circa 1840 – 1914

Topic: The removal of the Indians from the Grand River Valley coincided with the beginning of a mass immigration of millions of Europeans to America. The old frontier settlements along the Grand were soon replaced with many new walking neighborhoods. Dutch, German, Polish, and many other immigrants came to Grand Rapids from the mid-19th century until the beginning of World War I. The city became an intricate patchwork of different ethnic communities that primarily remained separate from the community at large and maintained their own, individual cultural heritages.

SECTION III TRANSPORTATION EXPANDS NEIGHBORHOODS

Time: Circa 1880–1960

Topic: Beginning in the 1880s, streetcars pushed the limits of Grand Rapids beyond the old walking neighborhoods. New "street-car suburbs" were created and allowed people a greater freedom of movement and more options in terms of residences, shops, places of work, and worship. Automobiles allowed people even more freedom of movement and by the late 1920s and early 1930s they had eclipsed the role of the streetcar altogether. People began to move out of the streetcar suburbs since the automobile and freeways provided nearly limitless possibilities.

POSTCARDS OF GRAND RAPIDS

SECTION IV   THE POSTWAR ERA

Time: 1960 to the present
Topic: Postwar transitions saw many residents moving out of the urban neighborhoods. Those remaining were left to deal with rising crime and neglect in their neighborhoods. Eventually neighborhood associations formed to battle the problems. Also, new people and businesses moved into the areas and have begun an effective urban revitalization movement. The future looks bright for the neighborhoods of Grand Rapids at the dawning of the 21ˢᵗ century.

Acknowledgements

This book would not have happened without Andy Schrier, who, at the start, was fresh out of Calvin College and possessed of an intuitive sense of the importance of neighborhood histories. His commitment to the project was evident throughout the one and a half years he worked conducting research, interviewing, and writing. More than 150 residents of Grand Rapids shared their memories and perceptions with him. Andy also recruited classmates Michelle Gundersen and Nate Bradford, who eagerly threw themselves into the work during the summer of 1999. Together they carved out a makeshift workspace in the dusty corners of the Public Documents area of the Grand Rapids Public Library. They worked on old computers donated by the City of Grand Rapids Community Development Office through the efforts of Bill Hooker, who valued this project as an opportunity to document important aspects of our urban communities from a unique perspective.

Lane Den Boer and Kevin Hommes contributed valuable research. MaryAnn Sabo found time in her own very busy schedule to meld many voices into one, through her skillful editing of raw material.

Calvin College and the staff of Heritage Hall deserve credit for sharing materials on the history of the Dutch in Grand Rapids. Dr. Henry Ippel and Dr. Herb Brinks provided answers to many questions about early Dutch life in the area.

Dr. Randal Jelks provided perspective on the formation and emergence of African American neighborhoods. Rev. Dennis Morrow, archivist of the Roman Catholic Diocese of Grand Rapids, shared his encyclopedic knowledge of people and places, past and present. Other writers and readers who collaborated in this production include Charles Honey, religion editor at *The Grand Rapids Press*; Dr. Michael Williams of Aquinas College, and individuals too numerous to name, who wrote or shared personal stories of their neighborhoods and cultural traditions.

The Grand Rapids Press, daily chronicler of our community's stories, was a valuable resource. Mike Lloyd, *Press* Editor, allowed us to use important information and photographs. Jim Starkey, *Press* photographer, deserves special mention for his willingness to dig through archived photos to find ones that fit particular needs.

The layout and design of a book of this magnitude proved complex. Aaron Phipps set the original style and produced the first segments of the book, while Steve Colthorp, Christine Sommerdyke, Sue Koppenol, Lisa Klynstra, and Walter Matzke contributed additional graphics work. Rebecca Near worked tirelessly checking all footnotes and photo credits through countless revisions, as did Ryan Noppen in preparing the Index after the book took shape. Diane Carroll snapped many hundreds of photos; Mary Isca Pirkola and Lorrie Menninga edited and proofed until the presses started to roll. Special appreciation is owed James and Peggy Falk of Falk Design for their talent, steadfastness, and perseverance in seeing this project through to completion.

Thanks to the unwavering vision and support of Bill Eerdmans, Jr., and Sandra DeGroot, William B. Eerdmans Publishing Company agreed to act as copublishers with the Grand Rapids Area Council for the Humanities, while graciously giving the Humanities Council full editorial control.

It is hard to express adequately our debt of gratitude to David Gilson of Gilson Graphics, whose level of confidence in the project matched our own enthusiasm; Gilson printed this book with a profound belief in future sales to offset his costs.

The Michigan Humanities Council has provided support to the Grand Rapids Humanities Council for almost three decades. The Steelcase Foundation, Grand Rapids Community Foundation, and the Sebastian Foundation were the first to believe this project was important, waiting patiently for the finished product. Meijer Inc., the Amway Foundation, the Frey Foundation, and the Dyer-Ives Foundation also provided funding. Dyer-Ives earmarked additional funds to ensure that copies of the book would be made available for use in the Grand Rapids Public Schools.

The taxpayers of the City of Grand Rapids deserve special acknowledgement for their financial support of the vast treasures of the Local History Department of the Grand Rapids Public Library. Few cities are fortunate to have collected and maintained such extensive archives, which were available for our research. City Historian Gordon Olson, Archivist Rebecca Mayne, and an ever-supportive and knowledgeable library staff—Betty Gibout, Karolee Hazlewood, Chris Byron, Martha Bloem, and Jennifer Morrison—assisted us ably, responding graciously to queries for information, source documents, and photographs.

M. Christine Byron and Thomas R. Wilson deserve special recognition for their great generosity in sharing their outstanding historical postcard collection.

Library Director Robert Raz and the Library Board of Commissioners were instrumental in forming an alliance midway through this project between the Grand Rapids Area Council for the Humanities and the Grand Rapids Public Library. This eased some of the burden of fund raising needed to bring the book to fruition.

Finally, the volunteer board of the Humanities Council gave this book its blessing, continued to believe in its eventual appearance, and never wavered in its conviction that *Heart and Soul* was a story worth telling. And worth waiting for.

Linda Samuelson
Project Director
Humanities Council at the Grand Rapids Public Library

HUMANITIES COUNCIL
GRAND RAPIDS PUBLIC LIBRARY

This project funded, in part, by

MICHIGAN HUMANITIES COUNCIL

Introduction

It is difficult to define a neighborhood. For some it may be the distance a twelve-year-old is allowed to go by bike. For others, it may be the block where everyone knows your name. It may be the distance one can reach out comfortably to borrow a cup of sugar or twenty dollars to tide you over until payday. It may be defined by the boundaries of the parish church, local school, census tract, or neighborhood association. For some it is a comfort zone, for others a danger zone. Usually there is an aspect of geography; frequently there is an aspect of socio-economic status or cultural identity.

People talk of their old neighborhoods with a sense of nostalgia. Neighborhoods can be evoked by a half-forgotten kitchen smell, the sound of an ice cream truck at dusk, the sight of a tree budding or losing its leaves, the remembrance of pick-up games in an alley or of the mom who passed out Popsicles or Band-Aids with abandon.

A neighborhood is a living thing, not just a random collection of streets and houses. Neighborhoods, it seems, are a lot like people. They have specific histories, distinctive appearances, attractive features, and problems that challenge those who know them best. In the course of preparing this book we have come to a realization that just as we can't know a person well without knowing his or her background, we can't know a neighborhood, or a city, without studying its past.

Seven years ago the Grand Rapids Area Council for the Humanities launched this neighborhood history, having forgotten the labor pains during the birth of its earlier book project, *Gathered at the River: Grand Rapids, Michigan, and Its People of Faith*, which enjoyed great community support and interest. From the beginning of this new project there were challenges.

Academically trained historical researchers were reluctant to start describing neighborhoods because of the lack of precise definitions. There was a fear that people would be disappointed to find their particular neighborhood or story left out, or relegated to a footnote. The scope of the project, we were told, was cumbersome, messy, might re-awaken ethnic or religious conflicts. Such caveats notwithstanding, the Humanities Council decided to proceed, believing that something of merit would emerge when the dust finally settled and the printer's ink dried.

In a throwaway, move-away society, it is my passionate belief that we must study and record our city's neighborhood histories. An awareness of local history gives city residents a sense of their urban roots and a way to understand often-dramatic change. It can form the basis for a deeper understanding and appreciation of our rich diversity. For residents of outlying communities, a history of Grand Rapids neighborhoods, told in the voice of those who know and love those neighborhoods, may create a realization that the city of Grand Rapids is the heart and soul of our wider metropolitan area.

Our community has a long, rich history. People who lived here before us contributed to what we enjoy today. From the Mound Builders to the People of the Three Fires. From pioneer families to succeeding immigrant waves. From abolitionists to suffragettes. From those who broke early racial barriers to those who still seek healthy, integrated neighborhoods. From those who ran mom and pop neighborhood businesses to contemporary entrepreneurs. From those who built trading posts and Victorian mansions to today's preservationists and neighborhood activists. These are the real-life people who are the heart and soul of this book. In telling their stories, in however abbreviated a way, we seek to honor their aspirations and dreams and emulate their desire to create a vibrant community along the Grand.

Linda Samuelson

Foreword

Once again the Grand Rapids Area Council for the Humanities has done the community a permanent favor by telling the story of our city from the perspective of neighborhoods. The Council's first literary gift to Grand Rapids was the book *Gathered at the River: Grand Rapids, Michigan, and Its People of Faith*, an important history of the city told through the prism of faith and religion. Both books focus on what the humanities are all about. They are histories of people as individuals and as part of the greater whole.

Gathered at the River is now the definitive history of how individuals of faith have organized themselves into church communities since Grand Rapids was a pioneer settlement in the early 19ᵗʰ century. This new book now records the history of the individuals and families who built their houses together and then made their neighborhoods home. Anyone who's ever lived in the city will find a piece of his own history written here.

Perhaps the ultimate success from this body, known as the Grand Rapids Area Council for the Humanities, is that they could bring a variety of individual writers together to write separate sections about Grand Rapids neighborhoods and make it work. Hidden away in the back room of the stacks at the Grand Rapids Public Library, Humanities Council Director Linda Samuelson and her "kids," as she called her writing team of new college graduates, got the job done. Yet as both the seer and overseer of this challenging project, Linda Samuelson is the one who deserves credit for a book that flows with the seamlessness of a single author.

One clear strength of the several writers has to be the depth and detail of information. The intimidating notes and index alone testify to the seriousness of their collaborative research. First the writers went into different neighborhoods and showed the residents how to record historical information. They then returned to conduct 150 separate interviews — the real "heart and soul" of this book.

Based on this primary research as well as their extensive background readings, the several writers' single thesis seems to be that the neighborhoods, so vital to the families who lived there, have been more fluid than static. As Linda Samuelson put it, "Neighborhoods are never used up."

This city's neighborhoods began changing when the first white Europeans started replacing the Indian settlements on the Grand River. In the next century, Henry Ford's technology also fueled a shifting of established neighborhoods from downtown outwards toward the suburbs.

Piece by fascinating piece, this book documents the history of Grand Rapids neighborhoods starting with the mysterious Mound Builders who vanished in A.D. 900. In the 1750s, the tribe of Odawas established the next neighborhood in the truest sense of the word. The Native Americans shared all the fruits of their hunting and fishing with the whole community. But when the Chicago Treaty of 1825 sent new Americans into the Michigan Territory to stake out their own piece of land, the Indian neighborhoods were doomed.

The early individualists, like wily Louis Campau and his rival Lucius Lyon, are documented, as are the saintly men like the Catholic priest Father Baraga, who fought for the rights of the Indians. Among the many wonderful photographs in this book are the comparison pictures depicting street scenes then and now, reminding the reader, for instance, that Monroe was once Canal Street. Similarly, the downtown area that Charles Belknap referred to as "Shantytown" in his history — the first neighborhood for many immigrant families — is now known as Heartside.

And while Grand Rapids is thought of as a Dutch community, this book makes it clear that this city blossomed into America's "Furniture Capital," thanks to the skills of immigrants from many countries besides Holland. Clustering into their own ethnic neighborhoods as they arrived were families from Ireland, Poland, Germany, Lithuania, Italy, Scandinavia, Greece, Syria, Lebanon, and Iraq. Likewise, African-Americans and Jewish families moved into the city, and they, too, settled into neighborhoods where their relatives and friends already lived.

The third section of the book focuses on specific neighborhoods such as Creston, North Park, and Eastown. Here's where the effects of transportation on neighborhoods are most thoroughly described. Two chapter headings say it all — "The Expressway Cometh" and "A Decaying Downtown, but Burgeoning 'Burbs." The last section records the racial strife in the 60s and 70s, the white flight to the suburbs, and the federal government's coming to help decaying neighborhoods.

The book also updates the many faith-based programs supporting city neighborhoods, such as the Inner City Christian Federation and Habitat for Humanity. The writers also credit the many active neighborhood associations, such as Heritage Hill, Baxter, Coit, and Roosevelt, for preserving the "heart and soul" of their neighborhoods.

To know Grand Rapids and to understand Grand Rapids, a reading of *Heart & Soul: The Story of Grand Rapids Neighborhoods* is a requirement. It is a well-compiled, well-written history and also a current description and analysis of the city's neighborhoods. While reading it, one feels carried along in the stream of Grand Rapids history and life, anticipating with hope that the current will carry the city to a successful future.

Arend D. Lubbers
President Emeritus
Grand Valley State University

I

Original Neighborhoods and American Expansion

The Oldest Neighborhood

"I never want to leave this country; all my relatives are lying here in the ground, and when I fall to pieces I am going to fall to pieces here."
Shunkaha Napin (Wolf Necklace)[1]

Muddy ruts lead to a corrugated tin shack that wears a NO TRESPASSING sign in unforgiving scarlet letters. The whir of machinery inside the old oil pumphouse, which stands barely out of sight from Indian Mounds Drive on Grand Rapids' Southwest Side, interrupts the harmony of bird songs.

Trucks barreling along Interstate 196 fill the air with their searing horns. In the distance, the beautiful stretch of woods adjacent to the Grand River is pierced by the freeway, its high banks marching across the horizon, hemming everything in like a wall that threatens to shut out all the light.

Lew Burroughs, an American Indian of Potawotami heritage, can go nowhere on this continent without constant reminders of the civilization that overran the natural beauty of the land. He has visited many places around the world and he carries a leather pouch containing soil from all of them. On a chilly November day in the last year of the 1900s, he brings some faraway soil as well as the tobacco from his peace pipe that he spreads around the base of the first mound he comes upon.

The Norton Mounds are remnants of the oldest known civilization to have populated this part of what we now know as West Michigan and Grand Rapids. Pinched between a road and a freeway, the mounds have barely escaped destruction. With reverence, Burroughs climbs the highest of the four visible mounds. He glares at an abandoned plastic bucket and uncovers a hole on the top of the mound.

"An animal knew I was coming," he laughs as he places his gift of soil into the vacant animal lodge and covers it with leaves.

At the beginning of a new millennium, three major civilizations that inhabited this region are represented: the mounds represent the extinct Hopewell people, Burroughs speaks for the American Indians, and the din of the freeway for today's world.

To Burroughs, all of the inhabitants dating back over the past three millennia have simply been visitors. The true host: the land.

FIGURES 1, 2, 3 **The Norton Indian Mounds just east of Indian Mounds Drive, southwest of Grand Rapids, along with artifacts recovered from the mounds**

The name Hopewell, immortalized by archaeologists because of an Ohio farmer whose land contained ancient mounds, applies to an unknown civilization of amazing scale.[2]

The incomprehensible millennium during which the Hopewells ruled the trading routes of an empire dwarfs the past 200-plus years that the United States has dominated this land. It seems unfitting to name an entire race and complex civilization of powerful traders after a farmer who knew nothing of the people who cultivated his land centuries before his existence.

However, attributing such a name to this fascinating group of people is almost a necessity since the Hopewell came to the Great Lakes around 100 B.C. and mysteriously disappeared between 500 and 900 A.D. without leaving a written record.[3]

The diverse array of mounds that have puzzled American Indians and professional archaeologists alike for centuries are all that remain of the vast empire that once stretched from the Gulf of Mexico to the Great Lakes, and from the Appalachian Mountains to the Great Plains.[4]

As many as 46 mounds once stood as symbols of the first known neighborhoods to exist at the rapids of the Grand River. Unfortunately, many inhabitants of Grand Rapids in the 19th century did not appreciate or understand the historical or cultural value of the mounds. Rather, they saw them as obstacles to paving roads and erecting buildings on the west side of the river.[5]

This historical ignorance was not confined to Grand Rapids. Across the Hopewells' former territory, their sacred mounds have been covered with railroads, expressways, buildings, and even military bases.

Increased interest in the puzzling mounds that pepper 21 present-day states in the United States, have resulted in the development of a complicated mythological concept of the mound builders. This myth lumped at least three distinct mound building peoples into one category.[6]

Quite possibly, the people did not live near the mounds. The best archaeological theories suggest multiple Hopewell villages came together for a special mound building ceremony. The frequency and length of these meetings is uncertain, but the mounds likely took a few hundred people a month or more to build.

The Hopewells looked forward to these communal gatherings. In addition to mound building, many events took place during this time: weddings, feasts, courting, business transactions, worshipping, storytelling, and exchange of news. During the rest of the year, they lived as hunters, gatherers, and farmers in large wooden lodges with bark roofs.[7]

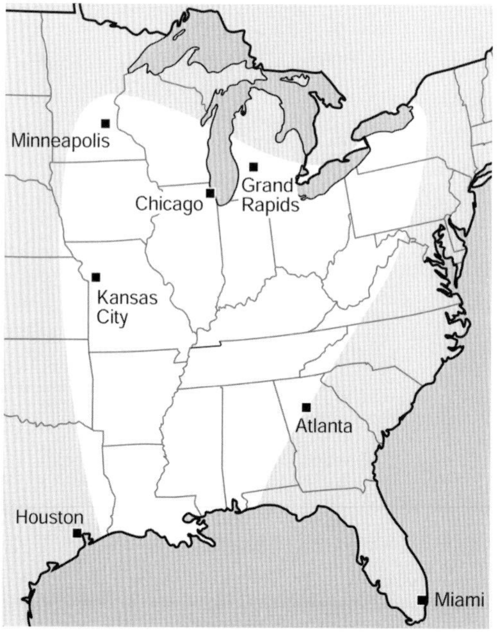

It is believed that the ancients built these mounds for the purpose of burying their dead. They took the earth from the area around the mound and carried basketfuls to the center and tamped the dirt into a hardened surface. When the mound reached its peak, they built a small house on the summit. After the completion, they conducted burial ceremonies using wooden crypts for cremated remains of their dead. Privileged individuals of a higher caste obtained the luxury of a flesh burial in a crypt

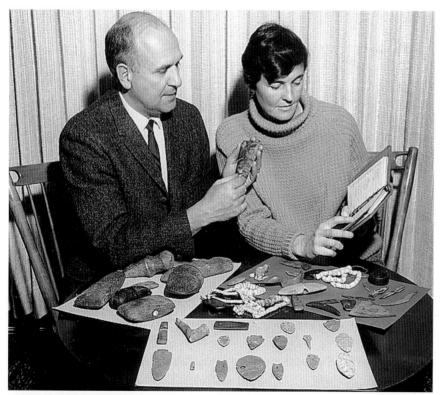

FIGURE 4 **Hugh and Nancy Lilly, members of the Grand Rapids Museum Association, one of the sponsors of the Norton Mounds excavation, review artifacts of the excavation.**

FIGURE 5 **The area in white shows the region where the Hopewell Indians flourished in river-valley settings.**

surrounded by a wealth of ceremonial objects. These objects ranged from pearl necklaces, copper trinkets, and pipes, to silver, obsidian, flint, and mica minerals. Because of the enormous amount of burial items, archaeologists believe that certain Hopewells in each village dedicated their livelihoods to making these ceremonial trinkets and grave articles for burial in the mounds.[8]

Two distinct groups of mounds exist near Grand Rapids: the Converse Mounds on the west side of the river between Bridge and Wealthy Streets, and the Norton Mounds on the east side of the river, just below the city. Charles Belknap, an early resident and a writer of Grand Rapids history, reported finding in the 1850s many objects in the remains of the Converse Mounds such as flint arrowheads, human remains, earthen vases, clay pottery, bears' teeth, pipes, copper, silver, stone trinkets, and clamshells.[9] But the Converse Mounds were destroyed during the latter half of the 19th century by the expanding city of Grand Rapids. The mounds were leveled and their contents largely unrecorded.

In 1874, backyard archaeologist Wright L. Coffinberry excavated many of the Converse Mounds that the city had not yet destroyed, discovering many similar objects. The mounds at the rapids ranged from two to 15 feet in height, and from 10 to 100 feet in diameter.[10] He concluded that close to one-third of the mounds excavated had originally existed for burial purposes.[11]

The remaining mound group, the Norton Mounds, are located just south of the city, between the east river bank and Interstate 196. Several groups have excavated the Norton Mounds, but they remain basically intact, although currently overgrown, littered with trash and beer cans. Perhaps the largest scare to those in favor of preserving the mounds came in 1962, when plans for Interstate 196 would have necessitated flattening the mounds. The work of W. D. Frankforter, former director of the Grand Rapids Public Museum, caused planners to detour Interstate 196 around the mounds. Other groups formed in following years, such as Friends of the Norton Mounds and the Norton Mounds Advisory Committee. They have advocated for the need for better preservation of the mounds as a historical site.[12]

Many American Indians in West Michigan feel strongly that the Norton Mounds should not be made into a public place. After all, it is a sacred place of burial and antiquity. But because of apathy and controversy, to date no further steps have been taken to acknowledge the Norton Mounds as a historical or sacred site.

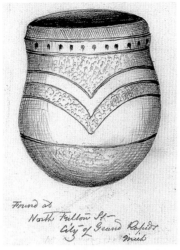

FIGURE 6 **Light brown, unburnt clay-colored pot**

FIGURE 7 **Wright Coffinberry**

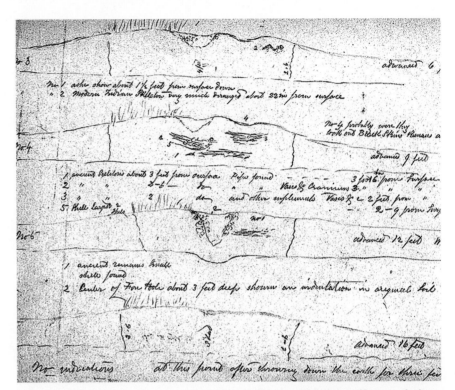

FIGURE 8 **This record of an excavation of an Indian mound listing artifacts and where they were found in the mound was drawn by Thomas W. Porter.**

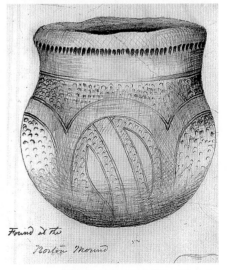

FIGURE 9 **Artifact from an Indian mound**

The Last of the Mound Builders?

To archaeologists, the mystery of the mound builders has proven somewhat divisive and incendiary.

As they pushed westward in the 19th century, Americans continued to discover intriguing earthworks, some built in the shape of animals and some astoundingly impressive in size. The inquisitive settlers associated the mounds with the Native American populations still living, but the Indians bore no clues to the mystery of the mounds, believing them remnants of a long-extinct race. As a result of the confusion, many developed theories concerning the mound builders, often associating all of the ancient earthworks with one legendary race of people who established a powerful empire across the continent.

One primitive archaeologist offered a solution that was perhaps crucial in the formation of this legend. In 1852, the Smithsonian rejected William Pidgeon's manuscript, but it was published by a less intellectual institution in 1858. The book became a big seller with the general population, and later with archaeologists themselves. Pidgeon claimed that while excavating mounds in the Mississippi River Valley, he befriended an old Indian named Decoodah, whose lineage extended to the extinct race of mound builders. Decoodah shared many traditions, stories, and lost secrets with Pidgeon, who reported everything in his book, relating them to his excavations. Reportedly, Decoodah was the last prophet of the Elk Nation, one of several nations who shared a religion and customs, yet vied against each other for power. A civil war between the nations destroyed them.

So convincingly written was Pidgeon's legend of Decoodah, and so extensive the romanticism, that it became accepted as gospel among archaeologists in the late 19th century. No one challenged Pidgeon's writings, until 1884, when an archaeologist named T. H. Lewis began to notice a pattern of fabrication. Lewis first noticed certain mounds in Minnesota that were not as Pidgeon had described them. This pattern of inaccuracy fit with other mounds reportedly excavated by Pidgeon. Lewis published his findings in 1886, the first established break from Pidgeon's theories.

Although many Americans believed in Decoodah and the Elk Nation, it is obvious from Lewis' work that Pidgeon fabricated much of his archaeological data. It is impossible to determine whether Decoodah himself is fictional, but the mere fact that Pidgeon's other data is false, as well as the extreme unlikeliness of a sole remaining member of the mound building race, leads to the conclusion that Pidgeon never encountered the last prophet of the Elk Nation.[1]

While standing among the cluster of mounds, it is difficult to fill in the gaps and imagine an ancient people who lived right on that spot thousands of years ago. Archaeologists may continue to hypothesize about these ancients, but the tool of imagination remains perhaps the best way to capture the soul of the place and the spirit of its history.

Though it remains impossible to determine the exact type of neighborhood that existed 2,000 years ago on the banks of the Grand River, we know this: a civilization of mound-building people thrived here as an outpost of a great trading empire. In other parts of the world at this time Christ was born, the Roman Empire rose and fell, the Byzantine Empire began, the Vikings started their sweep across Europe, and the Mayan Empire flourished in Mexico. These events add perspective to how long neighborhoods have existed at the rapids in the Grand River Valley. While the beginning of Grand Rapids is often tied to Louis Campau's settlement in 1827, in reality, the Hopewells lived here long before Campau's father country of France even formed in Europe.

And although whites usually view the mound builders as an extinct people, American Indians who followed the Hopewell hold a completely different perspective. They view themselves as descendants of the Hopewell, connected by a common history. This point is extremely difficult for whites to grasp from an archaeological standpoint without insight into Indian culture and oral tradition.[13]

FIGURE 10 **Thomas W. Porter**

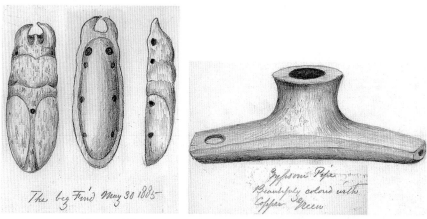

FIGURES 11, 12 **Thomas W. Porter's drawings of copper beetle and bone pipe found in mounds**

The Arrival of the Odawas

"One does not sell the earth on which the people walk."
Tashunka Witko (Crazy Horse)[14]

The survivors of the great battle had withdrawn to the bank of the river to wash their wounds and mourn for the fallen. The old Odawa warrior chief looked behind him to the field where the struggle took lives of both friend and foe. It was a brief and bloody conflict and many brave Odawas lost their lives in the victory over the Mushcodesh, who had once ruled proudly over this entire river valley.

The chief turned to the north, facing his people's old homeland. Their allies, the Potawotami and Ojibwe, formed a group known as the People of the Three Fires, or the Anishnabek. The long-time enemies of the Anishnabek, the Iroquois, now threatened the old homeland of the Odawa. A new race of white people from a far-off land had pushed the

FIGURE 13 **This longhouse is similar to those the Odawas built.**

sities. The river would yield fish, as well as provide transportation for their birch bark canoes. Some of the families would establish villages on the banks of the river, near the battlefield, and others would spread out across the region. Their name, Odawa, meaning "traders," defined their existence. From their vantage point on such a large river, the Odawa would become the middlemen of the trading route between the whites in Detroit and the other Indian tribes around them.

As he gazed south, the chief noticed several small, unnatural hills dotting the landscape all along the west river bank. Puzzled, he walked to the nearest mound and examined it. The mound was unusually steep, rising high off the ground. The old chief knew that some peoples buried their dead under huge earthen mounds, though he had never seen any until now.

Iroquois west, crowding the hunting grounds of the Odawa. Forced out of their intricate trading empire in Canada, the Odawa pushed south into the land of Michigan searching for new hunting and fishing grounds.

They found fertile land with plentiful game in the north at Mackinac Island, but trader Antoine de Cadillac invited all of the Indians of the area to live near Detroit and trade with him. In response to this offer, many of the Odawas and some of their allies moved farther south into Michigan.

Turning his gaze back to the river, the Odawa chief was pleased. This land would be ideal for the settling of his Odawa people. The large river flowed through a series of rapids that ended at his feet. The soil would be good for planting crops, and the woodland around them would yield plentiful quantities of game and other neces-

Though the chief knew not who had built the mounds, he knew that they were connected to the Odawas in the great circle of their history. He respected these mounds as the resting place of his ancestors, though he knew little about them.

The Odawa chief thanked the Great Spirit for blessing his people. At last they would be able to settle permanently and establish themselves among the surrounding nations. No longer would the Iroquois threaten them.

Yet his joy was mixed with foreboding. The people of the Great Spirit had existed long in this land, but the emergence of the new white race from a far-off land caused the Indian people to forget their calling to the Great Spirit. The upset in balance caused war, strife, and disease. The availability of alcohol added to the problems.

New technology caused a materialism that the red people did not know before. The chief solemnly wondered if the coming of the white people would be the end of this world and the beginning of another.[15]

The Odawas' New Home

In Odawa legend, the first landing party of Odawas to arrive in Michigan witnessed the hostility of the Mushcodesh who already lived there.[16] The larger party of Mushcodesh insulted and fired on the Odawa warriors who sought to land their canoes and establish a peaceful relationship with the inhabitants. Infuriated, the Odawas returned with a large war party and defeated the Mushcodesh. Thus began the bloody,

FIGURE 14 **Indians cut bark for a canoe.**

yet brief relationship between the Mushcodesh and the Odawa. Aided by guns from their French trading partners, the Odawas gradually pushed the less technologically advanced Mushcodesh out of the region and secured it for themselves.[17]

As the Odawa pushed south into Michigan, they established themselves on the west bank of what came to be known as the Grand River, developing two distinct communities around 1740 A.D. The southern village formed southwest of where the battle with the Mushcodesh took place, near the current intersection of Watson Street and National Avenue SW. Soon after, a northern village grew along the west bank of the river around present day Bridge Street.[18] Other Odawa villages were located on the Grand River, but these two remained cultural centers for the Odawas of the region.

Like many American Indian tribes, the Odawa understood the value of a neighborhood in a way that is difficult to grasp in our society. Indian life demanded that each participant of the community carry his own weight. The Odawa relied on hunting, fishing, gathering and agriculture for their food supply. They grew corn — a necessary ingredient for fry bread and other staple foods. Their methods of preservation allowed them to keep meat, fish, and produce all winter long.[19]

Swallowed by a Great Fish

Some Anishnabek legends closely resemble stories from Judeo-Christian sources. These stories are of great interest, as they are passed down through generations of Indians. Isolated from Europe and Israel, they had no knowledge of the Bible or the Torah. These legends, which grew independently out of Indian tradition and history, display much of Indian culture and morals.

One such story bears resemblance to the Old Testament story of Jonah and the whale.

A great fish in some lake had terrorized the Odawa people. While canoeing on the lake, people would be swallowed whole, canoe and all. After losing many of his tribesmen to this great fish, Nenawbohzoo, the great Indian trickster, made up his mind to solve the problem. He set out on this lake with his canoe, singing songs that dared the terrible fish to attack him. Eventually the fish swallowed Nenawbohzoo and his canoe. But Nenawbohzoo was prepared for this. Once inside the fish, he drew his weapons and wounded the fish so badly that it beached itself and died. Nenawbohzoo then climbed out of the fish that would terrorize his people no more.[1]

FIGURE 15 **Summer camp, on the east side of the Grand River, looks toward the Baptist Mission on the West Side.**

The concept of kinship among the Odawas pulled the villages together. Not only did the Odawas view the Potawotamies and the Ojibwes as brothers, but they maintained a strong sense of family ties within their own villages. Outside every family's longhouse, a totem pole marked the clan lineage of the family. This system insured that every family identified with the major clan of the village.[20]

Families also provided a system for instructing children in the morals of the tribe. The Odawa worshipped the Great Spirit, Ketchimatnedo, who they believed created the earth, people, and animals.[21] They openly worshipped him through singing and dancing around a beating drum, but also served him by following his moral standards.[22] The Odawa believed that the sun and moon were the Great Spirit's eyes through which he watched his people.[23] Therefore, they conducted their lives by living according to high standards of honesty and punctuality. The morality of Indian society caused peace and safety to reign in the Indian villages. Even at night, the Indians feared no vandalism or theft.[24]

During the winter, the community separated into small family groups fanning out across Odawa territory to trap and hunt. It was easier for the Indians to support smaller groups during the harsh winter. Family ties also grew much closer during this time of need and isolation, when they lived in smaller wigwams covered with reed mats and bark. These could be moved often as the Indians trapped, hunted, and cured their hides for the spring trading.[25]

The families returned to the village in the spring, their canoes loaded with venison, sugar, furs, bear meat and oil, and honey. Needing the community for large-scale tasks of agriculture, they began to plant corn, potatoes, and vegetables. During the summer the community lived in large longhouses, each housing up to nine families in a 130-by-24-foot area.[26] Framed with saplings and long wooden poles, the house was covered with bark. With two floors on either side running the length of the longhouse, each family could have its own defined area. Typically, the families in a longhouse were all related within their clan. Occasionally during the spring, the Odawas ventured far from home to trade the furs they had collected over the long winter months.

The strong sense of community complemented their value of respect for the individual. Each Odawa was judged for his own achievements and maintained a basic level of respect for other members of the community.[27] Males in Odawa society, for instance, enjoyed a great deal of social mobility. Each man had equal opportunity to rise to the level of a respected warrior or chief, regardless of birth status.[28]

In Odawa society the village shared all material wealth and any able-bodied individuals worked diligently for the good of the whole.[29] This communal connection reached much deeper than

A Great Flood Threatens Mankind

Nenawbohzoo had a faithful black wolf that accompanied him as his hunting dog. One day, the great spirit of the sea grew jealous of Nenawbohzoo's wolf, and killed it. He then served the wolf at a feast for all sorts of water spirits. This made Nenawbohzoo fiercely angry, and he decided to take revenge on the sea god.

He journeyed to a deserted beach where he knew the sea spirits often came out of the water to sun themselves. Then Nenawbohzoo, who could change himself into any human, animal, or object that he desired, assumed the shape of an old wooden stump. Suspecting no danger, the water spirits, including the sea god, came on shore and dozed. Seeing his chance, Nenawbohzoo snuck over to the sea god and shot an arrow through his heart, killing him. The other sea spirits awoke and furiously chased the Indian. As mountains of water, they chased him all over the earth until there was no earth left for him to run to. When the earth was almost entirely covered with water, Nenawbohzoo commanded a great canoe to appear. He entered the canoe, saving several animals who fled from the flood along with him.

He sent a beaver to find how deep the water was, but the beaver drowned. Nenawbohzoo revived the beaver and sent a muskrat to find the bottom. The muskrat also drowned, but not before reaching the bottom and tearing off a chunk of earth in its paws. After reviving the muskrat, Nenawbohzoo tied the earth around the neck of a raven and sent it into the air. After the raven flew back and forth over the water, it began to recede and the earth was restored.[1]

FIGURE 16 **A longhouse could hold up to nine families.**

9

Biological Warfare Against the Indians

One of the greatest problems that the Indians encountered after contact with Europeans was disease. Epidemics, most notably smallpox, devastated and even wiped out entire Indian villages. As their bodies were not accustomed to European bacteria and viruses, the Indians succumbed to the foreign toxins.

Oral tradition among the Odawa tells a story that took place before Pontiac's war against the British, at which time the Odawa were allied with the French. A British man from Montreal sold a box to an Odawa Indian, instructing him not to open the box until he arrived at his home. Dying of curiosity, the Indian traveled the great distance to his home at L'Arbor Croche, the largest Odawa village in Michigan. Once home, he opened the box to find a smaller tin within. He opened this tin to find another smaller tin, and yet another smaller tin after that. Finally, he opened the smallest tin, finding nothing but a few moldy particles. The elders of the village inspected these particles, not knowing what to make of the parcel. Soon, however, smallpox ravaged the entire village, killing large numbers of the Odawa and spreading throughout the countryside. The foreign disease killed all who caught it. The Indians realized much too late that the British intended the box to infect the Odawa population and destroy them.[1]

interpersonal relationships. Similar to most Native American tribes, the Odawa revered nature and believed in a circle of life in which humans, animals, plants, and everything on earth participated. The Indians reverently observed ceremonial obligations in which they paid their respects to these elements of nature. When the Indians took from nature, they did so with respect, thanksgiving, and efficiency and without wastefulness or greed.

FIGURE 18 **Pontiac**

The Odawa villages, therefore, embodied a deep understanding of neighborhood identity on several levels. Along with an interpersonal connection, the Odawas sustained interaction with the land and environment in which they existed. They treated each other and nature with incredible esteem. As a result, the Odawa villages maintained a balance of community fellowship and inter-dependency that defines neighborhood in its purest form.

Pontiac's Visit

More than 3,000 Odawas had gathered between the villages on the Grand River for the council to be held that spring evening. The visitor, a great Odawa warrior named Pontiac, felt the warmth of the hospitality; everywhere the visitor went he was treated with respect and honor. Many came forward and gave him gifts of food or trinkets. The youths whispered about him as he passed, proudly telling others of his importance. The feast ensued, as well as dancing, music, and storytelling. The visitor honored a group of warriors who had gathered around a fire telling war exploits. They eagerly anticipated the visitor's turn, listening closely as the pipe passed to him and he told a captivating tale from his vast repertoire.

After nightfall, the Anishnabek chiefs and warriors gathered in a small valley, so that all could hear and be heard. They circled around a fire, lit their pipes, and smoked for quite awhile in silence. Eventually one of the Odawa chiefs began the debate. Others joined in, resulting in an outpouring of articulate speeches until all sides of the matter had been presented, but no solution arrived at.

FIGURE 17 **An Odawa returns from a successful hunt.**

FIGURE 19 **Winter hunting was done in smaller groups among the Odawa.**

Sweat Lodge

Large pieces of bark provided a covering over the skeleton of saplings, trapping the heat and moisture inside the sweat lodge. The Odawa braves removed their clothes, placing them by the entrance as they entered the ceremonial wigwam. They sat in a circle as a youth used tongs to move the last of three hot stones into place. One man lit a peace pipe as the chief began to drip water onto the stones, uttering a solemn prayer as the ceremony commenced. The hissing steam rolled forth from the stones, releasing energy stored up from roasting in hot coals for three days. Trapped steam clouded the lodge, rendering their eyesight useless. One man wiped the dripping sweat from his brow and passed the pipe. The chief continued to utter prayers and drip water on the stones, as the men purified themselves by breathing deeply and meditating.

The chief began to call on the animals to show themselves. One man felt the wings of an eagle brush against his face. He heard the scream of an owl, the howl of a wolf, and felt the stomp of buffalo hooves. A mother deer and a fawn walked calmly in front of him, and he reached out his hand and touched the fawn's soft fur. One by one, the chief called and blessed all the good animals, each of whom were so important to the cycle of life.

The Odawas emerged from the tent exhausted; all those invited to attend the sweat lodge had to fast for at least a day. Not only was the ceremony physically draining, but it required an immense amount of mental concentration as well. The sweat lodge was a very important ritual for the Odawa, allowing them to express their appreciation for nature.[1]

Finally, the visitor rose to speak. All eyes focused on the honored guest. He spoke from the heart, and his eloquent delivery exposed the deep passions and emotions of a troubled soul. The fire behind him seemed to grow ever larger as his words shook the hearts and minds of every person present.

> "Drive the white race back to the ocean from whence they came!"[30]
>
> Pontiac

He spoke of the injustices of the British, and the contempt with which they treated all Indians. If the Indians could not stop the British, the British would take over their land, just as they had done to the French. The Odawa homes on the Grand River and across all of Michigan would be desecrated by the British invaders. The Odawas would be driven into the lake and their communities in this valley shattered forever. The French, on the other hand, treated the Indians with respect. The orator then displayed a fine belt of wampum, given from the great Father of France, as a promise to help the Indians in their quest to push the British back to the east. He appealed to the pride of the Odawas, asking them to join him and his confederacy of Indian tribes as they attacked the British and laid siege to Detroit. Of those who heard the visitor speak, not a soul remained who did not support the cause. Their homes on the river were too precious to give up.

Many families split apart the following morning as the warriors left on their quest with the great Odawa chief Pontiac. The visiting women and children withdrew to their homes, and the two Odawa villages on the Grand River lay quietly, waiting for their warriors to return.

Red Meets White

A white traveler named William Fitzgerald stood on Prospect Hill on the east side of the river, overlooking the entire Grand River Valley. Surrounded by Odawas, he predicted that in less than 100 years from that time, white man's culture and civilization would sprawl over the entire valley.[31] Fitzgerald's visit came in 1748, just a few years after the Odawa moved to the Grand River Valley.

Though it is not certain whether the story of Fitzgerald is fact rather than legend, such a message undoubtedly would have left a profound impact upon the Odawa.

FIGURE 20 **Indians parade down Monroe Avenue as part of Buffalo Bill Cody's Wild West Show.**

Fitzgerald's message was an omen of invasion to the Odawa, striking fear into their hearts. Fitzgerald's prediction of the destruction of their newly established neighborhoods could have played a significant role in influencing the Odawas to fight with Pontiac against the British 15 years later.

In April 1761, Pontiac visited the Odawa villages on the Grand River in his campaign to unite the Great Lakes Indian tribes into a confederacy to destroy the British influence in the area.[32] Many of the warriors from the villages at the rapids joined Pontiac's cause. Though they fought against a far-off enemy, they

FIGURE 21 **Tecumseh**

defended their beloved homes against a power that seemed far more brutal than their French trading partners. In 1763, he led these tribes, including a strong contingent of the Anishnabek brotherhood, against the white forts in Michigan, now controlled by the British after the French and Indian War. After a series of cunning victories, the Indians were stranded as the French reneged on their promise to help Pontiac and his supporters. The rebellion failed in its attack on Detroit, causing the confederacy to disband.[33]

Pontiac's defeat ushered in a new era of struggle for the neighborhoods in Grand Rapids, whose population had risen comfortably to around 200 to 300 people. Although Pontiac's attack failed, the ferocity of the Indians convinced the British government to restrict the colonies' settlement west of the Appalachian Mountains. However, the hope that Britain could contain the expansion of its colony began to fade when America won its independence in 1783.[34] The newly formed United States government organized the western territories, including Michigan, for settlement in the Northwest Ordinance of 1787.

It became apparent that they would have to fight to maintain their thriving center of trade and their cherished hunting and fishing grounds. They had worked hard to prosper here and were not about to have their land wrested from their hands by whites who fought under any flag. Building

FIGURE 22 **This painting depicts Indians shooting the rapids in the Grand River.**

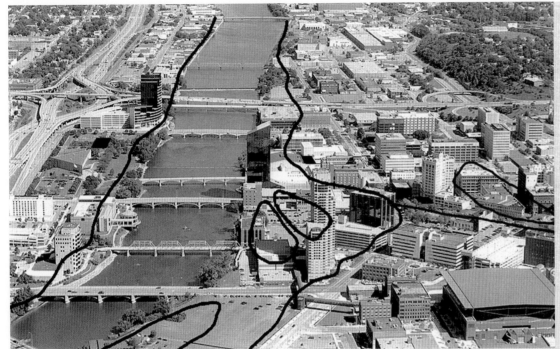

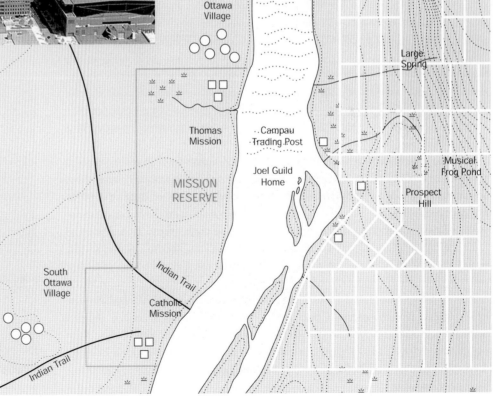

FIGURES 23, 24 **To get a better perspective on how wide the river used to be at Pearl Street, the old river boundaries have been overlaid on the 1997 aerial photo of Grand Rapids. The Amway Grand Plaza Hotel tower stands on reclaimed land in the old riverbed.**

Joel Guild built a home on land now occupied by the McKay Tower. A sketch of his house is pictured on page 16. See also page 40.

The map approximates the topographical features of downtown Grand Rapids during the 1830s. Each dashed contour line represents about ten feet of elevation change. A cross section elevation map at Pearl Street can be seen on page 47 showing how much land was moved when Prospect Hill was razed and the channels were filled in. For a different view of early downtown, see page 35.

on Pontiac's example, the Shawnee brothers Tecumseh and Tenskwatawa the Prophet organized a massive Indian confederacy, including tribes from the Gulf of Mexico to Michigan. Their unlikely birth as two-thirds of triplets, as well as their fiery speeches, qualified them as natural leaders.[35]

Many tribes, including the Odawa and Potawotami, sent warriors to Prophetstown, Indiana, in 1807, where Tecumseh's forces prepared for war against the Americans. As American General William Henry Harrison's forces drew close to the Indian army, the Indians decided to attack Harrison, against the orders of their absent leader Tecumseh. Harrison then counterattacked, annihilating Prophetstown and disbanding the army of Indians.[36] Desperation set in for the Indians, who realized that even a powerful confederacy of many tribes could not defeat the ever-expanding Americans.

Indians placed their hope in British restriction of American expansion and supported the British over the Americans as the War of 1812 drew near. The confederacy reunited, following Tecumseh and joining with the British in the War of 1812.[37] The Odawas at the Grand River sent many warriors to join Tecumseh, who fought mostly to protect British Canada from American invasion. At first, Tecumseh's forces succeeded, taking back

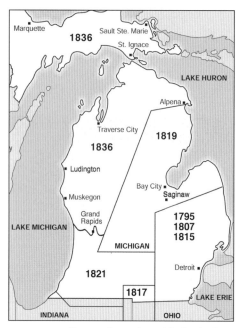

FIGURE 25 **Dates of treaties with the Indians show the land they lost piecemeal.**

many forts such as Detroit and Mackinac, and securing much of the region from the Americans. However, American Oliver Hazard Perry established naval control over the Great Lakes in 1813, cutting many of the British supply lines and eliminating the land superiority of the British and their Indian allies. Tecumseh's men covered the British as they hastily retreated into Canada. Tecumseh himself was killed at the Battle of the Thames in Ontario and the confederacy of Indians fell apart after his death.[38] From this point on, the Odawas would fight no longer.

America's victory over Britain in the War of 1812 solidified control over the territories west of the Allegheny Mountains and north of the Ohio River, beginning an era that changed life on the Grand River for the Odawa forever. As American colonists spilled west into unsettled territory, the American government remained under pressure to protect its citizens by securing land for their expansion. The American government responded by forcing the Indians to the negotiating table, resulting in a series of treaties nationwide.

The American government disguised its land hunger by proclaiming Indian removal as beneficial to the indigenous peoples. Theoretically, relocating Indian tribes west of the Mississippi would separate them from the whiskey and deception that white traders brought. Removal from this amoral atmosphere would allow the Indians to either enjoy themselves in separation from white culture or give them time to assimilate.

While proclaiming these advantages for the Indians, in truth, whites sought simply to clear Indian land for their own use.[39] The deception became multifaceted. In their determination to relocate the Indians west of the Mississippi River, American officials employed a multitude of devious tactics to make the Indians sign treaties that favored American policy. On several occasions, American officials bribed or slipped large amounts of whiskey to the Indian negotiators before signing a treaty. Many times, the Indians did not even understand what kind of terms they had agreed to, due to deliberate intoxication by the whites or unexplained sections of the treaty.[40]

The first treaty to have a major effect on the neighborhoods at Grand Rapids was the Chicago Treaty of 1821. This treaty ceded all Indian land south of the Grand River to the United States, while leaving the northern lands to the Indians. In addition, it gave the Americans one square mile north of the river, near Indian land, for the purpose of a mission. The treaty allocated an annual payment to the Indians forever, as well as funds for a blacksmith shop, a school, and other elements of "civilization" on this land. Michigan's governor Lewis Cass located the site for the mission on the west bank of the Grand River, near present day Bridge Street and Scribner Avenue.[41]

This treaty immediately began to affect the Odawas of the Grand River Valley. First, hunting grounds to the south of the river no longer belonged to the Odawa. For awhile, they continued to hunt there in spite of the treaty, but the influx of whites into the area seemed to happen overnight. Also, logging companies, speculators, and traders infiltrated the lands north of the Grand River in ever-increasing numbers. To the Odawa villages at the rapids, it appeared as though the whites would overrun them in a matter of years. Finally, the establishment of the mission within the bounds of the treaty spelled subjugation for the Odawa. The mission, along with its white religion, customs, buildings, and people, interrupted the peaceful northern village. Although unaware of how it would affect the village in the long term, the mission marked the beginning of the end of Odawa neighborhoods in the Grand River Valley.

FIGURE 26 **Rev. Isaac McCoy**

FIGURE 27 **Rev. Leonard Slater**

The Baptist Mission

The older of the two Odawa villages grew to the size of 300 by the 1820s under the leadership of Chief Muckitaoska (Blackskin). The individuals within Muckitaoska's village formed a cohesive community with themselves, with neighboring Odawas, and with nature. Their neighborhood thrived as a great trading center on the rapids, but the white man threatened to upset this balance.

Muckitaoska harbored a sincere distrust, if not hatred, for the white man. He thought that the whites could not be bargained with because of their insatiable desire to expand westward. As leader of his village, Muckitaoska was prepared to deal forcefully with the whites if they entered Grand River Valley.

Nunaquakezik (Noonday), chief of the Odawa village directly to the north of Muckitaoska's, did not agree with Muckitaoska. The two chiefs had enjoyed solidarity when they fought in the War of 1812 against the Americans. Muckitaoska, in a show of defiance against the Americans, had been the first to put a torch to the American town of Buffalo.[42]

Twenty years, however, greatly changed the agreement between the two chiefs. Muckitaoska still believed that the Odawa could not give in to any of the demands of the whites. Nunaquakezik, however, had changed his stance completely. When Nunaquakezik and the other Odawa representatives returned from negotiating the Treaty of 1821 in Chicago, Muckitaoska bitterly disagreed with the terms. He knew the whites had forced the Odawas into giving away half of their land and opening wide the door for white settlement of Odawa lands. Nunaquakezik, on the other hand, seemed to accept white presence, and even helped missionary Isaac McCoy establish his mission.[43]

McCoy built a blacksmith shop and a mill. In defiant response, Muckitaoska's disgruntled band burned the smithy.[44] Nunaquakezik was fiercely angry with him for this action. The whites continued to come in larger numbers, building many smithies, churches, and schools. Nunaquakezik felt an urgency to befriend the whites to avoid otherwise inevitable conflict.

In addition, Nunaquakezik and many other Indians received benefits from the mission. It brought the tools and knowledge of the whites to the Odawas, which helped them to grow crops more efficiently, and to build better homes, in the fashion of the whites.

However, the religion and schooling of the whites accompanied these changes. Some Indians had converted

FIGURE 28 **Grab Corners circa 1852. This is the same view as in the drawing below. Just past covered Bridge Street bridge is where the Baptist mission, shown below, was located.**

FIGURE 29 **Early Grand Rapids, showing Baptist mission across the river, Campau trading post, and island number one**

FIGURE 30 **Joel Guild's house, later the site of the McKay Tower**

FIGURE 31 **Joel Guild, one of the first settlers**

to the Christian ways preached by Rev. Leonard Slater and his assistant, Jonathan Meeker. McCoy had established the mission and left these men in charge, visiting periodically. Whether McCoy or Slater preached, a trumpet and a steel bell announced the morning church service on Sunday at the Thomas Mission. The morning service was preached in Odawa and the afternoon in English. Sabbath school followed the services, and the Lord's day was capped with an evening prayer service. Slater, Meeker, and others taught at the school during the week.[45]

Nunaquakezik almost always remained at the mission, preaching at his people to Christianize and quit drinking the white man's whiskey.[46] Muckitaoska did not think that the other chief's conversion to Christianity was very genuine. Rather, Nunauqakezik desired to "civilize" the Odawa so that the whites would see them as valuable, rather than destroy them. He also suspected Nunaquakezik of trying to garner respect and prestige in material wealth from the mission.

Even though the Indians found Jonathan Meeker's name difficult to pronounce, Muckitaoska at first welcomed him to the Mission in 1826, calling him "he who speaks good words."[47] Initially, the Indian chief believed Meeker cared genuine-

ly for the Odawas, but Muckitaoska's opinion changed as he witnessed the zeal of the missionaries.

An incident in 1827 further distanced Muckitaoska from the missionaries. Terror seized the Odawa villages as a meteor displayed itself in the heavens, exploding to the north of the rapids. The meteor alarmed Nunaquakezik so much that he asked McCoy if the Bible contained any wisdom concerning the meteor.[48]

Other Indians attempted to figure out what the sign meant. In their fear, some turned to Louis Campau, a French trader who built a trading post on the east bank of the river. Muckitaoska respected Campau, as did all of the Indians, and they asked the trader to explain the sign in the heavens. The trader told them that the meteor signified the coming of many Frenchmen.[49] This scared Muckitaoska, reinforcing his misgivings about the white man and underscoring his opposition to the mission. The following year, McCoy requested the chief's presence, and he refused to see the missionary.[50] Many Indians shared Muckitaoska's anxiety about the coming of the whites, and the Thomas Mission suffered as a result.

At Isaac McCoy's final visit in 1829, religious fervor at the Thomas Mission appeared very stagnant. Only 12 Indian students attended the Mission school he had founded. Drunkenness among some of the adult Indians had developed into a huge problem. As more traders moved into the area, they manipulated the Indians and their insatiable desire for whiskey, which could be purchased for 25 cents per gallon.[51] It was not uncommon to encounter groups of Indians who had bought liquor from some greedy trader. These frontiersmen went to any length to get the Indians to become hooked on the liquor that was totally new to them.[52]

"On account of erroneous opinions of Indian character, bad measures of government, and criminal neglect of Christians, the condition of [the Indians] has hitherto appeared less hopeful than that of any other upon the earth…. The apathy of Christians upon this subject has been unaccountable."[53]

Rev. Isaac McCoy

In McCoy's opinion, the Thomas mission had not improved the state of the northern village. Although some Indians had modernized, attempting to settle and cultivate the land, study the English language, build permanent houses, and wear the clothing of white people, most continued to live a traditional Indian lifestyle. Most Indians did not perceive the deceitfulness of the traders who often manipulated them into buying large amounts of alcohol.

The drunken fits of some Indians repeatedly placed both villages in danger and created deep divisions in the northern neighborhood. Those who had converted to Christianity and who abstained from drinking would often suffer verbal and physical harassment. In the days before the white man, evening for these villages usually brought peaceful hours of storytelling and smoking by the fire. Now they witnessed loud cavorting, debauchery, and violence. Witnesses were often surprised by the violence that occurred during these fits.[54] As a result, the northern village divided between Christianized and traditional Indians. The feeling of neighborhood among the Indians had become confused as values changed. Unfortunately, the unrestrained capitalism of the traders defied any attempt to stop their lucrative business of manipulating the Indians.

The Baptist missionaries at Thomas eventually grew very disillusioned with their work. Meeker, in his frustration with the mission, left the Grand River in 1831 for a position at a mission in Arkansas.[55] Meanwhile, McCoy's disgust with the stagnancy of the mission caused him to denounce Christians in America for not supporting or participating in missions to Indians. Slater, however, continued to preach to his few but faithful Indian subjects, including Nunaquakezik.

McCoy and Slater eventually butted heads over the land issues that presented themselves in the Treaty of 1836. The treaty makers in Washington desired all Indian land north of the Grand River to be acquired by sale or force. In their defense, the Indians enlisted the aid of any local acquaintances they possibly could, such as Indian traders Louis Campau and Rix Robinson, in the hope of gaining reimbursement for their lands. The traders feared that if a sale was not negotiated, the Indians would suffer the inevitable conclusion of having their lands taken by force. The Odawa and their Anishnabek allies held a council at the Grand River, expressing their overwhelming desire to hold onto their land. To stall for time, they sent a group of young

delegates to Washington, but purposefully withheld their authority to strike an agreement with the whites. Eventually, the government succeeded in bringing a real delegation of Odawa from Grand Rapids to Washington to negotiate the treaty, including Chief Kewaycooshquom and the Baptist missionary Slater.[56]

In Washington, Slater first campaigned vociferously that the Odawa would surrender their land under no circumstances. McCoy advised him to continue this position at all costs. Slater caved under pressure, however, and signed a treaty with the government on behalf of the Indians that paid him $6,400 to take his mission to another location.[57] This transaction ended the Thomas Mission at Grand Rapids. Chief Nunaquakezik and other Indians accompanied Slater to the new mission location at Gull Prairie, Michigan. Many of the Odawa continued to live at the northern village. Most, however, remained disillusioned about their identities and values. The great Odawa community had been divided, corrupted, and shattered.

FIGURE 34 **Professor Franklin Everett**

"Missionary zeal generally begins with theology, and woefully fails, not from lack of good intentions, but from lack of wisdom."[58]

Professor Franklin Everett

The Catholic Mission

Although the southern village experienced comfortable isolation from the Baptist mission, it also evolved after the foundation of a mission. Bishop Rese, of the Catholic Diocese of Detroit, commissioned Father Frederic Baraga to begin the first Catholic mission in the Grand River Valley. Baraga chose his location near the southern Odawa village, naming it St. Mary's. Although Muckitaoska and his followers had vehemently opposed the Baptist Mission 10 years earlier, they raised no complaint against Baraga's efforts. In the shadow of the failing Thomas Mission, St. Mary's effectively delivered its message to many Indians, who converted to Catholicism at a constant rate. The Odawa preferred this mission to the Thomas Mission because of St. Mary's more lenient rules, as well as their dislike of Nunaquakezik's subservient attitude to the whites.[59]

Meanwhile, Campau and other French Catholics enjoyed the presence of a Catholic priest, but did not respect government laws restricting the sale of alcohol

FIGURE 32 **Louis Campau**

FIGURE 33 **Rix Robinson**

FIGURE 35 **Father Frederic Baraga**

to Indians. Certainly, Louis Campau and the settlers' endorsement of the Catholic presence played a role in the success of St. Mary's as well. Most traders viewed Baraga as a hindrance to their business. They made a fortune by selling liquor to the Indians, but Baraga condemned this act by teaching and preaching against it. Campau, whose business prospects on the east side of the river lofted him high in the opinions of the white settlers, was no exception to the rule.[60]

In addition, the extremely influential Campau exerted pressure on Baraga in other ways. The trader desired to have Catholic services on the east bank of the river and pushed the issue by paying local farmer Barney Burton to move Baraga's chapel across the ice to the east bank. However, Father Baraga remained adamant about preaching on the west side. He viewed the Indian neighborhood as his first priority in ministry, and the whites as secondary.[61]

St. Mary's Mission was far from extravagant. At first, Baraga used an Indian's log house for a church and school. Eventually, he hired a carpenter from Detroit, named Isaac Turner, to build several other buildings. The completed mission consisted of a chapel building, a rectory for Baraga's quarters, and a school. The chapel was located between present-day Butterworth and Watson Streets SW, and between Tolford and Gelock Avenues SW. The rectory stood at present-day 223 Gelock, while the school building was located somewhere between the two. As many as 38 students attended Baraga's tiny schoolhouse. Though most of these were

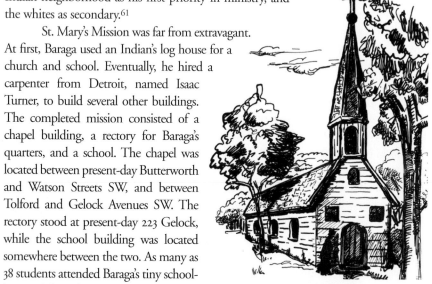

FIGURE 36 **St. Mary's Mission**

Odawa, some were sons of the traders and settlers across the river. The Indian converts of St. Mary's Catholic mission reached 91 in 1833, and French traders and Irish Catholic workers in the village often attended Baraga's services at the mission.[62]

Despite pressures from the Indians, the Baptists, the traders, and Campau, the determined Baraga managed the mission efficiently, pursuing his passion to convert the lost souls among the Indians. Of all the forces that weighed on Father Baraga, the U.S. Government Indian Agency remained his most constant burden. Against the

Attack on Baraga

Father Frederic Baraga sat at his desk in his rectory, improving his fluency in the Odawa language. The Slovenian maintained a busy and humble livelihood.[1] Father Baraga was happy in the Grand River Valley. With the exception of several vehement agitators from the Baptist Mission to the north, the Odawa had received Baraga and welcomed him to their community.[2]

Faraway voices ruptured the stillness of the evening, interrupting Baraga's concentration. He recognized the distraction as an all-too-familiar sound: a group of drunken Odawa disturbing the peacefulness that lay over the Grand River Valley. More disgusted than alarmed, Father Baraga rose from his studies and bolted the door and windows. Some trader had sold the Indians more whiskey, probably on credit, that the Indians would have to pay for with their government annuities. Many traders hated Father Baraga and treated him with contempt because he disrupted their business.[3] The more Indians he converted, the more business the traders lost.

As he listened, however, the riotous noise interrupted his reflections. The drunks had drawn incredibly close now, and many chanted his name. He risked a look at them from a window, and quickly bolted it again. His glance revealed a large group of Indians armed with torches. In fear, he knelt in prayer as the mob gathered around the rectory, pounding on the walls and the door and screaming for him to come out. He feared that the mob would set fire to the building. However, the Indians proved so affected by whiskey that they could not light the building on fire. Before long, a U.S. Marshal from the village heard about the commotion and journeyed over to the Mission, disbanding the mob.

Certainly, Baraga thought Slater had put these Indians up to this.[4] Baraga's disgust for the traders and their manipulation of the Indians' desire for whiskey grew. He remained on his knees thanking God for safety and vowing that he would never again touch a drop of alcohol in his life.

wishes of Indian agent Henry Rowe Schoolcraft, Baraga maintained a staunch defense of Indian lands, voicing his disgust with the Indian policy. Baraga wanted the Indians to stay so that he could minister to them. At first, he hesitated to build more buildings, knowing that the government might move the Indians off their land at any moment. He built anyway, reasoning that if the Indians were removed, the French Canadians would still need a chapel. Because of his staunch opposition to the Indian Agency's policies of annexation, Baraga was viewed by Schoolcraft as a thorn in his side. Campau, whose opinion carried a lot of weight with the government, also expressed anger at Baraga's refusal to meet Campau's demands.[64] As a result of these differences, Baraga left his position in 1835.

> "This has been the choicest, dearest spot to the unfortunate Indian, and now is the pride of the white man. Like other villages of the West, its transition from the savage to a civilized state has been as sudden, as its prospects are now flattering."[63]
>
> Father Andreas Viszoczky

After Baraga's removal, the care of St. Mary's Mission passed into the hands of Father Andreas Viszoczky. He began by preaching in the church that Louis Campau had moved to the east side of the river. In 1839, however, in a bold and defiant gesture, Viszoczky moved his pulpit back to the chapel at St. Mary's Mission, where he trained a choir of Indians to perform at Mass.[65] He still believed in ministry to the Indians as first priority, although by that time few Indians remained at the St. Mary's Mission. By 1842, Viszoczky still delivered sermons every Sunday in English, French, German, Odawa, and Ojibwe.[66]

Kewaykushquom, chief of the Odawa at Grand Rapids, negotiated the Treaty of 1836, acting with the belief that the Odawa should sell their land to the government. Before signing the treaty, however, he returned to Grand Rapids and reported the details to his people. They viewed his attitude as defeatist and overthrew him as chief. Megisinini replaced him as chief and went to Washington, signing the treaty in spite of the opinion of his people. Undoubtedly, both chiefs sensed the inevitability of the acquisition of their lands by the United States, and sought to get whatever they could from the government.[67]

FIGURE 37 **Henry Rowe Schoolcraft, Commissioner of Indian Affairs**

The End of the Odawa Villages

The Indian Agency sought to relocate all Indian tribes to land west of the Mississippi. The Treaty of 1836, as negotiated by Slater, turned all Indian land north of the Grand River over to the U.S. government in exchange for annuities to the Indians. The Indians could maintain hunting and fishing rights on lands not inhabited by whites. In effect, it allowed the Indians to remain on unsettled land, but forced them to search for new homes or ways of holding their land, because of the inevitability of white settlement.[68]

A carefully planned excursion by the government took a group of Michigan Odawa chiefs to Kansas in 1838 to display the land to them. Although the government agents presented the land as beautiful and sufficient, the Indians remained adamant. The flat, barren land in no way compared to their homelands in Michigan. The young Odawa delegates, who with the exception of Megisinini had no authority to negotiate a treaty, vehemently refused to relocate from Michigan.[69]

However, the displacement of the Indians over time forced many Indians to move to land north of the Pere Marquette River, or west of the Mississippi. By 1838, the Indians had virtually deserted the southern village and St. Mary's Mission, although a few inhabitants managed to find ways to remain on their beloved homelands.[70] After the desertion of the Thomas Mission, the northern village dwindled for the same reasons as the southern village. The government purchased the mission lands in 1843, doling out $12,000 to the Baptists, and $8,000 to the Catholics. Viszoczky, however, maintained the mission church building, preaching from it until 1849.[71]

Traditional Indian unity disintegrated as they assimilated to

FIGURE 38 **Andrew Blackbird documented many Odawa legends and customs.**

white ways. For those who attempted to remain, it became necessary to modernize and acquire personal land and property.[72] In addition, the Indians developed close alliances with influential figures, such as traders Campau and Robinson, and William Richmond, who later became an Indian agent.[73] The Indians began a drive to obtain citizenship, which the U.S. government granted only to those Indians who could prove that they had assimilated to white ways.[74] These Indians who owned land, managed to stay around Grand Rapids, melding into the community. Thus, the Treaty of 1836 annihilated the flourishing Odawa neighborhoods that had existed for almost 100 years. Kewaykushquom became the scapegoat for the loss of Indian lands, and in 1839 a fellow Odawa killed him out of spite over his negotiations.[75]

FIGURE 39 **William Richmond**

FIGURE 40 **The old yellow warehouse**

Following the dispersal of the Indians from their villages, the only remaining semblance of community occurred once a year, when the government parceled out its annuities to Michigan Indians. The annual handout, at the old yellow warehouse on Waterloo Street (now Market), brought a gathering of as many as 4,000 Indians on the banks of the river. This meeting, until it shifted to Petoskey in 1857, attracted both fur traders and whiskey dealers. The traders waited until the Indians had collected their payments, then demanded the currency for the settling of old debts. The Indians usually paid their debts, and bought whiskey with what remained of their funds. Thus, the annual meeting resulted in a tragic display of drunkenness, swindling, and backstabbing.[76]

The final blow to the Indian communities came in 1855 when the government negotiated the last treaty with the Indians. This treaty created permanent reservations for the Indians in the northern Michigan counties of Mason and Oceana. The government kindly paid all transportation dues. Any remaining Indians who could not secure a spot at the rapids, boarded a steamboat destined for the sandy reserves in the north.[77] To make the situation worse, the Indians later realized that a significant portion of the treaty they had signed had not been explained to them properly. This deceitful move by American officials significantly reduced the sum of annuities that the Odawa were to receive for their lands.[78] By the time of the treaty, the mission lands were purchased and well populated by German immigrants, who formed a new community in place of the Indian neighborhoods.

Some Indians remained, although forced to forsake their traditional ways of life. In the eyes of early Grand Rapids historians, the vanishing Indians became a captivating and mysteriously sad subject. Charles Belknap remembers Indians living in wigwams on the islands that used to exist below the rapids.[79] William Etten remembers Louis Campau entertaining Indian guests at his mansion, many of whom slept on the lawn or the porch.[80] These Indians, however, did not last long. Grand Rapids historian Albert Baxter sadly lamented that by 1859 Indians could no longer be seen spearing fish at the rapids.[81]

> "The Indian survived our open intention of wiping them out and, since the tide turned, they have even weathered our good intentions toward them, which can be much more deadly."[82]
>
> John Steinbeck

The First European Settlers

"The aesthetic beauty of the place as it was in nature is gone; its beauty now pertains to business uses, and the embellishments of modern civilized life and taste."[83]
Albert Baxter

Campau and Lyon

Louis Campau attracted controversies. He created tensions not only with Fathers Baraga and Viszoczky at the Catholic Mission, but also with prominent entrepreneurs of early Grand Rapids. He was a fascinating man with interesting methods and quirks, but beneath it all he was an enterprising capitalist. Some estimated "Uncle Louis" was worth $100,000 or more at his peak. Eventually, most of the city embraced the French Canadian for his charm, wit, and stories. He spent his final years at his mansion, one room of which he plastered with worthless bank notes, entertaining his Indian friends and telling frontier stories to the neighborhood children.[84]

In his first days at the rapids, however, Campau engaged less in the delightful and innocent practice of storytelling to children than in cutthroat business dealing. Commissioned by the government to trade with the Indians, Campau had a series of strict regulations to follow, including the prohibition of the sale of alcohol to Indians.[85] He built his trading post on the east bank of the river at the foot of present-day Monroe Avenue and Pearl Street, as close as possible to the Indians under the current treaty agreements.[86]

Campau enjoyed his status as the sole founder of Grand Rapids village until he sold the northern half of his plot to Lucius Lyon. The two began to compete for control of the area. While Campau called his village Grand Rapids and cut his streets parallel to his area of the river, Lyon called his village Kent and platted his streets on cardinal directions. The two tycoons battled for control of the area, each wanting to name the entire village after his own choosing. Kent, however, lost its bid for the village name when the Kent Company went out of business in the mid-1830s, and the entire village became incorporated in 1838 as Grand Rapids.[87] Many a driver has cursed the mismatched streets that remain as symbols of the battle between Lyon and Campau.[88]

FIGURE 41
Louis Campau

FIGURE 42
Lucius Lyon

FIGURE 43 **This view of Grab Corners is from the second-floor balcony of the Rathbun House (see page 28). The top of Sweet's Hotel is visible in the background. In 1870, Monroe Avenue emptied into Pearl Street and the street level dropped several feet from Monroe to Canal Street. In 1873, this part of Canal street was raised four feet.**

Sweet's-Pantlind-Amway Hotel Timeline

1830s–1850s: Bentham's restaurant is the heart of the old business district, serving venison and other frontier cuisine; Bentham's goes out of business in the late 1850s; a sawmill pond exists where Sweet's Hotel will be built.

1868: Martin Sweet founds Sweet's Hotel, which crowns the downtown area of Campau Square.

1898: The financially unsound Sweet's Hotel is bought by Old National Bank.

1902: J. Boyd Pantlind buys Sweet's Hotel from Old National Bank, remodels it to 125 rooms, and renames it the Pantlind.

1907–1909: Large additions are built as the hotel becomes the heart of conventions and the furniture business.

1913: Construction begins on the new Pantlind.

1916: U.S. Senator William Alden Smith toasts at the grand opening of the new Pantlind, with 550 rooms and state-of-the-art technology.

1936: The Pantlind suffers problems from the Great Depression and failed business ventures.

1981: The Pantlind reopens as the Amway Grand Plaza.

1873   C 1874

FIGURES 45, 46 **The picture on the top left was taken after the last buildings in Grab Corners were removed (see previous page). Later that year, this intersection was graded four feet higher. The arrowed line shows the new height of Sweet's Hotel after it was raised to match the new street level. The building across the street was not raised.**

C 1860

FIGURE 44 **Daniel Ball's Exchange Bank was later expanded to make Sweet's Hotel in 1868.**

C 1870

FIGURE 47 **Martin Sweet**

FIGURE 48 **Part of the hotel at left stands on reclaimed riverbed where the channel between the islands was filled in. The original level of the land would have been several feet lower.**

1888

1902

FIGURE 50 **The Police and Firemen's Review Day in Campau Square. The Pantlind Hotel is no longer whitewashed.**

FIGURE 49 **Sweet's Hotel during its glory days. In autumn of 2000, Michigan National Bank closed the branch office in the Amway Grand Plaza. An ATM machine is all that remains of 150 years of banking at this site.**

C 1920

FIGURE 51 **J. Boyd Pantlind**

1988

FIGURE 52 **The Pantlind is now part of the Amway Grand Plaza.**

FIGURE 53 **The new Pantlind Hotel that replaced the old Sweet's Hotel building, part of which had stood since 1859.**

FIGURE 54 **Looking west along Pearl Street, circa 1870. Crane's Museum of freaks, snakes, and whiskered ladies was located over Houseman and May's Clothing Store.**

Lovett Block

Sweet's Hotel

Covered Bridge

Pearl Street

Grab Corners and Business District

Perhaps the most interesting landmark in early Grand Rapids resulted directly from this battle. The abnormal junction of Monroe, Canal (now known as Monroe, north of Pearl), and Pearl streets became known as Grab Corners, the center of life in the village.

Geographically, Grab Corners situated itself in a wonderful spot to snare passersby who had to navigate the center of the business district. With Sweet's Hotel on one corner, the City National Bank on another, and many shops fronting Canal, Monroe Avenue, Pearl, and Waterloo Streets (later Market Street), travel through the Corners was almost inevitable. Not only did the Corners serve as the center of commerce, but the entertainment of gambling and drinking captured many a traveler on his way home from work.[89]

Flanagan's

Lovett Block

Canal Street (Later Monroe Avenue)

Pearl Street

FIGURE 55 **If we take figures 55, 56, and 58 and blend them together into a panorama, we can visualize the full sweep of Grab Corners and the business district hustle and bustle. The three pictures were taken at different times. The one above is actually two pictures pieced together, taken after 1873. Several changes have taken place since the 1870 picture at the top of the page. The Lovett Block has been enlarged and the building that currently houses Flanagan's pub has replaced the old museum.**

Here's how an early resident described Grab Corners: "All the activities of the town, good, bad, and indifferent, centered about Grab Corners in the sixties. There were many fine stores and some very good buildings. There were also two justice courts, half a dozen dives, two chuck-a-luck games, some poker rooms, and several basement bars where men drank whisky out of tin cups and where it was the rule to throw a drunk into the alley, leaving it to the police to come along and pound the soles of his boots as a test of life."[90]

The heart of the business district, according to historian and early resident Charles Belknap, was Bentham's restaurant at Grab Corners by Sweet's Hotel (now the Amway), which specialized in smoked venison. When Indian suppliers of venison left the area between the treaties of 1836 and 1855, Bentham's ceased to prosper.[91]

The nearby Arcade, a covered alley shortcut from Pearl to Lyon Street, distracted a great many of these hard-working travelers. This small stretch included newspaper offices, Powers Theatre, Leppig's, Loetgert's dry goods store, Eliza Hall's millinery store,

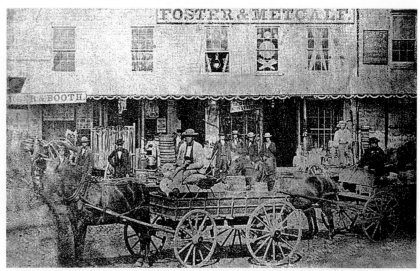

FIGURE 57 **Shoppers in front of Foster & Metcalf Hardware in Grab Corners**

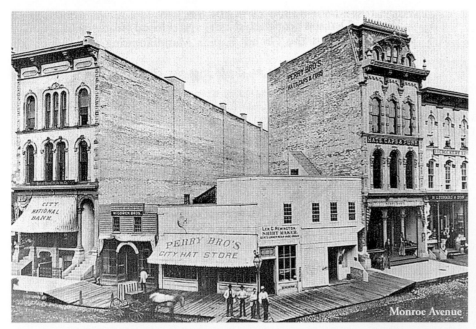

FIGURE 56 **Looking northeast, this 1860s view shows the bend in Monroe Avenue that ends at Pearl Street at the left of the picture. McKay Tower currently stands at this site. This picture was taken from in front of the Foster & Metcalf Hardware store, which can be seen in figure 57, as well as on page 27, just to the left of the Stone Commercial Block building.**

FIGURE 58 **Looking southeast down Monroe Avenue in the late 1870s completes the panorama. By the time this picture was taken, the old hardware store was long gone.**

FIGURE 59 **The Arcade adjacent to the Powers Theatre building in the 1970s, is now a parking ramp.**

and eventually a fountain that capped Power's well. This fountain was nicknamed "Iron John" because the volumes of cold water that flowed from it contained a large amount of iron. Similar to the actors who entered the theatre from the steps into the Arcade, the side alley grew in prestige and fame.

The refreshing water of the fountain may have served to cool the fuming tempers of the teetotalers, who declared holy war on the "18 licensed rum holes" located near the Arcade, by offering a pure and alternate source of refreshment to those of the taverns and bars. The availability of a less potent beverage, however, did not completely derail the crusades of the prohibitionists anywhere in Grand Rapids. As if to spite their efforts, the fountain was torn down in the 1970s, along with the last remnants of the Arcade, for a parking lot. To complete the

FIGURE 61 **Flanagan's in 1999**

snub, Flanagan's Irish Pub remains in an 1870s building on the north side of Pearl Street, a witness to a time when the Arcade thrived.

At the time the Flanagan's building was constructed, the most frequent visitor to Grab Corners and the Arcade may have been a beagle hound named Music. A saleswoman named Julie, from Eliza Hall's millinery store, reportedly took better care of the dog than anyone else, and attached the following poem around his neck with a ribbon:

> I belong to Aaron T.
> But he don't care a cent for me
> I wander up and down the street,
> Sniff at every one I meet.
>
> Through the dust and mud I wade,
> Part the time in the Arcade,
> Then in Leppig's stop awhile
> To see Leppig's happy smile.

FIGURE 60 **This late 1870s photo is about the same view as figure 54, but is expanded to include Powers Theatre. Sweet's Hotel is four feet higher with the street grading, though the Lovett Block was not raised. We have a small glimpse of the covered alley through the theatre.**

Then from there across the way
With Charlie Hall to have a play
Back again to Loetgert's shop,
There I have a happy lot.

Meat and crackers every day,
Not a single cent to pay.
Julie gives them all to me —
Happy may she ever be.

When some day I go to sleep
In the basket at her feet
She'll forget to wake me up,
Then goodby to this old pup.[92]

Such was the song of the most visible resident of Grab Corners and the Arcade. Ironically, the one who knew best the nooks and crannies and twists and turns of the old downtown was oblivious when it came to the temperance battles and business struggles that shaped the history of the area as it took place around him.

Perhaps Campau's wit served him properly, as he sold the northern half of his initial purchase at the rapids to Lyon.

Rathbun House

Foster & Metcalf Hardware

Stone Commercial Block

Daniel Ball's Bank

FIGURE 62 **This 1860 picture shows the slope down Monroe Avenue towards Grab Corners. From this angle it is quite apparent how much lower the ground level is at the Daniel Ball Bank building, where Sweet's Hotel will later be built. Recently, the Monroe Amphitheater that occupied the hardware store site was replaced with a park. Perhaps the dog in the lower right of this picture belongs to Aaron T.**

The southern half, as Campau developed it, was more geographically inclined to immediate prosperity. While Lyon attempted to start a line of mills and other industries in his Kent village by harnessing water power from the canals, Campau's village flourished because of the inevitable river traffic below the rapids. The yellow warehouse became the first landing place for boats at the corner of Fulton and Market, while the Eagle Hotel, Michigan House, and the Rathbun House competed for steamboat travelers.[93] These hotels also became bastions of communal activity, accommodating many social activities, conventions, meetings, dinners, and dance lessons. The shops of the business district continued northward on the east side of Canal Street (now Monroe north of Pearl) to Bridge Street (now Michigan), while the west side of the street featured shipyard forges, sawmills, livery stables, and factories.[94] This thriving business district became the heart of three early neighborhoods, providing work in

FIGURE 63 **A gathering in front of the National Hotel on Monroe Avenue at Ionia**

Water Street

Monroe Avenue

FIGURE 64 **Note the stagecoaches and the second-floor balcony at the Rathbun House.**

Rathbun House

FIGURE 65 **The Eagle Hotel was located just down Waterloo Street (later Market Avenue) from the Rathbun House.**

FIGURE 66 **Stage coach advertising**

factories, mills, shops, bars, forges, hotels, restaurants, and many other places.

A rustic plank road emerged as the main thoroughfare between Grand Rapids and Kalamazoo. As this road came into Grand Rapids at South Division Street, another business district evolved around the Division-Fulton street intersection. The heart of this district was the old National Hotel, which burned and later was built as the Morton House. Travelers who sought refreshment and lodging as they journeyed from Kalamazoo often frequented the district, located at the southeast edge of town.[95]

Fire remained a constant and all too often tragic scourge for the early settlers of Grand Rapids. They built most shops, hotels, and downtown buildings out of wood, and took few precautions. Mills and factories faced no restrictions on their safety standards and fire awareness, and invited disaster. Fires that began in mills or factories spread to adjacent buildings, causing severe damage to the city year after year. Many of these fires raged out of control until the 1880s, when the city finally began to develop effective methods of battling fires. Until this point, however, the brave but primitively equipped firefighters could not hope to rescue a building once it caught fire, but only to contain the fire and keep it from spreading to other buildings. On several occasions (an 1873 mill fire, for example), almost the entire downtown was destroyed by fire.[96]

The Intoxicated Firefighters

Charles Belknap reminisces:

"One afternoon in 1857, I occupied a reserved seat on the top of a house on Monroe Street, along with some 40 odd boys and girls, and saw 25 business places destroyed by a fire started in a drug store on Monroe between Waterloo and Ottawa Streets.

"There were three fire companies at that time and Number One and Number Two were in the crater, while Number Three was working to save surrounding property. It looked from my position as if all the people of the town were helping, throwing glass and china from upper windows and lugging feather beds down stairways.

FIGURE 67 **Volunteer fire department, Kent Street Company Number Two, with old hand pump, circa 1865**

"From one of the stores, many large boxes of dry paints were carried into the street. Every store kept whiskey in those days; none of them kept drinking water. As a result the male population, thirsty and hard pressed by the flames, got a little dizzy and began tumbling into the paint boxes. Yellows and greens and purple began to blend with the blue and gray of smoke and ashes. If any of you have a desire to know how funny a man really can look, fill his inside with fire water and his outside with the colors of the rainbow.

"Were it not that the wind-driven fire brands threatened the entire town, it would have been the most successful carnival the people ever put on the street.

"From a doctor's office, some fellows salvaged a pickling cask. It tipped into the gutter and scattered the contents, and an Indian with a scalping knife could not have stampeded a crowd more quickly.

"Number One and Number Two fire companies became badly demoralized by evening. Overcome by spirits and crusted with color, they disappeared from the scene of conflagration. Number Three saved the town by working until daylight next morning. The women keeping them going by carrying coffee and sandwiches. The following Sunday every church in town was given a sermon on temperance.

"As a reward of merit to Number Three company for keeping sober, the women of the town expressed their appreciation by the gift of a beautiful satin banner, which is now among the treasures of the Kent Scientific Museum.

"This fire had all the thrills of a great battle. It was the fireside story of the year and while it distressed many people for a long time, now that the paint is washed off they can smile, even at the foreman of the company, who, lying on his back in a box of red paint, waved his brass trumpet vaguely and shouted: 'Play away, Number Two.'"[1]

FIGURE 68 **Old fire truck circa 1926**

FIGURE 69 **Number Four engine house at Crescent and Bond before 1899**

Fulton Street Bridge

G. R. & I. Offices   G.R. & I. Union Station

St. Andrew's Cathedral

FIGURE 70 **View looking east toward Shantytown from the roof of the Phoenix Furniture Factory on the West Side**

Grandville Avenue Plowed by Domesticated Beast

According to early Grand Rapids historian Charles Belknap, Grandville Avenue was "blazed" by a homesick cow. At that time only a few settlers lived at the rapids, and they rescued the cow from a swamp. The path she trampled became Grandville Avenue.[1] More likely, Grandville Avenue began as an Indian trail, as many other streets such as Monroe, Butterworth and Robinson.

Shantytown

Because of its low elevation, the area directly south of Monroe Avenue has always met the housing needs of lower-class residents, even in the early days of the village. This area, stretching south of Monroe Avenue between Division Avenue and the river, where present day Heartside and U.S. 131 collide, began as a place for early immigrant workers to Grand Rapids to erect simple houses. Charles Belknap refers to this area numerous times as Shantytown.[97] Throughout Grand Rapids history, Grandville Avenue continued in this function, serving as the entry point into the city for immigrant groups of all origins. Generally, immigrants to Grand Rapids began in this area, moving out to better housing as their situation in this country improved.

Early entrepreneurs such as Lucius Lyon and N.O. Sargeant formed the Kent Company to build a canal and mills in Grand Rapids.[98] For this purpose, they hired many Irish immigrants, some of whom had worked on the Erie Canal in New York, and brought them to Grand Rapids in 1835.[99] The work continued for several years before the Kent Company went out of business. Irish immigrants became steady newcomers to the village.[100] Along with families of French traders, the Irish formed the first of many immigrant populations to inhabit Grand Rapids. As these families established their place here, they sought affordable housing and places for opportunity.

The location of Shantytown naturally matched this purpose. The foot of the rapids became a natural place for a village to develop; steamships could go no farther inland on the river,

and needed places to stop. Thus, the first business district in Grand Rapids evolved in the area around Waterloo (now Market) and Monroe Avenue.[101] As the French trading families increased, and the Irish canal workers came in the 1830s, they populated the area around and just south of this business district.

The inhabitants of Shantytown sought only to live their lives and make a living for their families, rather than attempt to boost their egos by building larger houses than their neighbors. The inhabitants of Shantytown built their houses simply, yet

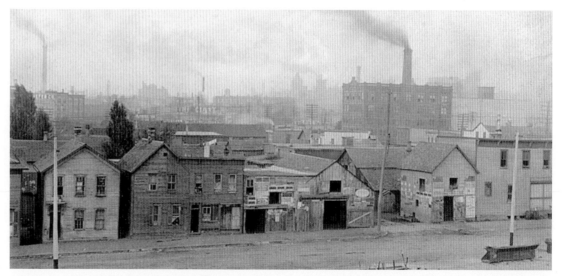

FIGURE 71 **The north side of Oakes Street between Summit and Waterloo Streets (Later Grandville and Market Avenues)**

30

FIGURE 72 **This house on Waterloo Street is typical of Shantytown.**

Chanties in Shantytown

Rafting men added interesting flavor to Shantytown, the shipyards, and the business district. Charles Belknap reminisces:

"Rafting developed a new type of man. Almost any man could run a boat down stream, but it required a peculiar skill and river instinct to keep a long fleet of lumber rafts out of the way of passing river steamers, to avoid sandbars and the lure of lost channels and bayous on the lower stretches where the wind was apt to struggle for the master hand.

"The sweeps for the steering must work in unison and so the men sang or chanted as they worked.

"The chanty man, as he has been called, had his beginning with what is perhaps the most beautiful work of man's hands — the sailing ship — and the 'chanties' are the working songs of the water. Many of them have been handed down through the generations and followed certain haunting melodies, but the songs of the raftsmen were usually improvised to suit the occasion. There was hardly a duty on the floating fleet of lumber which had not its own chanty to go with it, with one line solo and four lines chorus, in which all the events of the journey were told.

"I suppose the voice of the average raftsman was on a low level, but one could not be insensible to the charm of the song and the swishing of the sweeps that came to one out of the night or from above some river bend.

"Nearly all the raftsmen were French-Canadian. They worked in the lumber woods in the winter and drifted naturally to the river in the summer. Returning from the haven to the rapids by boat, the rest of their journey to the mills was on foot. The returning trip always included a day in town and meals at the hotel. On the way down the river, the captain bought supplies from the farms and they lived on the fat of the land."[1]

FIGURE 73 **Charles Kunze, left, Emil Reichel, and North Park Pavilion in background**

adequately; a wooden house, 16 feet by 20, with lean-to additions for each child born to the family, served as the model. Belknap reports that the census taker only had to count lean-tos and the clothes-line for information on each family.[102]

In most cases, the immigrants in Shantytown lived peaceful lives, happy for acceptance and a place in America for their families. Many, especially the Irish, had fled problems in their homeland and gratefully welcomed the wealth of opportunities offered by the booming village of Grand Rapids.[103]

Though the neighborhood of Shantytown was not exclusively populated by immigrants, it definitely maintained strong ethnic characteristics. Charles Belknap remembers acquiring French swear words more readily than the Irish and credits the language barrier for keeping fights between the two groups to a minimum. The French and Irish of Shantytown competed for transportation of the steamboat goods, each man pushing a cart, or "dray," to carry provisions to

Steamboats

The hardy, backwoods tastes of the early citizenry of Grand Rapids shone through in the 1837 christening of the steamboat *Mason*. Instead of the traditional champagne, the favorite town drink of whiskey was the obvious choice to launch the first steamboat to operate on the Grand River. Not only did the precious portion of whiskey expended on the steamboat's hull announce the commencement of a new vessel's life, it ushered in a new era for the city. Many additional gallons of the cherished liquid were consumed that day, celebrating the wealth and commerce that the new method of transportation brought to the city.

Steam-powered river travel opened wider the possibilities of trade and transportation with coastal cities such as Grand Haven, and even more lucrative interaction with other Great Lakes cities such as Chicago. With open arms, the village at the rapids welcomed its steamboat visitors. The business district of Monroe and Market streets offered housing, food, and entertainment to steamboat travelers, while the factories and shops benefited from the wealth of trading goods that the steamboats brought to and from the city.

By 1854, an entire fleet of steamboats gradually filled the void left by the *Mason*, which had wrecked at Muskegon in 1840. The *Michigan*, the *Empire*, the

FIGURE 74 **Steamboat *Barrett* was built in 1874 and lasted until 1894.**

Algoma, and the *Humming Bird* had appeared by 1854, joined soon after by the *Pontiac*, the *Nawbeck*, the *Forest Queen,* and the colossal *Olive Branch*. All these steamboats regularly ferried people and cargo between Grand Haven and Grand Rapids. Additional boats, the *Porter* and the *Kansas*, operated above the rapids, adding to the already dense river traffic of logs, rafts, canoes, and smaller boats.

The luxuries of steamboating were often accompanied by risks. The huge boats acquired their steam power by burning vast amounts of huge lumber slabs. Enormous pressure built up in these steam engines, causing fires and explosions, such as the one that destroyed the *Humming Bird*, allegedly causing damage to the fish in the river. Also, navigation on the river proved treacherous, as the changing depth of the water caused wrecks on sandbars and rocks.

Steamboat travel suffered drastically as a result of competition from the railroads in the 1860s and 1870s. However, the era of steamboats was crucial to the business prospects of the early settlers of Grand Rapids, the life of Shantytown, and the migration of new people to the booming village.[1]

FIGURE 75 *Valley City of Grand Rapids* at Church Grove on September 1, 1892

St. Andrew's Church   Second Reformed   Central High School   First (Park) Congregatinal Church

Summit Hill

FIGURE 76 **View in 1870 from the hill at Summit Street, now Grandville Avenue**

the appropriate shop or factory on Monroe Avenue, Waterloo, Canal, or Bridge Streets. Many worked in factories, shops, or at the hotels. Still others made their living as raftsmen, herding logs down the river to Grand Haven. According to Belknap, a steamboat traveler arriving at Grand Rapids would first see Shantytown and wonder whether he was in Killarney, Ireland, or Montreal, Canada.[104]

Whether Shantytown reflected a neighborhood spirit of communal unity is difficult to determine; first-hand accounts of old Shantytown are scarce. The neighborhood definitely did not maintain a communal identity such as that of the Indians. The immigrants banded together in Shantytown out of convenience and financial situation, whereas the Indians depended upon community for survival. As a result, neighborly relationships were perhaps cordial, though the language difference may have separated the French from the Irish and New Englanders during the early years.

Shantytown, however, by no means exhibited a hostile atmosphere. A general level of respect for one another's space and livelihood existed. Perhaps it was the beginning of the American ideal of pulling oneself up by one's own bootstraps. Everyone who came to America could understand the underdog concept that allowed one to take on American identity and prosperity through hard work and good luck.

A religious bond unified the inhabitants of Shantytown as well, as both the Irish and the French came from staunch Catholic backgrounds. If the immigrants maintained these ties, they undoubtedly participated in the Catholic ministry of

Fortune Teller Meets Firefighters

Perhaps the first icon of the Grand Rapids African American community was an energetic older woman named Martha A. Ball. She made her living as a fortune teller at her house at 74 (now 546) Stocking Street, between Second and Third where Interstate 196 now cuts through. This lucrative business made her enough money to support several children, as evidenced by the many lean-tos. She charged 25 cents per fortune, and snared her audience of daring children by way of a sign that read, "Goin' out washun dun here."

Many of the West Side children passed her place on their way to the Stocking Commons, a large vacant lot dotted with newly cut tree stumps. Kids often stopped while Martha Ball predicted that they would each fall in love soon, and then went on to a war dance around the blazing stumps in the commons.

One night, Ball entertained the African American church by hosting a church social at her house. As the children of several firemen danced nearby in the commons, they noticed a fire on the side of Madam Ball's chimney. Climbing the roofs of the many lean-tos, they finally reached the height of the chimney and dumped a solitary bucket of water into the chimney, putting out the fire. Until this point, the oblivious revelers inside Ball's house knew nothing of the fire. One young firefighter remembers: "One must have a fireman's experience to know what happened to the social below: a bang like a thunderbolt, soot, ashes, fire and steam. By the time the folks had the cinders out of their eyes and the fear of the Lord out of their hearts, the firemen sensed they had stirred up something. Faster running was done in getting away from that fire than was ever done in getting to another, and all that fall and winter the sons of Number Three [Fire Company] held their war dances in another place on the West Side."

Despite the dusting of ashes that the African American congregation received, Ball's house was saved. They continued the social without knowing whether it was the Lord's wrath or his grace, and Martha Ball continued telling fortunes at that house.[1]

Father Viszoczky and other Catholic priests. Although Viszoczky preached four sermons every Sunday in five different languages, many people of French descent attended the English service to enhance their English skills. Inevitably, many French worshipped alongside the Irish, a situation which undoubtedly helped to keep the peace in the neighborhood of Shantytown.

The First Garbage Collector

Charles Belknap remembers the first sanitation engineer, a West Sider:

"Everything must have a beginning and to the best of my recollection, this is how the collection of garbage began in Grand Rapids. In the early days nearly every family had its own cow, chickens, and pigs, and they very largely used up the household refuse. Not until the [18]70s did the city authorities make a determined effort to keep the hogs and cattle out of the streets. When they began zoning the town, the disposal of garbage became a problem, greatly magnified because nearly every voter had livestock of some kind and the aldermen were taxed to the limit of their wit trying to please them all.

"The first man to collect garbage had a pig yard on the commons at the north end of Front Street. He was equipped with a small two-wheeled cart with a barrel, drawn by a huge Belgian dog. The barrel made a seat for the driver except when it was full — then he walked.

"Nearly every boy on the West Side had a dog that watched for the swill cart and when half a dozen of them, large and small, engaged the Belgian, there was a riot in the garbage department. This man carried a whip and applied it to the dog in a way that aroused the ire of the men of the Number Three fire company, and one day they turned on the man a stream that nearly washed him into the next block.

"For some time this man was followed by a trained pig which ran squealing behind the cart until the marshal ordered his pigship shut up.

"For all this, business prospered until there were three dogs with carts and all the people in the vicinity of the piggery protesting. Then one day there appeared, also from North Front Street, a venerable old man driving a lone steer hitched between the shafts of a two-wheeled cart and guided by rope lines attached to its horns. He came from some foreign land and, unhindered, built a shack of sidings and tin can shingles. He went about hatless and often coatless, accompanied by a daughter built on solid lines, whom the boys soon named 'Sloppy Ann.'

"His piggery was a finishing touch to the atmospheric misery of the north end....

"A string butcher bought the pigs of both parties and they seem to have vanished over the alpine hills. Later on in garbage history, when the piggery was located south of town the early residents, sniffing the evening odors, sensed the ghost of the Belgian dog, Sloppy Ann, and the steer, circling in from the dusk, and every owner of a good watchdog had him out on guard."[1]

FIGURE 77 **Charles Belknap**

East and West

The rift between the east and west banks of the river has existed as long as whites have settled here. Transportation remains the main reason for the difference. Differences arose as early as 1833 and 1834 when Campau desired to have Father Baraga's congregation meet on the east side of the river for transportation purposes. Agreements with the Indians prohibited white settlement of the West Side until the treaty of 1836. In 1840, James Scribner and Eliphalet Turner bought and platted the area between Bridge and Sixth streets, and the whites began to spill over to the West Side. To facilitate the transportation, Scribner built a plank footbridge in 1843.[105] Canoes accounted for all other river crossings.

The toll bridge, built in 1852, increased tensions between east and west. Located at Bridge Street, the toll keeper charged one cent for foot passengers, two cents for a horse rider, and increasing tolls for larger vehicles. According to Charles Belknap, "It was this toll gate penalty that divided the east and west side, much the same as the Mason and Dixon line divided the north and south."[106] Young lovers would turn aside at the gate to the bridge to avoid the toll. Undoubtedly, the toll bridge posed problems for businesses as well. Belknap reports that it was the "financial problem" in town until the fire of 1856 destroyed the bridge completely.[107] Since the fire began in a mill at the east end of the bridge, and the West Side fire company lost a machine in vain, Belknap reports that, "... the East and West Side were not on social terms." Canoes and small boats handled all traffic until free bridges replaced temporary footbridges in 1858 at Leonard, Pearl, and Bridge streets.[108] Perhaps the differences in transportation gave rise to differences that exist even today between the East and West sides.[109]

Prospect Hill

Prospect Hill remains an enigma. A common mistake, for instance, is that Prospect Avenue is so named because of its location on Prospect Hill. This claim bears as much truth as the statement that the East and West side of Grand Rapids are similar, as Prospect Avenue lies about a half a mile east of where Prospect Hill used to take root.

Historians can thank fires for destroying some pertinent records concerning Prospect Hill, but their sardonic gratitude does not ease the painful task of reconstructing what Prospect Hill may have looked like.

Myths and baffling theories aside, the truth is that Prospect Hill, located just north of Grab Corners on the east bank of the river, was extremely important to the first settlers of the village of Grand Rapids.

An overwhelming majority of settlers in Grand Rapids came from New York state. The first large colony arrived in 1833, under the auspices of Samuel Dexter.[110] Many more New Englanders arrived with their families in the next four years. Land speculation increased rapidly, as well as prices of lots in the village. Many built houses of slab shanties and log cabins before the lumber mills began to thrive, improving the quality of the houses.[111] Many of the most influential and prosperous people in the history of Grand Rapids arrived during these years, before the recessed economy abated migration to the area.[112]

Most of these well-educated individuals became entrepreneurs, opening shops, restaurants, hotels, banks, industries, and all the businesses that made up the town. Those ambitious and assertive opportunists who did well, especially after the Depression of 1837–1846, became extremely influential in town finances and politics. Between 1845 and 1864, well over 80 percent of all officeholders in Grand Rapids hailed from New York and New England, showing that these New Englanders remained both economically and politically in charge.[113] Often, the home-building practices of these individuals reflected the class level of their social status. Early on, some of the sons of New England plotted the West Side in an area that became known as "Scribnerville." But most built homes around Monroe Avenue, with the wealthiest members of the upper class living on Prospect Hill.

In those days, Prospect Hill rose about 55 feet above the river.[114] At a time when the lower parts of town flooded often, especially the ever-present mud pits of Monroe Avenue and Canal Street, premium land located on high ground went only to those who could pay handsomely for it. By 1890, the city had gradually removed Prospect Hill, using the dirt to fill in these mudpits, and to raise the grade of the streets. Before this time,

FIGURE 79 **Looking east from the island in the river, Thomas W. Porter's depiction of what Prospect Hill looked like in 1833; the hill's height is a bit exaggerated.**

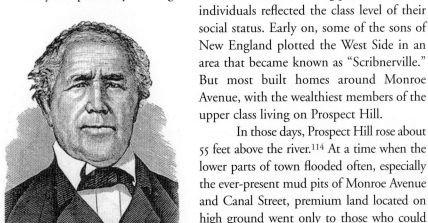

FIGURE 78 **Samuel Dexter**

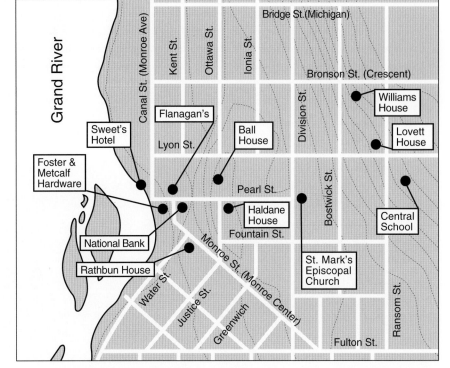

FIGURE 80 **The map shows the streets and their names as listed on an 1842 plat map; current street names are in parenthesis.**

Early Street Problems

The streets of a city are perhaps its most identifying landmarks. An extreme nuisance when clogged or under construction, the streets of a city become symbols of the neighborhoods or business districts they serve. These tendencies were no different in the early days of Grand Rapids, when the streets were much less developed than the streets of today's Grand Rapids.

Though street-plotting would have been much easier on the West Side of the river, the Indian treaties prevented settling of the West Side until the city building was well under way. Therefore, the early settlers encountered all kinds of geographical problems on the East Side as they insured that travel through their city would proceed smoothly, heightening the prosperity of the town.[1]

Since the first settling of Grand Rapids, its early residents struggled with flooding from the river. The northern half of Monroe, first called Canal Street, was infamous for the large amounts of stagnant water and mudpits that developed at certain times during the year. The quagmires on Canal Street slowed wagon traffic and inhibited business, while Division was a "musical frog pond."[2] These virtual swamps also became breeding centers for disease and mosquitoes during the wet months of the year. In dryer times the mud caked, producing clouds of dust that choked and blinded travelers and ruined merchant goods.

The settlers developed many methods of combating the problems caused by

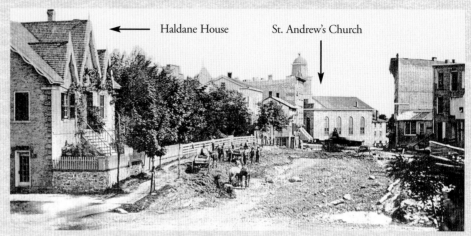

FIGURE 82 **The second grading of Ottawa Street, looking south from Pearl Street 1865**

flooding. Early attempts to smooth the flow of traffic through the quagmires included laying of planks, as well as dumping of stones, bricks and stumps into the mud pits. Also, many shopkeepers attempted to encourage travel in front of their shops by placing plank sidewalks in front of their stores.

An interesting innovation to handle the dust problem during the summer was the sprinkling wagon. In 1857, the merchants commissioned Thomas Sargeant to sprinkle the dusty streets in a contraption described as, "a watertight square box, with a trap door on the top and a sprinkler spout at the lower back end, and with a valve operated by means of a piece of rope." Sargeant would back his cart into the river at Fulton Street, filling it with buckets of water, until companies outfitted him with new tanks and pumps to ease his burden. The city later took over the job when it developed a water system of its own, but it must have been a sight indeed to witness Sargeant soaking the streets in his gerry-rigged contraption.

The final and most successful method of dealing with the flooding problem was the street-grading. In a series of projects from the 1850s through the 1890s, the city raised the level of the lower streets by several feet. Buildings on these streets were lifted on jack screws, as crews piled dirt underneath. Canal and Monroe were among the first to be graded, as Prospect Hill was flattened bit by bit. Some dirt was also taken from the mound flattening projects of the 1850s and 1860s. As the completion of some of the grading did not take place until 1890, some existing buildings in Grand Rapids endured this raising process.[3]

FIGURE 81 **Wooden sprinkler carts**

FIGURE 83

FIGURE 84

FIGURES 83, 84, 85 **Pictures show furniture industry pioneer William Haldane's home at the corner of Ottawa and Pearl streets situated on the top of Prospect Hill. The upper right photo shows the original land level and shape of the building. Note the Houseman Block in the left background built in 1883. The upper left photo shows how high the house, complete with fire alarm bell tower, sat above the graded street level. Dr. Shepard's house, right of the Haldane home, below, was also left about 15 feet above street level.**

FIGURE 85

The Park on Fulton Street

The square bordered by Fulton, Sheldon, Library, and Park streets at the end of Monroe, was first bought by Samuel Dexter, who gave it to Kent County. This square, now Veterans' Memorial Park, became a buzzing center of social activity in the early days of Grand Rapids. The first courthouse, built in 1838, burned in 1844, and was replaced by a small schoolhouse where all of the county's social events were hosted. The wide open space of the square also hosted county fairs and circuses until animal control became a problem. Others congregated to encourage patriotism during the Civil War by listening to speakers, singing, and talking at bonfires. City officials even scheduled a public execution to take place in the square, but the criminal's sentence was lessened to life in prison. After several years of neglect, the park received a face lift from Sheriff Thomas Gilbert. John Steketee also planted and nurtured trees, fighting diligently to resurrect the park. To Gilbert's dismay, the county fenced and locked the park, forcing lovers seeking a romantic walk in the park to scale the fence. In 1881, however, the county removed the fence, and Gilbert took measures to protect the park from stray animals. He was rewarded for his services in 1896, when local businesses erected a bronze bust of Gilbert. The existing building on Sheldon Avenue was built in 1918 as a public restroom. The building now belongs to the Children's Museum.

During the 1920s, the public wanted to rename the park in honor of Samuel Dexter, who had originally donated the land. However, the Supreme Court investigated the matter, deciding that Louis Campau had donated at least part of the land for the park, and Dexter's name should not be given to the park. The public was more successful in using the park as a memorial for soldiers who had died in World War I. The city added granite pillars engraved with the names of deceased World War I veterans on November 11, 1926. The name was changed to Veterans' Memorial Park in 1956, when the city added flowers, benches and new granite pillars dedicated to the veterans of World War II and the Korean War. Since that time, the city also has added veterans of the Vietnam War.[1]

FIGURE 86 **Old fountain in Fulton Park similar to the fountain in Crescent Park, circa 1895**

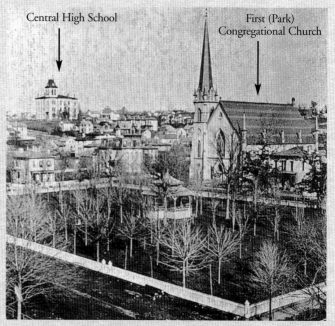

Central High School First (Park) Congregational Church

FIGURE 87 **In 1862 the picket fence was put up to keep cattle and swine from using the park.**

FIGURE 88 **First block of marble laid for the Veteran's monument pillars in Fulton Street Park, 1926**

FIGURE 89 **Monroe and Ottawa streets in 1865. Notice the slope up Ottawa to Prospect Hill.**

FIGURE 90 **The same intersection in 1999. Though the building remains the same, the hill is gone and Monroe Center at left is closed to traffic.**

FIGURE 91
Edward W. Chesebro

however, the prominent neighborhood of wealthy New England pioneers developed on Prospect Hill, mostly on Kent Street (now Bond), but also on Bronson (now Crescent), Fountain, Lyon, and Pearl streets.[115]

The "Yankee" neighborhood definitely maintained boundaries between itself and areas of immigrant housing. This trend of isolation is reflected by the fact that most early histories written by wealthy New Englanders show heavy favoritism toward wealth, prestige, and New England blood.[116]

It seems as though Prospect Hill sustained some semblance of community, or neighborhood, despite its lack of interdependence. During the 1850s, the steep slopes of the hill, the ponds at its base, and the many varieties of trees all over it, served as playgrounds for the children. The houseowners on the hill cordially entertained each other, while the children of the New Englanders coasted down the western slopes, skated and swam at the ponds, and climbed in the hickory, oak, and black cherry trees. These trees caused disputes between lumber companies, who fought in the courts for possession of the timber on Prospect Hill.[117] The parents of these children could afford to send their children to school, strengthening neighborhoods even more. One of the first organized schools met in a frame building on Prospect Hill, before later moving to a building on East Fulton, across from Jefferson Avenue.[118] Fountain School, founded in the 1850s, grew in prominence as a service to the neighborhood, with Principal Edward W. Chesebro playing a crucial role in the solidifying of the school, until his early death in 1857.[119]

One would expect that the New England bastion of Christianity and Puritanism would produce a plethora of church building and religious consciousness among its offspring in Michigan. However, many of these had come from the burnt-over district of New York, the center of the revivals in New England, and had obtained their fill of intense religion. Also, many had come to Michigan for the business opportunities. As a result, they focused not on religion, but on making their mark and their fortune. Whereas immigrant groups plugged into churches immediately

FIGURE 92 **St. Mark's Episcopal Church, circa 1860**

direction. They built more homes on Fulton Street, progressing eastward, and Division Avenue, south of Fulton. Many also built homes across the river, along Grant and neighboring streets between Fulton and Leonard.[121]

As the spread of prominent New Englanders continued eastward, homeowners continued to seek high ground to avoid the flooding of the river. As a result, two wealthy neighborhoods developed. In the mid-1840s, the earliest residents built homes east of Lafayette on what became Heritage Hill, and in the 1850s, some settled in the thin strip north of Michigan and east of Division that became Belknap Lookout. Both of these areas claim historical roots to this time period, but the neighborhoods themselves did not become well established until the 1870s.[122]

The concept of neighborhood, in these wealthy areas of proud New England business families, could not reach a strong communal identity. Though the children played together and the adults befriended one another, they did not band together in a strong, unified, definitive manner. Perhaps if they had rallied around their neighborhood, they may have been able to save the hill from destruction.

upon arrival, often depending on them for subsistence and community, religion for the New Englanders rose out of their desires, not from urgency to have a church. Their faith was by no means empty, but church did not perform the same role or importance in the life of the New Englanders as it did in the lives of immigrants to America.

Despite the differences, the New Englanders did build and attend churches, although not with the same tenacity as their forefathers, or urgency as the immigrant groups who would later inhabit Grand Rapids. The New England neighborhood included the Universalist People's Church of Grand Rapids on Monroe and then on Pearl, First Reformed Church on Monroe, St. Andrew's Church on Monroe, St. Mark's Episcopal Church on Division, the Congregational Church on Park Place, and the Baptist Church on Fountain Street.[120]

As the trees became lumber and each shovelful of dirt from Prospect Hill raised the grade of the downtown streets, the neighborhood of Prospect Hill gradually disappeared. The general migration pattern of New Englanders usually assumed an easterly

FIGURES 93, 94, 95 **Joel Guild built his 16 by 26 foot pioneer home in 1833. This site later became the National Bank building, middle photo, left building. Now the McKay tower stands at this site which used to be a few dozen feet from the river.**

FIGURE 96 **Campau Square on July 7, 1899. The National Bank building appears dwarfed next to the Wonderly building. Compare this photo with the photos on page 46.**

Lovett House   Lyon Street   St. Mark's   Central High School   Ransom Street

FIGURE 97 **The view east from Prospect Hill toward the budding Heritage Hill neighborhood. While St. Mark's remains today with its towers extended, virtually everything else has changed. Grand Rapids Community College has taken over the high school location and Kendall College of Art & Design has replaced the livery stables.**

Oak Hill Cemetery – Neighbors from the Past

Where in the city can you find a 35-foot-high Egyptian pyramid, carved out of gray granite, with lumber baron Marcus Brown's name carved into it? Oak Hill Cemetery, one of the oldest and most unique graveyards in the city, contains the Brown monument and many others.

When dedicated in 1859, Oak Hill Cemetery stood at the southeastern border of the city at the intersection of Eastern Avenue and Hall Street. Just outside the city limits lay a budding Dutch settlement known as "Dutchtown." But in future years, Grand Rapids outgrew those original borders and the area around the cemetery became home first to New Englanders, then to Dutch, and finally to African Americans and Latinos.

Oak Hill Cemetery remains, 140 years after its dedication, as a fascinating repository of city history. The designers of Oak Hill Cemetery held an enlightened view of death as a hopeful, peaceful, and bright occasion, rather than one marked by pain, mourning, and darkness. They captured this progressive view of death by creating a cemetery modeled after a recreational park, with benches, walkways, plants, trees, and ornate monuments.

The trend attracted wealthy families who hired architects to design both the mausolea and landscaping. They erected large and ornate monuments in the new cemetery to preserve their family names. Many of these mausolea and monuments reflect a trend of Greek Revival architecture in the United States that was popular from the late 1800s to the Great Depression. Many of the most influential and powerful names in Grand Rapids history lie buried in Oak Hill Cemetery: Houseman, May, Herpolsheimer, Steketee, Pantlind, Chesebro, Voigt, Vandenberg, Lowe, Waters, Withey, Giddings, and Friant. These city elite not only built elegant homes in Heritage Hill to live in, but ornate mausolea by which they could be remembered, even competing at times for the most memorable monument. The large stone tombs, usually carved by costly Italian stonecutters, have provided intriguing architectural study pieces for scholars at Calvin College and other institutions.[1]

FIGURE 98 **Amasa Brown Watson Egyptian-style mausoleum**

FIGURE 99 **Celtic cross on the Butterfield site**

FIGURE 100 **Bissell monument**

FIGURE 101 **Withey mausoleum**

FIGURE 102 **J. Boyd Pantlind headstone**

FIGURE 103 **Clark mausoleum**

FIGURE 104 **Marcus Brown Egyptian pyramid monument**

FIGURE 105 **A. B. Watson Post 395 memorial site to the veterans of the Grand Army of the Republic (GAR)**

FIGURE 106

Marshy area, possibly the outlet of the musical frog pond

Original width of river below Fulton Street

Daniel Ball House

Immanuel Lutheran

Covered Bridge at Pearl Street

Prospect Hill

Division Street

East Bridge Street

FIGURE 107

FIGURES 106, 107 The above 1866 view of Grand Rapids, looking southwest from East Bridge Street (Michigan Street), is the best overall view of Prospect Hill. This photo shows how the hill sloped gently from the left edge of the picture towards the Daniel Ball House then plunged sharply down to Canal Street and the river. In the same view at left in 1999, the river is obscured by large buildings and the area of Prospect Hill is now flat. Immanuel Lutheran has expanded and the sharp slope up Michigan Street, at left in the old photo, has been graded over the years and is now the new home to the first phase of the Van Andel Institute. This view is currently more congested as the new courthouse building cloaks the buildings that hide the river.

FIGURE 108

FIGURE 109

FIGURE 108 In the 1856 painting by Sarah Nelson, above, St. Mark's Episcopal Church is partially hidden by Prospect Hill. Just to the left of St. Mark's is the Daniel Ball house situated on the highest point of Prospect Hill.

FIGURE 110 Daniel Ball, an early banker

FIGURE 109 The upper right photo shows the Ball house after Pearl Street was graded in 1857. Just visible to the right of the house is Crescent Park and up on Heritage Hill is the Williams home.

FIGURE 111 The photo at right pictures the Ball house high on Prospect Hill after the grading of Pearl Street was complete. See page 46.

FIGURE 106 AND 108 establish that the Daniel Ball home was situated at the highest point of Prospect Hill. FIGURE 109 AND 111 establish the grading that leveled Prospect Hill. From these photos we can determine the height of Prospect Hill.

FIGURE 111

Flanagan's

Universalist Church

Federal Building

National Bank Building

Powers Opera House

Central High School

THE MERCANTILE AGENCY

BANK

PIERCE

JOB PRINTING

Pearl Street

Daniel Ball Property

Monroe Avenue

FIGURES II2, II3 In the 1880s photo above of Campau Square, the Daniel Ball property is just visible in the middle left part of the picture. Though the house is out of view, the ramp up to house level is visible, as is the fence and tree line just in front of the house. The photo below was taken in November 1999 just before the Monroe pedestrian mall was to undergo construction to reopen the road to automobile traffic. The Flanagan's building built in 1873 is the common building in both photos.

Flanangan's

OLD KENT

OLD KENT

Monroe NW

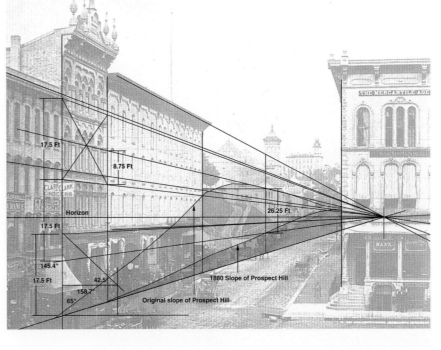

FIGURES 114, 115, 116 **By estimating the height of the present day Flanagan's building, a scale of measurement can be established for the historical photo. Once the scale is determined, it is relatively easy to calculate the height of Prospect Hill relative to the graded street level: approximately 26 feet. The historical record notes the height of Prospect Hill at about 60 feet, but gives no reference from what point they determined** its height. The record also mentions that the lower portions of Canal Street were once 15 feet lower than today. These facts combine to put Prospect Hill about 55 feet high from the old river edge before the islands were filled in. It is now possible, referring to historical maps, to draw a fairly accurate elevation profile of Pearl Street before all the earth works occurred that molded downtown Grand Rapids into what it is today.

Elevation Cross Section of Prospect Hill at Pearl Street

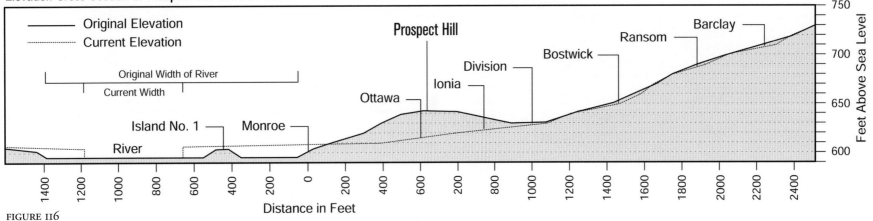

FIGURE 116

Crescent Park   Williams House   Second Reformed Church   Central School

St. Mark's Church

Federal Building

Unitarian Church Tower

FIGURE 117 **Photo looking northeast from the top of the 200 foot tower built over the old Haldane home (see figure 83). The Federal building is located where the Grand Rapids Art Museum stands today on the corner of Division Avenue and Pearl Street.**

FIGURE 118 **Fountain in Crescent Park. Henry R. Williams' house in 1865. Williams was Grand Rapids' first mayor. Note the lower grade of the street level.**

The Hill District Forms

When John Ball built his mansion at the top of Fulton Street Hill in 1838, it was a move that foreshadowed the movement of future city elite. During Ball's time, people would come to Grand Rapids, make their fortune and build a large, beautiful home on Prospect Hill. By the 1870s, however, this once-wealthy area of Prospect Hill faced destruction for city improvements, and anyone with a significant amount of money struck out for the nearest and largest hill — Fulton Street Hill.[123]

Louis and Sophie Campau later joined John Ball atop the hill. Furniture barons, politicians, lumber barons, prominent business owners, and bankers, each with their own fascinating tales, gradually bought up plots of farmland and built mansions. Unlike the Campaus, who were French Canadian, most of the first residents of what would become "Heritage Hill" were sons of New England.[124]

The early settlers of the hilltop joined Ball in the 1840s, mostly on Fulton Street, the main road into the downtown. One of the first residents, Damon Hatch, built on farmland at the present day corner of Cherry and Morris in 1845. Many

Grand River   Lovett House   Williams House

FIGURE 119 **Two photos pieced together form this view from Central High School bell tower looking north along Ransom Avenue. The Lovett House, on the bluff in the foreground, is where the Ford Fieldhouse is located today.**

parties for the neighbors were thrown there. The river limestone house remains as perhaps the oldest home on the Hill.[125]

    Another early settler to the Hill, druggist Samuel Sanford, began building a home near Cherry and Paris, not far from Hatch in 1847. When the frame of his house was completed, his fiancée died, leaving him heartbroken. He left the building before its completion and it became known as "Sanford's Folly." After a 17-year stint during which the house allegedly became haunted, Sanford returned and finished the house. It still stands at 540 Cherry Street SE.[126]

    Whatever the stories or legends behind them, the large houses were numerous by the 1880s and 1890s. Often, smaller houses built by working-class men were bought and destroyed as land on the Hill became sparse, and those who wanted it most could afford to pay for the demolition. Lots were unavailable by 1930, as large mansions of varied architectures and building materials filled the area roughly bounded by Union on the east, Pleasant on the south, Jefferson and Barclay on the west, and Crescent on the north.[127]

FIGURE 120 **Afternoon gathering at the Williams house in the 1860s**

FIGURE 121 **Stereoscopic view of the John Ball house on Fulton Street. To view this photo in three dimensions, hold the book about a foot away from your face and cross your eyes until a third photo forms between the two photos. It takes some practice to view the merged photo in focus. Sometimes it helps to hold and focus on a finger a few inches from your nose in order to get your vision to cross, then shift your attention to the photo.**

The Hill was "The Place to Live" in Grand Rapids for several decades, for those who could afford it. Nearly every prominent businessman or politician in the city once lived in the Hilltop. Typically, these men and their families had the best jobs and education, and frequented the wealthy Peninsular Club downtown. Most attended Fountain Street Baptist Church or First Congregational Church.[128]

Neighbors on the hilltop formed the "Good Government League" to combat corrupt city politics and conduct moral reform. The organization wanted to shut down saloons and beer halls, mostly working-class establishments.[129]

After the furniture strike of 1911, the power of the Hilltop reached its greatest strength. Reverend Alfred Wishart of Fountain Street Baptist Church, who lived on Terrace (present day Prospect) Avenue on the hill,

FIGURE 122 **Robert Irwin**

Heritage Hill's "St. Ann"

Known as "St. Ann" by her friends due to her nurturing, motherly presence, Anna Bissell is also well known for her extraordinary business accomplishments as a woman at a time when gender roles severely discouraged such behavior.

The daughter of a Scottish mariner, Anna Sutherland met and married Melville Bissell, moving to Grand Rapids in 1865. They first lived on Prospect Hill near St. Mark's Episcopal Church, but moved to 60 College Ave. on the Hilltop as Prospect Hill disappeared.

Frustrations with keeping their china shop on Canal Street clean during the 1870s led the Bissells to invent the Bissell Carpet Sweeper. As the pair sold the idea, they closed the china shop and turned their full attention to making carpet sweepers.

As an equal business partner with her husband until his death in 1889, Anna Bissell learned enough business and law to see the company through a disastrous fire at the sweeper plant in 1884. She served as president for 30 years, and the business became famous nationwide.[1]

In 1897, Bissell shared her company's financial success with the community by contributing to the building of the Bissell House, an inner-city children's mission to the "Bloody Fifth," a run-down area between Belknap-Lookout and the river. In addition to educating and helping children, the huge building served as a community center for lectures and music until 1912 when money ran out and the Bissell House was closed.[2]

FIGURE 123 **Anna Bissell**

became entrenched in the city politics and business, preaching the need for the most educated members of society to rule over it politically and economically. Furniture baron and Fountain Street Church attendee Robert Irwin, who lived just a block away from Wishart, epitomized the city elite from a business perspective. Irwin was on the board of four large furniture factories in Grand Rapids and several local banks, a trend shared by the entire furniture and banking industry. He was crucial in changing the city charter of 1916, to mold the opinion of city politics in favor of the hilltop.[130]

The Hilltop quickly became the place to live in early Grand Rapids, the first lasting symbol of its prosperity and pride.

Belknap-Lookout

The steep bluff that overlooks the city may in itself represent the reason why no prominent settlement existed on Belknap-Lookout until the 1870s, when a huge population growth in Grand Rapids quickly turned the obstacle into a prime housing settlement.

The bluff community that soon developed took the name of early Grand Rapids firefighter and historian, Charles Belknap. The community had maintained a water reservoir since 1874, capitalizing on the numerous springs of clear drinking water located on the bluff. The reservoir twice drenched the community below, as the retaining wall split in 1880 and again in 1900, causing severe damage to streets and homes.[131] The city repaired the reservoir each time, and population on the bluff continued to increase.

FIGURE 124 **Photos on this page show damage caused by the break in the old Livingston Reservoir on the morning of July 2, 1900. This break through the dike wall of the reservoir was on the east side, flooding the hillside east of Belknap Park. The break started at 5 a.m. Within an hour the flood of water had entered Coldbrook Creek and was carried into Grand River.**

FIGURE 125

FIGURE 126

FIGURE 127 **Roberta Griffiths**

Braille on Belknap

One of Belknap's early residents couldn't appreciate the view it offered of the rest of the city. Roberta Griffiths was blind.

She moved to the bluff in 1900 to be near her mother. Despite her handicap, she worked as a writer and real estate agent after attending various schools for the blind and Western Reserve University.

Her most amazing contribution to the neighborhood was the designing of her own house, which was constructed according to her plans. Unfortunately, when the resevoir on top of the hill broke in 1900, the gushing water filled her basement and destroyed much of her writing and music.

Among her other accomplishments are the founding of the Association for the Blind and Sight Conservation (now Vision Enrichment Services) and the American Association of Workers for the Blind, and the writing of a 6-volume Braille dictionary, the first of its kind. Before her death in 1941, she worked to prevent infant blindness as well as improve life for other blind adults.[1]

FIGURE 128 **Reservoir break damage, 1900**

Originally purchased in 1833 as part of a larger plot by New Yorker Samuel Dexter, Belknap-Lookout became a major settlement for the overflow population of the expanding class of New Englanders. The area originally served as a cemetery, but this was moved in 1855, clearing the way for housing.[132]

An age-old rule of city settlement states that wealthier residents take the highest ground and Belknap-Lookout followed that dictum. Fairview Avenue, along the western bluff, became populated by upper-middle class entrepreneurs and lawyers, while a blue-collar working force filled in along the gradual downward slope to the east.[133]

FIGURE 129 **Coit School**

FIGURE 130, 131 **The photo below shows Belknap hill before much of the hill was removed to make the earthen embankments used to elevate U.S. 131 through downtown. The top photo reveals how much land was removed.**

A microcosm of city growth during the same time period, Belknap's population exploded, increasing demands for both education and transportation. The city built Coit School at the corner of Coit and Trowbridge in 1880 to serve the needs of the swiftly expanding bluff neighborhood. Originally heated by four wood stoves requiring 30 cords of wood per year, Coit School was enlarged in 1908, 1922, and 1950, and still stands today as one of the oldest landmarks in the city. In the absence of another prominent building, the school has served as the neighborhood rallying point for 120 years, even between 1960 and 1980 when Belknap experienced the typical housing problems of an inner-city neighborhood.[134]

A horsecar route preceded a streetcar route that ran north on Coit Avenue to Trowbridge, east on Trowbridge and then north on Clancy until it dead-ended near Matilda Street. The short-lived streetcar line lasted from 1888 until 1914. Though the reasons for the removal of the streetcar in Belknap remain unknown, the disappearance suggests a lack of demand for streetcar service on the bluff. The stairway on the western face, built to aid pedestrian traffic in late 1880s, was likely all the neighbors needed for transportation.[135]

FIGURE 132 **Campau Square, circa 1870**

FIGURE 133 **Campau Square with the Wonderly building, circa 1890**

FIGURE 134 **Campau Square with the new National Bank building, circa 1923**

FIGURE 135 **Campau Square, August 1926**

II

Walking Neighborhoods

Immigration Fuels Explosive Growth in City
Ethnic Neighborhoods Form

Immigration Fuels Explosive Growth in City

"When people first arrive here, especially while they have had to borrow travel money, they have many expenses. It's like starting all over again and having to buy everything. It's tough." [1]

Jan Scheffer, immigrant

Through the streets of Grand Rapids, a Polish factory worker walks home. It is late in the evening in the spring of 1880 and he has spent hours working at the furniture factory. One of the young girls working for Valeria Lipczynski, a Polish employment agent, took him to the factory the very day after he and his family arrived in Grand Rapids. Her recommendation immediately got him hired, as factory owners always eagerly snatched up hard-working immigrants directed to them by Lipczynski.

Although moving to a different country is no easy experience, adjusting to life in America proves less difficult than expected for this man. Yes, the work is hard and the pay is not illustrious, but he can provide for his family. They live in a sizable city, but the neighborhood in which they live seems to be a small piece of Poland — not an American city at all. Like most Polish immigrants, he and his family settled into a Polish neighborhood where everything his family needs is within walking distance. A Polish grocery store provides the comfort of native foods. He can stop by a Polish hall to sip a pint of refreshing beer and share news with his neighbors. On Sunday, they walk to St. Adalbert's Catholic Church to worship in their native tongue, and on Saturday, his entire family treks to the casino club to visit with other Polish immigrants.

Like other growing American cities at the turn of the century, Grand Rapids was a walking city. Its rapidly expanding industrial center resembled a patchwork quilt comprised of factories surrounded by "walking neighborhoods" divided along ethnic lines and fueled by immigra-

FIGURE 1 **Before 1900, immigrants began forming "walking neighborhoods" around furniture factories and churches in Grand Rapids.**

tion. By the turn of the century, Grand Rapids was on its way from a small trading post on the Grand River to a successful city, its population skyrocketing from 2,000 to 90,000. That spectacular growth gave rise to the walking neighborhoods, small cities within a city, which sprouted up around Grand Rapids. The lack of public and private transportation made proximity a necessity. People lived, shopped, worked, worshipped, and played all within a short walking distance of their homes. Neighborhoods were not only a place to live, they were a microcosm of a 20th century city. Each neighborhood, therefore, contained a variety of businesses, stores, and employment opportunities all flavored by the ethnic stew in which they simmered.

Despite language and ethnic differences, all neighborhoods in Grand Rapids shared common ground. Adults and children established and maintained their social networks. People chose to live in areas where they felt a common bond with their neighbors. In the last half of the 19th century, those ties revolved around ethnicity and religion. Grand Rapids, as with most U.S. cities during this period, was home to a sizable immigrant population. As is common among immigrants, they tended to settle in enclaves where their language was spoken and their cultural heritage was shared. Neighborhoods developed as distinctly Dutch, German, Polish, Irish, Italian, African American, and others around the city.

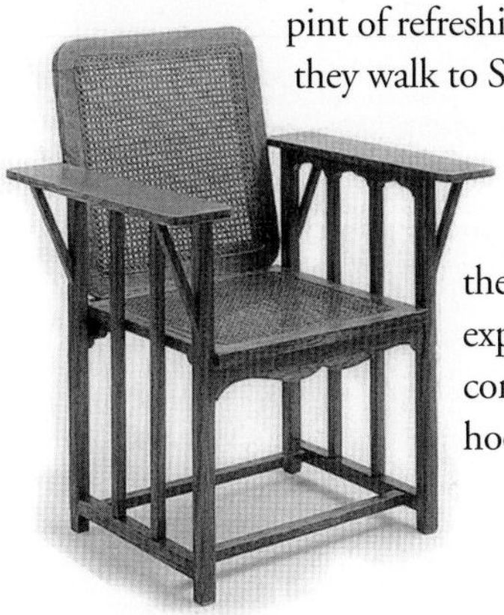

FIGURE 2 **Chair from Phoenix Furniture Co., circa 1894**

FIGURE 3 **Berkey and Gay furniture, circa 1875**

57

U.S. "Open Door" Immigration Policy

States located west of the Appalachian Mountains worked proactively to attract immigrant workers. Some states sent brochures and pamphlets to Europe encouraging emigration. Michigan sent a designated "immigration agent" to work the immigration docks in New York City. Perhaps the most convincing arguments, in the eyes of the Europeans toiling over the decision to emigrate, were letters received from friends and family members who were established in America. These letters described the positive aspects of life in the States, offering those frustrated by the European economy and leadership a very positive and viable alternative. As the demand for workers grew, Grand Rapids and other areas in Michigan soon began to publish brochures. The receipt of the brochures along with the letters written by immigrant residents of Grand Rapids resulted in a dramatic increase in immigration to the area.

Between 1882 and 1912, immigration regulations were set in place to restrict the great influx of immigrants. Castle Garden, located in New York City, served as the welcoming center for immigrants on the Northeast coast until 1892, when Ellis Island opened. Ellis Island, a larger, more modern facility, was better equipped to handle the masses of immigrants. It operated as the welcome center and inspection area for immigrants until 1932. By the 1930s, the number of immigrants to the United States had decreased so much that the number emigrating from the United States was greater than the number immigrating to the country.[1]

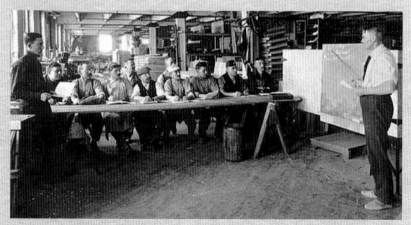

FIGURE 4 **Immigrant workers were often taught English at their workplace in Americanization classes such as the above class at Raab Chair Company.**

Before the population boom, though, the future of Grand Rapids was uncertain. Several local businessmen believed that Grand Rapids had the potential to become a great city. But they realized Grand Rapids needed more people to achieve its full potential, and they set about to recruit these future citizens.

Migration to Grand Rapids

Immigrants chose Grand Rapids for both macro and micro reasons. Many felt pushed to leave their homes because of poor economic conditions or worrisome political and social situations. Europe during the 19th century was in a state of economic and social unrest. Industrialization and changes in agricultural practices displaced both craftsmen and peasant laborers. At the same time traditional occupations for these classes disappeared, their populations increased. In addition, famines, such as the one caused by potato blight in Ireland, occurred in many countries. Nationalism across Europe peaked in the 19th century, so agitation for independence caused unrest.

FIGURE 5 **John Almy**

Most who came also felt the lure of money, freedom, food, and work pulling them to America, assuming that any situation they found in their new home would be better than what they had left behind. As the century wore on, the tide of European immigrants increased and diversified. The Irish, Dutch, and Germans came first, followed closely by Poles, Lithuanians, Italians, Scandinavians, Greeks, and other groups. In 1900, nearly two-thirds of Grand Rapids' 87,565 residents claimed foreign parentage.[2] An additional 12,200 men claimed foreign birth and, of those, nearly 35 percent had been residents of Grand Rapids for at least 20 years.

But other immigrants came as the result of a concerted public relations campaign by the city's industrial leaders. Despite the city's initial growth spurt in the early 1830s, residents and businesses in Grand Rapids experienced effects of the decade-long economic depression that swept the nation. Leading citizens who wanted to transform the village into an industrial town decided to advertise the advantages of living in Grand Rapids. They reasoned that by convincing people to move to West Michigan, they could fill their factories with workers — and the town would become prosperous.

In the spring of 1845, Michigan's Governor Barry established the government-funded position of "immigration agent" in the hopes that an agent, acting on behalf of the state, would attract recent immigrants to Michigan, encouraging them to settle its great wilderness and populate one of its few cities. Grand Rapids resident John Almy, on the recommendation of congressman Lucius Lyon, was chosen by Barry to fill the office and represent the interests of all Michigan in New York.

Almy was experienced in this business: He had been living and working in New York and Boston for the previous six months as a private immigration agent, hired by several West Michigan landowners to recruit immigrants. Michigan appointed Almy as its first immigration agent and gave him state funds to attract new residents to Michigan. Almy then joined with Edmund Bostwick to create a six-page booklet describing Grand Rapids in very favorable terms, highlighting reasons that a move would be beneficial. More than 5,000 copies of the booklet, which was produced in both English and German, were given to immigrants in New York City and to organizations and individuals who might encourage immigration. The promises and projections appealed to many who longed to emigrate from Europe. Almy served as Michigan's immigration agent until 1849 when a Flint resident replaced him.

In the 1850s, as the flow of immigration began to increase, the need for government subsidized agents such as Almy dissipated. Immigrants wrote letters home praising Grand Rapids for its plentiful jobs and abundant homestead land. In the 1850s, Dutch settlers in Grand Rapids established such a successful communication network with friends and family members still in the Netherlands that they created an immigration society to aid newcomers in finding housing and employment.[3]

Not all immigrants to Grand Rapids were foreign-born, however; many came north seeking economic advancement and better lives. Following the Civil War (1861-1865), Charles C. Comstock, the owner of a tub and pail company, attracted African Americans to Grand Rapids to work in his factory. He operated in conjunction with the Freedmen's Bureau, a federal agency designed to aid newly freed slaves and bring workers to the city.

Other local enterprises also banded together to finance recruiting trips. In 1871, the Grand Rapids and Indiana Railway paid for Grand Rapids minister J. P. Tustin to visit Scandinavia and encourage Norwegians and Swedes to make their home in Grand Rapids. His trip was successful. By the turn of the century, the number of Kent County residents of Swedish or Norwegian birth had more than doubled.

FIGURE 6 **In this early photo of Sixth Street, Comstock's factory is yet to be built. The curved dam in the river just above Sixth Street was built in 1849.**

FIGURE 7 **Constance Rourke**

Women of Consequence

Two women who made a difference lived just blocks away from each other in what is today East Hills.

Constance Rourke

A local proponent of American culture, Constance Mayfield Rourke lived on Luton Avenue SE. Between the world wars, Rourke wrote volumes of reviews, articles, and books, reacting powerfully against critics who said that America had no culture compared to Europe. Her legacy in literature is significant, though underestimated, as she helped pave the way for the American Studies movement and built American pride during a crucial era of its history.[1]

Minnie Sheldon Hodges

At the age of 16, Minnie Sheldon Hodges began a teaching career. She then worked as office manager of an insurance company before marrying Alonzo Hodges in 1887. Perhaps her early experience with desks at her first two jobs inspired the newlyweds to start Valley City Desk Company on Butterworth Street SW. After his death in 1905, Minnie ran the company shrewdly until selling it in 1913. During their married years, the couple lived on Holbrook Street, now Kellogg SE.[2]

Ethnic Neighborhoods Form

"It happened about that time that all Holland seemed to be climbing over the dykes…"[4]
Charles Belknap

East Side Dutch Neighborhoods

Most Dutch immigrants came to Grand Rapids in large groups, making the Dutch among the first Europeans to settle the area en masse. In 1846 and 1847, within two years of the distribution of Almy and Bostwick's pamphlet, Rev. Albertus C. Van Raalte brought 17 families from the Netherlands to West Michigan. The bulk of the group settled near Holland, but a small number settled in Grand Rapids. These Dutch immigrants opted to forego the pioneer lifestyle of clearing land and building homes in the wilderness; instead, they sought industrial employment and urban life, finding jobs in Grand Rapids' furniture factories.[5]

This group of Dutch immigrants in Grand Rapids settled near Fulton Street and Grandville Avenue in the Shantytown area today known as Heartside. Like the small groups of Irish before them, the Dutch sought out the most affordable neighborhood to meet their immediate needs. By this time, Shantytown had become a melting pot of the blue-collar working class of Grand Rapids. The hard-working community consisted of blacksmiths, shipyard workers, riverboat hands, warehouse workers, and restaurant and hotel employees. They lived close to the manufacturing district, yet they could still farm outlying areas.[6] Encouraged by the success of the first Dutch settlers, Dutch immigrants continued to flow into the city. In 1848 and 1849 significant numbers arrived and by June 1850 Grand Rapids was home to 53 Dutch households, or 222 people.[7] Sometimes entire congregations moved to Grand Rapids.

In 1849, a group of Dutch settlers in Grand Rapids formed the first Dutch-speaking congregation in Grand Rapids at Second Reformed Church, located on

Frans Van Driele and His Arrival

"…I left Holland for Grand Rapids and on July 5, 1848, found work as a laborer on the canal at the rate of $16 per month and board. But the days were long, from 6:30 in the morning til sunset. There was no money, and we were paid in store pay. I slept in a shanty on a straw tick. There were three bunks, one above the other. We had no blankets, for the weather was warm. My friends were 14 or 15 Irishmen who conducted themselves fairly well, considering everything. When evening came we all knelt in prayer. Each prayed by himself. They asked if I was Catholic. I answered that a good Protestant also said his prayers when he went to bed."[1]

FIGURE 8 **Frans Van Driele**

FIGURE 9 **Dutch Shantytown, looking down Oakes Street toward the Union Depot**

Piggeries in Grand Rapids

"The history of the piggeries was erratic and, at one point, hilarious. In one day's garbage there was a quantity of peaches pickled in alcohol. The pigs got drunk, squealing merrily, and staggering as their legs gave way, pitching them on their snouts."

— Dr. Richard Harms

As the 20th century began and the city's population approached 100,000, disposing of garbage became a major problem that required city action. During the 19th century, citizens had disposed of animal and vegetable waste from their kitchens by feeding it to livestock, tossing it in a remote corner of the yard or down abandoned wells.

A few city neighborhoods were periodically visited by pig farmers who hauled the kitchen waste back to their farms. They mixed this waste with water or sour milk to make swill (also called hogwash), which was fed to the pigs. For most of the rest of the city without this service, the garbage was left to rot. Vermin and insects were attracted to these mounds, and during the summer months the odor became very offensive. In 1895, garbage thrown into the Grand River became such a problem for river navigation that the Army Corps of Engineers complained to the mayor.

As a result, the city built a coal-fired garbage burner in 1897. Located on what was then an island in the river, now the 200 block of Market SW, the facility had a daily capacity of 39 tons. By 1905, health concerns caused the city to institute mandatory citywide municipal garbage collection. To handle the increased garbage volume that resulted, the city sought a more cost-effective means than the burner, which cost $6,000 annually to operate. After studying other municipal projects, city leaders decided that either burning the garbage to produce steam for heating and electricity, or reducing the garbage to fertilizer, was preferred.

Although the city sought bids for such a facility from several firms, all the proposals came with sizable construction costs. One alternative, presented by Alvah Brown of the Garbage Reduction & Utilization Co., was intriguing. Brown talked in vague terms of using "chemical means" to process the animal and vegetable waste component of the city's waste. Brown proposed paying the city $1,200 annually for this portion of the waste. The city was responsible for collecting and separating the waste. Since this garbage component constituted the bulk of the city's waste, Brown was given the contract.

Citizens were required to discard their waste in two containers, one containing animal and vegetable waste, and the other containing ashes, cans, glass, small dead animals. The material that could not be reprocessed was burned, while the rest was loaded onto wagons, later railroad cars, for shipment to Brown's operation, southeast of present-day Alger and Plymouth streets. To the surprise and anger of many, Brown's processing plant turned out to be a large pig farm.

Brown's piggery cooked the garbage and mixed it with water to make swill. The swill was delivered to the more than 500 pigs.

The raucous and malodorous "ranch" brought complaints from residents as far away as Oakdale School, nearly two miles to the northwest. In 1913, because of the complaints, the city gave the three-year contract to another bidder, the Grand Rapids Garbage Holding Co., which operated a 200-acre piggery south of White Cloud in Newaygo County. The city, however, had to pay the cost of transporting the garbage the additional 40 miles.

Three years later these transportation costs caused the city to accept the bid of Henry Hartman. When word circulated that Hartman was planning to reopen the Brown piggery south of town, residents of that area obtained a court injunction to prevent the city from disposing of the garbage at that location. As a result, Hartman opened his farm near Sullivan, west of Ravenna, in Muskegon County. In 1921, the contract reverted to the Garbage Holding Co., which had changed its name to the Grand Rapids Livestock Co.

The Livestock Co. held the contract until 1938 when the increasing amounts of chemicals and other non-digestible material in the garbage made the pork unpalatable to humans. Since there was no market for the meat, operating costs increased, and the city sought a piggery closer to town to save transportation costs. The Michigan Piggery operated by the Darling Co. of Chicago, was the only bidder. Its plant was located on Market SW, near the sewage treatment plant. The Michigan Piggery shipped fattened hogs to Ohio for use in producing hog cholera serum, their only commercial use due to the meat's flavor. In December 1952, the piggery was closed and the city began to use landfills for garbage. [1]

FIGURE 10 **Pigs formed the early answer to Grand Rapids' garbage woes.**

The Immigrant Experience

The choice to immigrate to the United States often was not easy. Many felt as though they had no choice: if they wanted to live, they needed to leave. Oscar Handlin, in his award-winning book, "The Uprooted," describes the socio-economic climate in Europe that set the stage for mass migration across Europe and to the United States.

"The immigrant movement started in the peasant heart of Europe. Ponderously balanced in a solid equilibrium for centuries, the old structure of an old society began to crumble at the opening of the modern era. One by one, rude shocks weakened the aged foundations until some climactic blow suddenly tumbled the whole into ruins.... Stability, the deep, cushiony ability to take blows, and yet to keep things as they were, came from the special place of these people on the land. The peasants were agriculturists; their livelihood sprang from the earth. Americans they met later would have called them 'farmers,' but that word had a different meaning in Europe. The bonds that held these men to their acres were not simply the personal ones of the husbandman who temporarily mixes his sweat with the soil. The ties were deeper, more intimate. For the peasant was part of a community and the community was held to the land as a whole.

"Always, the start was the village. 'I was born in such a village in such a parish' — so the peasant invariably began the account of himself. Thereby he indicated the importance of the village in his being; this was the fixed point by which he knew his position in the world and his relationship with all humanity.

"So the peasants held together, lived together, together drew the stuff of life from an unwilling earth. Simple neighborliness, mutual assistance, were obligations inherent in the conditions of things, obligations

which none could shirk without fear of cutting himself off from the whole. And that was the community, that the village — the capacity to do these things together, the relationships that regulated all.

"Upon arrival in the United States, immigrants struggled with language and money problems. Some sought out family members; others sought out anyone who shared their language or religion. The situation made many immigrants feel helpless and caused them to wonder if they might be wise to return to their homeland. Recollections of the struggles and difficulties experienced in their homeland reminded most of why they left and forbid them from returning. Slowly, they began to build new connections in this land they neither knew nor understood. Immigrants, though isolated, were eager to start a new life in America. Confusion and loneliness, coupled with the desire to build a new life, united immigrants. This is the beginning of immigrant neighborhoods and communities.

"Strangers in the immediate world about them, the immigrants often recognized, in dismay, the loneliness of their condition. Their hesitant steps groped around the uncertain hazards of new places and exposed them ever to perilous risks. No one could enjoy the satisfaction of confidence in his own unaided powers....

"In their loneliness and helplessness, the immigrants reached for some arm to lean upon. There came a time, they knew, when a man was like a stray dog, driven away by all folk, glad to be caressed by any kindly hand. At many steps in his life's journey, he came to points beyond which he could not go on alone; unaided, he was doomed. Then it was well if help could come from others like him.

"Consequently, the newcomers took pains early to seek out those whom experience made their brothers; and to organize each others' support, they created a great variety of formal and informal institutions. Then, at last, they came to know how good it was that brothers should dwell together."[1]

FIGURE II **Poster depicting the joining of Greek and American cultures**

Bostwick Avenue near Lyon Street.[8] Frans Van Driele, co-founder of Second RCA, claimed that the Dutch immigrants found unity within the church because they shared a "'deep inner piety' and a familiarity with Reformed theology."[9] As Van Driele once wrote: "We were all of one heart and one mind. We recognized each other as truly being of the faithful."[10] The church was a unifying factor within the Dutch community from the very earliest days of Dutch settlement. As immigration increased, individuals within the Dutch population began to define themselves less by their shared "Dutch-ness" and more by membership in a specific neighborhood church that preached a familiar interpretation of Reformed theology. Doctrinal interpretations divided the Dutch population in Grand Rapids, but united the members of the individual churches. Over time, many small immigrant Dutch neighborhoods established a church that reflected the religious beliefs of the residents.

FIGURE 12
Rev. Hendrik Klyn

Bonded together by language, religion, family ties, and need, the Dutch helped each other establish roots, find jobs and housing, and build community in their new neighborhoods. Unlike the Irish, the Dutch held fast to their language and did not learn English as quickly. This unified them even more, as they published many periodicals in Dutch and conducted church services in Dutch well into the late 20th century.[11]

Unified by their traditions and the proximity in which they settled, the neighborhood began to flourish. Bounded by Fulton and Wealthy streets, and Sheldon and Ionia avenues, this community boasted 74 Dutch families by 1860.[12] By the census in 1860, 10 percent of the population, or 867 people, claimed birth in the Netherlands. By 1870 that number more than doubled, rising to 2,944, or 18 percent of the population.[13] The First Christian Reformed Church, led by Hendrik Klyn and Wilhelmus Van Leeuwen, was organized in 1857 in a small building on

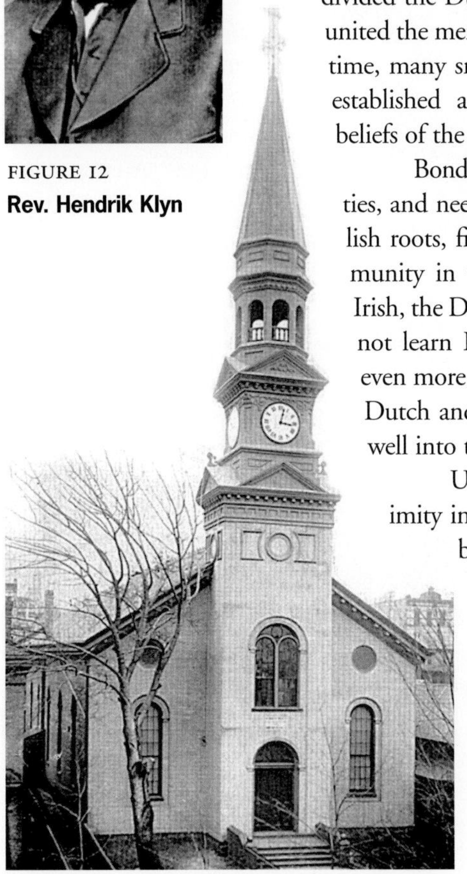

FIGURE 13 **First Christian Reformed Church on Spring Street (58 Commerce Avenue SW). It was torn down in the late 1950s.**

Ionia and Weston Street. Ten years later it had grown to 1,300 members in a church on Commerce Avenue.[14] This close-knit Dutch community established businesses such as a wooden shoe outlet, grocery store, clothing store, and feed store.[15] The Church even sponsored a Dutch-language school on Williams Street, opened in 1873 by W. H. De Lange.[16]

Soon after the first Dutch settled in the Heartside area, two other Dutch neighborhoods began to develop to the north. One enclave was near Canal Street and North Division Avenue, with many Dutch living near Coldbrook Street. As more Dutch settlers arrived from the provinces of Zeeland, Friesland, and Groningen, the

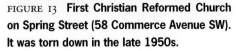

FIGURE 14 **Stryker's Mill at 668 (278) Grandville Avenue SW, on the northeast corner of Rumsey. The building stood until 1980.**

A Snapshot of Dutch Life, 1892

"In the immigrant neighborhoods, Dutch housewives, barelegged in wooden shoes, hitched up their skirts and scrubbed the front steps while their husbands filed into the furniture factories. Along the main streets the garish glow of electric streetlights had only recently replaced gas lamps. Several downtown business establishments were newly illuminated. So close to Lake Michigan, the climate favored clouds. Yet on clear nights, when a wind cleared the haze of coal smoke, city lights were no match for the stars."[1]

John Ter Braak: The Wooden Shoe Man

In 1873, Dutch immigrant John H. Ter Braak moved to Grand Rapids and opened a shop on Goodrich Street. Ter Braak and his employees produced wooden shoes worn by the area Dutch for work and for dress.

By 1888, Ter Braak's shop was located at 159 Spring Street SW. He had expanded production to make 60 pairs of wooden shoes each day — about 12,000 pairs per year. Local American and Scandinavian farmers, seeing the practicality of the wooden shoes, began to frequent his shop. Ter Braak's business, though supported by local patrons, was not entirely dependent upon it. Surprisingly, many of the shoes produced by this klompenmaker were shipped either to Paterson, N.J., and worn by employees in a silk factory, or shipped to Cleveland to protect the feet of steel and iron workers.

Ter Braak's shoes, worn by some for the sake of tradition and others for the sake of safety and practicality, were popular. This modest shop in the Grandville Avenue Dutch community is a great example of businesses building on the ethnic heritage of the surrounding neighborhood.[1]

Canal-North Division neighborhood expanded; however, it disappeared around the turn of the 20th century when factories laid claim to this residential area.

About this same time, Dutch immigrants moved into the College Avenue and East Bridge Street (now Michigan Street) area. By 1879, more skilled Dutch workers resided in this neighborhood than any other within the city. This neighborhood,

FIGURE 15 **Dutch language school at 43 Williams SW.**

because of its high rate of skilled workers, proved more stable than many other lower-income neighborhoods. Steady employment made purchasing a home possible and many of the families in this neighborhood owned their own homes.

South of the Canal-North Division and College-East Bridge neighborhoods, Dutch settlers bought land and homes near South Division Avenue and Lafayette Street. A majority who lived there migrated to Grand

FIGURE 16 **Newsboys were allowed to sell papers inside Bylsma's Saloon.**

Rebelling against Dutch Life, 1913

"Along our little street there was much rivalry among the different families to prove how non-Dutch they were. Many showed their non-Dutchness by mopping their floors daily not on hands and knees, but with a newfangled mop on a stick. Others would scrub their front stoops only on alternate days instead of daily. Some did away with the afternoon tea hour, or the morning coffee session, because those were so Dutch…. It was being non-Dutch and therefore meritorious, to buy your new furniture on the installment plan, to aspire to owning a Ford, to sing with a fancy trill in your voice, not to shake hands with your host or hostess when you entered their house — wasn't this a free democracy? — to read the comics in the daily papers, to leave the house by the front door instead of the back, to shun eating Leiden or Gouda cheese, to wear round patches on your pants instead of square Dutch patches, never to read or speak or admit that you understood one word of the abominable, lowly Dutch language, even though your poor old stubborn mother might have all the walls of the house hung with Dutch mottoes and Bible texts, and might turn away every salesman that came to the door by whispering guiltily; "No spreek Englels."[1]

Rapids from the Netherlands just after the Civil War, between the years 1865 and 1869. Originally, the bulk of the population worked as unskilled factory laborers, but as the residents moved up to skilled labor and professional employment, they remained in the area and elevated the status of the neighborhood.[17]

Later, as the city grew, Dutch immigrants settled the outskirts of the city near Grandville and Clyde Park avenues. From 1888 to 1900, about 600 households of immigrants moved there, with more than three-quarters coming directly from the Netherlands, mostly from Groningen in the north.[18] Like many Dutch immigrants, most worked in factories. This group tended to be skilled workers who had heard of the prosperous furniture manufacturers in Grand Rapids and left Holland ready to live, work, and raise families in the already-established Dutch neighborhoods of Grand Rapids.

About the same time the Grandville-Clyde Park neighborhood was settled, Dutch immigrants started to settle a northern neighborhood near Plainfield Avenue and East Leonard Street. This neighborhood, established around 1900, was one of 12 distinct Dutch neighborhoods in the city. New immigrants were drawn to this semi-rural neighborhood for the abundance of available land and for its proximity to the industrial area near downtown. The 300-plus Dutch households within the neighborhood created a need for businesses to serve them and many local residents not making furniture found employment in shops and other local businesses.

FIGURE 18 **Verbrugge Barber Shop in Dutch brickyards**

A Chosen Isolation

The Dutch and Polish brickyard neighborhoods, though located close to each other and focused on the same brickyards, operated virtually independently of each other. The Dutch lived in their enclaves and frequented the shops of other Dutch members of their congregation (or, if necessary, the shop of a Dutch person from a different congregation).

The loyalties of the brickyard Dutch were focused on those Dutch with whom they worshiped at church; what loyalty that remained was directed at other Dutch within the area. If an item could not be purchased, a business transaction made, or a spouse found within these two realms of loyalty, it is surprisingly possible that the item would be done without, the business transaction never completed, and the son or daughter never married.

For "the good Dutch" living in the Dutch brickyard, there was no mixing with Polish neighbors. This was a distinctively Dutch neighborhood by every possible measure. In 1900, 60 percent of the population declared themselves to be immigrants of less than 20 years. Dutch was spoken at home, at work, and at two of the three Dutch Reformed/Christian Reformed Churches. By most accounts, the neighborhood maintained its strong ethnic flavor until World War II.

After the war, residents of the brickyard began to move away to less crowded, more desirable neighborhoods. The tiny brickyard neighborhood, containing 103 Dutch families in 1900, was just a memory of a long-lost era. Times were changing, the brickyard as much as anything else.[1]

FIGURE 17 **Schaafsma Heating & Cooling now occupies the original home of Coldbrook Christian Reformed Church, here seen looking up the south side of Barnett Street east from Ionia Avenue.**

FIGURE 19 **Zevalkink Grocery was owned by Dutch grocer Barund Zevalkink, who stands at his storefront at 649 (255) Grandville SW.**

FIGURE 20 **Dutch funeral in the Brickyards, 1906**

North of this area was the Knapp and Wartrous Streets (now Lafayette Avenue) settlement. This neighborhood, comprised of 40-some blue-collar households in 1900, housed Dutch who had immigrated since 1880. Differing from other nearby Dutch enclaves, this neighborhood was the only entirely Dutch, entirely blue-collar neighborhood of the city. This community was a stable working-class neighborhood with a very high percentage of homeowners. Whereas other neighborhoods experienced a change in demographics as some homeowners were promoted to white-collar work and moved into larger and newer homes, the residents of the Knapp-Wartrous neighborhood continued to work their blue-collar jobs and remained in their homes.

The area near Wealthy, East (now Eastern) and Fifth (now Franklin SE) Streets also supported a Dutch neighborhood by 1900, with nearly 70 percent of the residents immigrating over the preceding 20 years.[19] Unlike other neighborhoods, few residents in the Wealthy-Franklin area owned their own homes, so people moved in and out of the community frequently. Still, it remained heavily Dutch. It was distinct because over half emigrated from Groningen and claimed a link to the Secession in the Netherlands.[20]

The Secession these Dutch claimed as part of their heritage was a schism within the Reformed Church in the Netherlands. This schism began in 1834, when Hendrik C. De Cock was expelled from the ministry. De Cock's expulsion forced him and his followers to proclaim that their religious beliefs were within Reformed doctrine. They accused the organized Reformed Church of straying from traditional Reformed doctrine as established during the Reformation. This accusation was not received favorably. Life for the Secessionists became increasingly difficult as the state attempted to repress the secession.

In 1846 Albertus Van Raalte and Rev. A. Brummelkamp, two men viewed as leaders in the secessionist movement, began to encourage those displeased with living in the Netherlands to emigrate. Many answered this and later calls by Van Raalte and Dutch immigration to western Michigan skyrocketed. This association with the Secessionists united the residents even after immigration, as it linked their strong, shared religious beliefs and personal experiences. A large portion of the population worshiped at Eastern Avenue Christian Reformed Church and its school educated many of the neighborhood children.

> "On Saturday nights young people marched up and down Leonard Street between Powers Street and the Grand River. The women were looking to be found and the boys were looking to find. Many couples found lifelong mates during this ritual which took on a great magnitude for them."[21]

A nearby neighborhood at East Fulton Street and Lake Drive won the moniker of "Brickyard" because of its location near several brickyards and tile manufacturers. The overlapping nature of this Dutch neighborhood and a nearby Polish enclave is a great example of how immigrants established homes in homogeneous neighborhoods, yet found daily interaction with neighboring ethnic groups. The Dutch and the Polish on the East Side of Grand Rapids interacted in a variety of ways. The Polish women enjoyed an occasional afternoon of browsing through the shops owned by the Dutch. Both Dutch and Polish men worked at the brickyards.

Interaction for the children most often took the form of friendly, or not so friendly, neighborhood rivalries. Ed Bala, a lifelong resident of the East Side Polish community, shares his memories of interaction with the Hollanders: "When we were kids,

FIGURE 21 **In the days before sporting goods stores and athletic sponsors could provide uniforms, neighborhood teams formed and played at the local parks. These were the West Side Bushwackers and the Alpine Shortstockings.**

the Hollanders used to chase us Poles down the hills, and we'd fight, and then we used to chase them up the hills, when we'd get our gang. And now most of them that we used to chase are married to Polish girls, or boys are married to the Holland girls."[22] However, this story is not shared by all that lived in these neighborhoods. Some residents of the Dutch neighborhood lived solely within their neighborhood, abhorring the idea of venturing out to make a purchase or meet a wife.

By 1900, within the boundaries of Fountain Street, Orchard Avenue (now Baldwin Street), Hermitage Street, Dennis Avenue and the Fulton Street Cemetery, Dutch households equaled three-quarters of the population, and of that, 75 percent had immigrated to the United States since 1880.[23] This area, beyond being a predominantly Dutch neighborhood, also supported three Dutch Reformed churches.

In addition, nearly 100 Dutch households were located near what used to be Oakdale Park within the boundaries of Alexander Street, Oakdale Street, East (now Eastern) Avenue and Kalamazoo Avenue.[24] The majority of these Dutch emigrated from Groningen, with most arriving between 1885 and 1894. This neighborhood was unique because immigrants of varied economic level lived there. Half of the residents held skilled-labor positions in 1900, one-third owned or worked for businesses that served the Oakdale Park community, and roughly one-fifth were employed as part of the unskilled work force.

FIGURE 22 **Eastern Avenue Christian Reformed Church**

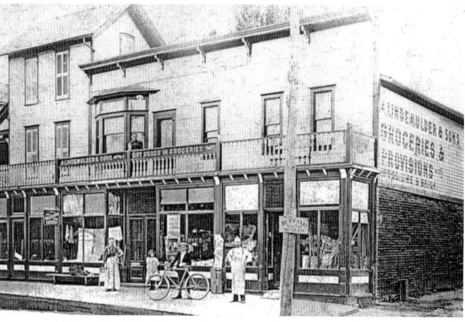

FIGURE 23 **Smoked hogs hung in front of the Thomasma Butcher Shop, located at the southwest corner of West Leonard Street and Turner Avenue.**

FIGURE 24 **Lindemulder & Sons Grocery Store at 816-20 Logan Street SE**

West Side Dutch Neighborhoods

On the west side of the Grand River, Dutch immigrants established themselves in neighborhoods near West Leonard Street and Alpine Avenue, and near West Fulton Street and Straight Avenue. Between 1880 and 1900, the West Leonard-Alpine neighborhood grew phenomenally, from 73 to 1,000 households, a majority of which were Dutch. This sharp rise corresponds to the great influx of Dutch settlers to arrive in Grand Rapids during those years.[25] Those 1,000 Dutch households represented more than 80 percent of the total population of the area and a great portion of the Dutch population within Grand Rapids. Most of these Dutch immigrated from the provinces of Zeeland and Friesland, finding strength in their common heritage as well as their sheer numbers. The residents of the West Leonard-Alpine area began mostly as manual laborers in the furniture industry, but they learned new skills at their jobs. Many did well enough for themselves so that by 1900, more than 100 residents were proprietors of neighborhood businesses.

The residents of the smaller West Side Dutch neighborhood, West Fulton-Straight, were unskilled laborers primarily from the province of Overijsel. The residents of this neighborhood worshiped at 9th Reformed at Watson Street and Deloney Avenue SW.

> "The people here do drink liquor but not on Sundays…. You can't even buy a glass of beer. The price of liquor or beer is about equal to that of Holland – a glass of beer is 5 U.S. cents – and for that reason it is often consumed in excess."
>
> Jan Scheffer[26]

German Neighborhoods

In 1888, thousands of Grand Rapids residents flocked to the center of the city to join in the bicentennial celebration of the German colonization of Germantown, Pennsylvania. The parade wound its way through downtown and across the Bridge Street bridge into the west side of the city. Residents of German ancestry sported traditional German clothing, while German bands performed traditional music. As they celebrated, the German Americans reflected on how the German immigrants had quickly become accustomed to American society, yet still managed to maintain many of their own traditions.

Some Germans came to Grand Rapids as early as 1836, but most came after 1848, fleeing problems in their homeland and responding to the immigration propaganda from Grand Rapids.[27] The influx of German Americans to the city was sizable. In 1870, the German population in Kent County topped 1,700, roughly 3.5 percent of the total population, but 20 years later, that number nearly doubled, making Germans the second-largest ethnic group in Kent County.

Most Germans began as skilled laborers in the factories of Canal Street. Acquiring reputations as strong, intelligent, and diligent workers, the Germans contributed to the thriving factory center around the intersection of Bridge Street,

The Schnitz

People told Gus and Martha Horn that they could never start a restaurant on Jefferson Avenue. In the 1930s, well before highways existed, yet after cars had become crucial, Division Avenue was the main north-south thorough-fare. Conventional wisdom told them that to succeed, they must locate on Division. But the Schnitzelbank was built on Jefferson, a parallel street to the east, full of houses and car dealerships.

Current owner Karl Siebert's father married into the Horn family in 1934. As German immigrants, the Horns faced open criticism that questioned their integrity and threatened the existence of their establishment. A visit to Germany just prior to the founding of the restaurant in 1938 raised specula-tion that they had received funding from Hitler himself. Since the family lived above the restaurant, light poured out of the upper windows long after closing time. Some used this as evidence to accuse the Sieberts of holding Nazi meetings. This same criticism appeared when Gus Horn would hang hats that customers had forgotten in the doorway. When the last customers left and saw hats still hanging and no one else in the restaurant, they assumed Nazis inhabited the place. On many occasions, the FBI questioned the owners as to their involvement with the Nazis, but found no evidence. Despite the caustic accusations, the Schnitzelbank survived due to a large number of loyal clientele. Many Germans in Grand Rapids, however, were not as fortunate; their credibility and careers were ruined by anti-German propaganda.

The restaurant continues to serve the only ethnic German cuisine in the city. The inside walls feature images painted by Siebert's uncle, Wilhelm Seeger.[1]

FIGURE 25 **Schnitzelbank exterior and new addition**

FIGURE 26 **Interior view of the restaurant**

FIGURE 27 **Karl Siebert's uncle, Wilhelm Seeger, had to repaint the ornate woodwork every year.**

FIGURE 28 **Germania Hall was built in 1886 on the east side of North Front Street at First Street. Later occupied by the Fraternal Order of Eagles, the building was removed for Bridgewater Place in 1990.**

(now Michigan), and Canal Street, (now Monroe). The Germans settled in this area and, in the absence of sufficient housing, spread to the West Side. On the East Side, Germans located as far south as Bronson Street (now Crescent Street). On the West Side, they located around Bridge Street at West Division Street (now Seward Avenue) and Stocking Avenue, and in the north at Leonard Street and Broadway Avenue.[28] The presence of a bridge linking the east and west sides of the city at Bridge Street encouraged the West Side population to line Bridge Street with their homes and businesses since they could easily travel to the more populated east side. German immigrants and their descendants dominated this area until at least the 1880s.

The east side of the Grand River enjoyed a prominent German settlement, prompting an early resident to state that this area could be known as Germantown.[29] In all likelihood, the very first German immigrants settled with blue-collar New Englanders, choosing to assimilate to English and American customs rather than form an isolated German ethnic settlement. As the German population in Grand Rapids expanded, the need for German immigrants to assimilate lessened, German businesses were established and German culture began to thrive.

Positive Effects of Beer

The beer-making industry, according to some, had a positive effect on the city of Grand Rapids. Historian Albert Baxter reports the health benefits of beer drinking:

"In 1847 chills and shaking ague were terrors of people afflicted with malaria, and sallow faces and feeble frames were familiar sights. In the eight years following came two experiences — a great growth in the habit of drinking lager beer, and the almost complete dying out of the shaking ague. It is not the province of the historian to moralize upon these facts, nor to attempt an explanation, but only to chronicle the coincidence."

The coincidence was actually due to the tapping of a pure water source by German brewer Christoph Kusterer that eventually extinguished the diseases from the city's water source.[1]

FIGURE 29 **The fine fellows of Frey Brothers Brewery. Perhaps the young gentleman of about 12 years of age sitting on the keg has a mug of root beer.**

The Germans maintained social contact with their brethren by establishing clubs and halls where they could dance, drink and eat. The Schwabenverein, on Front Street, was probably the only German Hall that appealed to members of a specific German region, that of Schwabia in southern Germany near Stuttgart.[30] The Austrians built a hall on Stocking Street. They would have protested being called German, though they often were lumped into that category because they spoke German.[31]

Other efforts to preserve German tradition included the Workingman's Aid Society, Landwer Hall, and Arbeiter's Club. St. Mary's also opened a school for the Germans, and a German-English School Society began on Front near Bridge. A gymnastic organization called the Turnverein was built, as well as Germania Hall on North Front Street.[32] Here, immigrants could exercise in the comfort of their native tongue.

The Germans brought two traditional arts that characterized all their neighborhoods. The first was beer brewing. German men enjoyed stopping on the way home from work to drink a beer and talk with their comrades before joining their families for dinner. With rye bread and cheese in one hand, and a glass of German-style beer in the other, they sipped and spoke of philosophy, religion, music, news, and politics of

FIGURE 30 **Jos. C. Herkner Jewelry Store, 148 (25) Monroe, in the 1880s**

FIGURE 31 **To compete on a national level, several local German brewers consolidated to form the Grand Rapids Brewing Co. in 1893.**

FIGURE 32 **Julius Wagner Grocery on East Bridge (Michigan) Street and Lafayette Avenue**

Kusterer's House   Immanuel Lutheran Church   Division Avenue School   Williams House   Central High School   Kusterer's City Brewery

FIGURE 33 **The following three pages show how the neighborhood around the intersection of Michigan Street and Division Avenue has changed over the years.**

FIGURE 34 **Christopher Kusterer and family pose in front of their home.**

FIGURE 35 **Employees of Kusterer's Cooper Shop, on the northeast corner of Michigan Street and Ottawa Avenue, pose for a photo in 1876.**

FIGURE 36 **Immanuel Lutheran Church, circa 1870**

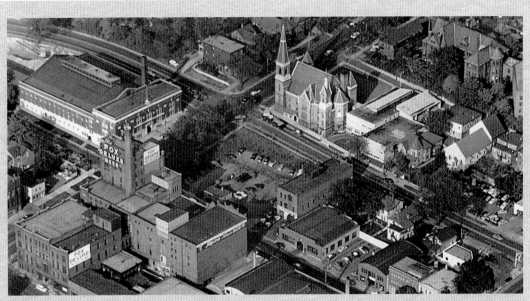

FIGURE 37 **In this aerial photo, taken before urban renewal and freeway construction, a newer Immanuel Lutheran Church exists, as does the National Guard Armory building. The Fox Brewery is located where Kusterer's City Brewery once stood.**

FIGURE 38 **Built in 1839 by Major Abel Page, this house was later sold to Mr. Kusterer in 1846. It was razed in 1915.**

FIGURE 39 **The Michigan National Guard Armory replaced the Kusterer home on Michigan Street between Division and Ionia Avenues. It was later torn down to make way for the I-196 freeway.**

FIGURE 40 **An 1870 drawing of Kusterer's City Brewery**

FIGURE 41 **Kusterer's, Grand Rapids, and Fox Breweries all used this site.**

FIGURE 42 **Michigan Street looking east from Monroe Avenue in May 1936. The Grand Rapids Press now occupies the Hermitage Hotel site shown above.**

74

FIGURE 43 **Abraham Killinger**

their homeland.[33] Despite the various temperance movements, many of the German breweries flourished as part of the culture of Grand Rapids.

Music also became a hallmark of the Germans. The Germans loved traditional music, using it as a method to contribute to the city and to become accepted as Americans. German Americans were foremost in teaching music and forming bands, choral societies, and musical performance groups. Many German performers were numbered among the best known musicians in the city.[34]

German immigrants formed five Christian churches and one Jewish Temple in Grand Rapids, several before the Civil War.[35] Catholics attended St. Mary's Catholic Church while Protestants chose either Immanuel Lutheran Church or German Methodist Church. German Jews founded Temple Emanuel, the city's first synagogue, to minister to its Jewish citizens. Both St. Mary's and Immanuel Lutheran opened schools to educate their congregations' children.[36]

In 1880, the Germans established a sixth church, St. John's Evangelical Lutheran Church. A number of dissenters broke away from Immanuel Lutheran, a Missouri Synod congregation that disapproved of lodges and secret societies. At one time, many German associations built halls that served as neighborhood social centers where people spent their free time.

FIGURE 45 **German Immigrant Adolph Rademacher and his daughter at site of present West Side Library on Bridge Street.**

Members of Immanuel Lutheran did not agree with the church's disapproval of such establishments, and created St. John's Evangelical Lutheran Church in response.[37]

FIGURE 44 **Abraham Killinger made violins and operated an instrument repair shop in Grand Rapids for more than four decades.**

FIGURE 46 **Abraham Killinger in his shop at 38 ½ Monroe Avenue (now Monroe Center) in 1948. He was born in Branch County on June 27, 1885, and died November 11, 1954.**

Queen of the Poles

Valeria Lipczynski was born in Tremessen (Trzemeszno) in the principality of Posen in 1846 to a professor and his wife. Valeria became one of the most ambitious and influential individuals within the Grand Rapids Polish community. Her life and her influence on Grand Rapids were well documented by Eduard Skendzel, a long-time resident and historian of Grand Rapids' Polish citizens. This excerpt, written by Skendzel, was first published in the Grand River Valley History:

"Valeria Lipczynski enjoyed a special prominence in the history of the Grand Rapids' Polonia. A devoted wife and loving mother, she was also a teacher, social worker, nurse, midwife, journalist, youth leader, feminist, godmother to innumerable youngsters, and the confidante of judges, men of the cloth, and ordinary citizens alike. Her profound faith, unfailing generosity, seriousness of purpose, unflagging industry, and a deep concern for others earned scores of admirers and a widespread reputation as La Grande Dame Polonaise, 'Mme. Lipczynska, Queen of the Poles.'[1] 'This little woman,' as the Grand Rapids Herald described her near the end of her life, 'is the mother to the whole community of Polish people, combining staunch loyalty to her new country with interest in the fatherland she left behind.'"[2]

FIGURE 47 **Anton Lipczynski and family, 1895**

The neighborhoods established by early German immigrants provide an intriguing microcosm of the society they left behind, blended with their New World. Though immigrants, these Germans assimilated in American society enthusiastically, learning English, working diligently, taking part in the community, and becoming friends with their non-German neighbors. However, they preserved many of their traditions and interests, offering them to the greater community around them.

The city's flourishing German culture ended abruptly with the advent of World War I. From the outset of the war, all eyes were on Europe, where Germany was seen as an enemy of freedom. The German Americans in Grand Rapids, like those across the nation, were forced to choose carefully where they would place their loyalties.

Polish Neighborhoods

In the late 19th and early 20th centuries, Polish immigrants established three neighborhoods within Grand Rapids, each supporting a Catholic church. Before these neighborhoods, the earliest Polish immigrants to Grand Rapids grouped themselves on the West Side with the slightly larger German population, and worshipped at St. Mary's Church. These Polish immigrants left an area of Europe then under German control, so most spoke German as well as Polish, sharing with the Germans both language and religion. However, as the number of Poles increased, they found ways to bring themselves together as a separate ethnic group.

FIGURE 48 **Father Simon Ponganis**

The large numbers of Polish immigrants to Grand Rapids and other cities in the United States is strongly linked to German Chancellor Otto von Bismarck's 1871 campaign of Germanization. Bismarck introduced this plan to "deprive Poles of land ownership, eliminate the Polish language entirely from primary and secondary education, state and self-government offices"[38] in the newly acquired Prussian partition. Thousands of Poles feared his plan, fled from their homeland and resettled in areas where they were free to speak their own language and to own property. Grand Rapids resident and promoter Valeria Lipczynski explained her reason for leaving in this way:

When I was 20, my husband and I came to the "land of the free." In Poland we had no liberty. The Polish language was being suppressed. Only German was being taught in the schools. The government was trying to make Germans of us and of our children. We could not stand that, so we came to this country that we might have the freedom to speak our own language and to teach Poland's history to our children. This is a great and grand country. Here we may be true to ourselves.[39]

FIGURE 49 **Monsignor Casimir Skory funeral at St. Adalbert's, March 11, 1935**

The Lipczynskis settled in Grand Rapids in 1869 and, together with other early Polish settlers in Grand Rapids, encouraged friends and family to join them.

As the Polish population steadily increased, they were able to establish a community with a separate identity from the Germans. In 1877, Bishop Borgess of the Detroit diocese granted 50 Polish residents permission to establish a fund to build a Polish Catholic church dedicated to St. Adalbert, the apostle of Poland.[40] Three years later, the organization purchased two lots at the corner of Fourth Street and Davis Avenue and began construction.[41] In May 1882, the Polish residents enthusiastically celebrated their new church's dedication. The parish opened a school and by 1888 listed 300 families as members. Only 30 years after the arrival of the first Pole, Rev. Julian John Maciejewski, Grand Rapids had a Polish church. In 1913, the Polish community around St. Adalbert's built a new church, which is still in use, and which in 1980 was designated as a basilica.

A growing population on the East Side of the city led to the establishment of St. Isidore's parish in 1897. The Lipczynskis, pioneer East Side Polish residents, were

FIGURE 50 **St. Adalbert's Catholic Church, corner Davis and Fourth in 1930**

St. Isidore's Neighborhood: The Brickyard

Who: Polish immigrants from the Wast Side of the Grand River, within the St. Adalbert's community, moved to the East Side and established the community that would come to be known as the St. Isidore's neighborhood. Most of the Poles to move from across the river immigrated from Austrian- and Russian-controlled Poland and spoke Polish, while many of the West Side Polish residents were earlier immigrants from areas of Poland that spoke German as well as Polish.

What: The neighborhood of St. Isidore's... the Polish brickyard... "Cegielnia (Tseh-gyel-nya)"

A three-quarter-square-mile area, relatively centered on the intersection of Michigan and Eastern, that became the central business district of the neighborhood. According to Ed Skendzel, "Though the Michigan-Eastern intersection was the visible physical center of this Polonian community, its heart and soul was St. Isidore's Church where in the 1912-17 time-span they built an almost $100,000 Gothic church without incurring any indebtedness." This Polish community is regarded as having been traditionally the most ethnically homogeneous neighborhood and was at one time 99.44 percent Polish. That is no longer true of the neighborhood, though it still maintains a general Polish Catholic identity.

Where: The original boundaries of the St. Isidore neighborhood were: *North:* Lydia-Malta streets; *South:* Lyon Street; *East:* Fuller Avenue; *West:* Grand Avenue

When: The Polish immigrants who established the St. Isidore neighborhood moved from the west side of the Grand River to the east side near Michigan and Eastern during the 1890s. In 1891, this east side Polish community purchased five acres of land on which they proceeded to build a Roman Catholic church and school.

FIGURE 51 **Girls from St. Isidore's in traditional Polish garb**

Why: The St. Isidore's neighborhood was located within walking distance of the brickyards of Michigan Street and Fuller Avenue. Polish men easily walked the distance to work in the morning. Women of the community walked to the business district to buy groceries and other supplies. The children could walk to school, to the neighborhood store, and to church. Residents of all ages could interact within a community of other Poles ... at work, at the store, at church, and for recreation.[1]

FIGURE 52 **St. Isidore's Catholic Church, circa 1930**

once again among the charter members of a Polish Catholic church in Grand Rapids. Initially christened St. Stanislaus by its founding pastor, Father Simon Ponganis, the parish was renamed St. Isidore's when Bishop Henry Joseph Richter, the first bishop of Grand Rapids, determined that no new Polish parish should bear the name of a Polish saint as its patron.

In 1871, the short-lived Wiarus, or "Old Faithful," was created as a mutual benefit organization to meet the immediate needs of Poles. Wiarus provided burial for the dead and aid for the impoverished.[42] The next year, on the recommendation of a Jesuit missionary, the Polish community launched the St. Adalbert Benevolent Society, which was affiliated with St. Mary's Church. The following years gave rise to roughly a dozen other Polish organizations. Like the St. Adalbert Benevolent Society and the Polish National Society, created in 1878, these associations served the community in many ways. They held cultural, patriotic, fraternal, and social activities. They also provided support to individuals or families who suffered sickness, personal tragedy, death, or other problems.[43]

A second Polish neighborhood developed in the 1870s on the east side of the city, between Leonard and Fountain streets and Fuller and College avenues. By 1900, about 150 Polish families lived in the

FIGURE 54 **Widdicomb Fifth Street factory, with St. Adalbert's spires in the misty background**

FIGURE 53 **The enameling department in the Widdicomb factory**

The Widdicomb Factory Family

The philanthropy of Widdicomb Furniture owner William Widdicomb influenced his employees in a thoughtful and personal manner. His factory, still in the same walking neighborhood on Grand Rapids' West Side, employed more than 400 men and boys in 1912. Each furniture maker was valued greatly by Mr. Widdicomb.

Sometime around 1900 a Widdicomb employee approached the owner with the unusual request of permission for a day off. The man wanted the day to prepare for his infant's christening. Mr. Widdicomb granted the request, and went one step further.

Touched by the employee's joy, Widdicomb wanted to do more. That infant was the first of hundreds to be given a christening gown by the Widdicombs. For decades following that first gift, the Widdicomb family happily welcomed each new son or daughter into the factory family with a christening gown.[1]

So How Big Was Furniture in Grand Rapids?

It was a warm spring night in 1911 during the ides of May, about 5:30 p.m. in the West Side Polish neighborhood near St. Adalbert's Catholic Church.

About 2,000 Polish men, women, and children, consisting of strikers and their families, congregated near the factory, their latent anger brewing as they waited for the Widdicomb Furniture factory workers who refused to strike. They had done this before in their month-long strike, but their anger reached a new peak, spurred by a recent taunting in *The Evening Press* from the Furniture Manufacturers Association that declared that all of the strikers in the 19 furniture factories in Grand Rapids were ready to start work again.[1] This time the strikers were joined by their families, who participated in the battle even more as their meals grew smaller and their mortgage payments went unpaid.

As the strikebreakers left the factory, the strikers hurled stones at them. Soon police arrived on the scene, the strikers' wives picked up their children and formed a wall between their husbands and the attacking policemen. The men now hurled stones at the policemen from behind their wall of loved ones. The fire department turned their hoses on the strikers to disperse them, but the water could not cool their fierce anger.

FIGURE 55 **Riot squad that tried to control the strikers. These were all policemen, but Ellis received criticism for hiring furniture workers who were striking to bolster the ranks of the riot squad.**

Harry Widdicomb, president of the company and object of the strikers' wrath, emerged from the building and made a dash for his car. On previous days, he had hurled insults at the strikers, once even brandishing a gun. On this occasion, however, the police officers' guns saved him from the violent crowd. He escaped to his home on the hilltop with several gun-toting policemen on the running boards of his car.

The crowd quieted for a brief visit from Mayor George Ellis, whose election their working class votes had supported three times. But their anger reappeared as soon as he left. They chased off the remaining police officers and hurled rocks at the factory until every window was broken. Finally at midnight the mob dispersed.

The Widdicomb riot was the climax of a four-month struggle, but in the end, the strikers did not achieve their goal of higher wages. Despite the violence displayed at the peak of the strike on May 15, the factory workers could not budge their intransigent employers.[2]

At no prior point in Grand Rapids' history were the lines of politics, economics, class, religion, and neighborhood so clearly defined as in the 1911 strike. Like no other event, the conflict of the furniture strike ripped a giant hole in the social body of Grand Rapids, baring the insides and providing the clearest view of how the city really functioned at the pinnacle of its industrial might.

The roots of the trouble began in 1906 when hilltop resident Ellis was elected mayor. While he lived among the wealthy management class, Ellis knew how to relate to the working class and won the support of wage earners and immigrants throughout the city. The working class wards outnumbered the votes of the industrial leaders and bankers who clustered on the hilltop. Ellis' unique way of relating managed to keep him in office for 10 years.

Ellis willingly set himself up for disagreement with the rest of his neighborhood. He openly tried to equalize the clout of the common man. During campaigns, he frequently visited the saloons that the elite "Good Government League" tried to shut down, buying a round of drinks for all present.[3]

The working class, most notably the Polish and Dutch, supported Ellis from the beginning. The great flood of 1904 had damaged many of their homes on the West Side,[4] only amplifying the huge debts on mortgages they owed to the banks. By 1911 their cost of living had increased significantly. Prices had increased, wages remained the same, and the factory owners drove home every evening to their mansions on the hilltop. Ellis represented hope that someone could fight for them.[5]

The same year that Ellis took office, his neighbor and adversary, Rev. Alfred Wishart, also began preaching at Fountain Street Baptist Church, which many of the furniture factory owners and bankers from the hill attended. Wishart fit perfectly into the bastion of wealth and its educated congregation located at the base of the hilltop neighborhood. While claiming an affinity for the working man, Wishart preached that industrial leaders should set fair wages and policies for their workers, but that unions and strikes only misled the uneducated workers into unnecessary actions. As an anti-Catholic, Wishart also denounced the main proponent of the strikers, Bishop Joseph Schrembs of St. Mary's Catholic Church.[6]

The industrialists fully accepted the teachings of Wishart that rationalized their right to rule, a position that placed them squarely opposite George Ellis. The furniture barons, who almost exclusively lived on the hilltop, controlled the banks and finances in the city at a time when unethical business practices nationwide could not be checked. Many of the 19 furniture companies shared board members with each other and with the banks of Grand Rapids — the same banks that held the mortgages of the Polish and Dutch homeowners. Price fixing and other business practices were not uncommon at the turn of the century, and the furniture industry of Grand Rapids was certainly not exempt.[7]

While the working class, Catholic, Polish in two West Side and one East Side neighborhoods supported the idea of a strike in 1911, the Dutch working class neighborhoods remained more fragmented and opposed. As a whole, their more conservative theology distrusted labor unions as secret societies and eschewed both violence and disloyalty to employers. Also, their economic status in the factories and adjustment to American life was slightly better than the Poles' due to their earlier arrival. Finally, the fractionalization of theological and provincial squabbles between the Dutch neighborhoods, who had settled in Grand Rapids almost by province, kept them from presenting a unified front in the strike.[8]

The Polish felt the brunt of occupying the lowest rung of the socio-economic ladder, especially after factory owners stubbornly rebuffed attempts at negotiations for higher wages. Although many Dutch workers struck as well, the Polish became the most vehement advocates for labor reform. When the strikers began the strike in mid-April, the furniture factories closed, operated on skeleton crews or hired "scabs" to take the place of the strikers.[9] The presence of these strikebreakers led to the violence that peaked on May 15. But the industrialists, spurred on by Wishart, remained convinced that labor reform would have to come from the employers rather than as a reward for strike violence. The strikers went back to work in August without achieving their goals.[10]

The industrial leaders went back to work as well. Frustrated with the methods Ellis employed in the strike, including the hiring of strikers for a "peace patrol," as well as just frustration with his policies, the hilltoppers pushed to reform the city government.[11] Led by Robert Irwin (hilltop resident, board member of four furni-

ture factories and several banks, member of the private Peninsular Club and of the Fountain Street Baptist Church), the "Good Government League" pushed for a new government charter.[12]

The new charter contained some groundbreaking features. First it reduced the mayor's power, drastically increasing the power of the commissioners (the number of which was reduced from 24 to 7) and created a position for the commission-appointed city manager who would wield the most governmental powers. Secondly, the charter realigned the wards, creating three large voting districts rather than the 12 distinct wards.

FIGURE 56 **George Ellis**

The boundary of the first two wards split the hilltop in half, effectively dividing its political influence and control over wards Two and Three. The First Ward was left as the West Side. The hilltoppers hoped that they could control the two East Side wards if the predominantly working class West Side would vote against their ideas.[13]

The charter went to the polls in 1916, the same year that the working class grew frustrated with the ineffectiveness of Mayor Ellis and voted him out of office.[14] The elitists on the hill sold their charter as a method of more effective government, which everyone in the city agreed was needed, especially after an arson outbreak burned several factories and other buildings in 1916. The working

FIGURE 57 **Alfred Wishart**

class was not completely informed as to how the charter would reduce the political clout of their unified neighborhood interests, and the charter passed.[15]

While the labor unions of the country eventually managed to improve working conditions, many of the scars of the strike still exist. Most of the changes made by the charter are still in effect today. Many West Siders still distrust the city government that isolated them 90 years ago.

area.[44] Although the Polish community near St. Adalbert's was larger, this neighborhood was more homogeneous.[45] Generally, men worked in factories, mills, or foundries; some were skilled tradesmen. Many residents found employment at the Grand Rapids Brick Company located at Michigan Street and Fuller Avenue.

For almost two decades, the Lipczynskis and other Polish families living in this East Side neighborhood walked two or three miles to St. Adalbert's for Sunday Mass. In 1897 they formed their own parish. In 1912 the congregation began building St. Isidore's church on Diamond Avenue, which was dedicated five years later.

A third Polish community began to take form around 1895 in the area near what would later become John Ball Park. Most of the men in the neighborhood worked at the local gypsum mine on the west bank of the Grand River.[46] These Poles differed from the other West Side enclaves in that they emigrated from European areas controlled by Russia and Austria. This group did not share the same ties to Germany, and some did not speak any German.

The two-mile walk from this southern Polish neighborhood to the school at St. Adalbert's posed a great concern for parents. While not unbearable for a family to undertake on Sunday mornings, the walk was too long for the elderly and also posed difficulties for children attending school. In 1903 a committee from this neighborhood petitioned to establish Sacred Heart parish on Valley Avenue, intending to open a school and convent as soon as possible. The Sacred Heart School opened a year later and the committee began plans to build an adjacent church. In 1924, 20 years after they first organized, the parishioners celebrated the opening of their permanent place of worship, Sacred Heart of Jesus Church.

FIGURE 58 **Sacred Heart Catholic Church at 151 Garfield Avenue NW in 1931**

Polish Name Changes

Immigration to the United States often meant name changes for entire families. The Polish in Grand Rapids are a good example of immigrants whose names in the United States differed from their names in the Old Country.

Sometimes exact translations resulted from name changes allowing, in a sense, for the immigrant families to retain their identity, if only in a different language. Kowalski, for example, is translated into Smith while Jaworowicz became Mapleton.

More commonly, Polish names of difficult spelling and pronunciation were transliterated (spelled in English as they should sound when pronounced in Polish) or abandoned entirely for an unrelated American name.

Miszkiewicz is transliterated as Mishkevich.

Walkowiak changed to Walker.

Wisniewski changed to Hudson.

Sniatecki changed to Snow.

Changes such as these make it relatively impossible to identify the place of origin of the families, but the changes made it easier for the families with Americanized names to blend into the lifestyle of their new neighbors.[1]

FIGURE 59 **In 1929, using a four-foot aerial about 100 feet underground, gypsum miners demonstrate their Majestic radio's good reception to visiting businessmen. They tuned in to stations in Illinois, Kentucky, Tennessee and Texas. The miners probably lived close to the mines, near Sacred Heart.**

Lithuanian Neighborhood

Upstream from the Sacred Heart community, a small Lithuanian neighborhood began to develop near Myrtle Street and Quarry Avenue NW around 1885.[47] These immigrants worked primarily in factories near the Grand River.

Unlike the Poles, many of whom spoke German and aligned themselves with fellow German immigrants in the early 1880s and 1890s, the Lithuanians felt little in common with the Germans. They did not share a language and they did not want to share a culture which had been forced on them by the oppressive Russian regime. Similar to the Poles at Sacred Heart and St. Isidore, the Lithuanians first attended St. Adalbert's Church and then went on to establish their own church. By 1904, the Lithuanians founded the ethnic Catholic parish of Saints Peter and Paul.[48]

"Lithuanian Town" released its residents from the hardships of their homeland where freedoms had been curtailed by Russian invaders. They developed a close-knit community, transplanting religion, language, and ethnicity to their new home. Despite these freedoms, Lithuanians experienced some tension as their loyalties to Lithuania challenged their desire to adapt to life in the United States. Leaders in the Lithuanian community felt the need to assimilate by learning English and embracing American culture.[49]

FIGURE 60 **Lithuanian women at work in the varnishing department at the Gunn Furniture Co. factory in the 1920s.**

FIGURE 61 **Saints Peter and Paul Church, 520 Myrtle NW, was dedicated in 1924.**

FIGURE 62 **Unable to stop at Fuller Junction, just north of the Lithuanian neighborhood, an eastbound Grand Trunk freight train plowed through a Pennsylvania freight train and tipped over, mid-1930s.**

To provide a structured system of aid to members of the Lithuanian community, the Saints Peter and Paul Aid Society was established in 1891. This group provided help during times of sickness or family hardship and offered burial assistance when necessary. In 1903, a second Lithuanian society was organized, St. George's Aid Society. Many people belonged to both organizations — membership in both guaranteed double the death benefits, something very helpful since the government decreed that aid societies could not operate as insurance organizations.[50]

The aid societies were crucial in times of trouble, but it was the *svetaines*, or social halls, that were important on a daily basis. Adults enjoyed entertainment reminiscent of their native culture at the svetaines, which became the center of the Lithuanian walking city. Lithuanians could attend plays, minstrel shows, concerts and choral presentations, parties of all kinds, lectures, political rallies, dances, and costume balls. The halls also offered Saturday morning Lithuanian language classes for youngsters, a women's auxiliary, and sporting activities such as boxing and wrestling. Politicians running for local office made their pitch for votes at the monthly club meetings, thanking attendees with a free keg of beer. Bridal showers, wedding receptions, baby showers, and funeral luncheons were regular clubhouse events. These beloved *svetaines* became "little Lithuanias," cultural havens in the midst of America. As one Lithuanian resident remembered: "I would go to church to cleanse my soul. But I went to my *svetaine* for a glass of beer and a good time."[51]

Snake Tonic Memories in Lithuania Town

Ed Gillis reports:

"Perhaps the most notorious of all Lithuanian folk medicines was what our Lithuanian old-timers called snake tonic. For thousands of years, snakes played an important role in Lithuanian religious practices. During the Middle Ages snakes were worshipped widely among Old Prussians, Latvians, and Lithuanians....

"In general, Lithuanians considered it fortunate to come across a snake, for such an encounter prophesied an upcoming marriage or birth. Snakes were said to bring happiness and prosperity, ensuring the fertility of the soil and the addition of children to the family....

"Although the Lithuanians who came to Grand Rapids in the late 1800s were far removed from the snake worshippers of old, they retained the respect for snakes that was a thousand-year-old tradition. And they believed in the efficacies of snake tonic, which was nothing more than a jug or bottle of whiskey into which a snake had been immersed....

"Ed Tuma remembers catching grass snakes as a boy and giving them to his father for snake tonic. Each spring, after the high waters had receded, he and a friend, using five-gallon pails as 'hip boots,' would search the grass hummocks just south of the Grand Trunk railroad bridge for snakes sunning themselves. They grabbed the unsuspecting reptiles, stuffed them into gunny sacks and carried them triumphantly home."[1]

FIGURE 63 **West Leonard Street farmer's market, located between Front Avenue and the Grand River. View is looking north in 1927.**

Svetaine Culture: Adding Spice To Lithuanian Life

"I would go to church to cleanse my soul. But I went to my *svetaine* for a glass of beer and a good time."

Anonymous Lithuanian

FIGURE 64 **Poker and suds were enjoyed at Sons and Daughters of Lithuania Hall on Hamilton Avenue in the 1920s.**

FIGURE 66 **St. George's Aid Society Hall on Quarry Avenue, was built in 1907.**

FIGURE 65 **Knights of Vytautas Aid Society stand in full-dress uniform in front of their club building at the intersection of Hamilton and Crosby in 1925.**

FIGURE 67 **A Sons and Daughters Aid Society drama production featured an all-female cast, except for the king seated in the front right.**

Neighborhood stores became the economic center of the Lithuanian population in Grand Rapids. Grocery stores featuring native ethnic foods and ingredients thrived, although they might be located only a block or two from each other. The matriarch of the family could send her child to the nearest store for one or two ingredients while cooking the evening meal. Store owners familiarized themselves with each family and their needs to meet the demands of the surrounding blocks. Neighbors met other neighbors at the store, which became another social center.

FIGURE 68

Father Salvatore Cianci

Little Italy

Italians, who began to immigrate to the United States in large numbers beginning in the 1880s, originally settled in the downtown area of Grand Rapids, often living in rented rooms above businesses or in apartments upstairs from their own businesses. By 1900, the estimated Italian population in Grand Rapids hovered around 300, and a small Italian neighborhood began to develop on the south side of the city. In 1895, two of the first Italian families in Grand Rapids purchased homes on Cornwall Avenue SE. Over the next 25 years, a noticeable presence of Italians developed in this area that was once predominantly Dutch. "Little Italy," as it became known, was centered within Division and Cass Avenues and First (now Buckley) and Fifth (now Franklin) Avenues.[52]

A second Italian neighborhood began to develop when Italians began working at the local gypsum mine on the west side of the river, around 1910. Many of the men purchased homes on or near Butterworth.[53] The larger Italian neighborhood, the East Side "Little Italy," became the anchor of the Grand Rapids Italian community.

As with other ethnic groups, the Italians wished to establish an ethnic church in the city so they could worship in their native tongue. As early as 1889, the Italian community had caught the eye of the local bishop, Henry Joseph Richter, who recommended Italian services be held at St. Andrew's Cathedral. By 1908, Father Salvatore Cianci was summoned from Sicily to shepherd the Italian population, with whom he shared a common language and Sicilian heritage.

Our Lady of Sorrows Catholic Church, constructed near the intersection of Sheldon Avenue and Hall Street SE, served as the anchor for the neighborhood. Father Cianci preached in Italian, but encouraged his parishioners to learn English and to make a place for themselves in the city's larger culture. Through the assistance of many of the Italian shopkeepers in the city, they enjoyed the comforts and foods of their native land. With the arrival of Father Cianci, the immigrant Italian population found an outspoken advocate for its growing community.[54]

FIGURE 69 **The Di Trapani Family in 1934 at their barber shop at 856 South Division in "Little Italy." The parents, Sam and Josephine, immigrated from Sicily around 1920 and attended Our Lady of Sorrows Catholic Church. At the far left, in the back row is Jerry Di Trapani, who now runs a barber shop with his son, at Fulton and Diamond.**

FIGURE 70 **Hibernian Band, circa 1910**

Irish Neighborhoods

The Irish were among the first groups of European immigrants to arrive in Grand Rapids, and they continued to arrive in significant numbers throughout the 19th and into the 20th century. As time went by, they established several neighborhoods outside the original Shantytown settlement on the river. Most of the Irish established themselves in either the Creston area or on the west side of the Grand River.[55] A majority of the church-going Irish worshiped at St. Alphonsus, St. Andrew's, and St. James Roman Catholic churches with Catholic New Englanders.

Irish people formed many societies in the 19th century, such as the Ancient Order of Hibernians, the Irish Fellowship Club, and Friendly Sons of St. Patrick. In 1883, the Hibernians, under the leadership of William E. Mahoney, built a hall on Canal Street for their members. The Order, composed of Irish Catholics with strong moral character, expanded quickly, and in 1889 built a larger hall at 415 Ottawa Avenue, near Michigan Street. The building included a bowling alley and billiard parlor. The Hibernians formed a 24-member band in 1907 and gave concerts in the hall's auditorium. By 1912, the Grand Rapids chapter of the Hibernians was the second-largest chapter in the nation, with only the New York City chapter claiming larger membership.[56] By 1915, the Hibernian membership reached more than 1,000.[57]

The Irish established Grand Rapids' first benevolent society in 1854. The congregation of St. Andrew's started the St. Andrew Benevolent Society.[58] Many of the congregations established such societies within their church; neighborhoods followed suit, launching similar secular organizations designed to care for the needs of recent immigrants and residents.

Prior to the establishment of St. James Catholic Church in 1870, West Side Irish worshiped either at St. Andrew's or at St. Mary's Catholic Church, a congregation composed primarily of German immigrants. Inspired by the example of their fel-

FIGURE 71 **St. James Catholic Church, 733 Bridge NW, circa 1931**

The West Side Ladies Literary Club

The Ladies Literary Club of Grand Rapids on the east side of the Grand River was founded in 1873. For $2 a year, "Any lady can become a member of this club." The club was progressive, influencing and creating educational experiences for women with the means to afford the entry fee and the luxury of time to attend club functions.

But what about women on the west side of the river?

The Grand River has always signaled more than a geographic division between residents in the city of Grand Rapids. It might seem that the progressive, educated women lived on the east side of the river, in the large homes on the hill, with their husbands and fathers at work in elite white-collar jobs in industry and finance. But the women on the west side also formed a club to allow expression of their desire to think, eat, and socialize with other like-minded women.

FIGURE 72 **The West Side Ladies Literary Club renovated the former firehouse at 518 Scribner NW.**

On April 3, 1875, fourteen women met and formed the West Side Ladies Literary Club. Just over a year later, the club reported attendance of 75 members or more at meetings. The purpose and vision for the club was stated by M.E. Holden in her "Address to the Club."

"And now we have it complete in all its perfection, a place where we may abide for years to come in all the serenity of a home unencumbered by debt, a place where women may congregate and rest if they are weary from their household cares, and for a time be carried beyond themselves, into the regions of art, science, education, and literature, unmolested from idle curiosity or sharp criticism. Among friends she may aspire to all that lies within her of the spiritually good."[1]

FIGURE 73 **St. John's Home original 1889 building on Lafayette and Leonard**

low German parishioners, they set about to build their own church. St. James, however, did not maintain the strong ethnic flavor of other Catholic churches, but instead became a melting pot where many English-speaking worshippers gathered.[59]

In 1888, Irish businessman John Clancy donated $60,000 to the Catholic Church in Grand Rapids to purchase land for and build an orphan asylum. The recent influx of immigrants had crowded St. Andrew's Cathedral, and Bishop Henry Joseph Richter of Grand Rapids chose to establish a new congregation in the northeast quadrant of the city with some of the money.[60] Partly a result of John Clancy's gift, St. Alphonsus Catholic Church was dedicated on January 6, 1889. The congregation, composed of residents living north of Trowbridge Street and east of the Grand River, filled the church.

By 1893 the congregation contained about 225 families and had begun plans to build a larger church. The new church, completed in 1909, also had a parish school, and, across the street, St. John's orphanage.

Scandinavian Neighborhoods

Scandinavians lived on the west side of the river, clustered near the furniture factories where they worked. Many had actually been wooed by local businesses during Rev. J. P. Tustin's recruiting journey to Scandinavia. Norwegians and Swedes, who had suffered

through difficult growing seasons in the 1860s, were receptive to his message of plentiful jobs.

Many of the Scandinavians who came to Grand Rapids did so based on Tustin's testimony. A majority, who were primarily Swedish, settled on the west side of the Grand River near communities of German and Polish immigrants. A sizable Swedish enclave existed near Bridge Street and by 1890 had established two Swedish churches. At least one furniture company in the city hired large numbers of Swedes as sawyers.

The first Swedish Evangelical Lutheran Church was built on Sinclair Avenue in 1874 and counted 100 members by 1878. The Swedish Mission Covenant Church opened in 1883 on Broadway near First Street NW. This Scandinavian congregation comprised both Swedish and Danish worshippers.[61] In 1889, the Swedish Evangelical Lutheran Church built a larger church on the West Side at Scribner and Blumrich NW. Now called Bethlehem Lutheran, the church has been located at 330 Crescent NE since 1929. These congregations served to unite the Scandinavian population within Grand Rapids.

FIGURE 74 **Rev. J. P. Tustin**

Like other immigrant groups, the Scandinavians established their own social and religious institutions, including the Danish (Dania) Aid Society Hall, the Norwegian Lutheran Church, Swedish Baptist Church, and the Swedish Hall.

FIGURE 75 **Swedish Evangelical Lutheran Church on Sinclair Avenue, 1874**

Greek Neighborhoods

Business thrives for the little bootblack shop on the corner of Market and Monroe Avenues. The owner, a Greek immigrant named Peter Smirlis, sees hundreds of customers a day. He also has interest in many transactions that do not take place in his store — nor do they involve the boots of his customers.

Many Greek immigrants know of Smirlis as a padrone, or employment agent. While no questions are asked about his bootblack store, his role as a padrone is somewhat controversial. Either Smirlis or one of his agents meets Greek immigrants right off the boat in New York harbor, pays their train fare to cities such as Grand Rapids, and arranges for jobs. Smirlis has sent many to Grand Rapids, including those who now work in his shop. The Greek entrepreneur not only keeps his store filled with loyal Greek workers, but he gets payments from the employers who hire the immigrants he sends.

It is an extremely lucrative business for Smirlis. Some who work for him view the padrone as a helper, but others see him as a manipulator who exploits Greek immigrants unable to speak English. Smirlis would contend that he provides a service to his fellow countrymen, many who have left their families to make money before returning to Greece.

Although Peter Smirlis and others like him were incredibly instrumental in bringing immigrants into America, the U.S. Immigration Act of 1909 severely limited the practices of these employment agents. The same law also placed restraints on the number of immigrants that could enter the United States.

Greek immigration had already reached its peak by this point. The Greek exodus began in the 1880s at a time when Greece suffered from a poor economy and domination by the Turkish Ottoman Empire. Young Greek men left their families to earn money for those left behind – and to avoid service in the Turkish army. By 1915, one-fourth of all 15- to 45-year-old Greek men had left their country for America.[63]

Unlike other immigrant populations, Greeks looked for financial stability elsewhere so they could one day return to their homeland. Traditional Greek culture made it difficult for immigrants to assimilate to life in the United States. Unlike other groups, Greeks left their families in Europe.

> Unlike other immigrant populations, Greeks looked for financial stability elsewhere so they could one day return to their homeland.[62]

FIGURE 76 **Greek coffee house**

FIGURE 77 **Greek shoe repair business**

89

Few temporary migrants from Greece were enticed to stay permanently in America. Further, Greek gender roles were very conservative, especially in dress and societal roles. Greek bachelors seldom met and married women in Grand Rapids.

FIGURE 78 **Greek school and choir**

FIGURE 79 **The Tolanas wedding party posed before the Castle Gate boarding house, circa 1919.**

A common drive within the Greek community, as with many other immigrant groups, was the desire to be self-employed. By 1910, Greeks in Grand Rapids owned laundries, shoe repair shops, shoeshine parlors, confectioneries, bakeries and restaurants. Many were located on Michigan Street NW. In the next 15 years, the Greek population perhaps reached its peak. During this time two confectioneries, two restaurants, two hat cleaners, and one shoe repair shop, all Greek-owned, existed between Ottawa and the Grand River.[64] But the success of such businesses in Grand Rapids was not enough to convince Greeks to remain permanently.[65] The original desire of many, to save money and then return to Greece, was foremost in the hearts and minds of most Greek men — and so they did. Only some of those who established businesses and assimilated effectively stayed in their new home.

FIGURE 80 **Greek Independence Day celebration program, circa 1932**

Grand Rapids' permanent Greek population was not homogeneous. The first Greeks who settled in Grand Rapids came from three different geographical areas within Greece: the Peloponnesus region in southern Greece, the Thessaly and Roumeli regions in central Greece, and the area surrounding Trabizond in Asia Minor.[66] Greek immigrants who arrived at different times did not necessarily feel connected to one another. As with other immigrant groups, established Greeks looked upon the most recent arrivals as foreigners.

The Greek Orthodox Church united this diverse population. After several years of making do with a Syrian or Russian Orthodox clergyman, the Greek community elected a church council — a symvoulion — and began to raise the necessary money to build or purchase a church and pay salary to a priest. In 1927, interested Greeks purchased a home at 1000 Cherry Street SE which they renovated and dedicated as Holy Trinity Greek Orthodox Church. In 1929, the Rev. Asterios Asteriou became the first Greek Orthodox priest in Grand

Rapids.[67] The church building on Cherry Street had a two-fold mission: the first floor served as the sanctuary and the second floor housed the Greek school. Students met here after the regular school day and learned according to Greek tradition, augmenting the American schooling that they received. Parents strongly desired for the children to learn their heritage, and sent their children to learn the Greek faith, history, values and language.[68]

Unity of the Greek population in Grand Rapids owes much to the church and community leadership of the Rev. Aristides Palaynes, who took great measures to foster understanding and pride in Greek heritage. For the children, he hired a teacher trained in Greece to lead heritage lessons. For non-Greek wives, he created the American-Hellenic Society to increase their knowledge of Greece and its customs.

Between 1929 and 1956, the most concentrated area of Greek population centered around Madison Square. Twenty-eight children attended Greek school and their families found camaraderie and support from each other. Other families lived away from this enclave. During the Great Depression of the 1930s, many Greek families returned to Greece and, for the first time in history, the number of Greeks returning to their homeland exceeded the number coming to the United States.[69]

African American Neighborhoods

The first wave of African Americans came in connection with the Freedmen's Bureau, which helped former slaves find work and housing after the Civil War ended. A Grand Rapids businessman, Charles C. Comstock, used the bureau to bring freed slaves and their families from Virginia and free blacks from Canada to work in his tub and pail company. Comstock built tenant housing located near his company on the east side of the Grand River. The housing, which became known as "Comstock Row," was located north of the downtown area and perhaps was the only strictly segregated African American neighborhood.

African Americans across the nation left the South and migrated to the North during and after World War I (1914–1919). In the South, industrialization eliminated many of the labor positions traditionally filled by African Americans. As the overall economy of the South declined, tight competition between white and black laborers for the few open jobs

Hattie Beverly

Hattie Beverly, the first African American schoolteacher in Grand Rapids, lived at 221 Prospect Avenue SE in the African American neighborhood. The school board almost prevented her from becoming a teacher because of her skin color, but she was able to proceed with her career. She began teaching in 1897 at Congress Elementary in present day East Hills. After three years of teaching, she married and left the profession. She died of turburculosis at a young age.[1]

FIGURE 83 **Hattie Beverly**

FIGURE 81 **Comstock Row was the first African American housing in Grand Rapids.**

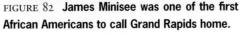

FIGURE 82 **James Minisee was one of the first African Americans to call Grand Rapids home.**

FIGURE 84 **St. Luke's African Methodist Episcopal Zion Church**

increased the strain on race relations, as one after another, white men were awarded jobs and equally qualified black men were turned away. Racial tensions, a poor economy, and the circulation of rumors that Northern living conditions were more welcoming made Northern migration a very attractive option for many families. One by one, black Southern families headed north in search of better living conditions. Most were destined for industrial cities like Cleveland, Chicago, Detroit, and Pittsburgh.

Few of the migrating African Americans left the South with a final destination of Grand Rapids. Grand Rapids did not have the same pull as those large industrial centers because it did not offer as many opportunities for employment. In Grand Rapids, furniture manufacturers and automobile manufacturers and suppliers locked out African American laborers. Even into the 1930s, many of the large employers of the area refused to hire black workers. Foundries and railroads hired a majority of African American men in Grand Rapids and a majority of African American women were hired as household servants. Despite the lack of open employment, the population increased.[70]

Unlike newly arrived European immigrants, the African American migrants had the advantage of speaking English. But to many employers, it did not matter. Most Grand Rapids employers would hire light-skinned immigrants with whom they could not communicate and refuse to employ African Americans with whom they were able to communicate. As African Americans found employment, they also found housing. As with other immigrant groups to the city, African Americans looked to neighborhoods with affordable housing located within walking distance of their jobs.

FIGURE 85 **A group of African American girls enjoy a band and choir concert at Henry School.**

FIGURE 86 **African Americans in Grand Rapids work as lumberers.**

An African American neighborhood arose around the turn of the century near Grandville Avenue SW and the railroad tracks. Here, the African American population settled among a variety of European ethnic groups.

In addition to the Comstock Row settlement and the Grandville Avenue neighborhood, a third African American community existed south of downtown near the Southeast Side. This area developed between 1870 and 1880 as the chosen area of housing for African Americans who were employed as servants and laborers in the Heritage Hill neighborhood.[71] It is within this community that the first black church was officially established. St. Luke's African Methodist Episcopal Zion Church served this neighborhood from 1878 until 1881 when it moved to a new location on Franklin Street at Thompson Avenue, the present site of the Sheldon complex.[72]

R. Maurice Moss, executive secretary of the Baltimore Urban League, conducted a survey in 1927. Moss was assigned the task to survey the situation African Americans faced, evaluate the information, and make suggestions regarding the future. As part of the results, Moss outlined three sections of the city where African Americans lived. Wealthy Street, Market Avenue, Cherry Street, and Division Avenue (including King Court) bounded the first section. Franklin Street, Buchanan Avenue, Buckley Street, and Jefferson Avenue bounded the second section. Franklin Street, Union Avenue, Wealthy Street, and Fuller Avenue bounded the third section. It was estimated that 589 African Americans lived in the first section, 500 in the second, 920 in the third, while approximately 400 African Americans resided outside these areas.[73]

For European immigrants, success was measured by social status and material goods. But among African Americans in Grand Rapids, respectability and social status were linked to church involvement.[74] Churches — virtually the only social institution African Americans could lead — began to develop in Grand Rapids. Between 1870 and 1915, the African American community built at least seven churches. As with the Dutch population, the African American community sacrificed some unity for a plurality of church options. In 1913, Reverend S. Henri Browne of Messiah Baptist

Richard Allen Home
for Colored Girls

195 Bates Street

Grand Rapids, Michigan

The Objects of the Home

1. To protect the girl on coming to the city in search of employment.

2. To raise the standard of domestic service, and recognize it as a profession.

3. To bring our girls together that they may realize their worth as a true woman.

4. To provide suitable accommodations for lady transients.

MRS. GOGGINS, President.

As the years come and go,
There is work for all to do.
Labor for the weaker brother;
Lend a hand to help each other.

FIGURES 87, 88 **Pages from a brochure for the Richard Allen Home, started by Minnie Goggins, at 721-23 Bates Street SE. Goggins later moved the home to 114 Wealthy Street SE.**

FIGURE 89 **First Community African Methodist Episcopal Church was located at 341 Commerce SW.**

FIGURE 90 **Mrs. Sara Glover helped form the Grand Rapids Study Club, which hosted speakers and intellectual discussions on a wide variety of issues.**

Church reported, "[It is] quite unfortunate to have so many churches among so few; while there is no law to prevent this utterly and useless multiplicity of churches, it seems that common sense ought to come to the reasons of this waste of energy — for two could do the work with far better results." [75]

In 1910, the U.S. Census reported that 665 African Americans lived in Grand Rapids. By 1930, this number grew to 2,795, yet African Americans remained less than 2 percent of the city's total population. In spite of this, the new migrant population was sizable enough to transform the local community that had already established itself in the late 19th century.[76] Prior to the influx from the South, the African American community in Grand Rapids voiced concern about social welfare and the respectability of urban living. The elite wanted an environment that stimulated intellectual, spiritual, moral, and skill development.[77] The arrival of migrants from the South heightened their concerns and increased the pressure on the already-struggling community of African Americans.

The strong push for the betterment of the African American community often came from the women. Wives, mothers, and women workers were strong proponents in the establishment of programs aimed at giving wholesome alternatives to the children and young people.[78] In June 1927, the Community Service Committee joined with the Interdenominational Missionary Union and formed the Interracial Council. This social welfare committee, born of Protestant women's networks, had the objective of addressing the recreational needs of young African Americans.[79] A social center was desired, one that was outside the white community. This increased the debate over integration versus segregation.

Jewish Immigrants and Settlers in Grand Rapids

The early Jewish population in Grand Rapids was first unified in 1857 when a French Jewish fur trader passing through the area died. The small Jewish community in Grand Rapids realized the need for a Jewish cemetery, so the Hebrew Benevolent and Burial Society was founded as the first official Jewish organization in Grand Rapids. The group purchased a half-acre of Oakhill Cemetery and buried the man. The founders of the Benevolent Society met weekly for educational meetings and worship at homes of the various members up to the Civil War. After the return of men from the Civil War, in 1871, twelve families and twenty single men rented a hall for the congregation at Monroe and Erie NW. The newly incorporated congregation, eventually named Temple Emanuel, was entirely of German descent.[80]

In 1882 the congregation dedicated a temple on the corner of Fountain and Ransom, a purchase made possible by money raised by the two charitable organizations, others within the congregation, and donations from area Christians.

Across the United States, Eastern European Jews tended to cluster together in the non-Reform congregations, while German Jews gathered in Reform congregations. About fifteen families of Eastern European immigrants to Grand Rapids formed Temple Beth Israel in 1892. The non-Reform Jewish population in Grand Rapids had experienced an increase due to ten years of Russian pogroms. As the numbers fleeing the pogroms increased, the migration of Jews from Russia and Eastern Europe rose steadily and the Jewish population in the United States increased rapidly. Some immigrants settled in Grand Rapids.

During the early years of its existence, the Orthodox congregation was a loosely connected organization that met at a store on Bridge Street for Sabbath services and for prayers. By 1903, the congregation was comprised of nearly fifty families and had been led by several rabbis. They purchased property at 438 Ottawa Avenue NW and built

FIGURE 91 **Temple Emanuel**

Temple Beth Israel. Within Beth Israel there existed a small population who wished to establish a congregation composed of only Orthodox believers.

During the High Holy Day services in the fall of 1911, twelve men left the congregation, joined the handful of Orthodox West Siders, and adopted the name Congregation Ahavas Achim. The congregation was small, only fifteen to twenty families, but it continued to grow. Within a few years they purchased a building at Scribner Avenue and Second Street NW to serve as a place of worship and meeting.[81]

Ahavas Achim and Beth Israel merged into the congregation Ahavas Israel, a Conservative Jewish synagogue, in 1937. This merger was precipitated by the rise of anti-Semitism that preceded World War II and by difficulty in financing two congregations within such a small population. The anti-Semitism also influenced the larger and wealthier congregation of Temple Emanuel to practice more traditional Judaism. For Jews who lived in predominantly Christian neighborhoods of Grand Rapids, the killings of the Holocaust were, in a sense, a wake-up call. They sparked a reawakening of cultural and religious pride, prompting Jews to revert to traditional practices.

FIGURE 92 **Hebrew School**

Julius Houseman

The influence of few Grand Rapids men can compare to that of Julius Houseman. Julius Houseman was born in Zechendorf, Bavaria, in 1832 and educated in Germany. By 1851, Julius was working in Ohio as a mercantile clerk. In 1852 he moved to Battle Creek, met and partnered with Isaac Amberg, and together they established several mercantile tailor and clothing shops in Grand Rapids and Battle Creek.[1]

Houseman was influential in both business and politics. His outstanding character made him respected and successful in both areas. He moved to Grand Rapids in 1852, working as a mercantile clerk at the Grand Rapids branch of the company. By 1855, the company had dissolved and Houseman became owner and operator of the Grand Rapids store for the next nine years. Around 1865, Alsberg, Houseman & Co. was formed in Grand Rapids, and later opened branches in New York, Baltimore, and Savannah. After four years as a partner in this company, Houseman sold his share in the out-of-state shops. He created a new and final partnership in the mercantile business, this time named Houseman and May. Houseman's numerous business ventures secured his place in Grand Rapids, where he remained a lifelong resident.

Houseman may have spent his days in the business world, but his heart was always in touch with the needs of all his neighbors. By many accounts, Houseman's greatest legacy was the philanthropic contributions he made to those in need — an organization, a family, or individuals.

The characteristics that made Houseman a successful businessman also helped him to succeed in the political world. Houseman served as a city alderman for three terms, from 1864–70, and was a state representative from 1871–72. From 1872–74 he served as mayor of Grand Rapids, and served as a member of Congress for the 5th District of Michigan from 1883–85. Houseman was known as a "true democrat, one of the most liberal and charitable men in the city."[2]

Another of Houseman's legacies centered on the contributions of time, money, and leadership he made to Temple Emanuel — the reform Jewish congregation in Grand Rapids. Houseman was one of 20 families who founded the congregation, and he was also its first president (1871).

FIGURE 93 **Julius Houseman**

For many years, Orthodox Jews could choose between attending Beth Israel, located on the east side of the river, or Ahavas Achim, on the west side of the river. Worshippers lived within walking distance of the temple, and for this reason two Orthodox Jewish neighborhoods developed, one on each side of the river. The east side, Beth Israel neighborhood, centered on Ottawa and Ionia Avenues north over to Coldbrook Street and east to Fairview Avenue. Residents of this neighborhood walked to Temple Beth Israel, and also walked to the Weiner Delicatessen and two kosher meat markets on Ottawa Avenue. In addition, living within the Ionia Avenue area were two shochets, men who killed chickens for Jewish people in the area.

A Jewish Childhood in Grand Rapids

Max Apple's grandfather, Rocky Apple, moved to the United States in 1914. Like many other men who chose to immigrate without their families, Rocky Apple immediately began to work long, hard hours to raise the money needed to send for them. During World War I, he worked, wrote letters to his family in Europe, and attended night classes where he learned to read and write English. When the war ended, the family joined Rocky Apple in Grand Rapids. The family home still stands at 700 Broadway NW.

FIGURE 94 **Max Apple**

Max Apple's books, *Roomates* and *I Love Gootie*, reflect on his experiences growing up Jewish in Grand Rapids. Max is a second-generation American, a grandchild of Rocky Apple, but writes of his experiences growing up in a household and neighborhood so similar to that of his grandparents when they were children in Europe: "In a gray clapboard house in the industrial district of Grand Rapids my family began, like many immigrants, to put all they had into their children. In our case the grandchildren were the children as well.

"At home we spoke Yiddish, but at school my sisters and I hung on to English like the life raft it was. Once we had the language, we polished it. The girls become paragons of fluency, high school debate champs. They brought home gilded trophies that thrilled us.

"Around the kitchen table, it was the 19th Century. In Yiddish the adults talked about the czar and pogroms — but in the dining room only the issues of the day passed my sisters' lips as they practiced debate before a large gilded mirror."[1]

The west side Orthodox Jewish neighborhood in Grand Rapids can loosely be defined as the area from First to Tenth Streets, from Broadway to Front Avenues. Temple Ahavas Achim served as the focal point for this neighborhood, which also contained the Hebrew School (used by all Orthodox Jews in Grand Rapids) at 657 Front Avenue NW, and the Workman's Circle (an organization to preserve the Yiddish language) just south of First Street. The Hebrew School served as the cultural center for the Orthodox Jewish community of Grand Rapids. This is the place where cultural affairs and community celebrations were held, such as weddings, anniversary parties, and Jewish plays. During the week, Hebrew School was held here and Jewish children from across the city would walk or take the streetcar up to the school for religious classes.

Transportation developments in the 1920s ushered in the era of the family automobile. This convenience eradicated the need to live near the chosen place of worship. A unique characteristic of the Jewish community lies in the fact that for reasons of faith, some members of the temple or synagogue choose to walk to worship on the Sabbath. Those families, though they live in diverse religious and ethnic neighborhoods, ensure a small representation of a Jewish presence in the neighborhoods surrounding Jewish worship centers.

Syrian, Lebanese, and Iraqi Neighborhood

A sizable collection of Syrians interspersed with Lebanese and Iraqi immigrants began settling on the north end of Grandville and Market Avenues in the 1880s. By 1905, the Syrians and "Assyrians," as *The Grand Rapids Press* labeled them, began to draw attention for their unusual wedding ceremonies and music.[82] A second wave of immigration brought more Syrians to Grand Rapids at the onset of World War I, swelling the total population to approximately 400 families.[83]

Until 1913, almost all Syrian immigrants attended St. George's Syrian Orthodox Church, where their own Rev. Philipous Assaley ministered in Arabic. The first structure was a brick basement building just off Grandville Avenue on Williams Street, then it moved to La Grave Avenue. St. Nicholas Syrian Orthodox split off in 1923, taking Assaley to its location at 328 Cass Avenue SE, where he served until his death in 1935.[84]

FIGURE 95 **St. George's Syrian Orthodox Church**

Immigration Restrictions

Most 19th-century Americans supported open immigration with the belief in the United States as a vast melting pot. But after 1880, as immigration rose dramatically and began to include groups from Eastern and Southern Europe in large numbers, this climate changed. Citizens who once believed that immigrants contributed to the nation's economy, growth, and stability began to fear that immigrant labor threatened the welfare of American workers. Concerns about the cultural and religious practices of these new immigrants came about and Americans began to wonder if the melting pot was beginning to overflow.[1]

Between 1882 and 1917, Congress created legislation in response to growing fears. These new laws barred people likely to require special public services, including ex-convicts and the mentally ill and imposed a literacy test upon those immigrants entering the United States.[2] The Quota Act of 1921 was designed to maintain the country's ethnic and cultural status quo.[3] It restricted the number of immigrants entering the United States by setting annual limits of given nationalities based on the census in 1910. This severely restricted the immigration of people from Eastern and Southern European countries such as Russia, Italy, and Greece. In 1924, the Johnson-Reed Act limited the yearly total of immigrants to 165,000, with quotas based on the census of 1890, a time when Eastern and Southern European immigrants were sparsely represented within the United States.

The limitations placed on immigration kept the ethnic, cultural, and religious component of the city of Grand Rapids stable. The status quo was supported and any increase in immigrant population was generally in proportion to the previous populace.

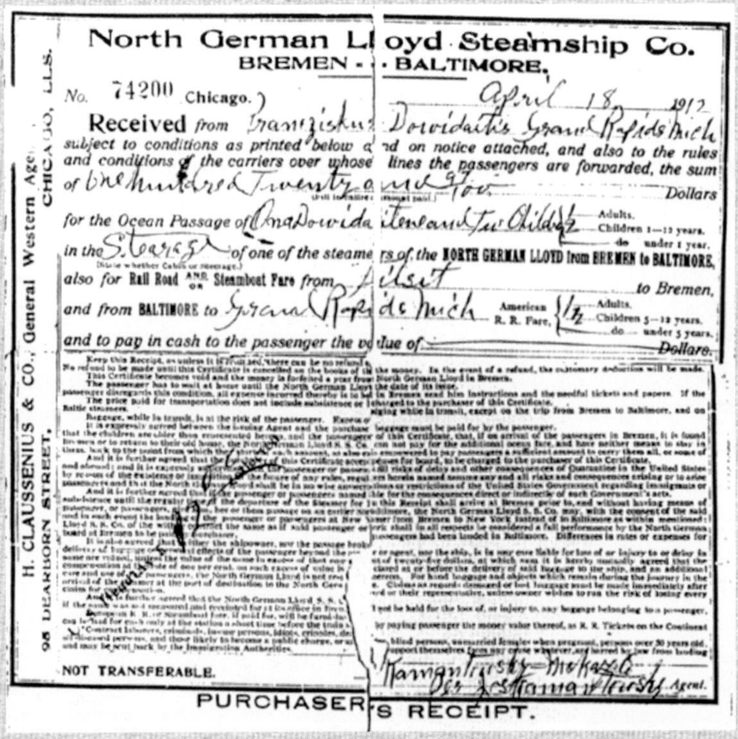
North German Lloyd Steamship Co.
BREMEN - - BALTIMORE,
No. 74200 Chicago. April 18 1912
Received from ... subject to conditions as printed below and on notice attached, and also to the rules and conditions of the carriers over whose lines the passengers are forwarded, the sum of ... Dollars
for the Ocean Passage of ... in the Steerage of one of the steamers of the NORTH GERMAN LLOYD from BREMEN to BALTIMORE,
also for Rail Road and Steamboat Fare from Tilsit to Bremen,
and from BALTIMORE to Grand Rapids Mich
and to pay in cash to the passenger the value of ... Dollars.
NOT TRANSFERABLE.
PURCHASER'S RECEIPT.
H. CLAUSSENIUS & CO., General Western Agents, CHICAGO, ILL.
98 DEARBORN STREET.

FIGURE 96 **In 1912, Prancziskus Dowidaitis, who later became the "Americanized" Frank Dover, arranged passage for his family from Tilsit, Lithuania, to Grand Rapids, by purchasing this ticket for $120.97.**

But in 1913, religious strife threatened to divide the Syrian colony on Grandville and Market Avenues. Although most Syrians in Grand Rapids practiced Eastern Orthodox Christianity, World War I in Europe had ballooned the Islamic Syrian contingent in Grand Rapids. The newly arrived Syrian Muslims reportedly declared war on Syrian Christians in Grand Rapids. According to a newspaper article, a small group of young Islamic fundamentalists armed themselves and collected funds to pay any legal fines that might be incurred against them for attacking their enemies. The storm passed quickly, however, as the talk was probably rumors about an extremely small group among a generally peaceful crowd of new immigrants.[85]

Besides religious diversity, the Syrians also had a varied range of economic opportunity. Unfortunate timing caused problems for the Syrians at first, as some of the earliest newcomers lived in houses near Market and Grandville that the city labeled "tumbledown shacks" and targeted for destruction. Apparently, the dangerous, crumbling structures served as nightly refuge for hundreds of Syrian men working to bring their families over and move to more permanent housing. Many were forced to find new housing after these structures were destroyed.[86] Many of these struggling immigrants first worked in the railroad yards or other jobs, such as grocery or dry goods sales. The wealthier Syrians also developed a significant middle class of doctors, engineers, lawyers, and teachers who benefited from a western education and learning the English language. Several became successful entrepreneurs, such as Kenneth Ellis and Michael Skaff of Ellis Parking.[87]

Syrians stood apart from other immigrant groups in Grand Rapids. All other immigrants who came to the city were European or African American. Arab immigrants, however, brought an entirely different set of ideals, culture, music, customs, and ideas about how society should function, all of which Grand Rapids had never before encountered. Syrians perhaps suffered a more difficult period of adjustment to

Grandville Avenue: The Gateway

Since the early days of Grand Rapids, no area of the city has experienced as much diversity as the north end of Grandville Avenue. The small stretch of isolated high ground has served as the entry point to the city for generations, providing affordable housing to a varied collection of immigrant groups from all over the globe.

"The Avenue" is well acquainted with the immigrant struggle of starting life anew in America. The very first Irish, French, and Dutch settlers on Grandville worked along the river, downtown, or in the furniture factories, saving their hard-earned dollars until they could afford to move to more permanent homes. Those that followed in various waves throughout the early 1900s — Italians, African Americans, Syrians, Lebanese, Hungarians — echoed the immigrant song of toil, eventually melding into the great diversity of the city. Since the 1960s, Hispanic immigrants — Mexicans, Puerto Ricans, Cubans, Guatemalans, Dominicans, Peruvians — have populated Grandville Avenue, once again blending a rich diversity of new cultures, languages, and ideas into Grand Rapids through one of its major gateways.

FIGURE 98

FIGURE 97

FIGURES 97–99 **These three photos, which reflect the diversity of the Grandville neighborhood, were taken at Finney School near Grandville and Wealthy in 1928.**

FIGURE 100 **St. Nicholas Orthodox Church schoolchildren are pictured with Helen Abadeelee Azarellah, FatherJohn Tertechny and Father Ellis Khouri.**

American life and were misunderstood a great deal more than many other immigrant groups in Grand Rapids.

In 1908, for example, Syrian customs conflicted with the city's "blue laws," which ordered grocery store owners to close their shops on Sundays. Most Syrians were accustomed to doing business on Sundays in their homeland, so they protested against the American law. Syrian grocer George Bashara was arrested when he violated the Sunday ordinance. To demonstrate the double standard, Syrians demanded that streetcars stop running, argued that milkmen should also be restricted from delivering on Sundays, and called for soda fountains to be closed.[88] Although their demands were not met, the confrontation sparked a healthy debate over the laws.[89]

Although the Syrians continued to maintain close ties with their homeland and sometimes clung fiercely to its customs, they also worked on becoming more American. In 1927, the creation of the Syrian-American Confraternity underscored their desire to promote good American citizenship among its members.[90] In 1927, the confraternity dramatized Shakespeare's "Hamlet" in Arabic at St. Cecilia's Music Society, displaying their knowledge of both Syrian and Western culture.[91]

The Walking City-Ethnic Neighborhoods Map
Footnotes and Boundaries

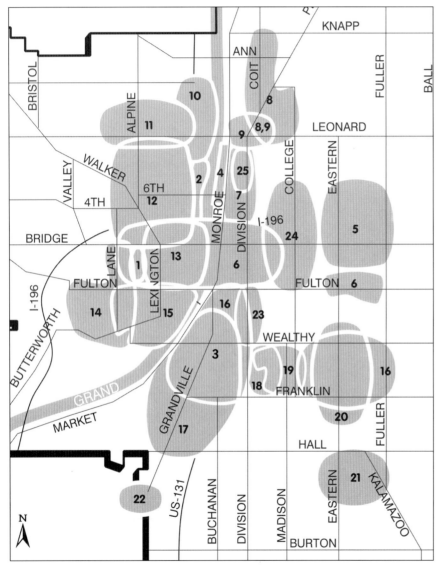

FIGURE 101

1. Germans were among the first immigrants to the city in the 1850s. Polish immigrants who spoke German settled easily among them from the 1870s on into the 20th century. Later immigrants to this area included Irish, Norwegian, Swedish, Danish, and Austrian, producing one of the most multi-ethnic areas of the city. Boundaries: N-2nd, W-Lane, E-Grand River, S-Lake Michigan.
2. West Side Jewish neighborhood — Temple Ahavas Achim, around 1900. Boundaries: N-10th, W-Broadway, E-Grand River, S-1st.
3. The Grandville Avenue corridor has been the city's "gateway" since the 1830s, when the city's very first Irish and French immigrants settled there. A host of other ethnic groups settled there at one time and moved on to other parts of the city, including Dutch, Hungarian, Syrian, Lebanese, Iraqi, African American, and Italian.
4. Comstock Row, the first African-American settlement in the city, 1865–1890.
5. St. Isidore's Brickyard Polish neighborhood, 1890s. Boundaries: N-Lydia, Arbor, Short, W-Grand, E-Fuller, S-Lyon.
6. Brickyard Dutch neighborhood, late 1840s. Boundaries: N-Fountain, W-Packard, E-Dennis, S-Baldwin, Hermitage.
7. Coldbrook Dutch neighborhood, 1860. Boundaries: N-Coldbrook, W-Monroe, E-Fairview, S-Trowbridge.
8. Knapp-Lafayette Dutch neighborhood, 1880. Boundaries: N-Knapp, Sweet, W-Center, E-Lafayette, College, S-Leonard.
9. St. Alphonsus Irish neighborhood, 1880s. Boundaries: N-Grove, W-Monroe, E-Lafayette, S-Coldbrook.
10. St. Peter and Paul Lithuanian neighborhood, 1880s. Boundaries: N-Ann, W-Davis, E-Grand River, S-11th.
11. West Leonard Dutch neighborhood, 1870s. Boundaries: N-Myrtle, W-Powers, E-Quarry, S-11th.
12. St. Adalbert's Polish neighborhood, 1870s. Boundaries: N-11th, W-Lane, E-Quarry, S-Bridge.
13. Scandinavian: Norwegian, Swedish, Danish neighborhood, 1870s. Boundaries: N-2nd, W-Straight, E-Grand River, S-Lake Michigan.
14. Sacred Heart Polish neighborhood, 1890s. Boundaries: N-Veto, W-John Ball Park, E-Indiana, S-Wealthy.

The Black Community in Grand Rapids
1865–1960

15. Southwest side Dutch neighborhood, 1900.
    Boundaries: N-Veto, W-Lane, E-Grand River, S-Wealthy.

16. African-American neighborhoods, 1890–1945. Eastern neighborhood boundaries: N-Fulton, W-Godfrey, E-Division, S-Franklin. Western neighborhood boundaries: N-Wealthy, W-Union, E-Fuller, S-Franklin.

17. Grandville Avenue Dutch neighborhood (Protestant and Catholic), 1850s.
    Boundaries: N-Cherry, W-Market, E-Ionia, S-Hall.

18. Little Italy neighborhood, 1890–1950.
    Boundaries: N-Wealthy, W-Buchanan, E-Cass, S-Hall.

19. African American neighborhood, 1945–1960.
    Boundaries: N-Wealthy, W-Division, Jefferson, E-Union, S-Pleasant, Franklin.

20. Eastern Avenue Dutch neighborhood, 1900. Boundaries: N-Evans, Buckeye (now Fairmount), W-Union, E-Fuller, S-Alexander.

21. Oakdale Park Dutch neighborhood, 1880s.
    Boundaries: N-Hall, W-Linden, E-Fuller, S-Crofton.

22. Clyde Park Dutch neighborhood, 1890s.
    Boundaries: N-High, W-Godfrey, S-Crofton, E-Century.

23. Heartside Dutch neighborhood, 1850s.
    Boundaries: N-Fulton, W-Ionia, E-Sheldon, S-Wealthy.

24. East Bridge Dutch neighborhood, 1870s.
    Boundaries: N-Bradford, W-Lafayette, E-Union, S-Fountain.

25. East side Jewish neighborhood, Temple Beth Israel, 1900.
    Boundaries: N-Coldbrook, W-Monroe, E-Fairview, S-Michigan.

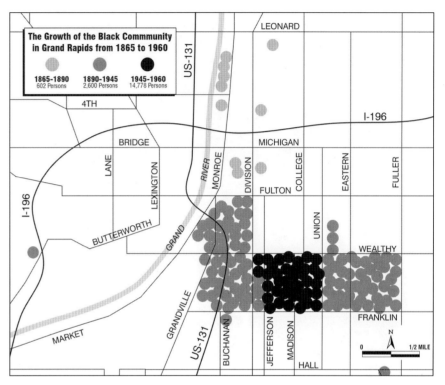

FIGURE 102

III

Transportation Expands Neighborhoods

Streetcars Launch Era of Opportunity
Autos Push the Boundaries

Streetcars Launch Era of Opportunity

"A city lives or dies, rises or falls, by its transportation, and Grand Rapids witnessed many of the most colorful
and exciting events in its history in the attempts of its citizens to get from place to place."

Z. Z. Lydens[1]

June 10, 1891, brought to a head the summer of violence that had boiled in Grand Rapids since May 19. Ever since the Street Rail Workers Union went on strike over the workers' rights to be in the union, chaos reigned in the city.[2]

The union publicly denounced any involvement with the stoning of street-cars, riots, and the brutal attacks on policemen and workers who filled in for the strik-ers. When the police department was openly criticized for not controlling the vio-lence, it commissioned many more men to help deal with the crisis. Mayor Edwin Uhl publicly condemned the violence and looked to the streetcar company to end the strike. Public opinion heavily favored the strikers, despite the few "midnight cowards" who continued to vandalize and terrorize after dark.[3]

But on the night of June 10, a tip about a planned attack led 21 police officers to lie in wait at the corner of Sweet Street and Taylor Avenue in the present-day Creston area. A huge armed mob stumbled blindly onto the greatly outnumbered squad of policemen, surprised to find opposition to their plans. They planned to dynamite the cable wheel pit, an act of vandalism that would tie up the streetcars for weeks, but the police interrupted their plans. Its anger provoked, the mob attacked the police and a hand-to-hand battle ensued. The police managed to fight off the mob, arresting 13 people.[4]

During the next several days, the shakedown revealed a conspiracy led by the Street Rail Workers Union, aided by various other unions, to destroy the cable wheel pit. The conspiracy ruined the credibility of the union and brought public outrage about such violence. Within a month, the strike died, the workers never receiving the concessions sought.[5]

The turmoil encountered during the rail-way strike brought the city's growing pains to the surface. In a way, the explosion of violence that June night only foreshadowed the explosion of population that Grand Rapids would experience throughout its next century of growth.

At the time of the strike, Grand Rapids had existed as a city for only 41 years. It consisted of a thriving downtown that boasted the Sweet's Hotel and several neighborhoods within walking distance. An outer ring of ethnic neighborhoods was developing around the core circle, each inde-pendent of the downtown in many ways.

These walking neighborhoods were crowded, noisy, and dirty. Many Grand Rapids residents, particularly those with solid financial status who had spent a number of years in the city, wanted to get out of this crowding.

FIGURE I **Grand Rapids electric streetcar, 1896**

FIGURE 2 **Canal Street looking North from Pearl Street circa 1870**

FIGURE 3 **Canal Street, looking North from Pearl Street circa 1890, shows the Pantlind Hotel, the first building at left.**

Another limiting factor in the 1890s was the lack of green space close enough to the downtown and its places of work. But a lot of farmland existed outside the city of Grand Rapids. To move to some uninhabited farm outside the city and commute to the downtown would have allowed thousands of city residents to build beautiful new homes and leave behind the racket of the city each day after work.

With the introduction of electric streetcars in 1891, moving out of the crowded downtown neighborhoods became a possibility. Although the city had experimented with various forms of public rail transportation for 25 years, electric streetcars proved to be a technological breakthrough. They combined efficiency for the rider and the streetcar entrepreneurs in a way that fostered their mass production, use, and city-wide expansion.

Electric streetcars ushered in the dawn of the age of opportunity in America and Grand Rapids. In great contrast to the area's initial European settlers, who found themselves content with owning a simple plot of land and a modest house, second- and third-generation Americans wanted more.

Transportation was the mechanism that launched this era of opportunity. First with the streetcar, then with the automobile, Americans extended the boundaries of their world. They could move beyond the confining borders of Grand Rapids to a place where they could build their own house, have a backyard, grow some trees and a garden, and yet still be able to commute to work. Also, for the first time, Americans could choose to live in a different neighborhood than their place of work, church, or social gathering.

Though the era of the streetcar was short-lived, its legacy was long lasting. Once America became addicted to the many options that transportation allowed, it was only a matter of time until technology offered her more efficient ways of feeding that addiction.[6]

FIGURE 4 **The city's first railroad depot, near Plainfield and Leonard, attracted many hotels to the area, 1858.**

The City Experiments

The Civil War actually provided the excuse for domestic improvement in Grand Rapids leading to the rise of public transportation. The journey by stagecoach or foot to the train depot, barely within the city limits at Plainfield and Leonard, was difficult for a family wishing to send its loved ones off to war. Union Depot had not yet been built downtown, so the citizens looked to the city to ease the burden.[7]

From the beginning, public transportation rose as a capitalist venture. The city asked a "citizens' committee" to look into the problems and come up with a solution. Without a doubt, Grand Rapids recognized that such an ambitious project as a system of public transportation would only come to life if it promised to make money. The committee members representing all of Grand Rapids included several prominent businessmen, such as C. C. Comstock, Martin Sweet, William Hovey and Freeman Godfrey.[8]

The citizens' committee recommended a horse-powered car on rails, looking to the models in other American cities. The early experimental routes proposed connecting the train depot (near Comstock's Pail and Tub Factory) to Campau Square

(near Sweet's Hotel) and to the plaster mills, with one route out Market Street (Freeman Godfrey's plaster mill) and the other near Butterworth Street on the West Side (William Hovey's plaster mill).[9]

When they opened stock in the company for public sale, these entrepreneurs found it difficult to obtain local investors due to the competing livery stable interests. However, three businessmen from Detroit, New York, and Saginaw couldn't pass up the opportunity to invest. The Street Railway Company of Grand Rapids formed, laid track along the recommended routes, and opened for business in 1865.[10]

The horsecar system proved effective in its first years, though it hauled fewer than 20 passengers at a time, at just above walking speed.

FIGURE 5 **Freeman Godfrey**

Creston

The street railway strike ended in June of 1891 when the police saved the cable wheel pit on Sweet Street from destruction. At that time, Creston experienced its most crucial growth period. The portion north of Sweet Street to Knapp had just been annexed to the Fifth Ward of the city, and the entire North End inherited the name "the Bloody Fifth."

The infamous name referred to the troubled area just south of Leonard, between Belknap Park and the river and north of Michigan. Before the annexation, the Bloody Fifth was inhabited by a mix of Canadian, British, French, and Irish immigrants, a fair number of New Englanders, and more than a few African Americans.[1] The conglomeration of factory and foundry workers lived in an overcrowded area of small houses, and the area suffered from crime, nelgect, and dilapidation.[2] As Creston was coming into its own during the streetcar era, it offered a step-up neighborhood for many of the working class from the Bloody Fifth who sought slightly higher-paying factory jobs and better housing.[3]

The 1891 annexation included the settlement of Dutch immigrants around Knapp and Wartrous (Lafayette), and a great deal of unset-

tled land east of Plainfield Avenue and north of Sweet Street. The area between Plainfield, Sweet, Monroe, and Leonard settled quickly as a fairly diverse neighborhood because of the train depot at Leonard and Plainfield. Several hotels, as well as a variety of retail businesses, sprouted along Plainfield Avenue near Grove Street, as the entire area benefited from the original horsecar line that ran from the depot to Grab Corners. Early settlers to the Creston area also included many Irish who settled around St. Alphonsus Catholic Church, and French who worked as lumbermen or railway workers.[4]

Furniture factories and lumber yards began to capitalize on the proximity to the railroad line, the canal, and free passage over Leonard Street bridge (1879), filling in the area between Canal Street (Monroe) and Taylor Avenue during 1880–1890s. Laborers for these businesses, mostly Polish, Dutch, and Irish, began to settle in the area between Plainfield, Sweet, Taylor, and Leonard.[5]

The sparsely settled area east of Plainfield Avenue towards College Avenue quickly became one of the prime development areas with the improvements in street-

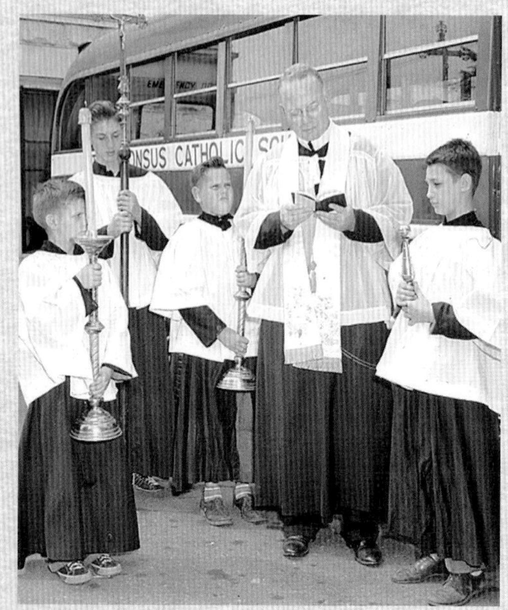

FIGURE 6 A St. Alphonsus parish priest blesses a new school bus, 1948.

FIGURE 7 View from Belknap Hill overlooking the Berkey and Gay Furniture factory, 1924

cars after the turn of the century. By 1906, 400 neighbors of the new community rallied to produce the first neighborhood organization in the city. Tired of the lackluster title "fifth warders," they sponsored a name contest that produced "Creston," after the hills near Spencer Street and Plainfield Avenue. They formed Creston Citizens'

FIGURE 8 **Kent Country Club has been in the Creston Neighborhood since 1901.**

FIGURE 9 **The Baldwin Hotel, at Leonard and Plainfield, was one of many new businesses to open when the train depot was built in 1858. The Baldwin was torn down in 1938.**

Association (CCA) to interact with city hall for various community improvements ranging from parks and street lights to increased police protection and attraction of retail trade.[6]

In a meeting commemorating CCA's accomplishments hosted by Second Congregational Church later in the year, Mayor Ellis and many other prominent citizens spoke praising CCA's accomplishments.[7] But the association was only getting started. Over the next 20 years, they placed sidewalks, laid out Briggs and Riverside Parks in 1917, installed electric lights, and campaigned for Creston High School in the neighborhood. Although business associations had grown quite influential in city affairs, CCA became the first to speak for the needs of its residents.[8] Its like was not seen again until after World War II.

By far the greatest achievement for CCA came in 1914, when it petitioned for and obtained an extension of the streetcar line north on Plainfield to Knapp. The area north of Sweet on the east side of Plainfield and north of Knapp on the west still contained numerous small farms. But, increased mobility to the area turned it into prime land for settlement, and the settlers came.[9] A business district also sprouted around Creston and Palmer schools, just south of Knapp Street. The area west of Briggs Park developed also during this era, as it was conveniently located on the streetcar line between the downtown and the Soldiers' Home. Evidence of this line can still be seen in the route of the power lines from the North end of Taylor Avenue to the Soldiers' Home, 70 years after the line was removed.

As automobiles became increasingly popular during the 1920s, Creston began to reflect the changes. The area known as Fairmount (not to be confused with present-day Fairmount Square in East Hills), just north of Knapp, grew significantly during that time period, as the Fairmount Theatre (later called the Roxy Theatre) crowned the storefront area. Neighborhood children played in the swampland behind Pasadena Avenue and skated there during the winter. The area also featured a golf course just south of Three Mile Road that catered to motorists, as the streetcar didn't extend past Knapp Street.

After World War II, Fairmount began to reflect the complete change to auto traffic, as the area continued to develop north of Knapp Street all the way to Three Mile and beyond.[10] Businesses accompanied the population growth along Plainfield, with parking spaces becoming a vital commodity. In 1949, Kay Pharmacy moved into its present location. In 1950, businesses in Fairmount formed the North Plainfield Improvement Corporation for the sole purpose of acquiring and maintaining a parking lot to share.[11] Many years later, this area chose the name Cheshire Village.

FIGURE 10 **The Dolbee & Kennedy Undertaker and Livery, on the northeast corner of Fountain and Ionia, later became the site of Bell Telephone Co.**

One company, the Valley City Street and Cable Company, pioneered the use of a cable car with winch houses at each end of Lyon Street, to serve what is now Heritage Hill and Midtown. One entrepreneur, Jeremiah W. Boynton, extended a line north on Scribner Avenue all the way to Webster Street in 1878. As a testament to the cutthroat competition between the railway companies, Boynton avoided paying some excess wages by driving one of the streetcars himself.[11] Cutthroat competition even led to duplicated lines as street rail mileage increased more than the population explosion during the 1880s.[12]

Competition included the use of entertainment to gain rail riders. Amusement parks or other attractions at Reeds Lake, Comstock Park, and North Park either formed because of or capitalized on street railway traffic. The Reeds Lake Street Railroad first experimented with steam-powered cars, but this was short-lived as electric streetcars soon came into vogue.[13]

In the same month that the street railway strike ended, electric streetcars became the rage. The new technology shattered its predecessors, eliminating the need for horses and stables, individually steam-powered cars, and the cumbersome cables that often broke and cost a fortune to replace. Centrally located electric power houses could feed an entire rail system of larger cars, each with enough room to hold forty people.[14]

The company built tracks on the major thoroughfares of Division, Scribner, and Wealthy.

The 1870s brought a flourish of new streetcar activity, as many businessmen tore the expanding market wide open. Several new companies sprouted, along with lines that serviced new areas of Grand Rapids. This fierce competition led to technological changes and experiments as each company tried to gain market edge over its competitors.

FIGURE 11 **O-Wash-Ta Nong Club, Reed's Lake, circa 1870**

FIGURE 12 **Before steam or electric streetcars, there was horse power.**

Just 20 days later, another roadblock began to dissolve when the Consolidated Street Railway Company bought out and centralized the remaining railway companies. The goal was to eliminate passenger headaches, such as changing lines and paying separate fares for each company on the way to one destination, as well as the confusing slew of tracks used by different companies.[15]

At that time, growth was also an issue — and a matter of significant pride to city residents. The city government anticipated a significant growth due to increased reliance on the streetcar

FIGURE 13 **Streetcar near Sweet's Hotel, 1872**

system and annexed seven square miles of additional territory in 1891. These new areas included Eastown, Creston from Sweet north to Knapp, Burton Heights, large portions of what is now Garfield Park, the South East End, Roosevelt Park, Ottawa Hills, Fulton Heights, and the low end of the hill on the West Side.[16]

Most of the areas annexed already included significant populations, as well as the vanguard of streetcar commuters who had begun to build houses and businesses in these areas. A total of 10,000 people already lived within these seven square miles, significantly raising the tax base of the city overnight.[17]

Unfortunately the massive consolidation and reconstruction effort that accompanied the merger ran into a major obstacle. A financial panic seized the country in 1893, forcing several notable Grand Rapids' furniture factories to shut down, significantly decreasing streetcar riders, and bringing the consolidation efforts to a screeching halt. The scars from the riots of the streetcar strike in 1891 did not help, and business limped along for several years. Consolidated couldn't muster the funds to complete the improvements.[18]

Finally, in April 1900, the Grand Rapids Railway Company took over Consolidated. It completed

FIGURE 14 **Privately owned and operated streetcar companies fostered competition and confusion for riders, necessitating additional fares and indirect routes.**

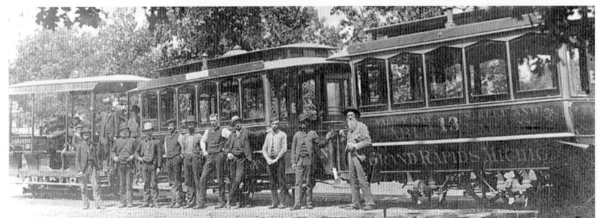

FIGURE 15 **Streetcars sit near the foot of Lyon Street hill, 1870.**

North Park

Charles Carter Comstock managed to involve himself in every profitable business that could possibly form in North Park. He and other tycoons, such as J. M. Nelson, E. L. Briggs, C. F. Nason, and Huntly Russell established North Park as a haven for several wealthy businessmen of the city.

Contrary to popular belief, North Park was named for a person, not a cardinal direction. The first American settler, Daniel North, set the tone for his successors in the area by building a sawmill and starting a logging business.

The entire region found itself littered with logs as a flood in 1883 swelled over the river banks. The logs piled up at the Grand Trunk Western Railway Bridge, creating a log jam eight miles long. Comstock built levies along the river that would help prevent such a catastrophe from occurring again.

He sold some land in the North Park area to the state for the building of the Soldiers' Home in 1886, and also opened the area around it for urban development. Most importantly, his creation of the North Park Street Railway Company in 1889 connected the quickly developing area to the city of Grand Rapids.

To increase the number of rail passengers over and above the usual Soldiers' Home crowd, the North Park Resort was created. The spot offered an inexpensive alternative for vacations. From the peak of the resort's roller coaster, vacationers could see canoeing and fishing on the river, a beautiful view of the Soldiers' Home, or a hot air balloon. Those who couldn't stomach a roller coaster ride found plenty of alternatives, and the resort quickly became a popular spot for parties, dances, picnics, and reunions. The attraction of the amusement park helped to justify the outrageous price, as Comstock's streetcar company charged three times the normal rate at fifteen cents per ride.

As the North Park Railway became part of the electrified Grand Rapids Street Railway Company in 1900, people flooded into North Park. Farmers who

FIGURE 16 **E. L. Briggs** FIGURE 17 **J. M. Nelson** FIGURE 18 **Huntley Russell**

FIGURE 19 **Michigan Soldiers' Home and Veterans' Facility is located in North Park.**

FIGURE 20 **Grand Army of the Republic decorated soldiers' graves in Soldiers' Home cemetery, May 30, 1926.**

owned land in the rapidly changing area, such as Robert Briggs, turned their land into dollars by selling huge lots to hungry developers. The new settlers of North Park could take the streetcars to work or find work within the neighborhood. One local business dug its fortune in clams along the banks of the river near North Park, selling them to button factories in the city.[1]

FIGURE 22 **Boat races were a popular activity.**

FIGURE 21 **North Park Pavilion, circa 1900**

FIGURE 23 **Sunday afternoon in the park**

FIGURE 24 **The North Park Resort dummy railroad passed the entrepreneur Comstock's home on its way to North Park, 1890.**

TROLLEY TOPICS

Vol. 3   MARCH   No. 4

Published Monthly By The
Grand Rapids Railway Company

A GOOD SPRING TONIC

Beware the ides of March!

Grand Rapids residents may soon expect the 59 different varieties of Michigan weather.

Rain, sleet, snow and all the others.

These can ruin a perfectly good shine, spoil a new hat, or playfully wreck a very good temper within a very few minutes.

Rubbers, galoshes, umbrellas and raincoats!

You may not be required to borrow any of these, but raincoats are not the only things that should be parked in garages during damp days. Take automobiles for instance.

Only as a necessity it doesn't help your car $30 worth to stand parked in a driving rain, or a sleet storm. It's said to be poor economy to use an auto at all in bad weather. Rain, mud, oil, sleet and snow are not good friends of varnish and lustre. Besides, the chance for accidents while driving an auto on slippery streets is increased.

You will be money ahead if you leave your auto at home and ride the street car. Sixteen cents, the round trip fare from home to factory or office, is small compared to the cost, everything considered, of operating an auto.

FIGURE 25 **Cover of *Trolley Topics* with graphics**

FIGURE 26 **Grand Rapids Railroad logo**

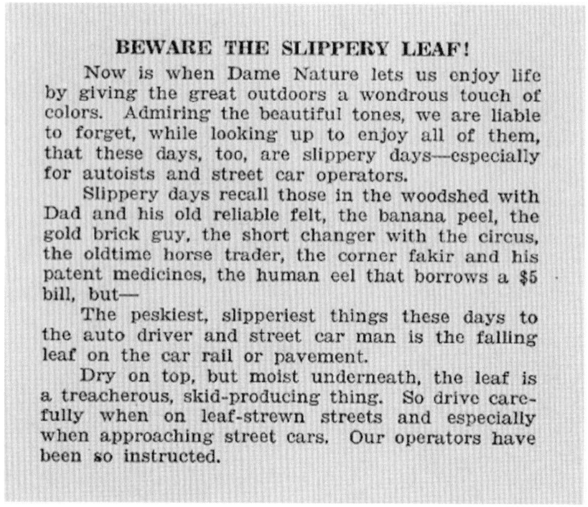

BEWARE THE SLIPPERY LEAF!

Now is when Dame Nature lets us enjoy life by giving the great outdoors a wondrous touch of colors. Admiring the beautiful tones, we are liable to forget, while looking up to enjoy all of them, that these days, too, are slippery days—especially for autoists and street car operators.

Slippery days recall those in the woodshed with Dad and his old reliable felt, the banana peel, the gold brick guy, the short changer with the circus, the oldtime horse trader, the corner fakir and his patent medicines, the human eel that borrows a $5 bill, but—

The peskiest, slipperiest things these days to the auto driver and street car man is the falling leaf on the car rail or pavement.

Dry on top, but moist underneath, the leaf is a treacherous, skid-producing thing. So drive carefully when on leaf-strewn streets and especially when approaching street cars. Our operators have been so instructed.

FIGURE 27 ***Trolley Topics* September 1926**

the reconstruction and improvements, unifying Grand Rapids under one system of public transportation.[19] The employers demanded that all riders be treated with courtesy and began publication of *Trolley Topics*, a pamphlet "devoted to the interest of the patrons" that passengers read for information and amusement. The pamphlet usually included an editorial that promoted the streetcar, a list of attractions, jokes, humorous stories, contests, and information about events to which streetcars could transport people.[20]

With labor issues resolved, consolidation under one company, and the efficiency of the electric trolley cars, the heyday of the streetcar began in earnest after the turn of the century. The evolution of the system into a reliable form of public transportation created a dependence on streetcars realized by both the city government and the people whom the system served.

The annexation of land in 1891, and streetcar service to those areas, met the demands that the city needed for expansion. A third ring of the city began to develop. This ring consisted of "streetcar suburbs," areas that maintained some

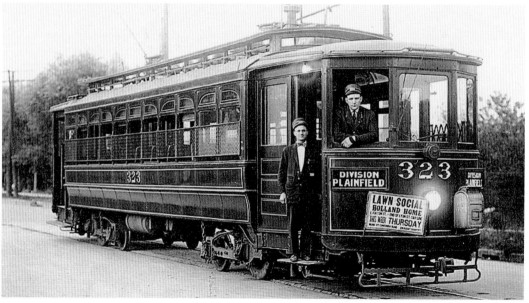

FIGURE 28 **Cars stopped at any corner for mail; note mailbox on front, circa 1910.**

ties to the downtown, but were largely independent of the rest of the city for their needs.

The capitalists who ran these streetcar companies realized an economic lesson. They could transport commuters to their work place all week long, but on Sundays, no one rode the streetcars. To collect profits on weekends and holidays, the railway company focused on the development of streetcar services for recreational use. This began by extending service to and promoting places like John Ball Park, Reeds Lake, and the fairgrounds at Comstock Park. Later, the owners began to create and promote their own resorts, such as North Park and Ramona Park.[21]

For the first time in the city's history, transportation choices dramatically expanded the options open to city residents. The streetcar offered mobility, allowing families to live in one place, attend church somewhere else, work downtown, visit friends in other areas of the city, and visit one of the streetcar company's many parks or resorts each weekend. Most streetcar suburbs developed their own business districts within walking distance of residents, each new development becoming a virtually autonomous entity.

For the first time, the city began to refer to Burton Heights as South Grand Rapids, while anything near Reeds Lake became East Grand Rapids. Creston and North Park were the North End and up the hill on the West Side became the Upper West Side.[22] These areas developed at a furious pace as city residents and newcomers left the first and second rings of Grand Rapids behind.

As quickly as Grand Rapids residents became accustomed to the convenience of public transportation, they also became

FIGURE 29 **Miller's Boat Livery on west shore of Reed's Lake**

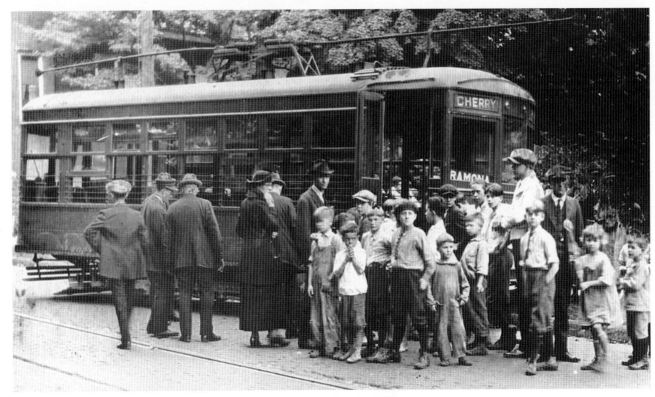

FIGURE 30 **Streetcars dramatically expanded options for work, church, and fun.**

115

Eastown

Few Grand Rapids neighborhoods have the same mythical quality as Eastown. Perhaps part of the aura lies rooted in the story behind Eastown's development. Reeds Lake was the place for everyone to go on the weekends, a vacation spot located three miles east of the city. Eastown sprang from a crossroads between the city and the lake, connecting the 9-to-5 work world with the land of summer vacation.[1]

The fact that Eastown developed into a community would have puzzled these early vacationers. They saw it as a place where the streetcars changed lines and were stored. But a community developed, independent of and separate from the lake. It preserved the nature of the crossroads neighborhood throughout its first 30 years, remaining a "bedroom" community. People slept in Eastown, but worked and worshiped elsewhere. Others stopped in on their way through to the lake.[2]

The East Building, a 1906 structure, stands at the heart of Eastown at the intersection of Lake Drive, Wealthy and Norwood. The changes this building has endured symbolize the changes experienced by the entire neighborhood. While the building once held a bowling alley and has recently housed several popular pubs such as the aptly named Intersection Lounge and Mulligan's Pub, it began as a streetcar barn, housing the streetcars that travelled on the old Indian trail to Reed's Lake.[3]

The gradual development of Eastown began with the platting and settlement of small farms by some well-to-do individuals who could afford the move to the streetcar suburb. The business district at the intersection developed to capture not only new residents, but streetcar passengers who waited to switch lines. No later than 1915, pedestrians could conduct almost all of their shopping in the district that spanned Lake Drive between Wealthy Street and Robinson Road.[4]

Most of the early development in Eastown depended on the streetcar lines. The streetcar company, though, wanted Eastown traffic to travel more on weekends. So like any good capitalist, the streetcar company created demand for weekend streetcar service by allying with Ramona Park at Reeds Lake in 1904. The popular amusement park brought more customers through Eastown than ever.[5]

Unfortunately for the wallets of the streetcar tycoons, they capitalized on the wrong people. Most of those who could afford to travel to Ramona Park every weekend were middle and upper-class families who could soon afford to buy cars. They continued to ride streetcars until they obtained cars that allowed them more indepen-

FIGURE 31 **Sailboat race at Wilcox Park, 1947**

FIGURE 32 **The intersection of five streets at Wealthy and Lake Drive was built to accommodate the street car lines.**

FIGURE 33 **The Eastown Theatre became one of many popular neighborhood theaters throughout the city.**

FIGURE 34 **The Laughing Gallery at Ramona Park**

FIGURE 35 **Reed's Lake, 1900**

dence. While streetcars proved crucial in the formation of Eastown, they soon dwindled in importance and faded from the mystique of the neighborhood.

The most expansive growth of Eastown came during the 1920s when cars began to replace streetcars. Almost half of the houses built in Eastown date to the 1920s. The business district also began to feel the effects of the commuter traffic. By acquiring some crucial parking lots and capitalizing on the walking traffic, the businesses of Eastown managed to survive negative effects that cars inflicted on many other shopping districts.

From its genesis, Eastown has been as diverse as the passengers that rode the streetcars and began to settle there. While African Americans could not settle in Eastown until the 1960s due to redlining and unspoken racial covenants, Eastown mixed white residents of many different ethnicities into a heterogeneous brew. The diversity of the neighborhood contributed to its character and style, a feature that would play a crucial role in the later story of Eastown.

The East Building passed from usefulness as a streetcar barn, to house buses for public transportation from 1932 to 1946. A fire in 1954 threatened to destroy the massive building, a foreshadowing of what the next two decades would bring to Eastown. But just as the building survived, so has the neighborhood.

FIGURE 36 **Dedication of new street railway car named for the Campfire girls, 1926**

Can You Find the Golden Egg?

The streetcar companies stretched their creative craniums to fill every seat on every streetcar with riders. During the summer of 1906, in an attempt to encourage riders to visit the amusement parks and entertainment sites, the newsletter *Trolley Topics* of the Grand Rapids Railway Company announced the hunt for the Golden Eggs.

As passengers traveled during that summer, *Trolley Topics* updated them on the hunt for several Golden Eggs that the railway company had placed in the various parks or attraction sites. The pamphlet urged readers to tour all of the attraction sites to search for the Golden Eggs. Those who located the eggs could redeem them for five dollars worth of streetcar tickets. This fortune would go a long way with a fare of only 5 cents.

Some riders criticized the Egg Hunt, which dragged on throughout July with no eggs in sight. *Trolley Topics* claimed that the eggs were located in plain view. The pamphlet answered any critics by stating that the hunt was "not about the nickel." In fact, they claimed, the eggs could be found in any downtown park that people could access on foot.

When someone did find two golden eggs, one in John Ball Park and another in North Park, it turned out that the eggs hadn't been initialed properly, a "safeguard" that the railway company had taken before planting the eggs. Someone, *Trolley Topics* claimed, had placed these false eggs as a hoax. Therefore, the contest would be closed the following week if the real eggs weren't found.

The contest closed on July 28, 1906 without a winner. *Trolley Topics* disclosed the location of five initialed eggs at Lincoln Park, North Park, Reeds Lake, and the bleachers of the baseball park on Market Avenue.[1]

dissatisfied with it. Perhaps the perception that the streetcar company raked in money hand over fist led to open criticism by commuters.[23] The companies tried to meet the demands of the city, as residents purchased 30 million rides in 1915 at the cost of a nickel each.[24] But commuters complained that the company did not create new streetcar routes to accommodate the transportation needs of newly developing areas. *Trolley Topics* responded by barraging its readers with statements that most of the money collected in fares was spent on wages or improvements.[25] Unfortunately for the streetcar company, the new communities in the streetcar suburbs began to outgrow the efficiency of public rail transportation.

Automobiles quickly became the popular answer to the shortcomings of public transportation during the late 1910s and early 1920s. While autos offered the utmost in convenience for their owners, they also featured incredible inefficiency in both production and congestion of the city, yet were affordable to only the richest in the city. Nonetheless, auto ownership tripled to over 9,000 between 1915 and 1917, at great cost to the streetcar company.[26]

A propaganda war developed. The streetcar company fought for its life as each new automobile meant one or more fewer streetcar riders per day. *Trolley Topics* frequently contrasted the inefficiency of a large chunk of metal that carried one or two passengers with the streetcars, which could carry 40 commuters at a time. Collisions between streetcars and autos grew more frequent. The streetcar company blamed the carelessness of the drivers, stating that streetcar riders were safer than both drivers and walkers. It also poked fun at drivers who had to search for parking places or battle the clogged arteries of the downtown auto traffic. Ironically, the streetcar company criticized the inability of autos to carry as many passengers as the streetcars, yet conducted a moral crusade against drivers who picked up other passengers, especially for money.[27]

Despite the hard-fought battle for survival, the streetcars lost in the end. The trolleys, driven by one centralized electrical power system, could not compete with gasoline engines that encouraged freedom. A 1924 fire that raged through the Hall Street car barn sent the future profits of the streetcar industry up in smoke and foreshadowed the end of the era.[28] Owner Louis J. De Lamarter replaced the cars and attempted to hold on to the street railway business until 1935, but it soon gave way to buses. He switched the name of his company from the Grand Rapids Railway Company to the Grand Rapids Motor Coach Company and created a bus system of public transit.[29]

The last streetcar, the "J. Boyd Pantlind," made its way from Campau Square to Ramona Park on August 25, 1935. This last ride spelled the end of the streetcars, and symbolized the shift of focus away from the downtown and the hotel that the streetcar's namesake operated.[30]

While the streetcar relinquished the public transportation feud with automobiles to its successor, buses did not create dependence on public transportation to the same degree as the streetcars. It was not a case of streetcars giving way to buses so much as the role of public transportation diminishing as consumers chose the convenience of their own automobiles. Beginning with the streetcar era and continuing with buses, Grand Rapids has always faced a tension between public transportation and private privilege.

FIGURE 37 **Mr. Toot of the *Grand Rapids Herald* put papers on the street cars for the first time in 1927.**

FIGURE 38 **The interiors of the streetcars were made comfortable with folding seats, lights, ventilation, and advertisements for distraction.**

FIGURE 39 **After the last ride in August, 1935, the streetcars were burned.**

Autos Push the Boundaries

"Private transportation drove public transportation off the rails and into the ditch until there was not thoroughfare enough to carry the load. The freeways… seemed to alleviate only a little the travel congestion that threatened to engulf civilization itself."
Z. Z. Lydens[31]

As automobiles increased in popularity during the "Roaring Twenties," a decade of prosperity and booming entertainment for Americans, demand for cars in Grand Rapids increased greatly. Autos embodied two aspects of the culture of the decade: speed and convenience. Not only could motorists travel faster than the streetcars (and buses for that matter), they could also come and go as they pleased without being subject to the times and tracks of public transportation.

Development pushed the streetcar suburbs beyond their previous limits, as speculators, developers, and land-hungry middle-class families snatched up every available parcel within the city limits. Neighborhoods such as Creston, Burton Heights, Roosevelt Park, and the West Side stretched along their main boulevards, forming business districts. Ottawa Hills was hailed as the last available land within the city limits in 1922, but the city splurged and annexed yet another ring of land between 1924–1926.[32]

Businesses began to cater to the needs of cars rather than pedestrian traffic. New storefronts pulled back from the roads, leaving parking space in front. Where room was scarce, stores chipped in for a common parking lot. Roads had to be widened because of street parking and increased traffic.

The battle of small neighborhood grocery stores to stay in business perhaps best exemplifies the effects of automobiles. During the 1930s and 1940s, larger grocery stores like Kroger's and A&P appeared with large parking lots on main thoroughfares. Grocery stores that specialized in ethnic foods and captured walking traffic struggled throughout the next two decades.

A Time for Survival

October 29, 1929 brought a screeching halt to most of this activity as the stock market crash plunged America into the Great Depression. Survival, not prosperity, became the key word for all but the wealthiest individuals. Many families lost their homes. Others, such as young Richard DeVos' family at 60 Wallinwood Avenue NE, were forced to rent out their houses and go live with other relatives just to keep their homes.[33] Where the ethnic neighborhoods had not yet dissolved, neighbors banded together for support. For example, in the Lithuanian neighborhood on the Northwest Side, ethnic grocery stores helped the community. The storeowners knew everyone well enough to offer food on credit to needy families.[34]

FIGURE 40 **As streets were widened in the 1920s and 30s, the streetcar rails and ties were removed. By 1935, Grand Rapids relied solely on buses and autos. This view looks south on Division at Fulton.**

Furniture factories, the lifeblood of Grand Rapids' working class, closed or laid off workers as the companies suffered economic starvation. Unemployment mounted, as workers with no jobs fought to feed their families.

The citizens looked to the government for help. Before the federal government could act efficiently, City Manager George Welsh introduced a keenly devised and well-intentioned plan in 1929. Those who needed work could perform tasks assigned by the city in exchange for "scrip," paper that could purchase food and other basics, but only at the city store that was run by scrip laborers.

The plan fell under criticism by a panel of citizens chosen to investigate its effectiveness. They pinpointed several reasons why the plan should be scrapped, mainly because it didn't jive with capitalism. Businesses that had somehow remained open, most notably neighborhood grocery stores, lost customers to the city store. Though the city wanted these businesses to survive at a time when every dollar counted, it provided a form of socialist monopoly that removed their only means of survival.[35]

FIGURE 41 **Grand Rapids scrip labor constructed Belknap Park. Those who needed employment during the depression in 1929 could work for the city in exchange for scrip.**

The Loss of Neighborhood Grocery Stores

One trend that took place in the 1930s and 1940s, robbing neighborhoods of the ethnic flavor and specialization of small, neighborhood food stores, was the rise of huge supermarkets, such as A&P and Kroger's. George Harper describes how this trend affected the Dutch in the Eastern Avenue neighborhood during that period:

"In the 1930s there were still many small shops in the Eastern-Wealthy area. The A&P had begun to destroy the market for these shops, but many hung on, serving a dwindling clientele. Most of the shops were family enterprises, and in some cases the family lived behind or above the shop. The shops had large front windows, which were used to display some of the goods. And often the family cat would lie in the window absorbing sunlight, under the 'glass curtains' that hung from brass rods at the top of the window…. The shop often had a warning bell attached to the door frame which jangled whenever a customer opened the door. The shopkeeper would then emerge from the back room and do business.

"But not only business: Often the customer entered in expectation of news as well as merchandise. The most sought-after news was church news; then came gossip about families in the area, or of political matters in the city or neighborhood, or excited descriptions of recent catastrophes such as streetcar-automobile collisions. The shops functioned as message centers also — when few had telephones, one way to communicate with others in the community was to leave a message with the shopkeeper or his assistants. The shops were more than mere commercial enterprises; they had important social and political functions."

In 1926, no more than 10 large grocery stores existed in Grand Rapids. By 1940, the A&P supermarket chain alone had 12 stores. Several other chains also developed: Food City Stores, Matt Heyns Serve-Self Grocery, Kroger's, C. Thomas Stores, Inc., and John Wawee's Market.[1]

FIGURE 42 **Shopping at the A&P Super Market**

Burton Heights

Some very gracious donors, Charles and Jessie Garfield, did their best to secure the future of their neighborhood by donating the land for what became Garfield Park. But the Garfields' legacy to what was then, in 1906, called Burton Heights was more than just land. Their spirit of community and caring lived on for many years in the neighborhood.[1]

Perhaps the closeness of Burton Heights, formed around the major intersection of Burton Street and Division Avenue before it became a part of the city, developed because of its physical isolation from the rest of the city. Several geographical features put Burton Heights on the map as a farming settlement. First, Division Avenue had been in service for many years as a plank road to Kalamazoo, offering a major thoroughfare to farmers. Secondly, the proximity to Plaster Creek provided a good source of water. Finally, the slight elevation of the area made the land more valuable. Several noted farmers, such as Edward Feakins, George Griggs, and Barney Burton, inhabited "the Heights" in the late 1800s.[2]

Major settlement did not happen until streetcar lines reached the intersection in 1893. Though Garfield Park was extremely popular within the developing neighborhood, it was not advertised as a major resort by the streetcar company. Those who came to settle in Burton Heights came for the attraction of the unsettled land and its beautiful location.

FIGURE 43
Charles W. Garfield

The land north of Burton Street developed first and was annexed to the city in 1891. South of Burton quickly followed, but the vote over whether to annex south to Alger Street split the neighborhood in half three times. Many residents liked to remain outside the city and its taxes, while others wanted the availability of city services. After many heated battles, those who voted for annexation finally won in 1916.[3]

Before long, the neighborhood became known as "South Grand Rapids" and quickly developed its strong character. The Burton Heights Businessmen's Association ("men's" disappeared later) formed in 1924 to help the retail interests of the

FIGURE 44 **An early duplex on Division Avenue in "South Grand Rapids"**

FIGURE 45 **Burton School grounds, 1929**

neighborhood. In 1952, the organization worked for the widening of Division Avenue, an improvement that eased the traffic flow of what was then U.S. 131 through the neighborhood.[4]

The diversity of the neighborhood is displayed in the variety of its early churches. By the Depression, 11 churches of many different denominations thrived in Burton Heights. Many of these churches survive today, adding a distinct faith-based element to the neighborhood. Several schools had also sprouted throughout the neighborhood, most notably South High, Burton Junior High, and Buchanan and Dickinson Elementaries.

Centered on the land that the Garfields donated, Burton Heights grew into a close-knit, thriving neighborhood before the Great Depression.

FIGURE 47 **City Welfare Department Sewing Room, where old clothing was repaired and sold for scrip**

In 1932, Welsh's plan gave way to the federal government's plan. President Franklin D. Roosevelt's New Deal programs, such as the Works Projects Administration (WPA) and the National Youth Administration (NYA), paid workers cash to improve parks and public property. During the Depression, the city capitalized on the abundance of labor and workers drastically improved the city's parks, buildings, roads, and the river. Labor ranged from the building of Roosevelt Park and the construction of a wooden walkway up the western face of Belknap Hill, to the reconstruction of the riverbank.[36]

The city did not expand much during the Depression, as Grand Rapidians scrounged for necessities rather than cars and land. Except for Alger Heights, the only area of the city to experience significant growth during the Depression and World War II, development of the city had to be shelved.[37] The era of opportunity lay dormant, waiting for prosperity to rise again.

Ten years of the Depression stifled the prosperity that the city had become accustomed to during the 1920s. World War II brought another five years of struggle for survival, but it ended the Depression and restored America's pride.

FIGURE 46 **The Burton Heights Methodist Episcopal Church at Burton and Horton SE in 1931**

FIGURE 48 **Transporting food supplies for the City Welfare Department**

While the war restrained the growth and expansion of upper-class, white, male America, it allowed other groups valuable time to catch up. With a dearth of men in the working force, women and African Americans walked into previously unattainable factory positions, setting the stage for the Civil Rights movement. While they could not yet assure themselves a position at the table of prosperity that white males dominated, they made strides that would allow them to take part in the feast.

FIGURE 49 **Grading and widening of Eastern Avenue at Maybelle Street, November, 1931**

FIGURE 50 **City snow removal on Monroe Avenue, 1929**

FIGURE 51 **Several fire stations served as scrip stores, giving out bread and milk.**

FIGURE 52 **By the mid 1930s, bus service replaced the streetcars.**

A Time for Prosperity

Prosperity. This theme reverberated in every American after World War II as they were eager to recapture the opportunities of the 1920s. The Depression and World War II had acted as a 15 year barrier to the growth and development of the nation.

A new foe had risen from the ashes of World War II that drove the ideology of prosperity with a newfound intensity. As the infamous "Cold War" set in, America feared the spread of the oppressive communist ideology to other nations and fought to preserve democracy and capitalism. The U.S. government felt that it must stay technologically advanced to prove that capitalism could produce a stronger nation than Russia and her socialist allies.

On the homefront, Americans worked feverishly in scientific fields, pressing their children forward as proponents of the generation who would save America from the

FIGURE 53 **Tubbs Oil Co. ran one of the early corner gas stations that became popular in the neighborhoods.**

125

FIGURE 54 **West Bridge Street during the 1904 flood**

West Side

When the 1904 flood swept through the lower West Side near the river, the torrent of water buried hundreds of homes. Many families waited for the water to recede, only to find their homes in need of serious repairs.[1]

Without a doubt, unsettled land up the hill to the west reached a premium after the flood, especially as politicians tarried for several years to protect the West Side from such destruction ever recurring. The prime years of the electric streetcars had arrived and those who could afford to move to dry ground used the streetcars to travel to their places of work.

Part of the demand for streetcar lines was due to the fact that few existed on the West Side in comparison to the web of street rails that had tangled the East Side of the city by 1904.[2] Perhaps another factor was the thriftiness of the working class Polish, Dutch, and Lithuanian immigrants who could easily walk and save their nickels for more important — and less capitalistic — gains. While the East Side featured this mentality as well, it was far less prevalent as the area featured a more diverse array of ethnicities and economic abilities than the West Side.

At least in the earlier years, the south end of the West Side benefited more from streetcar traffic than the north. One of the three original horsecar lines extended down Butterworth Street, connecting Godfrey's plaster mill to the central city. During the next years of development, lines extended down West Fulton and north to the business district on West Bridge Street. Most importantly, a line extended out Shawmut to John Ball Park, an amusement area that the railway company advertised and modified to increase streetcar traffic. As the park became an attraction for people from all over the city, the area around John Ball Park began to settle more heavily.

FIGURE 55 **The flood damaged hundreds of homes on the lower West Side, like these which still stand on Fourth Street between Turner and Broadway.**

By 1914, the West Side obtained additional lines out Bridge Street and Leonard Street. As cars became more popular, settlement occurred even farther up the hill. The Covell/Shawmut Hills area became settled after World War II, often by those who had grown up on the West Side. Similar to North Enders, West Siders continued to settle the West Side, gradually moving farther from the downtown.

Although the West Side developed due to streetcars and automobiles, the rings of development are not as extensive as in other parts of the city. Perhaps this is mostly due to the close-knit ethnic neighborhoods that remained virtually intact until the freeways came in the 1960s.

Russians. American businessmen prospered as well, trying to further the cause of American capitalism and the success it brought.

The government soon had to adjust to the changes. Not only were already-established families feeling cramped within the city limits, but returning soldiers were getting married, launching the "baby boom." With a healthy economy and a country that could focus on events at home, cars and houses were produced at an amazing rate. Rather than programs aimed at survival, new programs such as government-funded housing encouraged city growth.[38] For example, Congress encouraged veterans' dreams of starting their new family in a new house through the Veterans Housing Act of 1944, which promised a mortgage to all returning veterans.[39] An estimated one-fifth of all new single-family homes built in the twenty years after the war were funded by this GI Bill.[40]

At first, new homeowners in Grand Rapids capitalized on government housing and the availability of "Leavittowns," quick and cheap housing developments, and filled in the last remaining lands between the city and adjoining villages. The outskirts of the city limits filled with commuter neighborhoods such as Ken-O-Sha, Millbrook, and Eastgate in the southeast, parts of the North End, portions of the Upper West Side such as Shawmut and Covell Hills, the Richmond Park on the lower West Side, and Michigan Oaks in the east.

Mother and Daughter Keep Women Forever Young

Before her second marriage to J. C. Carr, Nora Husted ran a boarding house. She sold her own cosmetics made from a legendary recipe on the side, but had dreams to turn it into a full-time business.

Despite years of depression and financial panic that ruined businesses everywhere, Nora began the Marietta Stanley Company in 1895 to sell the product known as "Sempre Giovine", eventually renamed "Sem-Pray Jo-Ve-Nay" for easier pronunciation. The family manufactured and sold the product from its home before expanding to a plant at Fourth Street and Turner Avenue in 1904.

At her death in 1915, Nora bequeathed the company's management to her 16-year old daughter, also named Nora, who ran the company effectively for 20 years. The company finally closed in 1951, but had kept the West Side young for over 50 years.[1]

FIGURE 56 **Mayor George Welsh signed leases for veterans' housing in 1946.**

FIGURE 57 **Nora Carr and her daughter manufactured cosmetics out of their West Side home.**

Ottawa Hills

During the heyday of the streetcars, the area south of Franklin Street (then Fifth Avenue) and east of Giddings Avenue that became Ottawa Hills escaped development because of a nine-hole golf course that sprouted on the former farm of Nelson Higbee in 1905. Knowing the importance of streetcar traffic at the time, the first owner, W. H. Symons, attempted to stretch the streetcar line down Fifth Avenue (now Franklin Street) to the golf course, then at the eastern edge of the city. The history of the golf course began with the failure to obtain the streetcar line and included cutthroat business competition, a fire that burned one of the clubhouses, and eventual relocation of the clubs that occupied the course by 1922.[1] When the last golf club left in search of better business, the settlement of Ottawa Hills began.

Since demand for land within the city limits was so high at the beginning of the "Roaring Twenties," it is doubtful that attaching a myth and name to the area would have been necessary. The planner and developers, who laid out the streets of the settlement according to curving natural contours of the land, advertised Ottawa Hills as the previous home of Ottawa Chief Pontiac. Despite the deception, over the next six years, developers sold increments of the old farm and golf course at incredible rates, barely able to keep up with the ravenous demands.[2]

Boasted as "The Best Place in Grand Rapids to Live," Ottawa Hills appealed to the upper and middle classes who couldn't afford, or didn't want, the elegance of Heritage Hill, but they had money and automobiles. They built an eclectic variety of architecturally styled homes amid the winding streets featuring Indian names and abundant maples and oaks that characterized the "Indian Village" neighborhood.[3]

The development was so rapid and steady that the city approved a high school to be built in Ottawa Hills. The developers gave up a marshy area between Fisk and Alexander Streets that gradually filled with dirt from the excavations for the new houses. The high school was built in 1925 on the former swamp, later changing to Iroquois Middle School when the new high school was built on Burton Street in the 1970s.[4]

In fact, the entire neighborhood had risen just before the Depression halted development during the 1930s. In a mere eight years, Ottawa Hills had grown from a struggling golf course to a wooded neighborhood with a beautiful new school that brought people from all over the city. As a purely residential neighborhood, it experienced little change during the Depression and World War II era. But it was the first automobile neighborhood, as most others came after the war.

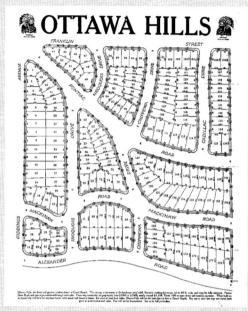

FIGURE 58 **Map of Ottawa Hills development**

FIGURE 59 **As it was not on the street car lines, Ottawa Hills was marketed to middle and upper classes with automobiles.**

OTTAWA HILLS
AT GIDDINGS and FRANKLIN ST.

The latest, greatest, and most interesting residence plat ever recorded in the annals of Grand Rapids' history. Every lot fully restricted. Single homes only will be permitted and to cost not less than $7,000 to $10,000.

Featured particularly with beautiful winding driveways, grand boulevard 80 feet in width and no street less than 66 feet wide. All homes to set well back from the street line, all public utilities service to be placed at rear of lots, no poles in streets, no fences except in line with houses.

The Ottawa Hills Land Co. reserves the right to take action on all improvements immediately when 75% of the present sale is completed, which, from present indications, will be a mighty short time. Dark asphalt pavements only will be permitted.

We urge you to spare a few moments to run out to this beautiful Plat, look about you and visualize how grand and delightful this wonderful home proposition will be, comprising as it does 160 acres altogether, fully restricted and fully improved and built up with attractive homes. Being so fully restricted, one lot is practically as good as another.

From 1912 up to about 1920 vacant property, owing to building conditions, was practically at a standstill. Activity started really in 1921 and those able to judge the conditions say that good lots will be in heavy demand for the next ten years. Grand Rapids now enjoys a very healthy growth and present building does not keep pace with the increase. As population grows, land values advance accordingly.

This property is located right at the apex of present operations in home building in the best part of Grand Rapids. Car service will pass

it. Splendid schools nearby, and one of the finest parks in the city two blocks away.

If you can find a good fifty-foot lot still left for sale on any of the better streets in the east end or in the Village of East Grand Rapids where there are practically no restrictions and merely on straight streets, you will find the owners ask anywhere from $3,000 to $3,500. No lots in Ottawa Hills less than fifty feet. Prices range from $1,000 to $1,900, and a lot you pay $1,500 for, when fully improved, will cost you in the neighborhood of $2,000–about half of the price in other districts. Terms are very easy, being 10% down and 1% monthly and 6% interest payable semi-annually. The improvements will probably be on the five-year plan.

An investment in one or more of these lots, either for a permanent home or investment, will be just as safe as in government bonds and more profitable.

The streets are plowed showing the lines, all lots numbered in plain figures on white stakes, and if you will call at any one of the Land Company's offices, secure a plat, or you may get one out there at the club-house, which will guide you over the property enabling you to make your own selection. Act quickly if interested, as they are moving rapidly. Salesmen on the ground Monday and part of each day during the week.

Within five years Ottawa Hills will be the best and most beautiful place in Grand Rapids to live.

S. R. FLETCHER
307-311 Michigan Trust Bldg. Citz. 69424; Bell M. 544
ADRIAN DOOGE
1013-1015 Michigan Trust Bldg. Citz. 64889; Bell M. 99
HAROLD T. FLETCHER
307-309 Michigan Trust Bldg. Citz. 69424; Bell M. 544
WM. H. GILBERT
336 Powers Theater Bldg. Citz. 51719

FIGURE 60 **Ottawa Hills was promoted as the latest, greatest, and most interesting residence plat ever recorded.**

By 1950, the only incorporated cities near Grand Rapids were East Grand Rapids and Grandville. The townships of Paris (present-day Kentwood), Wyoming, Walker, Alpine, Plainfield, and Grand Rapids filled in the outlying areas of the city.[41]

Wyoming, Grandville, East Grand Rapids, Paris, and Walker were more than crossroads for farmers, but they were not yet urban communities. Never before was such a drastic movement out of the city possible.[42] Thanks to the increased availability of the automobile after the War, suburban life became possible for more people than the streetcars and autos had removed from town during the first three decades of the century.

The tremendous residential growth that took place in the postwar boom created many new neighborhoods that would later join Grand Rapids. However, it also began a series of problems for the central business district of Grand Rapids, the established neighborhoods of Grand Rapids, and the relationship of the city with its immediate neighbors.

The postwar housing boom created many new neighborhoods that would later join Grand Rapids.

FIGURE 61 **Postwar housing on Kelsey NE. One fifth of new homes in the 20 years after the war were funded by the G.I. Bill.**

Annexation as the Answer

Over the decades following World War II, Grand Rapids was home to a continually smaller percentage of Kent County residents. In 1940, Grand Rapids housed 67 percent of the county's population, but in 1950 the percentage dropped to 61 and fell further to 49 percent in 1960.[43] A spot check of housing starts in 1954 shows that both city and suburb were growing, but the 1,479 homes that went up in the suburbs greatly overshadowed the 600 built within Grand Rapids.[44] The mass exodus was as much a journey for new houses and greenspace as it was an escape from the decaying inner rings of the city whose residents did not have the power to leave.

Grand Rapids leaders became concerned about the exodus and sought a way to combat the problem of a shrinking tax base. Annexation was the natural solution. In the past, outlying residents desperately wanted to be part of the city because of the social identity as well as city services such as water, sewer, and fire protection.[45]

But unlike earlier annexations, the city faced opposition from now-established suburban communities.[46] Suburbanites disliked the feel of a larger city as well as higher taxes that supported large city amenities such as museums and libraries.[47] The suburbs provided relief from these concerns, allowing residents to enjoy all the cultural benefits of the city-funded programs while only paying for the services that would specifically help their smaller community. These factors made annexation unattractive to most suburbanites.

While suburban cities could resist, township governments were vulnerable because these areas could be annexed with a majority vote of those who lived in the area. The township of Wyoming incorporated as a city in 1958, realizing that a municipal government wielded more defensive power than a township. Other townships soon followed Wyoming's lead.[48]

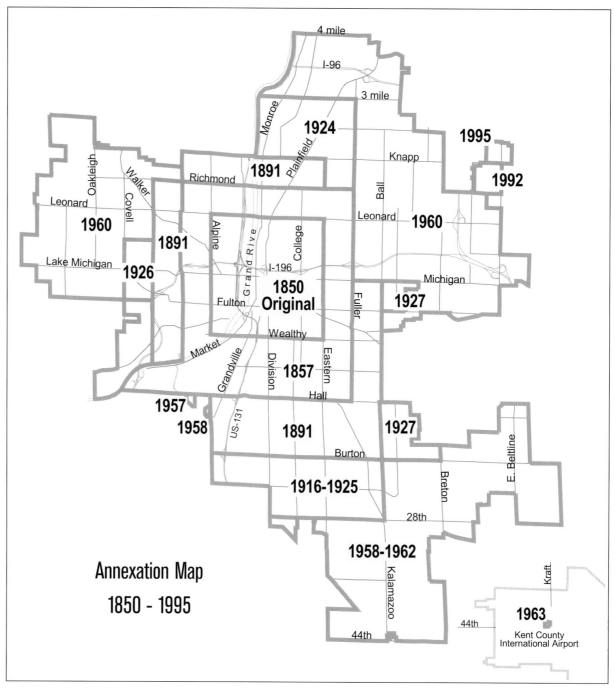

Annexation Map
1850 - 1995

FIGURE 62

130

Grand Rapids, on the other hand, hoped for a "New City" and campaigned ardently for unification of a large area that would drastically increase the city's population and tax base. The city's original proposal called for the greater Grand Rapids area, including Cascade, Rockford, and Grandville, to fall under one government.[49]

City services became the heart of the debate over the New City in 1959. Suburban residents would gain municipal conveniences of water and sewage utilities as well as police and fire protection if they joined the city. If they stayed apart, then they would retain home rule. Although Grand Rapids residents supported the consolidation by a two-to-one margin, the suburbs defeated the proposal soundly in a vote on December 8, 1959.[50]

With the "New City" plan defeated, Grand Rapids Mayor Stanley Davis and attorney Albert Dilley spearheaded the annexation of almost 18 square miles using a new strategy. The pair enacted a "no-extension" policy, meaning that all services stopped at the city limits.[51] Residents in newly developed areas found themselves without services under the new policy, but were given the option of joining the city.

FIGURE 63 **The laying of the city's first water pipeline from Lake Michigan began in 1939. City services were the "carrot" in the annexation debate.**

Fulton Heights

Located just east of the brickyard Dutch neighborhood near present-day East Hills, the neighborhood now known as Fulton Heights began to develop at the turn of the century. Many families were second-generation Dutch from the brickyards, near Fulton Street and Eastern Avenue, either self-employed or middle-class. Holland Home's Fulton Manor, which grew out of Holland Union Benevolent Association at Michigan and College, indicates a Dutch relocation from the brickyard. Mayfair Christian Reformed Church echoes this trend, relocating from Dennis Avenue CRC in the Dutch brickyards to Mayfair Avenue in 1955. But overall, the neighborhood grew to be more diverse than the brickyards.[1]

FIGURE 64 **Young Rich DeVos and family**

Streetcars proved crucial to the growth of the neighborhood, as the Fulton line ended at Wallinwood Avenue.[2] A number of businesses located on Fulton Street, to serve the residential area or to capitalize on its labor resource, such as Michigan Lithograph Company at Fulton Street and Carlton Avenue, Fulton Heights Foods (bought out by D&W in 1999), and Buth-Joppe's Dairy Ice Cream.[3]

Richard DeVos, who lived in Fulton Heights from 1928 to 1948, witnessed a crucial turning point in the neighborhood as the city switched from streetcars to buses and autos. But the survival of several businesses, churches, and faith-based ministries, such as the Salvation Army, indicate that the changes of the neighborhood did not undermine the conservative mindset of those who first settled there at the turn of the century.

DeVos' future business partner, Jay Van Andel, lived on Mayfair Avenue only blocks away from the DeVos household. With ambitions molded by their difficult childhood years during the Depression, the pair of aspiring entrepreneurs became friends not because of the neighborhood they lived and played in as children, but because of a car that Van Andel owned and drove to Grand Rapids Christian High School. But no school could teach DeVos and Van Andel the lessons that the neighborhood impressed on the minds of the young friends. According to DeVos, who paid Van Andel to drive him to and from school every day, the neighborhood was the most efficient way of communicating the important rules of life about hard work and tradition.[4]

After school, they entered World War II together. While on leave, in the garage of DeVos' home at 60 Wallinwood Avenue, the two young soldiers made the decision to go into business. Their company, Amway Corp., eventually developed into one of the most successful corporations in the country. The success and ethical business practices of DeVos and Van Andel are a tribute to the Fulton Heights neighborhood that helped them achieve those values.

Stanley Davis and the Polish West Side

Trucks roared by and fat snowflakes fell on Butterworth Street SW as Stanley Davis looked around the neighborhood where he had grown up some eighty years before.

"Every one of those houses was full of kids," Davis said, nodding at the plain, two-story structures across the street near the corner of National Avenue SW. The names from that World War I era began to come back to him.

The boy who would become one of Grand Rapids' longest-serving mayors and a state representative got his start, along with many other Polish immigrants, in one of the humble, hard-working families living near John Ball Park. The area known in the early 1900s as "Krakowo" was settled largely by families seeking jobs and homes better than they could hope for in Poland. Many worked in the gypsum mines, on farms west of the city, at furniture factories, or set up small businesses. They also formed their own close-knit community, founding Sacred Heart Parish in 1904 and nurturing tradition through Polish halls and parish societies.

Among these was the family of William and Angela Dyskiewicz, who came to Grand Rapids in 1914. Stan was only six then. Eighty years later he could still remember hiding from the Russian cossacks in the Polish village of Janowo.

"They would go into a village and tell you what they wanted," Davis recalled. "You had to give them fresh bread. Everybody was hiding from them. They were mean people."

It was a grim life the Dyskiewicz family left in Russian-controlled Poland. Their one-room adobe hut with a dirt floor was typical. They had one acre on which to raise vegetables, a pig, chickens, and a cow they shared with other villagers. Baked bread was also shared to conserve strictly rationed firewood. Stanley slept in a niche carved into the wall.

"The reason they came here was to better themselves, because there was no future (in Poland)," Davis said of the immigrants. "Everybody was going to the place where the streets were paved with gold."

William Dyskiewicz was followed by his wife Angela, Stanley, his sister Mary, and an uncle. Walking by night to avoid detection, they trekked some 300 miles to the German port of Bremen, where they boarded a boat to the United States.

A train took them from Ellis Island to Grand Rapids. There, name shortened to Davis at the suggestion of a citizenship clerk, the family built a new life in a new land. At first settling in an apartment at Williams Street and Division Avenue, near St. Andrew's Cathedral, they moved within a few years to the West Side. There Davis' father bought a house near the corner of Butterworth and National. It had a coal stove, no electricity, and an outhouse in the back. They got water from a spigot at the curb. Nothing about the house, or the neighborhood, was elegant. Tanneries and factories abutted one-story homes and saloons. But it was a far better life than Janowo.

FIGURE 65 **Stanley Davis, one of Grand Rapids' longest serving mayors, immigrated from Poland at age 6 with his parents, William and Angela Dyskiewicz.**

"There was nothing on the West Side that was run-down," Davis reflected. "Everything was kept up, because of the nature of the people that lived there. They had knowledge of tools and they were used to work."

Work they did. Poles, Italians, and other laborers walked down brick-paved Butterworth to the nearby gypsum mines, toiling from early-morning darkness until night. Davis, his mother, and three sisters walked to pick fruit at the farms west of town.

Davis also helped his father build a shoe shop next to their house, hauling bricks from a dump on Wealthy Street. To generate extra income, his father rented out part of the shop to a barber and remodeled the house to accommodate a renter.

Davis learned the shoe trade in his father's shop, sewing and sanding after school. "It kept me off the streets," he said matter-of-factly.

Then there was Island Park, located by the river near what is now Market Avenue SW and U.S. 131. It was a summer home to semi-pro baseball teams and enterprising lads.

"We used to shag the balls that were knocked into the river, and get admission for bringing the balls," Davis said. "A couple kids drowned going for those balls."

The drug stores provided abundant materials for mischief. Kids would stuff weeds or corn silk into cigarette papers and light up like the grownups did; bottles of alcoholic ginger flavoring, sold to bakeries for cakes and cookies, sometimes made their way to children's lips. More exotic compounds made for flashier diversions. A mixture of potash and sulfur, properly packaged in a paper bag and put on the street car track, was especially rewarding.

"When the street car went over it, boom! Oh, the kids would run," Davis chuckled.

The center of much social, cultural, and religious life, however, was Sacred Heart and its parish activities. Davis' parents worshipped there but didn't have much time to frequent the area's Polish halls, where Stanley would later campaign for office. Davis learned his lessons in Polish and English from the Sisters, sometimes pumped the church organ at Mass, and helped hoist one of the church bells into its tower when a new church and school were built in 1923.

He stayed within earshot of those bells until graduating from Union High School and marrying his first wife, Gladys, at age 21. He was still helping his father in the shoe store when William Davis died at age 49.

FIGURE 66 **West side neighborhoods were self sufficient with shops of all kinds, a bank, churches, and restaurants.**

Starting with the F&W Grand Store repair department, he eventually set up his own shoe shop on Bridge Street NW. True to their West Side roots, the couple bought a home near Lincoln Park.

Soon he began his long political career, as a solid working-class Democrat serving first as a city commissioner, then as mayor from 1949–1950 and from 1958–1964. Next came four terms in the state Legislature and other legislative posts until he retired in 1983, at age 75.

After 35 years of marriage, Gladys died in 1964. Davis remarried social worker Marjorie Hoxie, despite her Republican background. Living on the Northeast Side, and maintaining a cottage on Reeds Lake, he rarely had reason to visit his childhood haunts in old Krakowo.

But he often picked up the newspaper and saw the familiar Polish names of people he grew up and worked with — in the obituaries.

In his unsentimental, plain spoken way, Davis summed them up with perhaps their most telling obituary, "They were all people who worked hard."[1]

FIGURE 67 **Mayor-elect Stanley Davis with outgoing Mayor Paul Goebel**

While older township residents had enjoyed their independence for many years, residents in the newer areas felt less angst toward the city. From 1960–1963, they supported the city's piecemeal annexation votes.[52]

But when Grand Rapids tried to annex a large area of Wyoming, a court order halted these piecemeal annexations. The courts said both governments had to agree on the annexation for it to be legal.[53] With the exception of a small annexation in 1992, along the East Beltline in northeast Grand Rapids,[54] this decision cemented Grand Rapids borders as they are today.

FIGURE 68 **Attorney Albert Dilley helped spearhead the annexation of nearly 18 square miles to the city!**

FIGURE 69 **Alger Heights was the only neighborhood to develop during the war.**

FIGURE 70 **Built in 1947, this business district provided everything for families.**

FIGURE 71 **Robert and Bernice Lalley were early residents and still live in Alger Heights today. Their seven children all had the same kindergarten teacher, Katherine VanHouten, at Alger School.**

Alger Heights

Almost every other area of the city remained virtually unchanged during the Depression and World War II, but Alger Heights sprang up almost overnight during the early years of the war.

While there was a handful of houses along Alger Street in 1939, the quick housing spurt of 1940–41 left few vacant lots. The new inhabitants were primarily middle-class men and women who were stable enough financially to build a new home. It quickly became a neighborhood of young families.

The area residents between Alger Street, Kalamazoo Avenue, 28th Street, and Eastern Avenue shopped elsewhere for several years until the real estate partnership of William Duthler and John Simerink began to develop the business district at Alger and Eastern in 1947. Mersman's Supermarket, located at 2420 Eastern Avenue SE, anchored the business district that soon offered independence from other shopping areas to its residents.

The people who came to Alger Heights fell in love with the physical beauty of its trees and Plaster Creek, as well as the good-natured spirit of those who already lived there. It grew so quickly that Alger School and Seymour Christian Reformed Church and School could barely contain the incoming population.[1]

The Expressway Cometh

As early as 1919, West Point graduate Dwight D. Eisenhower had recognized the need for a system of highways to move military traffic across the country quickly and safely. While directing the Allied invasion of Germany during World War II, General Dwight D. Eisenhower noted with fascination the high-speed autobahns that enabled automobiles to hurtle across the German countryside at an incredibly efficient rate. When he became president in 1952, he sought to emulate the German freeway system. Such traffic arteries would be highly efficient for moving troops, as well as evacuating cities in case of attack. Also, the public could use freeways during times of peace, making them an economically viable commodity.

The Eisenhower administration's creation of freeways coincided perfectly with the prosperity of middle- and upper-class white America. The government hoped that freeways would help suburbanites commute from the downtown area to their homes outside the city, keeping the central core of the city healthy and thriving. Meanwhile, an aggressive plan called "Urban Renewal" would help to replace areas of the inner rings of the city that were beyond restoration.

To its credit, once the federal government realized that the downtowns of central cities were in trouble, a concerted effort came from all levels of government to bring them back to life. Unfortunately, projects to renew downtown life required the destruction of many historic buildings, neighborhoods, and community treasures.[55]

Like other developing cities, the clogged arteries of Grand Rapids were not prepared to handle the post-war boom of the automobile. Despite the costs involved, both city and state officials recognized the need for faster throughways. They worked to meet the transportation needs with the expansion of U.S. 131 from a two-lane highway to a four-lane expressway, a project funded by both state and local governments. The construction began in 1955 and ended up running $10 million over the original estimate of $17 million. Despite tensions between the local and state governments over the excessive price tag, the roadway opened for traffic on December 22, 1961.[56]

The Eisenhower administration passed the Federal Highway Act of 1956. The act provided 90 percent of the funding for freeway construction, asking local and state governments to split the remainder.[57] Interstate 196 came from this new source of funds, providing an east-west corridor through the city. With the north-south U.S. 131 and Interstate 196, a trip downtown no longer meant frustrating stop-and-start traffic. Expressways gave people the freedom to live further from their place of employment and shop further from home. The increase of cars and suburbs accelerated faster with the new expressways.

Under the label of Urban Renewal, Congress passed the Housing Act in 1954, which funded the demolition of blighted neighborhoods and replaced them

FIGURE 72 **In 1956 the Eisenhower Administration provided ninety percent of the funding for freeway construction.**

135

FIGURE 73 **Freeway construction cut a wide swath through the city and its old neighborhoods.**

136

FIGURE 74 **Automobiles and new expressways gave people the freedom to leave Grand Rapids and build homes in the suburbs.**

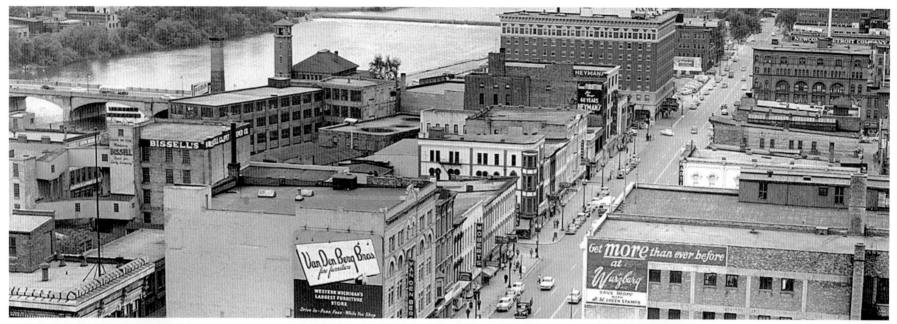

FIGURE 75 **Lower Monroe, circa 1950**

FIGURE 76 **Federal Urban Redevelopment funds enabled the re-building of downtown; the Grand Center was built in 1979.**

FIGURE 77 **On lower Monroe, Kresge's, Green's, and Woolworth's dime stores were a shopper's delight for over 70 years.**

FIGURE 78 **The "Dimestore Block" was removed when Monroe Avenue was extended to Fulton.**

FIGURE 79 **The Monroe Mall Amphitheater replaced the dimestores.**

FIGURE 80 **The midnight sky at the millenium shines through the design by artist Maya Lin at Rosa Parks Circle, 2001.**

with new, low-income housing. In response to the cries of local governments for viable business districts, revisions to the act allowed for 35 percent of the funds to go toward central-city economic renewal.[58] Urban renewal gave inner neighborhoods of Grand Rapids a new image.

In the 1960s, under the guidance of City Planner John Paul Jones, Grand Rapids approved the demolition of 40 acres of what Jones and other officials considered "blight."[59] A mix of houses, schools, businesses, theaters, and other structures, bounded by Ionia Avenue, Lyon Street, the river, and the newly constructed Interstate 196, succumbed to the wrecking ball.[60] City officials realized that downtown could not compete with the suburban retail centers, but Jones felt that downtown could transform "from the city's major retail area to a center of government, finance, entertainment, and other services," and workers in the area would support many specialty shops.[61] Down came many historic buildings such as Keith's Theater and the old Kent County building — 128 structures by 1966. In their place sprouted a mix of government and private office buildings, parking garages, DeVos Hall, and the Grand Center.[62]

While the positive effects of the expressway and urban renewal should not be trivialized, they also caused many problems. Before the construction of the expressways, long-standing neighborhoods thrived in the area. Some residential destruction occurred east of the river in the community near St. Isidore's Catholic Church, but the majority occurred in West Side neighborhoods because both U.S. 131 and Interstate 196 plowed through them.[63]

On the south side of the city, U.S. 131 followed a glacial riverbed that contained miles of railroad tracks and little development. The tracks divided up the area long before the construction of the freeway began, so it did little to disjoint the community there. However, once the highway reached north to the site of the present-day Van Andel Arena, the construction plan called for destruction of buildings.

Union Station was a major casualty. The train depot served as the site of the many emotional good-byes and hellos in Grand Rapids for decades, but fell in a move symbolic of the change in American lifestyles. A highway exit-ramp replaced it.[64]

FIGURE 81 **The old City Hall was one of 128 structures demolished on 40 acres of downtown Grand Rapids to make room for new development.**

FIGURE 82

FIGURE 83

FIGURE 84

A Decaying Downtown, but Burgeoning 'Burbs

While the federal government's plan sought to revitalize downtowns, the attention of the residents of Grand Rapids shifted towards the newly developing suburbs by 1950. The city realized that its days as "The Furniture Capital" were over when much of the furniture industry moved south in search of cheaper lumber and labor. Life along the river never returned to the industrious days of the early 20th century when downtown teemed with activity. Once the heart of retail, convention, and entertainment, the central business district's vitality had weakened to a faint pulse as industry relocated and downtown parking problems convinced motorists to shop at outlying retail centers.[65]

The population shift away from the center of the city, made possible by car ownership, also attracted retailers to the suburbs.[66] Shoppers enjoyed the ease of driving right to a store and avoiding the troublesome drive from their new homes to the downtown area.[67] Stores along Monroe Avenue, such as Wurzburg's and Baker Shoes, either left for 28th Street or yielded their business to stores where parking spaces were plentiful.

These changes gave rise to a 1960s retail trend: indoor malls. Rogers Plaza opened its doors in 1961, beginning a movement that would establish 28th Street as the second busiest thoroughfare in the state.[68] Stores began to fill in along 28th Street and, once again, tensions between Grand Rapids and the suburbs arose. This time the battle was over competing mall projects.

FIGURE 85 **Steketee's Department Store president Richard Steketee and Wurzburg's president Phil DeJourno review building plans for the move to Eastbrook Mall.**

FIGURE 86 **Sarret's was only one of many shops to move to the Mall.**

FIGURE 87 **Woodland Mall opened in 1970; note the new Sarret's.**

Eastbrook, built on property in Grand Rapids, opened for business in September 1969. Despite attempts by Grand Rapids officials to stop the Kentwood mall across the street, Woodland Shopping Center opened six months later. John Paul Jones feared the competition from Woodland, but appeals to the Kent County Commission's Zoning Committee were fruitless. Jones claimed that the city had no jurisdiction to prevent a second mall. Sears, Roebuck & Co.'s decision to set up shop in Woodland and not Eastbrook only increased the ill feelings of the Eastbrook backers toward the Woodland project. With these two malls now anchoring the new retail center, commentators began referring to the district as a second "downtown."[69] 28th Street continued to add retail stores into the 1990s. Other suburban areas developed thriving shopping centers as well. North Kent Mall opened in 1970, paving the way for a successful retail area along Plainfield Avenue in the Northeast Side and Alpine Avenue would develop into the shopping hub of the Northwest Side.[70] Finally, in 1999, Grandville got into the mix with the opening of River Town Crossings.

This began the pattern of urban sprawl characterized by thriving retail centers away from the downtown area. It forced central cities across the country to find new ways to remain healthy. In Grand Rapids, the flow of revenue shifted to the outskirts of the city. The wealthy no longer lived on the hilltop, but in Ada or Cascade. Residents no longer shopped at smaller, neighborhood grocery stores, but at large supermarkets. Fewer downtown restaurants and businesses survived, but moved to main thoroughfares on the outskirts of the city. The face of the city had changed dramatically.

FIGURE 88 **Woodland Mall, 1975. Malls became the new "neighborhoods" with park benches, fountains, sculptures, and plant scapes.**

FIGURE 89 **Woodland Mall in winter, 1975. Accommodating thousands of cars, suburban retail centers shifted people and revenue out of the neighborhoods.**

Postcards of Grand Rapids

Greetings from Grand Rapids, circa 1940

Monroe Avenue looking east from Campau Square, circa 1940

Monroe Avenue looking west toward Pearl Street, circa 1950

Monroe Avenue looking west from Division Avenue, circa 1955

Old Post Office, Ionia Avenue, between Pearl and Lyon, circa 1910

Court House, Crescent Street, between Bond and Ottawa, circa 1910

City Hall, Lyon Street, between Ottawa and Ionia, circa 1910

Police Headquarters, Crescent Street at Ottawa, circa 1910

Campau Square and Monroe Street, circa 1910

Monroe Street, circa 1910

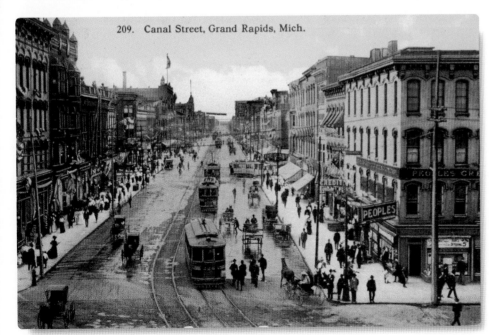

Canal Street, circa 1910

Division Street, circa 1910

Grand Rapids Art Gallery, East Fulton Street, circa 1950

Masonic Temple, East Fulton Street at Lafayette, circa 1950

Grand Rapids Public Museum, Jefferson Avenue at State, circa 1940

Civic Auditorium, Lyon Street at Monroe, circa 1940

YMCA, Ionia at Pearl, circa 1910 (Now the Federal Square Building)

Grand Rapids Public Library, Library Street at Bostwick, circa 1910

St. Cecilia Building, Ransom Avenue, circa 1920

Ladies Literary Club, Sheldon Avenue, circa 1915

*Grand Rapids' Greatest Department Store,
Grand Rapids, Mich.*

FINEST CLOTHING STORE IN MICHIGAN

Largest Clothing Store in Western Michigan

HOUSEMAN & JONES, GRAND RAPIDS

THE NEW HOME OF "THE HOME STORE"
PAUL STEKETEE AND SONS

Herpolsheimer's, Monroe Street and Ottawa Avenue, circa 1915   **Housman & Jones Clothing Store, Monroe Avenue, circa 1920**   **Steketee and Sons Department Store, Monroe Avenue, circa 1915**

Kresge's 5 & 10 Store, Monroe Avenue at Market, circa 1910

Foster Stevens & Company, Monroe Avenue near Pearl, circa 1915

Steketee's Ready-to-Wear, Monroe Avenue, circa 1920

Herpolsheimer's Infant's Department, Monroe and Ottawa, circa 1910

237. Evening Press Building, Grand Rapids, Mich.

Evening Press Building, Fulton at Sheldon, circa 1915

River Front showing Citizens' Telephone Building, Grand Rapids, Mich

P67271

Citizens' Telephone Building, Louis at Grand River, circa 1910

6927. Grand Rapids Brewing Co.,
Grand Rapids, Mich.

Grand Rapids Brewing Company, Michigan at Ionia Avenue, circa 1915

STAR MILLS

CRESCENT FLOUR

Capacity, 1200 Bbls. per day

Voigt Milling Company and Crescent Flour, circa 1920

The Coliseum, Commerce Avenue between Oakes and Cherry, circa 1920

Federal Building, Ionia Avenue between Pearl and Lyon, circa 1915

Fire Engine House, West Leonard at Quarry Avenue, circa 1910

Water Filtration Plant, Monroe Avenue at Coldbrook, circa 1915

Pearl Street Bridge, circa 1940

Monroe Avenue looking west, circa 1955

Kent County Airport, Madison at 32nd Street, circa 1941

Greyhound Bus Station, Market Avenue, circa 1955

Grand Trunk Depot, Michigan Street at Grand River, circa 1910

Interurban Bridge, Lyon Street at Grand River, circa 1920

Union Depot, Ionia opposite Oakes, circa 1910

Union Depot Train Sheds, Ionia opposite Oakes, circa 1915

AN ENTIRE CITY BLOCK OF HOSPITALITY.

PANTLIND HOTEL, GRAND RAPIDS, MICH.

Pantlind Hotel, Monroe Avenue at Pearl, circa 1930

HOTEL PANTLIND, GRAND RAPIDS, MICH.

Pantlind Hotel suite, circa 1930

HOTEL PANTLIND, GRAND RAPIDS, MICH. LOBBY

Pantlind Hotel Lobby, circa 1930

HOTEL PANTLIND, GRILLE GRAND RAPIDS, MICH.

Pantlind Grille, circa 1920

Morton House Hotel, Monroe at Ionia Avenue, circa 1915

Livingston Hotel, Grand Rapids, Mich.

67299

Livingston Hotel, Fulton and Division, circa 1915

CODY HOTEL, GRAND RAPIDS, MICH.

9396

THE CODY

Cody Hotel, Division Avenue at Fulton, circa 1915

HOTEL ROWE, GRAND RAPIDS, MICHIGAN

16

ROWE

Rowe Hotel, Monroe Avenue at Michigan, circa 1950

Pythian Temple, Ionia NW, circa 1910

National Bank Building, Monroe at Pearl, circa 1940

Michigan Trust Building, Ottawa at Pearl, circa 1910

Fountain Street Baptist Church, Fountain at Bostwick, circa 1910

St. Mary's Church, Turner Avenue, circa 1910

St. Andrew's Cathedral, Sheldon at Maple SE, circa 1915

Grand Rapids National Bank, Monroe at Pearl, circa 1920

West Leonard Street, circa 1915

Canal Street, circa 1910

Monroe Street, circa 1910

John Ball Park Pavilion, circa 1920

Ramona Park Pavilion, Reed's Lake, circa 1915

North Park Pavilion, Grand River at North Park Bridge, circa 1915

Grand River, Bridge Street Bridge, circa 1915

St. Mary's Hospital, Cherry Street, circa 1920

City Hospital, Fuller Avenue, circa 1920

Butterworth Hospital, Bostwick Avenue at Michigan, circa 1940

Blodgett Hospital, Wealthy at Plymouth Road, circa 1940

No. 172 New High School, Grand Rapids, Mich.

Central High School, Fountain near Prospect NE, circa 1915

330—Ottawa Hills High School, Grand Rapids, Mich.

Ottawa Hills High School, Iroquois Drive SE, circa 1930

Aquinas College Administration Building, Grand Rapids, Michigan

IC-H1621

Aquinas College Administration Building (former Lowe Estate), circa 1950

Calvin College, Grand Rapids, Michigan

3A-H1414

Calvin College, Franklin Street Campus, circa 1940

Furniture Exhibit Building (now Waters Building), Lyon at Ottawa, circa 1915

Furniture Museum (now Davenport University), on Fulton near College, circa 1950

Klingman's Furniture Building, Ionia Avenue NW, circa 1915

Furniture Temple (now Commerce Building), Lyon at Division, circa 1915

Oriel Cabinet Company, Monroe Avenue between Mason and Walbridge, circa 1915

Stickley Brothers Furniture Company, Godfrey Avenue, circa 1910

Michigan Chair Company, Godfrey Avenue, circa 1910

Imperial Furniture Company, Broadway Avenue, circa 1915

The Fox Residence, Cherry Street, circa 1910

Stratford Arms, Morris Avenue, circa 1915

Madison Avenue, circa 1925

Oakwood Manor Apartments, Cherry Street, circa 1955

Michigan Avenue, circa 1910

West Bridge Street, circa 1910

West Leonard Street, circa 1915

Madison Square, circa 1915

John Ball Park Pavilion, circa 1920

John Ball Park, circa 1910

John Ball Park Lake, circa 1910

John Ball Park Grotto, circa 1910

313—Fountain and Part View of Zoo, John Ball Park, Grand Rapids, Mich.

John Ball Park Zoo, circa 1925

BEAR CAGE, JOHN BALL PARK, GRAND RAPIDS, MICH.

John Ball Park Zoo, circa 1925

215. DEER PARK, JOHN BALL PARK, GRAND RAPIDS, MICH.

John Ball Park Zoo, circa 1925

JOHN BALL

JOHN BALL PARK, GRAND RAPIDS, MICH.

1A3290

John Ball Statue, circa 1930

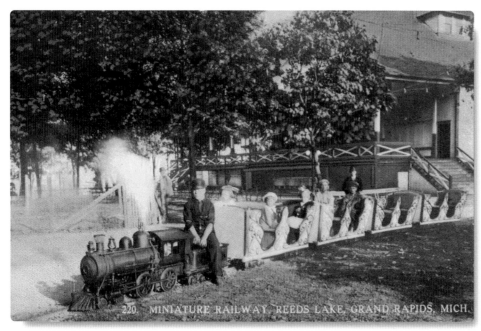

Reeds Lake Miniature Railway at Ramona Park, circa 1915

Reeds Lake Playgrounds at Ramona Park, circa 1910

Ramona Park Derby Racer, circa 1920

Reeds Lake Boat Landing at Ramona Park, circa 1910

Lake Side Club House at Reeds Lake, circa 1910

Ramona Theatre at Reeds Lake, circa 1915

Ramona Park Dancing Pavilion, circa 1920

Manhattan Bathing Beach at Reeds Lake, circa 1915

244. Grand Rapids Boat and Canoe Club, Grand Rapids, Mich.

Grand Rapids Boat and Canoe Club at North Park, circa 1915

Grand Rapids, Mich., Grand River Freight and Passenger Line.

Grand River Freight and Passenger Line, circa 1910

250. Canoeing on Grand River, Grand Rapids, Mich.

Grand River, circa 1915

223. VIEW ON GRAND RIVER, GRAND RAPIDS, MICH.

Grand River, circa 1915

North Park Pavilion, circa 1910

North Park Bridge, circa 1915

Soldiers' Home at North Park, circa 1915

Soldiers' Home, circa 1915

226. Highland Park, Grand Rapids, Mich.

Highland Park, College Avenue north of Railroad Tracks, circa 1920

Grand Rapids, Mich,
Antoine Campau Park.

Campau Park, Division at Delaware, circa 1910

FOUNTAIN, RYERSON PARK, GRAND RAPIDS, MICH.

Fulton Park (now Veterans Park), Fulton Street, circa 1915

67295   MONUMENT PARK, GRAND RAPIDS, MICH.

Monument Park, Division and Fulton, circa 1915

Lookout Park, Fairview Avenue at Newberry, circa 1940

Lincoln Park, Bridge Street, between Marion and Garfield Avenues, circa 1920

Franklin Park, Franklin Street at Fuller Avenue, circa 1940

Garfield Park Lodge, Burton at Madison Avenue, circa 1940

Holly's Restaurants, circa 1955

Charles Street Restaurant, Charles at Cherry SE, circa 1950

Fox Deluxe Brewing Company, Michigan at southwest corner of Ionia, circa 1940

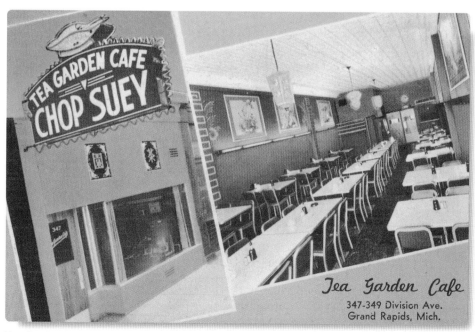

Tea Garden Cafe, South Division Avenue, circa 1945

IV

The Postwar Era

Idealism and Strife of the Sixties and Seventies
Neighborhood Profiles

Idealism and Strife of the Sixties and Seventies

"In the 1950s the familiar America began to call itself 'the affluent society.' While this discussion was carried on, there existed another America. In it dwelt somewhere between 40,000,000 and 50,000,000 citizens of this land. They were poor. They still are."
Michael Harrington[1]

With prosperity restored to America in the post-World War II years, few people ever anticipated that the second half of the 20th century would cause so much pain. Yet battles continued with the Cold War, Korea, and Vietnam. Domestic struggles with unprecedented racial violence, a credibility gap, busing, housing issues, suburbanization, urban renewal, crime, and political disgust, combined to radically change the social, economic, and political scene in America.

Not long after the freeways opened in Grand Rapids, Michael Harrington wrote a groundbreaking book, *The Other America*. This heart-wrenching work spoke about the plight of those in poverty in America, including the urban neighborhoods that the new commuters drove past every day. Harrington looked at the affluent society born out of the 1950s and called the nation's attention to the mess that the prosperity boom had left in its wake.[2]

In 1963, President John F. Kennedy read this book, and was moved to take on domestic poverty as a national enemy, including poverty in the rapidly declining inner-city neighborhoods. No matter how well intentioned Kennedy's plans, which produced his "New Frontier" platform for reform and technology, they ran into a host of complications.

Government could not simply wave a magic wand to solve all of the problems that had developed in its inner cities. While the explosion of affluence and prosperity had occurred quickly after World War II, the scars left behind by suburban-

FIGURE I **The 1960s and '70s unveiled a host of economic, racial, and social adversaries that America had to struggle against.**

ization would take much longer to heal. During the 1960s and 1970s, "the other America," those who had not previously had a voice, found their voice and made it clear that they would be included as Americans, too.

The 1963 assassination of President Kennedy, who had championed the cause of the "other America," foreshadowed the turmoil that was to come. With the first symbol of hope extinguished, others would have to carry the torch and fight the battle. At the same time, the battles for women's rights and civil rights became national issues. These proved crucial within the inner city of Grand Rapids.

Opposing Segregation

Decades after the Civil War, racism in the South thrived. White racists burned crosses and wore bed sheets while Jim Crow sat on all the town councils. But housing patterns in the northern cities hinted that the Mason-Dixon Line in no way represented a barrier for racial prejudice. In fact, residential segregation dominated northern cities during the 20th century.[3]

Grand Rapids was no exception;[4] suburbanization only compounded the segregation of neighborhoods. During the 1960s, the overwhelming majority of those leaving the central city were white, and the freeways became another link in the chain that pulled the races apart. The downtown area benefited from the accessibility of the freeways; drivers certainly spent less time on asphalt, but Grand Rapids' white tax base took these new roads straight to the suburbs, leaving African Americans behind.

A Fighting Family

Obtaining equality for everyone requires tremendous effort to break down the walls that hold certain groups back. One family in Grand Rapids stands out as particularly aggressive in refusing to accept the limits imposed on African Americans. Helen Jackson Claytor dedicated her life to fighting for equality between the races.

Helen Claytor's life began in Minneapolis in 1907. She spent her entire childhood living in a house her father, determined to put his four girls through college, built as close to the University of Minnesota as possible. Claytor graduated from Minnesota in 1928 with a teaching degree, cum laude and Phi Beta Kappa, yet found little demand for an African American teacher. Fortunately, she knew better than to let her talents be swept under the carpet because of her skin color and took a job with an African American branch of the YWCA in Trenton, New Jersey. Her marriage to journalist Earl Wilkins took her to Kansas City, where he wrote for an African American newspaper. The happy years of marriage soon turned to tragedy as Earl succumbed to tuberculosis. He died in 1940 and Helen went back to work for the YWCA.

She quickly rose within the ranks of the YWCA. Her position in the national organization as secretary of interracial justice brought her to Grand Rapids in 1942. During her visit, she met Dr. Robert Claytor and they married the following year. Robert Claytor was the son of former slaves and one of 13 children, six of whom, including Robert, attended Meharry Medical College in Nashville and went into the medical professions. Robert Claytor not only broke through a color barrier with his profession but also served on the

FIGURE 2 **Robert Claytor**

board of the Community Chest, now the United Way.

Prior to Helen coming to Grand Rapids in 1944, Robert needed to purchase a house for his new family. There were two distinct African American neighborhoods then and according to Helen, "You could almost count on the fingers of your hands the black people who lived outside of these particular areas."[1] Robert had fair skin, green eyes and straight hair so realtors would show him houses outside the "Negro District" until they found out he was African American. He was then told that all the houses they looked at were sold. Frustrated with the realtors, he went looking on his own and found a house on the Northeast side

FIGURE 3 **Helen Jackson Claytor**

that the owners were selling themselves. He quickly bought the house but then the owners discovered his race. They scrambled to buy the house back but Robert refused. Initially, the other neighbors protested and resented the Claytor's presence, but within a couple of years the neighbors overcame their initial prejudices and welcomed the Claytors.[2]

Helen continued to rise within the ranks of the YWCA after moving to Grand Rapids. Here she became the first African American president of a community-wide YWCA when she took over this position in 1949. While raising her children, Roger, Sharon, and Judith, she managed the local responsibilities of the YWCA along with many national duties of the organization. Her area of expertise was interracial relations. With this interest and knowledge she traveled to China, Lebanon, Ghana, and Greece as a representative of the YWCA. In 1967 she was elected to the National Board of Directors and then appointed president. She served in this capacity for six years and takes pride in the justice and equality imperative that the YWCA adopted in 1970 under her leadership. The imperative states that the YWCA will work for "the elimination of racism wherever it exists and by any means necessary."

FIGURE 4 **Opened in the Madison Square neighborhood in 2000 by St. Mary's Hospital, the Claytor name is remembered on the non-profit health clinic.**

Within Grand Rapids, the accomplishment of which she is the most proud is her work to establish the Human Relations Commission. She was appointed by Mayor Paul Goebel to a committee charged with determining the need for a permanent race relations body. Initially, many members of the study committee did not think a permanent body was necessary. However, Claytor and three other women kept prodding the study committee to carefully examine the racial situation in Grand Rapids. The final report of the study committee highlighted clear discrimination in the community. They recommended the establishment of a permanent body focused on alleviating discrimination. This body was first called the Human Relations Commission but is now known as the Equal Opportunity Office.[3]

Helen Claytor's son, Roger Wilkins, followed his parent's legacy by documenting the racial struggles in his life, including his growing-up years in both Harlem and Grand Rapids, in a book titled *A Man's Life*.

In June of 2000, the community remembered the Claytors' service by naming the Browning Claytor Health Center in Madison Square after Robert Claytor.[4] Their names will always be remembered as a fighting family who dedicated their lives to the community.

The African American population increased after World War II, but their housing options did not. Racial covenants, redlining, and racial steering practices kept African Americans confined to distinct neighborhoods, which were becoming exclusively non-white as block-busting occurred, while white residents were leaving for the suburbs. These neighborhoods were becoming increasingly less desirable and falling into disrepair.

African Americans in Grand Rapids were still at the bottom of the job market. They worked the most physically demanding jobs, received the lowest pay, the fewest promotions, were the last to be hired, and first to be fired.[5] A higher percentage of African Americans than whites rented their homes, whose upkeep was all too often neglected by their landlords.[6]

Through a practice called redlining, banks identified some areas as "declining." The lenders' refusal to give loans in these areas caused home prices to fall, allowing outsiders to make large profits by buying them up and renting them out. Often, landlords' lack of maintenance caused homes to fall into disrepair. Even homeowners who wished to refinance and make improvements found themselves unable to get a loan. The banks' designation of a "declining" neighborhood became a self-fulfilling prophecy.[7]

African Americans also suffered from racial steering, in which real estate agents would only show potential African American home buyers houses within the black neighborhoods. Since African Americans purchased homes in a controlled market, they were forced to pay higher prices relative to whites for homes of lesser quality. Realtors argued this practice kept housing prices from plummeting in the white neighborhoods. Studies proved that housing assessments plunged when African

FIGURE 5 **On July 4, 1925, a statewide gathering of Klu Klux Klansmen marched in Grand Rapids as seen here on Bridge Street at Indiana Avenue.**

Paul I. Phillips

FIGURE 6 **Paul I. Phillips**

Arriving in Grand Rapids in 1947, Paul I. Phillips brought the African American community in Grand Rapids through the heart of the civil rights movement. His death in 1977 ended his lifelong work of improving race relations.

Educated at Marquette and Fisk Universities, he came to Grand Rapids to direct the Grand Rapids Urban League, quickly establishing himself as a leader.[1] He spent the bulk of his first 10 years at the Urban League developing job opportunities for minorities. Prior to the enactment of civil rights laws, he expanded employment opportunities for African Americans, placing some of the first minorities in factory jobs, as nurse trainees, hospital workers, teachers, sales people, clerical workers, and bank employees.[2]

Phillips became the first elected African American in Grand Rapids when voters placed him on the Grand Rapids Charter Commission in 1951. In 1962, he became the first African American on the Grand Rapids Board of Education. As a member of the school board for eight years, he fought hard for equality. Phillips supported school busing, though he never thought it was the best way for integrating. "We will never integrate our schools until we integrate our neighborhoods," he said. "If the whites don't want busing, they will have to learn to live with others."[3]

Phillips worked toward this end by moving into an all-white northeast side neighborhood despite the bomb threats against him and his family.[4] On the national scene, he advised President Gerald R. Ford on minority concerns.

He recognized progress for African Americans in many areas, yet never felt satisfied. The Nebraska native said, "Grand Rapids is the kind of community in which gut hatred does not exist, but prejudicial attitudes do exist on the level of not wanting to recognize the problem or to get involved in solving it."[5]

The work of Paul I. Phillips did more to improve the conditions for African Americans than any other individual in the city's history. His legacy inspires many others to continue the task of improving race relations.

Americans entered a white neighborhood, but only due to the whites' fear. Values went back up after the initial panic subsided.[8]

While realtors certainly practiced institutional racism, they did not create it. Many racial covenants written into the housing deeds of white homeowners stated that the home could not be sold to African Americans. Many whites desired to live in areas surrounded by those of similar color, and their fears limited the growing African American community to land-locked neighborhoods desperate for repair.[9]

The social climate after World War II prevented African Americans from gaining equal access to homes, jobs, schools, and services. It was not until the civil rights movement of the 1950s and 1960s that America began facing its deep-rooted hypocrisy: It was a democracy founded on individual rights for everyone, yet it prevented whole groups of citizens from enjoying the same freedoms.[10]

Ironically, the same economic boom and prosperity that left a large population of inner-city African Americans stranded in decaying neighborhoods also helped the cause of civil rights. First, the creation of more jobs allowed more economic empowerment for African Americans, without taking the jobs of whites, so whites did not see the increased employment of African Americans as a threat. Secondly, economic prosperity allowed whites to leave the city, and the more economically-powered blacks eyed the vacant homes in areas that hadn't begun to decay. The braver African Americans began to try to buy these homes in mostly white neighborhoods, challenging the racist practices that had barred them from buying houses in these areas.[11]

FIGURE 7 **Paul I. Phillips, Mary Baloyan, Miss Clinton, and Rev. Albert Keith look at a map of the area served by the Brough Community Center, 1948.**

Another factor was the higher visibility of the national civil rights movement because of the rise of broadcast news, coupled with more television sets around the country. Blacks in the North watched Martin Luther King, Jr. and other African Americans march across the bridge in Selma, Alabama, only to be turned back by the brutal violence of the police and their fierce dogs. The black community in the North and South became unified, and many whites joined the cause as well, appalled by the violence of segregation in the South and moved by the elaborate speeches of King and other civil rights activists.

In addition, African Americans looked to their forefathers in Africa, where many African nations won their independence from European domination during the 1950s and 1960s. These revolutions, in turn, placed intense pressure on the U.S. government, as the world pointed fingers toward the racial upheaval that occurred within its borders.

A final development that created the atmosphere necessary for civil rights action occurred in colleges and universities across America. Academic research began to destroy older arguments that other races were scientifically inferior to whites. Economic prosperity also accounted for a much larger population of young people attending college during the 1950s and 1960s. The atmosphere fostered in the universities incubated a mentality of social justice that exploded in the beatnik and hippie movements, anti-war demonstrations, music, and writing across the country.

The civil rights movement capitalized on this tense atmosphere of change developing across the country. The NAACP's victory in the Brown vs. the Board of Education case in Kansas paved the way for integration of schools. Firm enforcement of the integration of schools by the Kennedy administration, as well as civil rights legislation passed in 1964 and 1968 by the Johnson administration, helped to solidify minority rights championed by Martin Luther King and Malcolm X.

In Grand Rapids, such voices as Paul Phillips, director of the Urban League, and Helen Claytor, president of the YWCA, called for changes in the policies that limited African Americans. Phillips, in particular, convinced the city government to follow the lead of many other cities throughout the country and examine the problems of racial discrimination within the city limits. In 1953, the City Commission directed Mayor Paul Goebel to appoint a committee to study Grand Rapids' racial situation and recommend solutions. The result of the two-

"The problem with the ghetto was not that Negroes clustered together. The problem of the Negro was that Negroes were unfairly clustered together and had limited mobility."

Dr. Randal Jelks[12]

FIGURE 8 **Two young musicians search for an agreeable audience at Henry Street School, 1949.**

FIGURE 9 **Looking west on Wealthy at Jefferson SE, ca. 1930. Until the 1960s, African Americans were primarily living south of Wealthy. In 1967, this area was hit hard by riots; stores were burned and looted.**

Roger Wilkins

In his book, One Man's Life, Roger Wilkins writes about his family's move to northeast Grand Rapids.

FIGURE 10 **Roger Wilkins**

"When Pop bought the house here, the seller didn't know he was a Negro. Your Pop didn't say whether he was or he wasn't and the man didn't ask."

"I glanced at my stepfather, whose green eyes were glinting amusement and then turned back to my mother. Well, at some point they found out that he was a Negro and the neighbors started to have meetings about our moving into the neighborhood. There was even some talk about burning a cross or something, but everybody thought that was crazy except the wild man who suggested it. And so they decided that the thing to do was to try to buy the house back and they tried. But Pop told them that he had bought a house for his family and he needed it and he didn't intend to sell it. They told him they thought he would be happier with 'his own people across town,' but he told them that he hadn't found a house across town good enough for his family and that he assumed that the people around here were Americans and that those were 'his own people' so he didn't feel uncomfortable. They tried a couple more conversations, but then they gave up. They all seem pretty reconciled to it now except Mr. Stuits across the lot. But he doesn't do anything but bang his lawnmower into the fence. And since it's his fence that's fine with me.

That night I thought about Stuits and the other people on the block. Our house was just about the biggest in the neighborhood, and we had a nicer car than anybody on the block. I was pretty sure that none of the other men was a doctor and that the women probably hadn't even gone to college, much less been Phi Beta Kappa. And, though that bit of social calculus was somewhat comforting, when it was all done, the other people were still white and I was still a Negro. There was no getting around it."[1]

year study by the committee was the creation of the Human Relations Commission, made up of 15 members, including Claytor and a full-time executive director. It became the vehicle in charge of securing equal rights for all citizens and carrying out education programs which promoted racial harmony.[13]

The formal attention given to the racial situation in Grand Rapids did little to end the long-standing fears and prejudice that prevented racial harmony and integration. The history of Grand Rapids' neighborhoods reflects sharp boundaries between different ethnic groups. Despite the Human Relations Commission and Grand Rapids Urban League success stories, such as the abolition of restrictive covenants and a new housing ordinance passed in 1956 to help African Americans with their housing problems, segregation and prejudice remained.[14]

FIGURE 11 **Mayor Paul Goebel (left), 1950**

The civil rights movement ushered in a heightened awareness of racial problems by both African Americans and whites. African Americans were more open in expressing their anger over prejudices and whites were either more protective of their power or confused about how to properly share it. In 1964, a group of African Americans in Grand Rapids started an African American settlement called Auburn Hills in the North End, in spite of the persecution they faced. In the words of folk singer Bob Dylan, "the times, they were a changin'"— drastically — and the instability caused tensions to mount. Beginning in 1965 and lasting for a few years, these tensions would explode in different inner cities across the country.

By 1967, frustration for African Americans boiled to a new level of intensity.[15] Locked into deteriorating neighborhoods, they were incensed by the slow changes coming from the Civil Rights Act. The assassination of Malcom X in 1965 and the changes brought on by busing culminated in a summer of violence that ignited riots across the country.

Two days after the major riots in Detroit during July 1967, Grand Rapids became unhinged by its own racial uprising. Warned of an incoming mass of troublemakers from Detroit, resident and police tensions ran high.[16] On Monday, July 24, two days of unrest began when a young group of African Americans, fueled by the

FIGURE 12 **Police keep bystanders in line on Jefferson near Sycamore during the riots.**

FIGURE 13 **A storefront burns at Lafayette and Hall during the 1967 riots.**

FIGURE 14 **Police patrol South Division Avenue and Wealthy Street during the race riots.**

unrest in Detroit, smashed in a storefront window on the corner of Division and Delaware. Police squelched the initial disturbance, but throughout the night of July 24 and the following night, unruly groups banded together to loot and vandalize stores and private property.[17] While police spent their time chasing people, the fire department raced to put out the 52 blazes that were set throughout the two days.

Most of the trouble took place along South Division, but disturbances occurred throughout the area which caused Governor Romney to declare a state of emergency for Grand Rapids, East Grand Rapids, Wyoming, Kentwood, Grand Rapids Township and Plainfield Township.[18] After the second night, police gained control of the streets for good. The final tallies stood at 348 arrests, 44 injuries, and an estimated $175,000 of property damage.[19]

Though police gained control in two days, the impact of the racial uprisings would not die as quickly. The positive impacts resulted from those who saw the turmoil of the central city and recognized the need to bring understanding and healing to the area. Police met with African American residents to open lines of communication and ease tensions. Many feared the violence and poverty of the inner city and simply left. The violence pushed many white residents into those quieter neighborhoods away from the central city.[20]

The increased flight of white residents to the suburbs further consolidated African American neighbor-hoods. In 1967, the African American "ghetto" was bounded by Cherry Street, switching to Wealthy Street at Union Avenue on its north side, Fuller Avenue along its east side, Hall Street on its south side, and U.S. 131 to the west with some spillover across Fuller Avenue and Hall Street.[21]

While the 1967 riots certainly caused more whites to leave the inner city, they also had positive effects. Some African Americans claimed that whites assumed a complacent attitude after civil rights reform, not wanting the winds of change to blow too quickly. Paul Phillips hoped that the riots would help to shatter the complacency of those in power, and they did.[22] The violence awakened the city to the housing and employment problems of blacks. Previously, Grand Rapids had ignored the problems in its neighborhoods, but the riots forced the focus of the media and politics onto the necessity for reform.[23]

On a city-wide level, citizens realized that they must do something to relieve the pressures on African Americans. Local churches had also come under fire as not being in touch with their congregations. Members in the inner city and local ministers became extremely influential in the push for reform.[24] Since meetings and panel discussions between real estate establishments and concerned entities, such as churches, the Urban League, and the Human Relations Commission, were fruitless in bringing about change, citizens turned to the government for answers.

FIGURE 15 **Children playing on Calvin Avenue near Martin Luther King Park, 1969. As African Americans moved into the neighborhood, paranoia gripped many white homeowners, who fled for the suburbs. Note the "For Sale" sign across the street.**

A Neighborhood that Broke the Color Barrier

Written by Pat Shellenbarger, Grand Rapids Press[1]

J. E. Adams knew his reception would be anything but cordial. As the one chosen by his three partners to make the initial inquiry, it was his duty to walk into Grand Rapids city hall that summer day and ask about buying 20 acres of land the city had put on the market. He has never forgotten the response.

"All the typewriters stopped," recalled Adams, now a retired schoolteacher and administrator. City employees stared. "It was a frightening situation. 'You want to bid on it?' If they could have said 'No,' they would have."

The four men hoped to develop an attractive subdivision of 50 or 60 medium-priced homes. Yes, the vacant land on the city's Northeast Side was for sale, Adams was told. Yes, it was zoned for residential development. That wasn't the problem.

The problem was Adams and his partners were black.

And it was 1962. In the South, James Meredith was trying to enroll at the University of Mississippi. Martin Luther King Jr. wouldn't deliver his "I Have A Dream" speech for another year, and the federal Civil Rights Act was still two years from passage.

In Grand Rapids, four Negro men (the terms "black" and "African American" hadn't come into vogue) were pursuing a couple of basic American dreams: the right to own a new home, the right to live where they chose.

They would pursue them in the face of vocal public opposition, despite anonymous threats, lawsuits, and efforts by city officials to dissuade them. Thirty years ago, the first resident of the Auburn Hills subdivision turned the key in the door of his new home and became one of the first black residents in the solidly white neighborhood.

Three decades after its start, Auburn Hills has become an integrated neighborhood. While most of the 51 homes still are owned by African American families, a dozen or so homes and duplex units are occupied by Whites.

And the larger neighborhood around Auburn Hills has become more integrated. In 1960 — four years before construction began in Auburn Hills — about 4 percent of the residents of the census tract, roughly bordered by Fuller Avenue, Knapp Street, I-96, and I-196 were Black. By 1990, their portion had grown to nearly 17 percent, according to U.S. Census figures.

FIGURE 16 **Sam Triplett, Joe Lee, and J. E. Adams, along with Julius Franks were responsible for the creation of Auburn Hills neighborhood.**

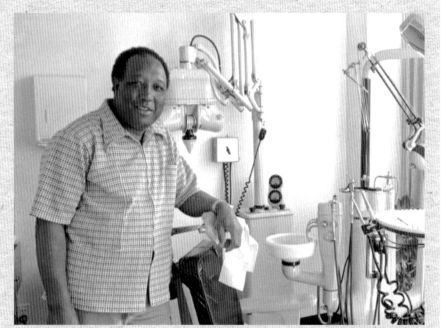

FIGURE 17 **Dr. Julius Franks**

"We looked on the Southeast side, but they wouldn't show us anything. We wanted to raise our family in a nice home with a yard and a pool. This neighborhood was our answer."

Leona Spencer

FIGURES 18, 19, 20 **Auburn Hills Neighborhood**

Sam Triplett contends that Auburn Hills was a catalyst, opening much of the city to blacks. Previously, they were largely confined to Southeast Grand Rapids, he recalled.

"That was the big problem," said Triplett, one of four developers of Auburn Hills. "At the outset we didn't know if we'd get anybody to build for us. There were no minority builders."

Eventually the city commission approved the sale, and, after a lawsuit by neighbors was dismissed, work began on Joe Lee's home in 1964. Fifty more new homes would follow — ranches, two-story colonials, and bi-levels, priced at about $20,000, moderate for the day.

When it was clear there was no stopping the project, many whites in the area put their homes up for sale, prompting the city Human Relations Commission and the Board of Realtors to impose a 90-day moratorium on home sales to blacks to quell the panic. Eventually, the scare subsided.

FIGURE 21 **Edward and Leona Spencer pose in front of their Auburn Hills dream home, complete with swimming pool.**

Initially, all but one of the new homes were occupied by black families, a reality that continued until recent years.

But like all neighborhoods, Auburn Hills would change. Most original residents have reached retirement age. Some have died. Others have moved. In recent years, young families with children, some white and some black, have happily acquired their dream homes.

And all these years later, Auburn Hills remains a quiet, attractive neighborhood of well-kept homes and groomed lawns.

"Absolutely it's been a success," stated Julius Franks, the only one of the business partners who never moved into Auburn Hills, though he lives nearby. "You can sit around and talk about discrimination and what you don't have. This was a positive step. The most important thing, I think, is the freedom of opportunity for housing and giving a choice."

Race

FIGURE 22 **Children can be oblivious to racial differences.**

Roger Wilkins reflects on race relations in the Creston neighborhood before civil rights:

"With my friends in the north, race was never mentioned. Ever. I carried my race around me like an open basket of rotten eggs. I knew I could drop one at any moment and it would explode with a stench over everything. This was in the days when the movies either had no blacks at all or they featured rank stereotypes like Stephen Fetchit, and the popular magazines like *Life, Look, The Saturday Evening Post,* and *Colliers* carried no stories about Negroes, had no ads depicting Negroes and generally gave the impression that we did not exist in this society. I knew that my white friends, being well brought-up, were just too polite to mention this disability that I had. And I was grateful to them, but terrified just the same that maybe some day one of them would have the bad taste to notice what I was. It seemed to me that my tenuous purchase in this larger white world depended on the maintenance between me and my friends in the North End of our unspoken bargain to ignore my difference, my shame, and their embarrassment. If none of us had to deal with it, I thought, we could all handle it. My white friends behaved as if they perceived the bargain exactly as I did."[1]

Phillips and other community leaders praised the city commission as it responded to the pressure by passing a revised fair housing code in January of 1968 by a 5 to 2 margin.[25] The measure was the beginning of obliterating the housing restrictions on African Americans. Those who had enough financial backing to break through redlining practices began to buy houses in white neighborhoods.

The African American buying spree during the late 1960s and early 1970s produced an interesting phenomenon in southeastern neighborhoods, such as Madison Square, Garfield Park, Eastown, Ottawa Hills, and the South East End. As African Americans began to shatter the chains of their confining neighborhoods and move into all-white areas, whites in those areas grew scared of racial violence and fled. Again, prices of houses in these areas decreased, allowing minorities to purchase and move into them.

In some cases it took the intervention of concerned residents, neighborhood organizations, or churches to calm the fears, but eventually the racial tension subsided. For example, in 1973, the Ottawa Hills Neighborhood Association formed in response to the flight, placing a moratorium on "For Sale" signs and realty practices that tried to capitalize on and encourage the paranoia. They succeeded and the neighborhood stabilized.[26] In Garfield Park, it took several years of careful work by Principal Jim Swanlund of Dickinson Elementary School, his teaching staff, churches,

FIGURE 23 **Members of the Human Relations Commission received support from Our Lady of Sorrows Catholic Church, 1973.**

and the neighborhood organization to steady the tensions. It was not until 1978 that a new state law put a stop to racist redlining practices in lending institutions, but most of the fear and flight had subsided in most neighborhoods by that time.[27]

Government and the Neighborhoods

The voices of the people in America and in the "other America" became increasingly vocal. As more people began to successfully protest the urban renewal campaign of solving problems through destruction, the government began to change its philosophy of "fixing" inner cities. Although previous government programs allocated money to destroying blighted areas, they now began to rebuild them.

In 1967, President Lyndon Johnson's Model Cities program began the federal government's first large-scale attempt at working with neighborhoods. The program was developed in the Kennedy administration, but his death delayed its implementation. Model Cities gave money to neighborhoods suffering from deteriorating housing, crime, and unemployment. These neighborhoods were primarily African American and it was no secret that the goal of Model Cities was to help struggling inner-city neighborhoods.[28] The most notable aspect of the Model Cities program was the recognition that urban renewal efforts should include the opinion of residents of the affected area.

Plans also called for a select few "model cities" to receive funding. However, many congressmen would not approve funding until it included their constituents. Therefore, dozens of neighborhoods across the country received millions of dollars in federal aid.[29] The inclusion of the whole country in a program intended for a few select cities opened the door for Grand Rapids to benefit.

Planning for Model Cities began in 1967, but without an understanding of the problems in individual neigh-

FIGURE 24 **Katie Cuncannan, Don Jandernoa, and Carol Townsend began meeting weekly in 1973 to organize the Garfield Park Neighborhoods Association.**

borhoods. Its implementation in Grand Rapids proved to be neither smooth nor efficient. Model Cities' funding fell within the boundaries of Wealthy Street, Union Avenue, the Chesapeake and Ohio Railroad tracks, Hall Street, Oakland, and Godfrey, causing distinctly individual neighborhoods to fight each other for funding.[30]

Another early activity was creating citizen participation in the form of a 41-member elected committee. The committee, known as the Model Neighborhood Citizens' Committee (MNCC), represented the non-governmental advising component of the program. By 1969, the city appointed Joseph Zainea as the first director. Zainea, the city, and the MNCC then had the job of spending money. They began with an $85,000 budget that went to hiring a six-person staff, including Zainea, and establishing an office.[31] It also was given $2.2 million to spend in its first year. Over the next five years, Model Cities used this money to complete both physical improvements and human service projects but, according to Zainea, its biggest achievement came in the level of community involvement.[32] Citizens and the city butted heads constantly, but the experience prepared the local government for working directly with concerned citizen groups.[33] Before Model Cities, the government sent down decrees with little invitation for citizen opinion, but after Model Cities, citizen participation was a critical element to most community development programs.

FIGURE 25 **Principal Jim Swanlund hugs some students outside Dickinson School, 1975.**

Whether it was the knowledge gained from the failure of Model Cities, or a changing of political parties in Washington, the government learned some very important lessons. No one in Washington, D.C., could become familiar with each individual crime and housing blight problem on Wealthy Street, Division Avenue, Eastern Avenue, and Union Avenue in Grand Rapids, Michigan. Consequently, no umbrella program designed in Washington to create structured programs for helping neighborhoods could meet the needs of each individual neighborhood across America.

Those who saw the federal government's attempts at change stop just short of allowing benefits to filter down to them grew frustrated. Instead of waiting for the central government to make the changes it saw fit to the neighborhoods, the neighborhoods created and implemented their own agendas. They formed neighborhood organizations in a grass-roots effort to change from the ground level.

The peculiarity of this movement was defined by its boldness and ingenuity in rerouting the system of change. Rather than forcing Washington to become aware of local problems, the ideas and institution of change came directly from the people who desired it most. Their own passions and experiences molded the institutions to meet the characteristics of each of their own neighborhoods.

While Model Cities was the first program to invite citizens in on the planning, the switch to citizen involvement was timed perfectly with new legislation formed under President Richard Nixon. The Nixon administration merged eight programs aimed at helping urban areas, including Model Cities, into one initiative. The Community Development Act of 1974, signed into law under President Gerald R. Ford of Grand Rapids, relocated the funds from the eight combined programs and doled the money out in the form of Community Development Block Grants (CDBG). To receive these grants the government required cities to involve citizens in the distribution process.[34]

Grand Rapids responded by creating four target areas and the Community Development Citizens Council (CDCC). The city, along with the CDCC, designated the target areas by circling the most troubled areas of the city. They intended to fence in the troubled areas, then work from the outside inward in the hope of revitalizing them. The original four target areas were the Stocking area on the West Side, Belknap in the northeast, and the Baxter and Madison neighborhoods in the southeast. A 15-member board served each target area. Originally, CDBG money went to infrastructure improvements: the boards designated the streets, curbs, and sidewalks that needed repair. Although giving the boards and CDCC this power met the stipulation that citizens remain involved in the allocation of the money, the citizens and government of Grand Rapids went further.[35]

FIGURE 26 **Joe Zainea was director of Model Cities and a former Grand Rapids City Manager.**

FIGURE 27 **Demolition in 1961, near Turner Avenue and Fourth Street NW, makes way for the US 131 Expressway.**

FIGURE 28 **Vacant, trash-littered downtown storefronts convinced city leaders that changes were needed. Urban renewal designated many buildings for demolition and replacement.**

FIGURE 29 **Mayor Lyman Parks, the first and only African American mayor of Grand Rapids, speaks to an Eastown Community Association Meeting. Eastown was one of the first neighborhoods to begin working with the city to accomplish its goals.**

FIGURE 30 **The Calder Plaza and sculpture in downtown Grand Rapids were both created with the help of federal funds.**

Neighborhood associations saw the potential for using this money and began to apply to the city for the block grants. Early neighborhood groups like Roosevelt Park, Belknap, and John Ball Park were the first to obtain CDBG funding, which usually went to hire a full-time director and crime prevention organizer. The availability of CDBG money made it possible for an organization to focus money and people on the problems within their neighborhood.

Other neighborhoods noticed the advantages that a friendship with the city created. Soon neighborhood associations outside Stocking, Belknap, Baxter, and Madison called for target-area designation. Many other residents organized new neighborhood associations with a desire to gain CDBG money as well. By the mid-1980s, most areas of the city had a neighborhood association representing them. They did more than designate how grants should be spent. Each association also quilted its neighborhood together through block parties and lobbying for neighborhood issues in city hall.[36]

The growth of neighborhood associations made target area boards obsolete. Each neighborhood took over the job of identifying the infrastructure improvements in its area and united to implement a neighborhood level, city-wide crime prevention program called Safe Guard. The city put its trust in the associations' ability to find the most pressing problems in the neighborhood and gave them a lump sum of money without requiring specific reports of its distribution. Though it proved to be very effective, this relationship would not last through the Reagan years.[37]

Grass Roots

Modeling after the earlier examples of Eastown and Heritage Hill, other neighborhoods began to organize around issues of crime, violence, and housing. The combination of government-appropriated money in CDBG and other programs, together with intensified organization of local citizenry, resulted in an explosion of neighborhood organizations. In addition to government funding, they conducted their own fundraisers and fought tooth and nail over the problems that plagued each of their neighborhoods. These organizations grew in power and, in some cases, forced the city to confront the plight of the inner-city neighborhoods. The city responded and began to work with the neighborhoods rather than against them.

By 1979, neighborhoods had become a force to be reckoned with. Disgruntled residents not yet organized began to look at the successful measures taken by neighborhood organizations with a hopeful eye. Neighborhood associations had proven to be an effective problem-solving method. Despite their differences in size, need, funding, and issues, each had arisen because of people who chose not to avoid problems in their neighborhoods, but to confront them.

The formation of the Council of Neighborhood Associations (CONA) exemplified the changes. In 1979, the Catholic Human Development Office donated money to start CONA. Thirteen neighborhood associations quickly became involved. Although CONA's role and definition changed throughout its existence, it first served as a neutral territory where all the neighborhood organizations could meet to discuss issues. It also helped many new associations develop and organize around the issues that they faced in their neigh-

FIGURE 31 **Sadie Branchaud, a community activist, and once a prominent milliner in Grand Rapids, joined with others for twenty years at City Hall to voice her opinion. She always wore a hat.**

borhoods. In addition to its start-up fund, CONA received most of its operating money from CDBG money allocated by the city.[38]

The city and CONA often disagreed on CONA's role. While the city desired an overseer of the neighborhood organizations and their funding, CONA itself sought to maintain its original identity.[39]

The Reagan administration began to squeeze the Community Development Block Grants by changing the nature of the Office of Housing and Urban Development (HUD). Reagan thought that the private sector should clean up cities, so he changed HUD from an action-oriented agency to a monitoring body, hoping to use it to eliminate CDBG funding altogether.

In an effort to keep CDBG money coming in, the city required the neighborhood associations to report all their expenditures to the city through CONA. The new red-tape leash did not fit well on the directors of the neighborhood organizations, who soon refused to report anymore. As CONA was not an administrative arm of government, they could not keep all of the neighborhood organizations in the fold.

Disagreement between CONA and the city continued. CONA and its executive director, John Peterson, never wanted to babysit the neighborhood organizations, but to facilitate their growth. The city commission was forced to terminate CONA in February, 1993. The following year the city created the Grand Rapids Alliance for Neighborhood Development (GRAND), which currently functions as an organization to assure that CDBG funds are spent wisely.[40] Unlike CONA, GRAND has limited power to restrict CDBG funding of neighborhood organizations.[41]

FIGURE 32 **Ground Breaking for Pleasant Prospect Homes. U.S. Senator Donald W. Riegle, Jr., Jonathan Bradford of ICCF, John Canepa of Old Kent Bank, Etta May of SECA, U.S. Congressman Paul Henry, City Commissioner Linda Samuelson.**

FIGURE 33 **This Pleasant Prospect Home was built by ICCF.**

While most neighborhood associations have lost the power and energy with which they shook city politics during the 1970s, they achieved many significant goals and rerouted the chain of command. Out of neighborhood organizing came drastic improvements to city housing, crime prevention, and general livability of the inner ring of Grand Rapids' neighborhoods. Neighborhood organizing forever changed the face of city operations.

FIGURE 34 **Federal Community Development Block Grants have contributed over $125 million to neighborhoods throughout Grand Rapids.**

Neighborhood Profiles

"In the long run, there can be no real joy for anybody until there is joy finally for us all."
Frederick Buechner[42]

Belknap Lookout

Coit School, a massive brick structure built atop Belknap Hill, has remained the bedrock for the Belknap Lookout neighborhood for 120 years. The oldest school in the city, Coit has served as the center for community battles since the newly settled area first needed a school in 1880. Much like the school, the neighborhood is no stranger to heated battles. Yet both have faced increasingly tough challenges over the past four decades and are preparing for perhaps their toughest battle yet.

The Belknap Lookout received its first major wound in the late 1950s when the construction of I-196 amputated Michigan Street from the main body of the neighborhood. Many stores became isolated from the community, and the freeway became a psychological barrier from the city to the south. Lafayette, Coit, and College Avenues remained connected to Michigan, but all other routes into the hill district were cut off. Many adjusted by driving to supermarkets outside of the neighborhood. To those who had to walk to Michigan Street for groceries and other necessities, the few remaining stores became vital.[43]

The incision, accompanied by the trend of migration to the suburbs, threatened to destroy the neighborhood Many residents chose to sell their houses on the hill or rent them out to lower-income residents. Belknap began to spiral into urban blight.

Remaining residents formed the Hill District Improvement Association (HDIA) in 1962, attempting to interrupt the cycle of decay. They organized block by block in reaction to a negative *Grand Rapids Press* article that predicted destruction of

FIGURE 35 **Coit School was built in 1880 and still serves as an anchor for the neighborhood.**

the inner-city neighborhoods unless something drastic happened. Although little is known about HDIA's tenure, it appears to have been quite active with the city commission in issues of paving streets, installing curbs, controlling traffic, enhancing property, housing and preserving the engine house on Barclay Avenue. Under President Walter Husted, they met at Coit School and maintained as many as 100 members. Although HDIA defined itself as the area bounded by Michigan Street, Fairview Avenue, Coldbrook Street, and College Avenue, many pushed for the inclusion of what is now Heritage Hill, but the freeway isolated them too much.[44] HDIA appears to have been the first active neighborhood organization in the post-World War II period.

Despite efforts to stop the immediate effects of the freeway, blight and deterioration continued throughout the 1960s into the 1970s. In 1968, the Grand Rapids Housing Commission built Creston Plaza, a low-income housing development on a portion of Mary Waters Park just north of the railroad tracks and west of Lafayette Avenue.[45] Several remaining homeowners left the Belknap area out of fear that the development would lower the status, safety, and value of the neighborhood.[46]

By the mid-1970s, owner-occupancy in Belknap dropped further as renters, including a large population of college students, moved into the area to fill the vacuum left by the previous occupants. Because of its college flavor, it became known as

FIGURE 36 **A Fairview Avenue home. From the backyard one sees the view shown below.**

"Hippy Hill," and was populated mainly by whites.[47] The tenant makeup of Belknap made community organizing extremely difficult, quite possibly leading to the disappearance of HDIA at an unknown date.

Throughout the 1970s, rental occupancy continued to increase and the area experienced high resident turnover. The beautiful houses deteriorated rapidly without homeowner occupants to care for them. Crime increased as landlords relaxed leasing standards, caring only about steady rental checks.

By 1978, an outside force determined that the Belknap area needed to organize. An Arkansas-based organization called ACORN sought to cultivate a neighborhood association in Belknap. It began by teaching classes at Coit School on community organizing and the value of a sense of history within a neighborhood.[48] Then ACORN members knocked on doors to encourage residents to join a neighborhood association. They worked with the neighbors, first rallying around what ACORN felt were high gas rates forced on homeowners nationwide. They also petitioned and obtained a stoplight at Coit Avenue and Michigan Street, which had become a dangerous intersection.[49]

An early dispute arose, however, when the organization applied for and obtained Community Development Block Grant funding from the city in the Belknap area. A power struggle between the outsiders from ACORN and the neighbors arose as to who would control the money. The neighbors appealed to the city, who gave them control over the money. This decision ended Belknap's successful relationship with ACORN, which later sued over the creation of the independent Neighbors of Belknap Lookout (NOBL), built and led by Belknap residents.[50]

The 1980s brought the 100th anniversary of Coit School and the surrounding community. The long-time white population began to diversify as an increasing number of African American and Latino renters appeared in the neighborhood. Like its predecessor HDIA, the infant NOBL found it difficult to rally such a transient population who rarely owned their homes, had no history in the neighborhood, and sometimes didn't speak English.[51]

While many homeowners desired gentrification to improve the general quality of the neighborhood, the nature of the houses, especially near the east end of the neighborhood, made gentrification an impossibility. The small, modest homes simply did not appeal to wealthier speculators who sought to move into and renovate old houses. They did, however, appeal to dealers and users of crack cocaine, the extremely addictive drug that surfaced in the late 1980s. Across the city, "crack houses" became

FIGURE 37 **This is the view of the West Side from Fairview Avenue, atop Belknap Hill, the highest place in the city.**

an established phenomenon. By the early 1980s, the 800 block of Clancy Avenue had become one of the worst blocks in the city.[52] Unchecked, the drug dealers on Clancy, which some called "Clancy Street Boys" held a firm grip over several blocks.[53] The entire neighborhood began to notice the effects of the invading drug traffic.

At the same time crack infiltrated Belknap, Butterworth Hospital (now Spectrum Health) became concerned, realizing the need for a strong healthy neighborhood on its northern border. The hospital began to work on its relationship with the neighborhood and eventually recognized the need for increased home-ownership in Belknap. Unfortunately for both parties, a long and heated debate arose between the hospital, a corporate organization attempting to make money, and NOBL. Many felt that NOBL had goals that conflicted with the hospital and that no common ground could be maintained.

As the hospital expanded to meet the increasing need for health services, its borders began to collide with the Neighbors of Belknap Lookout. To establish a dialogue with Belknap, in 1988 the hospital created the Butterworth Good Neighbors Program, to give back to the community. This included the hiring of Dorothy Munson as a full time employee to interact with area residents.[54]

Unfortunately for both parties, the program was overshadowed by a controversial issue that divided NOBL and the hospital for many years to come. The hospital had purchased a failed grocery store on Michigan Street, promising neighbors that another retailer would soon occupy the building. After a few failed attempts, the hospital decided that the location was not suited to retail and gave up the idea, much to the dismay of the residents.[55] Belknap neighbors, led by members of NOBL and then-Director Frank Lynn, felt threatened by the hospital's expansions.[56]

The tensions between NOBL and the hospital continued into the 1990s, but Munson persisted, often meeting with residents in their living rooms and listening to their needs and concerns. After awhile, the neighbors responded to the services offered, despite the tensions, although they remained careful to stay out of the bat-

FIGURE 38 **Butterworth Hospital assisted over thirty employees in buying homes in the Belknap Neighborhood.**

FIGURE 39 **Dorothy Munson, neighborhood advocate**

tle.[57] Drawing on the resources of Coit School and neighborhood churches, the hospital sponsored programs including food pantries, clothing banks, tutoring, Christmas presents, and health care.

To bring more stability to the neighborhood, the hospital instituted the Butterworth Home Ownership Mutual Endeavor in 1993.[58] The program helped over 30 hospital employees buy homes, increasing the pride of ownership and helping to stabilize the area.[59]

The goal of the hospital was to equip the community to meet its own needs. A perfect example is the Belknap Commons, a medical center and much more, spearheaded by Butterworth and funded by a collaboration of businesses. Once the ideas were proposed and plans laid, the neighbors got excited and performed the work.[60]

Located at a crucial place in the neighborhood, Belknap Commons featured a variety of services to the neighborhood which continue today. The Commons contains a health clinic and mental health services based on a sliding-fee scale. A clothing bank, food pantry, laundry, and computer lab is also available, but only to Belknap residents. The neighbors exchange volunteer hours at the Commons for services.[61]

FIGURE 40 **Belknap area children attend a bike safety meeting sponsored by Butterworth Good Neighbors, 1997.**

Though some may still doubt the sincerity of the hospital's motives, its results are unmistakable. Most residents of the community feel that the hospital has helped the area tremendously, leaving a huge impact and empowering the neighbors.[62] Without a doubt, tensions began to ease in the mid-1990s. The positive forces in the neighborhood began to collaborate with each other, and those who took sides on the hospital issue grew fewer as the residents realized the increasingly positive outlook of the neighborhood.[63]

One of the first efforts took aim at the heart of the Clancy Avenue drug problems. Steve and Carol Faas had planted roots in Belknap Lookout in the form of Clancy Street Ministries, a branch from the Reformed Church that began by working with youth in the neighborhood in 1992. As the ministry progressed, the couple began to confront the drug dealers, involving both the police and neighborhood association. As a result of their ministry and the work of other concerned parties, the outlook of Clancy Avenue has improved dramatically.[64]

Creston Plaza has also improved tremendously during the 1990s. According to Belknap's community police officer Kelly Bowers, the government-funded housing development had become a "shooting gallery" through which even the police feared driving.[65] Poverty, high turnover among renters, gunshots, open drug sales, assault, and vandalism tormented the low-income housing district as unruly individuals made life difficult for the many law-abiding citizens present.

FIGURE 41 **Leslie Wilkinson, Belknap Commons volunteer**

When Steve Ladd came as director in 1991, he and the Grand Rapids Housing Commission adopted a one-strike-and-you're-out eviction policy for drugs, crime and violence. The policy, birthed by Housing Commission Director Carlos Sanchez, began to eliminate crime as residents grew more serious about the area where they lived.[66] Ladd also arranged the construction of the HUB, a

FIGURE 42 **The Faas family, and friends gather in front of the first Clancy Street Ministries building, 2000.**

Clancy Street Ministries

One night as a group of drug dealers stood outside a house on Clancy Avenue, Carol Faas walked out with a video camera. Although Faas had forgotten to press the record button, the camera produced the desired effect. The dealers grew scared and fled, realizing that Faas and her husband were there to stay.

The couple began Clancy Street Ministries in 1992 as an outreach of the Reformed Church of America's North Classis. Moving into the Belknap neighborhood shortly afterward, they started working with the youth. Their ministry's focus changed quickly as they worked with the police to break the hold of drugs on Clancy Avenue. The ministry expanded to offer other services to the neighborhood as well, including a church service on Sundays.

More than anything else, Clancy Street Ministries helped to empower the neighbors to stand up for themselves and work with the Police Department against the drug dealers. The bold spirit of Steve and Carol Faas has helped to restore Clancy Avenue to a community of hope.[1]

building that serves as a community center to provide a computer lab, a gym, job placement, English classes, a homework club, numerous youth activities, and an office for Officer Kelly Bowers.[67]

Ladd credits the housing commission for going beyond its defined role by providing for other community needs aside from housing. It realized that a variety of factors have an influence on the livability of a community.[68]

The housing commission also introduced to the Creston Plaza one of the most effective home ownership programs in the city. The program allows tenants who would not otherwise be able to own a home to obtain mortgages and move from government housing.

The positive changes in Creston Plaza have attracted a significant immigrant population of 40 percent Hispanics, 15 percent from African nations such as Ethiopia and Somalia, and 4 percent Asian, adding amazing diversity to the neighborhood.[69]

Finally, Ladd, the Faases, and others acknowledge the importance of Officer Bowers. Since 1997, Bowers has worked diligently with residents, various ministries, and NOBL to eliminate crime and to build trust within the neighborhood.[70]

Just across from Creston Plaza lies another fairly new ministry to the community, but one that has had a remarkable impact. Formed as an outreach of Coit Community Church on Lafayette, His Place ministers to broken families and hurting people in the neighborhood. Ken and Lois Blake came to Belknap in 1995, rehab-

FIGURE 43 **Steve Ladd, of the Grand Rapids Housing Commission, helped over 20 families, like the Gonzalez family, move from renting in Creston Plaza to home ownership.**

bing a crack house and turning it into a ministry.[71]

Supported by Coit CRC and Pastor Jerome Burton, as well as the Blake's church, Westend CRC on Leonard Street, His Place has taken root.[72] Though it reaches out mostly to adult males, it defines itself as a family ministry with Bible studies and a drop-in center.[73] The pair gives all the credit to God for leading this ministry. "As hard as I work," Ken Blake said, "I can never accomplish in a lifetime what God can do in a twinkle of his eye. So I'm going to let him twinkle."

The community spirit has even caught on in the newer and more stable housing east of Lafayette Avenue to College Avenue, where neighborhood volunteer Ed Ohman has lived for 43 years. Ohman first noticed the problems in the neighborhood when he was forced to walk over the hill to work and back after his car broke down. He knew that the neighborhood needed some work, so

FIGURE 44 **Officer Kelly Bowers represents police officers in Grand Rapids who have left their cars to walk and bike through the neighborhoods, getting to know the residents and helping to keep order.**

he volunteered at the Commons and eventually became a board member. Although the strip between Lafayette and College Avenues does not have as many challenges as the hill or Creston Plaza, they still maintain a significant presence in the neighborhood.[74]

The spirit of community empowerment has helped reunite Belknap Lookout. NOBL continues to fight for the neighborhood, and former director Frank Lynn, who no longer lives in the neighborhood, continues to visit and help residents. The ministries of His Place and Clancy Street work together with Coit CRC, Trinity Methodist Church, and Creston Plaza. The hospital continues to work with neighborhood volunteers through the thriving Belknap Commons and Officer Kelly Bowers helps maintain stability.

Marian Hall, who has lived on Fairview Avenue near the top of the bluff for 58 years, has seen more changes in this neighborhood than virtually anyone. She has volunteered with city organizations since her husband passed away 10 years ago. More than anything else, Marian enjoys the cool air that comes up from the river as she sits on her porch at midnight remembering her husband, her children, and her life.

"I would like to see this neighborhood come back because we love it so much."[75]

Michigan Street: This Was My World

by Bonnie Barber Hamlin

FIGURE 45 **Van's Handy Market**

FIGURE 46 **Hill Drug Store**

FIGURE 47 **Calvary Undenominational Church**

FIGURE 48 **Runstrom's Funeral Home**

Michigan Street, bordered by Belknap-Lookout and Heritage Hill, was for several decades a bustling center of neighborhood activity. For three generations my family frequented the area on a regular basis. There, our needs for daily living were met while we were entertained and socialized with our neighbors.

Groceries were purchased at Filer's, where bins of fresh produce lined the entrance. Aisles were stacked high with canned goods and fresh meats were abundant behind a glass case. On to Van's Bakery for rye bread and a handful of crispy peanut-butter cookies. The beauty parlor specialized in pageboys, DA's, and pixies. For flat tops with butchwax and other styles requiring Vitalis, there was the Hill Barbershop.

On Saturday, Dad would fill the family car with gas at Betty Trill's Texaco station where Lucky Strikes and Chesterfields cost twenty-five cents, gas was less. Next a stop at Goudzwaard's Hardware where handymen ambled along sloping wood floors, imbedded with the scents of rubber, tin, and freshly cut wood. Pine barrels held nails sold by the scoop and weighed on a scale hanging from the ceiling.

During the mid-1950s, Michigan Street was the favored after-school spot. Seitz's Five and Dime Store, that later became Cook's, offered penny candy, pots and pans, long johns, satin bras and girdles, Pancake makeup, and Evening in Paris cologne. The three area drugstores, Reagan's, Nellist, and Hilltop, all boasted soda fountains, though only one had a jukebox. We shared malteds, tin roof sundaes, green phosphates, and discovered peroxide for spit curls.

Hamburgs, hot dogs, and icy mugs of root beer were best at the Ramblin Inn. Weekends were synonymous with double feature matinees at the Family Theater where Bambi, Marilyn, Roy, and Elvis were headliners, all for a dime.

I recall Butterworth Hospital on the south, Calvary Undenominational Church and Runstrom's Funeral Home on the north, and an abundance of life to be experienced in between.[1]

FIGURE 49 **Seitz's Five and Dime Store**

FIGURE 50 **Gordon Foods and Cities Service Gas Station**

FIGURE 51 **Family Movie Theater**

FIGURE 52 **Ramblin Inn Diner**

FIGURE 53 **Trill's Texaco Service Station**

FIGURE 54 **Mrs. Charles Roelofs and Mrs. Frank DeJong, of the Heritage Hill Association, look over plans for an open house at five historic homes.**

Stopping the Wrecking Ball: The Heritage Hill Model

Prior to 1968, the central city neighborhood known only as "The Hilltop" faced a mountain of problems. What was once the center of affluence in the city was becoming the door for the downtrodden. White flight left the area with dwindling property values and a less economically stable population. The drastic increase of rental property and the negligence of absentee landlords dimmed the beauty of the neighborhood. The race riots of 1967 weakened the neighborhood further, scaring banks into not approving home mortgages in the area. Banks even denied a mortgage for the Frank Lloyd Wright-designed Amberg House.[76] The downward slide of the neighborhood made the Hill a perfect target for bulldozers. The city, with an eye toward capturing urban renewal funds, produced reports that portrayed the area as overcrowded, full of substandard housing, and rampant with blight.[77]

A particularly determined resident grew frustrated after being denied a mortgage. Linda DeJong, who would buy the Amberg house, organized the first meeting of concerned neighbors, Izzy and Wendy Warnock and Pat and Ed Shea. Others soon joined the five, as they shared their frustrations and hopes to raise their neighborhood standards.[78] Among the newcomers were present-day Mayor of Grand Rapids John

Logie and his wife, Susie, and Barbara Roelofs. In the following years it would be Roelofs, the Logies, and DeJong leading the neighborhood out of the path of the wrecking ball and bulldozer.[79]

The destruction of the Ball House on East Fulton provided their impetus to act. One of their first steps was to define their neighborhood. The borders were, and still are, Lafayette Avenue on the west, Crescent Street on the north, Union Avenue on the east, and Pleasant Street for the southern border.[80] To emphasize the neighborhood's historical legacy, they added the word "heritage" to their association's name.[81] The new name stuck and the area has been known as Heritage Hill ever since.

The association knew that the neighborhood was historically significant but needed to convince city planners and developers to respect its history. They persuaded the city council to declare a moratorium on demolition while they sought status as a National Historic District. The Heritage Hill Association (HHA), with the help of the National Trust for Historic Preservation, hired two nationally recognized historic preservationists, Carl Feiss and Russell Wright. Their research found that of the 1,300 structures within Heritage Hill, 500 were architecturally significant buildings of exemplary status.[82]

In March 1971, the area was registered as a National Historic District, making it the largest urban historic district in the country at that time. With the city's moratorium coming to an end, the National Trust for Historic Preservation advised DeJong, the Logies, and Roelofs to invoke the Historic Preservation Act of 1966.[83] This act stated that federal money could not be used to harm a historic district unless alternatives had been considered. The College Park project sought the demolition of two entire blocks of homes for its own expansion plans. The school board never considered other options, so the project died when the HHA basically extended their moratorium.[84]

FIGURE 55 **Barbara Roelofs, John Logie, and Linda DeJong gather at the 30th Anniversary of the Heritage Hill Association.**

FIGURE 56 **Frank Lloyd Wright visits the Meyer May House with his wife Olgivanna.**

The Heritage Hill Association's celebration over its first victory was short lived. Unfortunately, historic designation did not stop projects that did not use federal money. Small construction projects continued to threaten homes and buildings in the area. The danger of more home destruction encouraged the Heritage Hill Association and its allies to patrol regularly for "midnight" bulldozing. They lost some battles, but they kept fighting and measured success with every saved property.[85] Often, they went to court to gain temporary injunctions against construction. To fund these efforts, the association sold grilled chicken, chocolate mousse, and iced tea at a Festival booth.[86] They also fought to save their neighborhood by lobbying legislative bodies for new laws.

Michigan passed new preservation policies in 1972. In 1973, the city commission designated Heritage Hill as the city's first historic district. Along with the designation came the formation of the Grand Rapids Historic Preservation Commission, which became responsible for reviewing exterior changes, other than paint. With these new laws in place, the association's board had more tools to prevent the demolition of Heritage Hill homes.[87]

Breathing easier, the Heritage Hill Association started concentrating on restoring homes to their original condition and improving other aspects of the neigh-

borhood. To get around the banks' ignorance of the neighborhood, DeJong helped others to obtain Federal Housing Association (FHA) mortgage approval. According to some residents, this act saved the neighborhood as much as historic designation.[88] In addition to getting around the banks' redlining practices, DeJong also helped terminate the redlining practices of realtors. These two achievements laid the groundwork for replacing the absentee landlords with homeowners who not only had capital investments, but personal interest in the neighborhood. The association also began a successful neighborhood watch program that helped reduce crime. The efforts of the Heritage Hill Association saved the neighborhood from becoming a patchwork of parking lots. It once again became a beautiful neighborhood, recognized nationally for its architecture and looked to locally as a model historic district and neighborhood.[89]

In the 30 years following the activism that saved Heritage Hill, the neighborhood improved drastically, but now faces new problems. Despite the diversity in the race and income of residents, the portrait of Heritage Hill is usually viewed as an elitist, white, high-income neighborhood. While some areas of the Hill do represent this often-painted image,[90] others contend that this portrayal lacks a few brushstrokes. Some African American residents of Heritage Hill fear that unless action is taken quickly, it will be too late and the misconception will become the actual picture.[91]

The early organizers never wanted to change the demographics of the area.

FIGURE 57 **The Friant Residence is now Mayor Logie's house. When the Logies were refused a mortgage in this neighborhood, they joined Linda DeJong and others to form the Heritage Hill Association.**

FIGURE 58 **Campau Mansion on East Fulton**

FIGURE 59 **The Gay Mansion was built in 1883 on the same location. The apartment building to the right was formerly a stable and built with wood from the Campau Mansion.**

Since the HHA's early days, it resisted the all-too-common phenomenon where rich, white residents, economically capable of restoring an urban area, replace poor minorities who are not. Fortunately, Heritage Hill managed to avoid the unwanted displacement, known as gentrification. In a demographic survey conducted by *The Grand Rapids Press*, the ratios of whites to blacks in the neighborhood changed little from 1970 to 1996. Both showed that African Americans made up about 30 percent of the population.[92] Logie reports this as the most satisfying outcome of his Heritage Hill experience. In his view, the 30-year Heritage Hill project took place slowly enough to avoid the displacement of residents.[93]

Though the neighborhood has maintained its diversity, the overall portrait still lacks accuracy. The same *The Grand Rapids Press* study showed that, while the percentage of African Americans has not changed much, the number of African American homeowners dropped from 32.7 percent to 21.5 percent.[94] Despite the best efforts of the neighbors, these numbers show that African Americans are being replaced in the neighborhood. Also, some areas of the Hill are much more diverse — socially, economically, and in the types of problems faced — than others.[95]

An interesting comparison between two areas of Heritage Hill provides insight into the stereotype of the Hill. The North College block (around the College-Fulton-Fountain area) reflects the general perception of Heritage Hill: Though there is some diversity, it is mostly an upper middle-class, white neighborhood with beautifully restored historic homes, many of which are shown on the annual Tour of Homes. Further south, where Sherman Street begins at Union Avenue, however, a different picture comes into place. A stretch of homes that once housed drug dealers has become a safe place once again because the other residents fought back.[96] Also, the area is predominantly African American, in contrast to the common image of Heritage Hill.

A renovator of neighborhood crack houses, Chuck Assenco of 553 Union Avenue SE cautions that his area is not representative of the typical image of Heritage Hill. "In this area," he says with gravity and pride, "we are still fighting things, not throwing elaborate parties."[97]

If the southern blocks of the Hill neighborhood continue to improve while staving off unwanted displacement of its residents, then Assenco and his neighbors will one day be able to celebrate their accomplishments with their northern neighbors.

LEAVING
HERITAGE HILL
Historic District

A NATIONAL REGISTER
HISTORIC SITE
ESTABLISHED 1971

PROPERTY OF CITY OF GRAND RAPIDS

Chuck Assenco

Chuck Assenco could only live with the raccoons for so long. Usually they just milled around in the piles of trash in the kitchen left by the previous inhabitants and Assenco didn't mind so much. But when the boldest of the three varmints chattered at him one morning from his bedroom doorway, he'd had enough. With a few well-placed barriers and a lot of shooing, Assenco managed to chase the last of the previous inhabitants out of the house for good.

The place had been a crack house until he bought it and moved in, hoping to restore it to its original condition. The house at 553 Union Street SE was Assenco's third and worst project on the block. He and cohort Marvin Smith had already restored two other former crack houses, one across the street and one next door.

In an unsuccessful city commission campaign years before, Assenco had visited the block and its neighbors. Extremely impressed by the activity of the community despite its rough surroundings, Assenco told them he would return someday, and hoped to live on the block. The residents dismissed Assenco's proposition as political propaganda, but he returned several years later and soon befriended 94-year old Callie Simmons, a resident just up the block who calls Assenco her guardian angel. A resident of 532 Union Avenue since 1950, her fiery spirit still anchors the block.

FIGURE 62 **In 1995, the block club of 500 Union picketed the Greenville home of an absentee landlord whose house at 523 Union Avenue SE had become a crackhouse. As punishment, the judge made the landlord live in the house. He then sold it.**

FIGURE 63 **Chuck Assenco**

In the last 10 years, Assenco, Simmons and others have rallied to imrpove the neighborhood. For exercise, Simmons used to walk downtown to run errands and ride the bus back to her house. But one of the houses she walked past became a crack and prostitution house, and the fights, screaming, and drugs scared her and the other neighbors. Concerned about his elderly friend's safety, Assenco refused to let her walk past the house anymore.

The block also refused to let the crack house terrorize the neighborhood. They channeled their anger and went out to Greenville to picket the landlord. Even Simmons, almost 90 years old at the time, accompanied the group. The block caught the attention of the city, which forced the landlord to live in his house for 30 days before he could sell. The house has now been restored beautifully, and other houses on the block are in high demand for renovators.

The block is quiet and friendly once more, says Simmons. She doesn't expect to live forever, but she is "in no hurry to go!" Meanwhile, Assenco is driven on by the memory of the drug-related shooting of his 19 year old son on Wealthy Street 11 years ago. He continues to restore drug houses in Heritage Hill and other neighborhoods.

FIGURE 60 **553 Union SE was a "crack house."**

FIGURE 61 **The same home today after restoration.**

Back to the Future at Fountain School

FIGURE 64 **Fountain School, on College Avenue NE, was built in 1918.**

FIGURE 65 **Mark Dykstra shares a smile with some of his fifth grade students at Fountain School, 1998.**

Fountain School, located at the corner of Lyon Street and College Avenue NE, is one of the oldest in the city. Built in 1918, it has a lot of ornate exterior trim, including small sculptured faces chiseled near the entrances. Two hundred fifty students attend pre-kindergarten through sixth grade, in a school ranked among the best in MEAP scores.

In 1997, Mark Dykstra's fourth-fifth grade class scoured records at the Grand Rapids Public Library and the city assessor's office to find out when their houses were built, who lived in them over the years and what those people did for a living.

The students also interviewed Heritage Hill residents to learn more about the neighborhood and how it had changed over the years.

Michael Lawrence explained, "it was cool because we got to look up how our house was a long time ago and talk to people who have been living here awhile." He discovered that three generations of one family had lived in his own house, which was built in 1913.

I think everybody had fun," Michael said. "You could consider it school work, but you could consider it a fun thing."[1]

Eve Tunnicliffe was interviewed by Kiera Trotter:

FIGURE 66
Eve Tunnicliffe

Our family lived in the same house for 57 years, but it was on two different streets! The house was moved around the corner from Lyon Street to Prospect Avenue when the area around Central High was expanded. I've watched the changes in the neighborhood and this is definitely a more desirable place to live. The value of the home has increased about 80%. I love this neighborhood and see few problems. It is a safe and pleasant place to live.

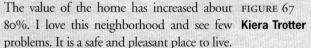

FIGURE 67
Kiera Trotter

FIGURE 68 **Eve Tunnicliffe's home, Prospect NE**

FIGURE 69 **Renwick House, Prospect NE**

Mayor John Logie was interviewed by Sam Simmons:

My wife and I bought our home in 1969. The house was vacant, and needed repair, yet the banks were not giving any mortgages in this area. We believed there was a future for these old Heritage Hill homes and wanted to see the neighborhood saved. The value of the property has increased over fifteen times what we paid for it. It is a beautiful, friendly neighborhood where we raised three children. We have no plans to leave.

FIGURE 70
Mayor John Logie

FIGURE 71
Sam Simmons

Alverrine Parker was interviewed by Theo Harrison:

My husband James and I have lived here since 1962. At that time many parts of the city were redlined for blacks, but this was the best location for us then. I like the positive changes. Heritage Hill is the inner city, but everyone is improving the condition of their homes. I enjoy my neighbors and am proud that my sons have much better oportunities than I had.

FIGURE 76
Alverrine Parker

FIGURE 77
Theo Harrison

FIGURE 72 **Mayor John Logie's home, Cherry SE**

FIGURE 73 **Sam Simmons' home, Union SE**

FIGURE 78 **James and Alverrine Parker's home, College SE**

FIGURE 79 **Theo Harrison's home, Fountain NE**

FIGURE 74 **Steketee House, College NE**

FIGURE 75 **Stickley House, Prospect NE**

FIGURE 80 **Students of Mr. Dykstra taking photos of Heritage Hill Homes**

FIGURE 81 **Gerald R. Ford's childhood home, Union SE**

Betting on Baxter

On the north side of Franklin Street, between Fuller and Giddings Avenues, stand the original buildings of Calvin College, located here since 1917. Calvin College followed the Christian Reformed Dutch contingent as they moved from an even older Dutch neighborhoood at Franklin Street and Madison Avenue. In 1960, Calvin College once again followed its Dutch contingent to the city limits at the East Beltline and Burton Street.[98]

Over on Eastern Avenue stands a Christian Reformed Church, founded by ardent Dutch believers who once tore up the streetcar tracks because the streetcar ran through their neighborhood on Sundays.

The land nestled between Eastern and Fuller Avenues and Franklin and Wealthy Streets used to be the site of a city dump and a graveyard, but the Dutch came and went, and many African American families now populate the neighborhood.

Long-time resident Beverly Farrow remembers how Baxter was when racial restrictions in real estate broke down and African Americans became mobile. Her family was one of the first black families on the street, yet she never saw any racial tension. She fondly

FIGURE 82 **Beverly Farrow**

remembers the neighborhood spirit of her youth: "In those days, kids didn't hang out. If somebody saw a kid doing nothing then they called his parents and told them their kid wasn't where he should be and the parents did something about it. Back then, the parents had control.

"But I've seen so many changes," she added, sadly.

Over the past 20 years, dozens of headlines telling of murders, rapes, and drug activity in the neighborhood ran on the front pages of *The Grand Rapids Press*. Residents like Farrow are more concerned about the negative events affecting the neighborhood than the newspaper coverage. Her eyes are well-trained to see the problems. As a former president of the Baxter Neighborhood Association (BNA) Board of Directors she well knows what upsets the community.

Current data confirms what Farrow said: Baxter has changed. According to Marian Barrera-Young, current Director of BNA, Baxter homes are now 55–65 percent rental units. This trend always means a drop in housing quality and, "Poor housing breeds crime," states Barrera-Young.

This two-headed monster of poor housing and crime is the beast that residents and others working to improve Baxter continually mention as the biggest enemy of the neighborhood. The combination of landlords not keeping up their property and tenants not caring about the property keeps many homes in shambles and brings down neighborhood pride.

The Wealthy Street business district has long served the neighborhood as a center for commerce, both legal and illegal. However recent improvements, such as increased police foot patrols and more concern from the business owners, cleaned the street of some of the drug activity. But the dealers moved from the edge of Baxter to the interior streets.[99]

For years drugs have plagued the neighborhood. The introduction of crack in the late 1980s particularly hurt Baxter and other inner-city neighborhoods. Crack houses in Baxter became common, increasing crime as well.[100] Fear grew among the residents, keeping them behind locked doors and shut off from their neighbors. But Baxter is battling back.

FIGURE 83 **Calvin College was established on Franklin Street in 1917. The college moves to the East Beltline and Burton Street in 1960.**

FIGURE 84 **This former Calvin College Building is now the Grand Rapids Public Schools Administration Building, 2002.**

The neighborhood spirit of times past never left completely. As long as there have been big problems in the community, there have also been bold residents willing to tackle those problems. The fortress from which most attacks were launched was the Baxter Community Center. Programs have come together within the center's walls with the hopes of building a stronger community. It offers day care for young children, an after-school program for school-age children, mentoring programs for older children, a health care center for everyone, an infant program, help finding jobs, and training for young fathers. However, it took valiant efforts by many of the Baxter volunteers to keep the center running.

Baxter Community Center began in 1966 after the Christian school, which had been there since the late 1800s, closed its doors. The white, Dutch community was leaving the neighborhood and without their support, the school had no students. Originally, the building was to be sold to a private business, but a clause in the deed ended the sale. When Eastern Avenue Christian Reformed Church opened the school in the 1880s, the founders stated that should the school ever close, the building was to be given back to the church. Upon the discovery of the clause, Eastern Avenue realized it now had a powerful weapon to help fight many neighborhood problems.

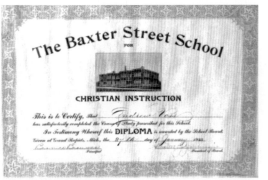

FIGURE 85 **Baxter Street School began educating children in the 1880's.**

FIGURE 86 **Baxter Community Center has been a haven for children since 1966.**

After a couple of years under Director Denny Hoekstra, Herschell Turner emerged in 1968 to champion the neighborhood improvement cause and begin helping the neighborhood children. An African American and a semi-pro basketball player who had spent some time with the Harlem Globetrotters, he worked with the predominantly African-American children in the neighborhood at the Baxter Community Center gym. Turner had risen to leadership status in both the black and white communities during the riots as part of the task force of African Americans assigned to calm the incendiary situation.[101]

Mr. Turner remained at the center for several years, despite the racial tension of the 1960s and early 1970s. The largely white board of directors, the majority of whom lived outside the neighborhood and practiced conservative Calvinism, placed considerable restraints on Turner's methods. In early 1977, Turner stepped down from his position at Baxter to focus on his lifelong love, art.[102]

After Turner left, the center went through five directors in two years and incurred a $60,000 debt. Baxter Community Center was on the brink of closure. Then, in 1978, Gene Proctor stepped into the job. Originally, all parties thought that he would not be at the position long, but six months grew to one year,

FIGURE 87 **Gene Proctor's brilliant fundraising efforts rescued Baxter Community Center from bankruptcy.**

which then became two. Somewhere not long into his tenure, people realized Proctor was capable of rebuilding the center. He ended up staying at the post for 18 years and his name became synonymous with the center and the neighborhood of Baxter.

With his unique background as an African American, Christian Reformed, Republican, he managed to get a foot in just about every door in the city. Partnerships with major corporations in the city, such as Amway and Steelcase, quickly brought in enough money to bring the center out of debt. Proctor also secured a great friendship with the United Way, which brought in a large amount of funds to help the community. Proctor's gift for raising money gave the center the boost it needed to become a model non-profit business and neighborhood center. In fact, Proctor's efforts, along with the work of his staff, including assistant director Jim Talen, were so successful that the organization earned a place in the book *Profiles of Excellence*, which featured 10 of the best non-profit organizations in the country.

Proctor retired in 1996, but left the neighborhood with a hallmark center offering a wide array of programs for the local residents. The torch has since passed to Melanie Beelen. Proctor has recently moved back into the neighborhood after living many years in a retirement community. Quite simply, he missed the neighborhood so much that it drew him back.

As the living remnant of the Dutch predecessors in the neighborhood, Eastern Avenue CRC did not exit, but stayed and became a rock in the current community.

FIGURE 88 **Baxter kids, under Proctor's direction, made and sold their own barbeque sauce.**

FIGURE 89 **Eastern Avenue Christian Reformed Church did not exit the neighborhood, but stayed and expanded.**

Wealthy Theatre

FIGURE 90 **Dotti Clune, Gail Peterson, and Carol Moore believed that saving the Wealthy Theatre would save the neighborhood.**

Carol Moore believes passionately that the newly restored Wealthy Theatre can bring to Wealthy Street what Van Andel Arena brought to downtown: a focus. Moore and several other concerned volunteers have spent 10 years in SEED — South East Economic Development — an organization dedicated to the revival of Wealthy Street and the theater. But for the theater to become the catalyst for the revival, Wealthy Street must first overcome the reputation that it has acquired over the years. People must be drawn to Wealthy Street, rather than avoid it for fear of the druglords and gangs who once ruled the area.[1]

The tyrants of yesterday are no more, claims Moore, who tackled the Wealthy Street Theatre renovation in 1999. Allied with Dotti Clune, Gail Peterson and Chuck Assenco, this group convinced the City Commission to sell the theatre to SEED, rather than spend $30,000 to demolish the historical landmark.[2]

FIGURE 91 **The Wealthy Theatre during renovation, 1999**

Built in 1911, the quaint theater once thrived. A streetcar route that ran up and down Wealthy Street between Reed's Lake and the central city helped the theater capitalize on the traffic until the mid 1930s, when the streetcars disappeared. Despite the suffering economy and the death of the streetcar, the theater thrived during the 1930s, completing a major renovation in 1934.[3]

The theater began deteriorating in the late 1960s and early 1970s as the surrounding area experienced the effects of the white flight and deteriorating housing stock. A victim of abandonment, the theater closed in 1973, as crime and fear were creeping into the neigbhorhood. Vacancy took its toll on the building throughout the 1970s and early 1980s as the area continued to decay.[4]

Although the White Rabbit Lounge, located across the street

FIGURE 92 **The Wealthy Theatre was built in 1911.**

from the theater, was once a reputable gathering place for college students and neighbors, a change in ownership led to its decline in the 1980s. It soon became the problem center of the entire area.[5] Drug deals and violence cast a dark shadow over the once-proud neighborhood. The fear of Wealthy Street spread like a virus throughout the area, depriving Wealthy Street's business district of the traffic it so badly needed for survival.[6]

The theater remained vacant and subjected to the elements for 15 years before the community around it began to fight back. The closing of the White Rabbit Lounge in 1986 proved to be the turning point.[7] By this time, city leaders saw the old vacant theater as an eyesore and a hazard that needed to be torn down before it collapsed or caused a major fire. At this point, SEED intervened and bought the theater from the city for 4 dollars.[8]

Any initial thrill in their purchase could easily have disappeared when two-thirds of the mosaic-tiled lobby floor collapsed into the basement as new owners investigated their purchase. However, they put a bridge over the hole, choked back their fears, and began renovations.[9]

Sheer determination carried them through the project. The volunteer organization raised $1.5 million over the next six years — including a huge grant from Peter Wege — funding restoration of the theater to its former condition.[10] They also purchased the building next door for offices, handicap-accessible restrooms, and other facilities. Both buildings were declared an Historic District in 1993. In 1999, the theater reopened for business, including live performances of choirs and plays, as well as its original function of showing movies.[11]

Wealthy Theatre's continued success hangs in the delicate balance of the surrounding environment. SEED is dedicated to the rejuvenation of Wealthy Street, not just the theater. By renovating some of the older buildings and working with the Wealthy Street Business Alliance,[12] they have tried hard to restore the pedestrian atmosphere, with a narrow and well lit street, sidewalk-front shops, and the continued removal of criminals and delinquents.[13]

FIGURE 93 **The Wealthy Theatre, 2002**

Roosevelt Park

The story of Latino immigration echoes the struggle faced by the inhabitants of the Grandville Avenue neighborhood since the early days of the city. Since the 1830s, the Avenue has served as the entry-point for many of the city's immigrant populations.

The hardships of immigration are told by one of the first Latino immigrants to Grand Rapids, Miguel Navarro, former owner of El Matador Tortilla Factory. Although Mexican-American, Navarro sympathizes with all Latino immigrants and their familiar story. Latino immigrants from Central and South America have become the most recent population to migrate en masse to Grand Rapids.[103]

Mexican immigrants make up the most numerous portion of Latinos but a significant portion are not from mainland Mexico, but from Texas, and are known as Mexican-Americans or Chicanos. Mexicans established themselves in Grand Rapids in the 1920s, but the most significant population did not arrive until after World War II. Proud of a heritage dating back to their Aztec ancestors, some Mexicans strongly believe that the Southwestern United States was unjustly taken from Mexico in the Mexican-American War.

Puerto Ricans are the second most numerous group of Latinos on the Avenue. American citizenship has eased the journey somewhat for this group, though the transition to American language and culture still presents many difficulties.

Cubans, also well represented in Grand Rapids, arrived in two main waves. Many chose to leave their island country during the 1960s after Fidel Castro's rise to power. In 1980, however, Castro sent many criminals and mentally handicapped refugees in a boat lift from the port of Mariel. Some of these criminals arrived here and caused problems in Grand Rapids for a brief period. The second wave of Cubans struggled more with assimilation than the first wave.

FIGURE 94 **Our Lady of Guadalupe graces the Family Party Store on Grandville Avenue.**

Other Latino groups include El Salvadorans, Dominicans, and Guatemalans. The language barrier becomes the first obstacle for any Latino immigrant. Over 70 percent of *el barrio* ("neighborhood") residents speak Spanish as their first language; very few understand English when they arrive. Many Guatemalan immigrants speak their own Mayan dialect rather than Spanish, which further complicates the problem. As a result of the language barrier, new immigrants find it difficult to apply for services, locate jobs, fill out forms, obtain health care, and assimilate into American life.[104]

Miguel Navarro feels that the Spanish-speaking population must unite as one political voice if they are to gain any recognition in the community. The "Hispanic community" is often unfairly seen as a single, homogenous group. While many look at *el barrio* on Grandville Avenue as a solid Hispanic entity, the Spanish-speaking immigrants have come from very diverse cultural backgrounds. Considering their diversity, as well as their lack of economic empowerment, it is not surprising that the "Hispanic community" does not present a more unified political and social front.

Just as the Latino community is not unified, the population of Grandville Avenue is not composed entirely of Latin American immigrants. James Van Brunt represents the Dutch community that has left its mark on the neighborhood. A resident of the neighborhood since his service in World War II, Van Brunt can rattle off every old Dutch store, house, and church in the neighborhood.

Although Van Brunt chose to stay on the Avenue even after his wife's death, most other Dutch who settled the Avenue during the early 1900s have left.[105] A close look around the neighborhood reveals several Dutch surnames, buildings, and businesses, most of which are vacated. Many left for better housing conditions, moving

FIGURE 95 **The M&M Bakery is an entrepreneurial success story. The building formerly housed Jurgens & Holtvluwer Men's Store.**

The Navarros

Miguel Navarro is thankful for life. He appreciates a listening ear so much that he forgets to take his medication, plucking one fond memory after another from his suffering heart. He has survived four bypass surgeries and his wife, Isabel, won a bout with tuberculosis.

It is hard not to view Navarro as the Padre of the Hispanic community on Grandville Avenue, which he affectionately calls *el barrio*. At 72 years of age, the founder of El Matador Tortillas at Franklin and Ionia has spent 51 years on "the Avenue."

Orphaned after his father was shot to death by a Texas ranger, Navarro bounced between jobs before moving to Grand Rapids to look for a home not long after World War II ended.

Although he eventually struck success with his tortilla business, his life has not been easy. The community where he now employs many workers did not want the Navarros when they bought their first house on Tulip Street in 1957. But the Navarros refused to budge. In fact, they dug their heels into the neighborhood and the community.

FIGURE 96 **Miguel Navarro**

"This is a forgotten world, a no-man's land, but I have suffered here and I want to stay."

Miguel Navarro

Isabel Navarro volunteered at Hall Elementary in the Parent and Teacher Association and created a local Girl Scout troop. Then she went to school and obtained her teaching certificate and began teaching fourth grade at Hall School. Meanwhile, her husband began teaching a boxing class for neighborhood kids in the basement of the Roosevelt Lots.

Miguel Navarro still feels the injustices that abound in his community. As he recalls some of the instances of hatred and discrimination against the inhabitants of *el barrio*, he almost breaks into tears. "This is a forgotten world, a no-man's-land," he said. "But I have suffered here and I want to stay."[1]

to the suburbs or into other areas of the central city as the Hispanics began to pour into the neighborhood during the 1960s.[106]

As a result of the language barrier, cultural differences and racism, Grandville Avenue developed a violent side. Gangs of unruly teenagers formed during the 1970s and 1980s as a reaction to the economic and racial hardships of the neighborhood. Much of the gang violence focused on the differences between the two most populous immigrant groups, the Mexicans and the Puerto Ricans.[107]

June Whitehead, a resident of African American and Cherokee descent, remembers working at Hall School when the Latino gangs roamed the streets. A hard-nosed advocate of old-fashioned ethics, June has worked with the children of *el barrio* for years.

She is known by her neighbors as "the investigator," "the warden," or the "FBI" because of her forthright way of tackling tough issues and sniffing out crime as

FIGURE 97 **The Lamar Hotel and Horseshoe Bar on Grandville Avenue at Goodrich Street was a very popular "speakeasy."**

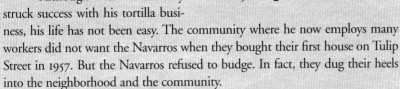

James Van Brunt, a Dutch Catholic, was denied a job by the Hekman Cookie Company whose owner was Christian Reformed. VanBrunt now lives in Hekman's old house on Grandville Avenue directly across from the factory.

FIGURE 98 **James Van Brunt and the former Hekman Cookie Company**

a long-time block captain. To the children at Hall School, Whitehead presents this same tenacity combined with loving care and hopes to see every child grow up responsibly, no matter how challenging the odds. She spends the majority of her time in the playground at Hall School for which another neighborhood warrior, Mary Angelo, raised almost $250,000.[108]

Although the gangs once ruled the neighborhood by trafficking drugs and causing violence, the people who cared the most refused to remain intimidated. Angelo, Director of the Roosevelt Park Neighborhood Association, and Julie Niemchick, Crime Prevention Organizer, worked with the gang leaders of both the Latin Kings and the Disciples, as well as Police Chief Harry Dolan, to develop programs where the gang leaders cleaned up the graffiti. Police arrests of several of the most problematic gang members, and graffiti removal by others helped to improve the neighborhood both physically and psychologically. By 1997, the fear of the gang lords no longer gripped the Avenue.[109]

St. Mary's Hospital witnessed a need for health care in the impoverished community and responded in 1990 by opening the Clinica Santa Maria, which uses a sliding-fee scale. Virginia Moralez, head of Clinica, recalls standing up to some gang members who had made the clinic their turf. Many of the clinic's walk-in clientele went without necessary services due to their paralyzing fear of the gang leaders loitering outside. Moralez approached the gang leaders and convinced them to leave.

In order to expand and serve a growing Hispanic population in *el barrio*, the clinic has since moved to a different location at Grandville Avenue and Franklin Street. It combats the language problem by hiring bilingual doctors, nurses, and staff. Many others volunteer their time to the clinic.

Moralez feels that good health care is critical. Hispanic immigrants, who often take whatever jobs they can get, cannot afford to make health care a priority. As a result, many miss work due to illness, part of a downward spiral that the Clinica hopes to interrupt.[110]

FIGURE 99 **June Whitehead with kids at Hall School**

Education presents another obstacle to the Latino immigrants. In 1996, a young Latino student walked into the Neighborhood Association office on Grandville Avenue and asked Angelo for an atlas to complete his homework. Unfortunately, she didn't have one to loan, so the student's assignment remained unfinished.

Angelo remembers looking out her window to an old house across the street and deciding that the neighborhood needed a library. The house across the street would be a perfect location. The owner of the house

FIGURE 100 **Mary Angelo, spirited neighborhood warrior**

virtually donated the house for the cause, and Angelo raised another $250,000 to convert it into a library.[111]

Dominican Sister Joan Pichette, who runs the library, says her goal is to serve the neighborhood children. She understands that the members of the Latino community do not feel comfortable in big libraries geared toward an English-speaking population. Such a place can be quite embarrassing for those who struggle to learn English. Lack of transportation also presents problems for reaching many of the Grand Rapids Public Library branches.

FIGURE 101 **Director Virginia Moralez at the Clinica Santa Maria**

This library sees 50 to 60 students every day, who come to read the bilingual children's books, to improve their English, to do their homework, or to use the recently donated computers. Sr. Joan still faces difficulty gaining the acceptance of Latino parents, many of whom see a library as a service to the wealthy. However, the library's impact in its three years of existence is unmistakable in the attitude, self-esteem, and respect reflected in the children who frequent the library.

"It's like a beacon of hope in this forgotten neighborhood," she said, "that is as isolated as the hollers of Appalachia." The library offers an alternative lifestyle to the gangs, drugs, and poverty that, all too often, the children of Grandville Avenue have been forced to accept as a harsh reality of their isolated environment.[112]

The success of the library led to another idea that has been put into action. When Sister Kathi Sleziak wanted to invest in the neighborhood, Angelo shared her idea about an arts center. Angelo then raised $1.7 million for a structure built on the corner of Graham Street and Grandville Avenue, north of Franklin Street. The project provides another safe haven for children in the area north of Hall Street. Sister Kathi runs the Arts Center as her ministry to the neighborhood.[113]

Angelo has also worked to fulfill a dire need for good housing in the area of Grandville Avenue and Roosevelt Park.

FIGURE 102 **Grandville Avenue Academy for the Arts**

In 1996, she arranged a bus tour of the neighborhood that brought together several non-profit housing developers and city planners. After the "magic bus tour," Dwelling Place Director Dennis Sturtevant took the lead role in a collaborative plan to build new housing in visible places throughout the neighborhood. In 1998, Dwelling Place, Grand Rapids Housing Commission, and ICCF built 18 new homes between Grandville and Godfrey Avenues, and Rumsey and Wealthy Streets. The effort was supplemented by several Habitat for Humanity homes on Hogan and Lynch Streets in the south portion of the neighborhood. Angelo anticipates that the new housing will help to stabilize the area even further.

FIGURE 103 **New homes on Grandville Avenue**

A remarkable accomplishment has occurred recently, embodying the positive changes in the neighborhood, especially in the south end. Several small Hispanic business owners have taken root in the neighborhood, bringing life and revenue to the community. Rather than fading away after a short stint in the neighborhood, as most Hispanic businesses had done previously, businesses like Yvette Rayez' M&M bakery have purchased and renovated older buildings to house their businesses. Rayez' building, the old Jurgens and Holtvluwer structure near the intersection of Clyde Park and Grandville Avenues, will soon become a pedestrian mini-mall featuring many other Hispanic retailers.[114]

Facelifts Through the Years

FIGURE 104 **Grandville Avenue home in the late 1800s**

FIGURE 105 **The same house in 1995**

FIGURE 106 **The home today with an adobe style**

Across from M&M stands Grandville Avenue Christian Reformed Church, a remnant of the Dutch community that once inhabited the neighborhood. As almost all of the Dutch have left the area, the church redefined itself by diversifying to accommodate the needs of the current neighborhood. Roosevelt Park Ministries spun off from the church to minister directly to the community. Run by director Steven Drewry, RPM helps immigrant families in a number of ways, including language development and translation.[115]

FIGURE 107 **Roberta Lovell works with Aurelia at Homework House, a ministry on Grandville Avenue.**

On the north side, in Smith Memorial Church near Grandville Avenue and Hall Street, a United Church of Christ Outreach Ministry has provided services for over 12 years. While it features a huge food pantry, Angelo stresses the impact of the ministry's Homework House that sends volunteer tutors to Hall and Franklin Schools.[116]

FIGURE 108 **Franklin School**

Grandville Avenue is a neighborhood that has invested in its future. Therefore, children become the most valuable resource, and the schools at Hall and Franklin became hubs of the neighborhood. The schools are better equipped to communicate with the Hispanic population. They teach the children to acquire the skills necessary to get a good job and assimilate life in America. "I've never lost the fact that I'm Cuban, but I'm Cuban-American," Franklin School Principal Mayda Bahamonde-Gunnel stated. "In this school, we can preserve that."[117]

The old Franklin School building has been a part of the community for many years and witnessed many of the neighborhood's changes. The schools on Grandville Avenue will perform the same function for the neighborhood: helping the immigrant community and others to gain a foothold in life.

The Black Hills

The Black Hills is a unique community of about 1,000 souls. Geographically isolated between Godfrey, the Grand River, and the railroad tracks, it maintains a certain self-sufficiency with its own school, church, park, and grocery store. Residents show off flowers and kids parade through the streets during Daffodil Days each spring. The neighborhood association has painted over graffiti, cleaned up alleys, and taken children to amusement parks.

FIGURE 109 **Sign placed in 1983 by Black Hills Citizens for a Better Community.**

"We're a community all our own," said Judy Rose, a one-time neighborhood association president who moved to the neighborhood in 1960.[1]

Many believe the area took its colorful name from the thick stands of black oak and black walnut that once created a forest dark enough for hoboes to hide in. Another version is that it was named Blackbird's Hill after the Indian chief whose tribesmen once summered there, according to historian Charles Belknap.

It was bought by nineteenth-century developers the Coit brothers, who named its streets after their native England. For years it was an idyllic place for city residents to picnic, gather wildflowers, and hunt. It wasn't until the early twentieth century that trees were felled and development began.

Into this little pocket of wilderness moved a mix of Dutch, Polish, and Germans who toted lunch buckets to the nearby railyards and factories, such as Stickley Brothers Furniture and Keeler Brass. Their numbers grew from a scattering of families in 1910 to about 175 homes by the mid-1930s.

Kensington School, a stately golden-brick building surrounded by mighty maples, became a prime social center. The other popular spot was the Coit Park Club House on Dorchester Avenue, which

FIGURE 110 **Daffodil Days parade in the Black Hills**

FIGURE 111   **Judy and Jerry Rose, community activists in Black Hills, moved to the neighborhood in 1960.**

hosted square dances, birthday parties, and Christmas celebrations.

"Oh golly, it was a big neighborhood social center," resident Russell Moore recalled warmly.

Though it had its own grocery on Oxford, the neighborhood was not entirely self-contained. Moore and his friends originally had to hoof it to Grandville Avenue to catch a streetcar downtown or hop on the interurban railway. The faithful had to seek sustenance at churches elsewhere, such as the Christian Reformed and Catholic congregations on Grandville Avenue. It wasn't until 1947 that Hillcrest Community Church was founded and became a social center of its own.

Even after cars and freeways took over the city, access in and out of the Black Hills was always an issue. In the early 1990s Kensington School installed a washer and dryer for low-income residents who had difficulty getting to a laundromat. Earlier, homeowners had lobbied for a bus run as a vital link to services and jobs. But residents took a quiet pride in their isolation, requiring as it did a sort of de facto self-sufficiency.

FIGURE 113   **Habitat for Humanity Homes in the Black Hills**

FIGURE 112   **Dave Rozema, future Detroit Tiger, crouching at right for the South West Little League Champs in the Black Hills, 1966. Coach Rose is standing upper left.**

By the early 1990s, the Hills were home to an economically marginal, racially mixed, and relatively young populace, according to a city planning profile. Its residents were 68 percent white, 23 percent Black, and 5 percent Hispanic (a percentage that has risen sharply over the last 10 years); median household income was less than $19,000; more than 12 percent were unemployed; only half those 25 and older were high school graduates; and the median age of the residents was 24.

Not quite 60 percent owned their homes, due in part to the subsidized Hillcrest Apartments for low-income families and seniors. About 25 struggling families became homeowners thanks to Habitat for Humanity houses built along Woolsey, near where Quonset huts and apartments had housed GI families after World War II.

With the changing population came more crime. Barbara Jones worried about drug dealers, thefts, and occasional shootings. She didn't worry about these things in the peaceful neighborhood of the early 1970s.

Yet she hasn't given up on her unique neighborhood. She still serves on the Black Hills Neighborhood Association, including a time as president. She also helps run the Daffodil Days festivities each spring, when the Black Hills bloom with yellow and neighbors bustle with enthusiasm.

"Sounds like something out of a storybook," Jones said wistfully, "but it's really true."

Peter C. Cook:
Firmly Rooted in Grandville Avenue

FIGURE 114 **Peter Cook with his father, Cornelius, 1914**

FIGURE 115 **Cornelia & Cornelius Cook with baby Peter when the family lived at 569 Shamrock SW. Cook described Grandville Avenue as a "family type neighborhood."**

Every day the welcome ring of the bell signaled the end of the shift at Kelvinator. The endless line of refrigerators stopped. The entire work force dropped its work and headed for the door in unison. At the end of the line, the spray paint department — workers who applied coats of thick paint to each product — dropped their hoses at the sound of the bell and followed suit.

One day during the factory's mass exodus, a line worker named Peter C. Cook noticed that the daily ritual left one man behind. The shift supervisor was left to clean the hoses in the spray paint department. Knowing he would receive no pay for his actions, Cook stayed to help the supervisor with his daily task. The supervisor never forgot Cook's act of service.

Before long, the factory decided to create another shift. Cook, who had worked only at menial jobs on the assembly line, had been recommended by his supervisor to become the line supervisor on the new shift. He accepted the position, as well as a 200-percent wage increase. This was merely the first step in Cook's career.

He had put aside his college aspirations to help support his parents, Cornelius and Cornelia, and his four brothers on Grandville Avenue.

FIGURE 116 **The Cook family moved into this house on London Street in 1922, when Peter was 8 years old.**

Born in 1914, Cook spent the first few years of his life in a crowded two-bedroom apartment at 569 Shamrock Street. His parents purchased a new home a few years later at 650 London Street, where his mother lived for the rest of her life.

Cook recalls the Grandville Avenue neighborhood during the Great Depression, describing it as a "family type neighborhood." Neighbors, church

FIGURE 117 **Peter Cook, 2nd from left, at Citizens Military Training, held under the auspices of the War Department at Fort Sheridan, Illinois, July 26 to August 24, 1928**

FIGURE 118 **Cornelia and Cornelius Cook and sons. The senior Cooks lived on London Street for the rest of their lives.**

members and their families intermingled, providing an intricate support network for those who needed help. His parents played their roles as Cornelius repaired automobiles and Cornelia canned food to give to friends and neighbors.

While the adult social ring kept the families in the neighborhood above water, the children entertained themselves. Soccer was the favorite game, followed by hockey, which Peter and his friends played with tree branches and an old can for a puck. The hodge-podge variety of sports helped to melt away ethnic barriers in the neighborhood. Many were Dutch, but children of other ethnicities were also present, including an Irish family down the street.

As the oldest child in his family, Peter had the weekly responsibility of walking his parents' house payments to London Brothers, located in the Jurgens & Holtvluwer Building at 1508 Grandville Avenue. The family also walked to Grace Reformed Church at Caulfield and B Streets, where Peter met his future wife. He also walked to Hall Street School for his early education, and received his diploma from South High School in 1932.

After the Kelvinator experience solidified his finan-cial status, he enrolled in secre-tarial, accounting, and econom-ics night classes at Davenport Business College. But it was his hands-on experience as an accountant in a failing business that laid the foundation for his future success.

He left the struggling business to work as an accoun-tant for Howard Sluyter, a busi-nessman with a keen eye for for-eign cars. While investigating to purchase a Jaguar in New York, Sluyter discovered that he could get more for his money by buy-ing six of the British cars. He kept one and Cook sold the other five for a handsome profit, discovering a wide open market for foreign cars in West Michigan. They formed Import Motors, which Cook eventually took over, selling a variety of for-eign cars and doing quite well.

Throughout his success, Peter Cook never forgot his roots. He continues to support the neighborhood that has been such a large part of his life. Still a member of Grace Reformed Church, he has remained in touch with the neighborhood. He has contributed to the schools in the neighborhood, and their efforts to offer children a better learning environment.[1]

FIGURE 120 **Peter and Emajean Vander Sluis Cook stand outside their Eastern Avenue home, 1941.**

FIGURE 121 **Grandville Avenue's favorite uncle, Peter Cook, made major contributions to the Hall School playground, Grandville Avenue Library, and Peter and Pat Cook Academy for the Arts.**

FIGURE 119 **Grace Reformed Church is where Peter met his wife Emajean Vander Sluis.**

Eastown

Like Heritage Hill, Eastown is known today as a strong community with a distinctive personality. With businesses like Wolfgang's, Brandywine, and Kava House, Eastown is known as the meet-and-greet place, where people from all over the city come for breakfast or coffee.

Unlike Heritage Hill, this personality does not come from spectacular architecture; rather, the people are the pride of Eastown. Walking the streets between Fuller Avenue, Franklin Street, Fulton Street, and the city limits is like looking at a patchwork quilt of humanity:[118] middle-income and lower-income families, college students and elderly couples, African Americans and whites, heterosexual and homosexual couples, Baby Boomers and their children all live side by side.

A similar reflection is seen in the business district, which stands along Wealthy Street and Lake Drive. It caters to the residents with a strong night life, art-related businesses, two used bookstores, a number of antique shops, coffeehouses, and many one-of-a-kind restaurants and stores. These establishments give the neighborhood a distinctive feel, prompting the labels of "the Greenwich Village of Grand Rapids" and "the hippest neighborhood in GR."[119] This distinctive sense of identity came, in part, from the fight that residents undertook to rescue their neighborhood.

Like Heritage Hill, the cannon was aimed right at Eastown and the community had to pull together to keep from going under. Unlike Heritage Hill, the ammunition did not come from developers and city planners but from new technology, fear, racism, and greed at the beginning of racial blending of the neighborhood in the 1960s.[120]

By this time a few African American families jumped over the invisible boundary of Fuller Avenue and the phenomenon of white flight swooped into Eastown. This migration opened the door for unscrupulous, block busting real estate agents to add fuel to the fire of white fear. Residents report that a swarm of realtors came knocking on doors trying to scare them into thinking that the neighborhood was now unsafe and the value of their homes was dropping.[121]

The initial selling panic came in the early 1960s. African Americans first moved into the blocks between Wealthy Street, Ethel Avenue, Franklin Street, and Fuller Avenue, causing the area, a smaller neighborhood in the southwest corner of Eastown now known as WEFF, to be the major hotbed for the struggles with integration.[122]

"Black families were as scared of us as we were of them," recalls Irene Wiersma, who still lives on the 1300 block of Logan Street. "They were struggling to fit in, too."[123]

FIGURE 122 **Dan West**

Dan West, an African American resident of the neighborhood at the time, downplays the tension that existed. He looks back on the time living in WEFF and his neighbors there with fond memories, patiently reminding, "If we were to take a good look, we'd find that we are all more alike than different."[124]

FIGURE 123 **The Brandywine Restaurant**

FIGURE 124 **The McKendree Building**

FIGURE 125 **The Yesterdog Restaurant**

Through a string of neighborhood meetings, residents of all races vented their frustrations and fears about the new form their neighborhood was taking. Residents began to get to know each other, and the panic selling subsided: people realized that they were, indeed, more alike than different.

However, the troubles did not end then. When many people move out of an area at one time, housing prices fall. This gives low-income residents, speculators, and landlords an opportunity to purchase homes at cheap prices. The low-income residents do not have enough money to keep up the homes properly, while the landlords and speculators often do not have the desire.

Adding to these troubles was the loss of Calvin College from the WEFF area. From the mid-60s to the early 1970s, Calvin was slowly moving out of its campus on Franklin Street in the south end of WEFF to the Knollcrest campus on the East Beltline and Burton Street. The movement of this anchor institution, which also took many professors with it, added to the instability of the neighborhood.

Two residents noticed the new trouble that WEFF was in and decided to do something about it. William and LaVerne Blickley felt like the city was forgetting about their neighborhood, specifically the crime situation and the deterioration of Sigsbee School, and rallied their neighbors to attack these problems. In 1970 the organizing effort turned into the WEFF Neighborhood Association.[125]

The intention was to bring all neighbors together, black and white, to improve the neighborhood while keeping the association as informal as possible. This recipe worked. The association, with the help of a grant from the Dyer-Ives Foundation, started a successful neighborhood watch program called Neighborhood Stewards. WEFF improved street lighting to help curb the crime in the area, and became the first area to have its alleys lit.[126] The association also achieved the less tangible goal of having neighbors get to know each other, thereby increasing neighborhood pride.

FIGURE 126 **LaVerne and Bill Blickley would not let the city forget about their neighborhood.**

Meanwhile, on the north end of Eastown, a separate effort to improve the community began to take shape. Aquinas College did not suffer from lack of space like Calvin, but concern about neighborhood safety threatened the health of the school. Under the leadership of its new president, Norbert J. Hruby, Aquinas began a campaign to save the neighborhood.

FIGURE 127 **President Norbert Hruby, Sister James Rau (standing), Professors Linda Easley, Thomas Edison, and Michael Williams (seated), the early organizers of Eastown**

The plan proceeded in several phases. First, in 1971 city officials and college representatives conducted a year-long study of the area to determine the best course of action. Next, an urban geography class at Aquinas College conducted a survey to determine the college's level of involvement. Finally, two community meetings for residents and merchants took place early in 1973. From these discussions came a task force which developed into the Eastown Community Association (ECA).[127]

The project received another boost when the W. K. Kellogg Foundation awarded Aquinas College a $129,836 grant in January 1974. The grant went toward creating close ties between the community and the college in order to promote development of the ECA and its programs.

The ECA recognized that it could not return the neighborhood to its old form. Instead, the organization helped the residents of Eastown define a new identity. However, this did not happen smoothly. There were many different ideas and attempts to accurately represent the needs of the entire community. The structure of the organization went from a volunteer-based steering committee to a volunteer-based community council, changing finally to an elected community council in 1976.[128] To the delight of the Blickleys, the ECA also swallowed the WEFF Neighborhood Association, thereby conserving resources and bringing WEFF residents in partnership with a larger community. Despite the numerous growing pains, the ECA made a significant impact on the neighborhood by focusing on housing, businesses, streets, parks, and education.

FIGURE 128 **Hammer & Cortenhof Hardware Store has been a neighborhood institution since 1912.**

Eastown Community Association — with the second word of the name chosen deliberately as the emphasis of its mission — stands as one of the best models of grassroots community organizing in the city. Its strength lay in its ability to empower individual members of the neighborhood by providing a forum for them to speak about their community concerns. People who had never seen themselves as leaders began expressing their ideas and taking leadership roles in the organization.[129]

Mary Alice Williams may be the best example of this phenomenon. As a stay-at-home mother, she became personally involved with ECA in 1974, when a neighborhood petitioner came to her door and invited her to attend some meetings. She took her two young daughters to the meetings, and before long she was hooked. Her husband Mike, an Aquinas professor, had already been exposed to the struggles of the neighborhood and by 1976, Mary Alice Williams had accepted a part time position as director of ECA.[130]

Although she had started as a fund raiser, Williams became entrenched in the issues of housing, public safety, and traffic. The young association began to confront the police department, which they believed had written off the neighborhood to blight and crime. One night in 1979, after a particularly frustrating meeting with police at Sigsbee Elementary, the neighbors regrouped at the White Rabbit Lounge on Wealthy Street (it was a reputable place before the mid-1980s) and convinced Williams to run as a write-in candidate for the city commission. She ran and won on a neighborhood platform.

The ECA began by recognizing the key components of the community that promoted a healthy, stable environment. Along with viable housing and a sound commercial center, the ECA identified streets, parks, and education as items on which to focus.[131]

With the strength of the neighborhood association behind them, Eastown's residents convinced city leaders to serve them. Eastown successfully thwarted a plan to widen Lake Drive, and a proposal to expand the Fulton Street-Fuller Avenue intersection which would have eliminated many key business structures. Although residents fought to prevent loss of land to automobile use, they campaigned to improve existing streets. Throughout the WEFF community, new lights, new curbing, and many new traffic signs helped the flow of traffic.[132]

Neighbors in Eastown also worked together to improve playgrounds. Wilcox Park, located in the northern-most section, had long served as Eastown's only recreation spot. Like the rest of the neighborhood, it suffered from vandalism, rowdiness, and disrepair. Through the efforts of many concerned citizens, fields and tennis courts were added or improved, and increased police surveillance made the park safer.

> "Black families were as scared of us as we were of them. They were struggling to fit in, too."
>
> Irene Wiersma

FIGURE 129 **Irene Wiersema, longtime Eastown resident**

FIGURE 130 **Mary Alice Williams began as a neighborhood organizer and became a Grand Rapids City Commissioner.**

FIGURE 131 **Robert Verhey, second from left, and his family at Verhey Carpets never gave up on Wealthy Street.**

The ECA then lobbied the Board of Education for improvements to Sigsbee School, beginning with the creation of a park on its property. The Board complied and Sigsbee received a $154,000 park and a "park school" designation. The ECA did

not stop at a mere park, however. Like the surrounding homes, the school needed many physical improvements. In 1975, along with the new park came a new school building. The new Sigsbee Park School became a source of pride for the neighborhood and place of recreation as well as education for the children.[133]

Residents also grew tired of the abandoned and burned-out houses in their neighborhoods. In one two-month period in 1974, fire destroyed five houses in the WEFF area.[134] Determined residents petitioned city hall, convincing the city to remove many dilapidated, burned-out structures. Residents also made the city enforce the policy of boarding up abandoned houses, which decreased the number of house fires. The removal of neighborhood eye sores spurred homeowners to take better care of their houses. Many different organiza-

FIGURE 133 **Eastown Street Fair reinforces the area's hip image.**

Former streetcar barn

FIGURE 132 **Five streets converge at the main intersection of Eastown, the site of the former streetcar barn.**

FIGURE 134 **Kava House, part of the coffeehouse culture of Eastown**

The Eastown Street Fair, featuring live music, artists, and hand-made crafts, reinforces its new, hip image. Three successful bars, two of which offer live music, stay open late and keep the area humming into the early morning hours. By 1973 a new mini-mall attracted more arts and crafts establishments. It also brought two new restaurants to the area and a small theater aimed at attracting the business of local residents. Many of the new businesses would not become permanent fixtures, yet the climate was and still is healthy.[136]

tions from churches to the government helped with home repair services.[135]

Despite all the efforts to fix up houses, Eastown will likely always have homes in some stage of disrepair. Most of the structures in the neighborhood are over 70 years old and subject to wear and tear. Yet the excellent craftsmanship of Eastown homes, characterized by solid frames and hardwood interiors, adds character that is difficult to find in newer construction.

Again, the business district is a good marker of the change. Small specialty shops now occupy once-vacant storefronts.

FIGURE 135 **The excellent craftsmanship of Eastown homes gives pride to the owners and encourages beautiful landscaping.**

The Wonders of the West Side

The physical differences catch the eye first. When driving by downtown on U.S. 131, a quick comparison reveals a stark contrast between the landscape and features of the East and West sides. The East Side has huge buildings, luxurious houses on hills and baby skyscrapers spanning the downtown. The West Side, however, remains predominantly flat, with the spires of St. Adalbert's, St. Mary's, and St. James churches dwarfing the modestly built homes and rivaling several huge furniture factories.

In the distance, the flat land begins to rise, giving way to the hills of the upper West Side. The expanse between those hills and the river is a melting pot of ethnicities, preserved traditions, and hard-working individuals, born of the immigrant groups who settled the area a century earlier.

Father Dennis Morrow, a walking encyclopedia of both West Side and Grand Rapids history, affectionately calls his native home the "United Nations" because of the amazing ethnic diversity, especially moving east toward the river.[137] Remains of significant Native American, Polish, Lithuanian, Irish, Dutch, and German populations can still be found throughout the West Side. Traces of Armenian, Jewish, Latvian, Hungarian, Italian, Greek, Swedish, Danish, and various other immigrant populations are also present and important to the unique flavor of the West Side.

One of Fr. Morrow's fondest memories of the area is the Leonard Street Market, an open-air bazaar where farmers brought their animals and vegetables to sell. It is gone now, partly because of the freeway. Fr. Morrow is quick to point out that

FIGURE 137 **The West Side freeway swath destroyed many homes and businesses. St. Adalbert's is in background.**

refrigeration contributed to the downfall of Leonard Street market and the many ethnic corner grocery stores. A chaplain for the Grand Rapids Fire and Police departments, as well as pastor of SS. Peter and Paul Church, and archivist of the Diocese, he has given presentations that document the numerous buildings destroyed by the freeway.[138]

The construction of the freeways rocked the world of everyone on the West Side. Interstate 196, the east-west expressway, sliced the St. Adalbert's community in half. The asphalt mass replaced hundreds of homes and businesses in a two-block wide strip from First to Third Streets. U.S. 131, the north-south highway, was perhaps more devastating. It destroyed not only Polish homes and businesses, but those of Lithuanian, Dutch, Greek, Swedish, Italian, and German as well. Buildings that escaped physical removal often suffered a slower, more painful death, choked by lack of walking traffic, now impeded by freeways.

Borders of neighborhoods were rewritten in the process. A neighborhood that had centered on church, halls, and grocery stores within walking distance of each other, suddenly found itself divided by an impenetrable concrete barrier. The government offered those who lost their homes a sum often less than the value of their house. Many families gave up their sense of community and pride when forced to find a home somewhere else.

Those who moved into the vacant homes, whether homeowners or renters, did not maintain the same spirit of unity, accountability, and pride in their properties. The great migration experienced by the rest of the city compounded on the West Side as many residents, disillusioned by the freeways, flocked either to the suburbs, the newly developed commuter neighborhoods, or up the hill to the west.

FIGURE 136 **Father Dennis Morrow, SS. Peter and Paul Catholic Church, is also Chaplain to the Grand Rapids Police and Fire Departments.**

Grand Rapids Indians at the Millennium
by Levi Rickert

FIGURE 138 **Levi Rickert**

We are known by several names. Some refer to us as American Indians, others call us Native Americans. Although we generally accept one or both terms, we know ourselves principally by our tribal designations. Historically, we are Potawotami, Odawa (Ottawa), or Ojibway (Chippewa). Together these three tribes make up the People of the Three Fires, a confederacy pre-dating the founding of America. But if you go a little deeper, we will tell you that we are all Anishnabek — "the people," the original people, the first people.

As we embark on a new millennium, the Grand Rapids Indian community is comprised of many more Indian nations than those of the Three Fires. A survey collected responses from members of 27 different tribes from across the United States. Although the approximately 5,000 member Indian community is not concentrated in any specific neighborhood, a little more than half, 52.3 percent, occupy the near west side neighborhoods of Grand Rapids.

American Indians view history through the lens of pride. Our pride is predicated on the fact that our ancestors were the first

FIGURE 139 **This Native American Pride Wall at Broadway Avenue and Third Street was painted by fifty young people in 1999.**

inhabitants of Grand Rapids and the surrounding areas. When I walk through the Monroe Mall towards Ottawa Avenue, I know I am walking past one of the sites of our former villages. And when I stand by the Norton Indian Mounds, listening to the birds and insects, I stand before a reminder that our people have been here for thousands of years.

American Indians also feel pride because we know that our people never unconditionally renounced their citizenship. We have steadfastly managed to maintain a dual citizenship in our tribal nations and in the United States of America. Both are valued possessions of today's Indian.

We are also proud because our culture is coming back. Our native languages were not passed down through the generations. But American Indians are now learning native languages, taught by elders and even through cassette tapes. As American Indians learn their language, their sense of pride becomes vastly restored.

Beyond learning language, other areas of American Indian culture are also seeing resurgence. The elders are once more passing on the art of basket weaving and bead making to the younger generation. Traditionally, powwows were a time for American Indians to come together to celebrate their culture through storytelling, dance, and food. For the past two decades, each year there are two powwows held at Riverside Park: the "Homecoming of the Three Fires" Powwow in June and the Grand Valley Lodge Powwow in September. This renewal has allowed American Indians to regain their sense of community and pride in who we are as Indian peoples.

Beyond the rolling hills that replicate the burial mounds of our ancestors, standing tall, surrounded by thick tall grass, is the Nishnabe Gemaw — Michigan Indian Leader — a sculpture in Ah-Nab-Awen Park. The park sits between the Grand River and the Gerald R. Ford Presidential Museum. Nishnabe Gemaw, a gift to the City of Grand Rapids from the superstore co-founder Frederick Meijer, is a tribute to the American Indian community of Grand Rapids. Amidst the noise and traffic of the freeway system that intersects nearby, Nishnabe Gemaw faces the river and looks towards Grand Rapids' downtown skyline. We gave our names to streets and landmarks, and each day we contribute to the continuing story of life in the Grand River valley, a place we know as home.[1]

The Near West Side, perhaps most concentrated between the river and Gunnison Avenue, contains many closely grouped old houses. The distance from the powerful Polish churches, Sacred Heart and St. Adalbert's, may explain why this area deteriorated more quickly than the areas close to the churches. In any case, many lower-income families, mostly renters, moved into this area during the 1960s to fill the void of those who left. A large contingent came from the poorer regions of Appalachia. African Americans did not spread to the West Side at that time, and a hostile racism kept it that way until much later.[139]

FIGURE 140 **A street of closely grouped houses in the shadow of St. Adalbert's**

According to Reverend Dick Ter Maat, a West Side resident and activist for 35 years, the emerging presence of rival gangs confirmed the breakdown of family values that occurred with the dissolution of the Polish community. In 1964–65, the Confederates and Outlaws fought for turf near Straight School playground, south of Fulton Street. According to Ter Maat, most of the gang members were glue-sniffing teenagers, and the violence between the two white gangs presented significant challenges to the neighborhood and the Police Department.[140]

Near the center of the neighborhood at Watson Street and Deloney Avenue, the Ninth Reformed Church had felt the strains of the changing times. Many of its Dutch members had moved to the Richmond-Alpine area, up the hill, or out of the city altogether. When only 30 families remained, the church faced a crucial decision: Should it remain in the neighborhood, move out, or fold?[141]

In 1964, the church hired a rural Dutch pastor, Reverend Dick Ter Maat, and his wife, Helen,

FIGURE 141 **Ninth Reformed Church became Servant's Community in 1978.**

to minister to the congregation. Under new leadership, the congregation chose to adapt to the reality of the struggling neighborhood. The church first reached out to the gangs by renting out a vacant storefront on Fulton Street near Frank's Market and turning it into a neutral place for members of both gangs to hang out. Volunteers taught the teens to build and repair bikes confiscated by the police department. They helped to teach the children "another way" than violence and drugs, and Otherway Ministries was born.[142] The ministry helped to get the teens off the streets and end gang activities.

More importantly, Otherway Ministries unified the church and helped it take root in the neighborhood. From 1964–1974, the church almost tripled in size.[143] By 1974, Ninth Reformed had a different image that reflected the diversity of the neighborhood. It hosted African American, Italian, English, Irish, German, and Dutch families.

FIGURE 142 **St. Adalbert's Casino Society, also known as Fifth Street Hall, has been a gathering place for over 100 years.**

Otherway had also gained quite a foothold in the neighborhood. The church put more resources into the neighborhood ministry, expanding into its own building on Fulton Street. Rev. Ter Maat eventually left the pulpit to direct the ministry full time. Otherway developed a variety of services to meet the needs of the people without becoming a rescue mission.[144] In 1978, Ninth Reformed became Servant's Community Reformed Church.[145]

A key factor for the West Side during the 1970s was integration, especially at Union High School. The long-standing neighborhood school had remained almost completely white until busing began in the 1970s. As most African Americans lived on the East Side of the city and very few lived on the West Side, the race riots of 1967 did not flare as severely on the West Side as on the East.[146] Talk about busing and integration, however, caused anxiety at Union, but it blew over as the school adjusted and African Americans began to move into the West Side for the first time.[147]

FIGURE 143 **Rev. Dick Ter Maat, Otherway Ministries Director**

Ter Maat at Otherway Ministries

The small office on West Fulton and Gold is often crowded with West Siders from all walks of life. Some are American Indians, others are white, African American, old, young, poor, mentally handicapped, or homeless. Usually they just drop in and stay awhile, then go on their way. What attracts this diverse group of neighbors to Otherway Ministries? It may be the free coffee and donuts, the company, the warm atmosphere, or the welcoming smile of the volunteers, but most likely, it is a tribute to the ministry that has meant so much to the neighbors of the near West Side for over 35 years.

Developed out of Ninth Reformed Church's ministry for gangs, Otherway Ministries has become a multifaceted ministry that attempts to meet all needs of the community. Otherway is the heart of the near West Side, having served the neighborhood longer than most of its current residents have lived there, remaining the bedrock among the transience and hardships of one of the oldest neighborhoods in the city.

Director Dick Ter Maat refers to the target area as "Westown," roughly bordered by the Grand River, Butterworth Street, the hill on the West Side and I-196. In addition to the drop-in center, Otherway features youth ministries, job-training, counseling, and housing improvement through its offshoot company, Westown Jubilee Housing. Otherway helps people "learn to fish and own a pond," and empowers the residents by investing in their lives and showing Christian love to them. Ter Maat is amazed at the results of placing hope in the residents, who have responded by taking ownership of their lives, homes, and neighborhood.

Ninth Reformed, which initiated the hope for change within the community, thrives at the same location as Servants Community Church. It continues to serve the neighborhood and also accommodates a few Latino congregations in its building.

As president of the West Fulton Business Association and a member of the West Grand Rapids Planning Committee of neighborhood and business associations, Ter Maat is quite concerned about the "tough guy" mentality of the West Side that often places it at odds with city politicians. He perceives that the neighborhood needs more long-term renters who care about the area, more homeowners, and more indigenous pride.

Although he grew up in a rural Wisconsin setting, Dick Ter Maat maintains that he has been thoroughly blessed by the urban ministry to the neighborhood. "These people are very real," he said emphatically. "Maybe they haven't learned to camouflage their authenticity." The integrity of the community makes the ministry possible for the workers and volunteers at Otherway, no matter what their training. "The neighborhood schooled us, and we just fell in love with it," Ter Maat said.[1]

FIGURE 144 **Otherway Ministries started out by teaching neighborhood teens to repair and rebuild bicycles confiscated by the police department.**

About the same time, members of Polish Sacred Heart Catholic Church grew concerned about blight creeping into the neighborhood. Father Ed Kubiak feared that Grand Rapids would experience the full effects of housing blight that plagued Detroit. He and several other members of the church formed the John Ball Park Neighborhood Association (JBPNA) to attack the problems that had struck the near West Side.[148]

Early members Joe Mentalewicz, Bill Abendschein, Ed Salvin, and Joe Bulgarella helped Kubiak to minister to the needs of the older Sacred Heart members, as well as others in the area. They developed house inspection and paint programs, knocking door to door to assess needs and offer services. Most of the housing work went into old homes on Butterworth Street, where federal Community Development Block Grant (CDBG) funding eventually allowed them to target.[149]

The Polish patriarchs noticed that an entirely new generation of people had moved into the neighborhood, many of them renters. Absentee landlords presented a huge problem and housing appearance declined drastically. Many homeowners were shut-ins who could not keep up their properties. Unfortunately for the association, the proud, independent mentality of the older residents prevented many of them from asking for help.[150]

Squabbling within the association accounted for its fall from grace in the eyes of the city. Tension and fighting among the second- and third-generation members, over how the funding should be spent, caused the city to remove all funding during the 1980s.[151] Without funding, JBPNA still exists, but remains only a shell of its former strength. One frustrated member, Shirley Sieting, broke away and organized South West Area Neighbors (SWAN). Eventually, this organization won the respect of the city and gained CDBG funding for a neighborhood organizer and crime prevention worker. It remains a powerful force in community affairs, working with housing, crime, and other issues. Meanwhile, JBPNA struggles to survive independently, but refuses to fold.[152]

Sacred Heart continues to minister to the community in its own way. Despite the fact that many Polish members have moved away, it continues to thrive. Its immense church building towers over the houses in the far southwest corner of the city, near John Ball Park Zoo.[153]

A steady increase in the numbers of Latino immigrants has occurred on the West Side, adding a new flavor to the predominantly European melange and changing the services offered by Otterway Ministries, SWAN, Sacred Heart, and JBPNA.

FIGURE 145 **The 1970 Union High Basketball team showed the effects of busing and integration. They were city champions that year.**

FIGURE 146 **Neighbor vs. Neighbor: In the 1980s, South West Area Neighbors broke away from the John Ball Park Neighborhood Association.**

The Latinos have concentrated below Bridge Street, due to the affordable housing.[154] As the newest immigrants to the melting pot of Grand Rapids, the Latinos changed the diversity of the neighborhood, adding restaurants, like Martin Morales' Little Mexico which relocated from Grandville Avenue to Bridge Street.

John Szczytko, a Polish descendant who still lives on Fifth Street near St. Adalbert's Basilica and Stocking Avenue, writes memories from the West Side for the West Grand Neighborhood Organization's newsletter. The series, entitled "Looking Back," focuses on memories of places like Gogulski's Valley City Bakery at Fourth Street and Stocking Avenue, later run by Mayor Stanley Davis. He also remembers Sparta Ice Cream Parlor at Sixth Street, Frank's Tavern at Fourth, Soukup Hardware and Tin Shop on Fifth Street, and Vidro's Grocery in the same building that WGNO now inhabits.[155] Passersby can still read "Vidro 1890" on the front of the building, and at the corner of Fourth and Stocking one can see the sign for the "Wisla," a Polish restaurant that closed some years ago.

FIGURE 147 **Marshall Chavez, owner of El Sombrero Restaurant at 527 W. Bridge Street**

FIGURE 149 **John Szczytko is a walking history book of the West Side.**

Szczytko shudders as he compares the pride of his Polish grandparents, who carefully used every inch of their backyard as a garden, to the thoughtlessness of absentee landlords, who now control most of the properties in the Stocking area north of the freeway. They control them, but they don't live in them or care about them as the old Poles used to, he says.[156] This is perhaps the main problem facing WGNO, a CDBG-funded group that serves the community north of I-196. The story from this point is quite similar to any other neighborhood in the city: the lack of pride and ownership gave rise to crime and blight. WGNO works closely with the police and neighborhood watch program to fight crime and the absentee landlord battle.[157]

FIGURE 148 **The original Adobe Drive-in Restaurant stood out as a West Side landmark for over three decades.**

FIGURE 150 **Frank's Market opened in 1933. The business remains family owned by son, Fritz Stanitzek.**

The plight is the same for the old Lithuanian neighborhood tucked in the northeast corner of the West Side. The community is still anchored by SS. Peter and Paul Church on Myrtle Street, where Father Dennis Morrow preaches and lives. He fondly points out several Lithuanian halls, some still in existence; and some remaining corner grocery stores, most of which have other uses. Fr. Morrow carries a police monitor in his car, reports to many crime scenes, and is well aware of the ugly statistics of the West Side.[158]

Despite the West Side's problems, Morrow maintains faith in the heart and persistence of the community. In his opinion, "It is a great place for people who like the concept of neighbors." The close housing and amazing diversity of the West Side allow for an intimacy that seems rare in society today. "Cars and freeways allow us to move to the suburbs and have big backyards rather than front porches that help us to get to know our neighbors," he said with a measured amount of nostalgic loss.[159]

Father Morrow is right: the West Side is a place filled with landmarks, rich history and intimate settings. Those who know it, and understand it, can continue to make it

a better place, but their pain over what has been lost may take long to heal. Above all, the West Side is about irreplaceable people. Many have gone, many have come, and those who are left of the old guard find it difficult to continue when so many of the new don't care and don't understand. When the old guard leaves, the new generation will have to step up and restore the West Side, or the mystique will become mythology.

New landmarks have risen, including the Gerald R. Ford Museum, the Van Andel Museum Center, and the expanded downtown campus of Grand Valley State University. In 2000, Grand Valley made another major investment in the West Side by building the Pew Campus on a ten-acre gift from Steelcase, along West Fulton Street. President Arend Lubbers' goal was to create an academic village in an urban setting. The Richard M. De Vos Center is a collection of connected buildings around a public square, attracting over 7000 students per year. Secchia Hall will eventually provide housing for over 400 students. The Grand Valley presence is creating yet another community, adding to the West Side's already rich history.

FIGURE 151 **Grand Valley State University's Pew Campus is a new community on the West Side of downtown Grand Rapids.**

Garfield Park

Until the 1970s, African Americans could not own any land south of the railroad tracks north of Cottage Grove Street. The civil rights reforms of the 1960s, especially those in real estate, allowed African Americans the option of crossing the tracks. The tracks augment a strip of industrial buildings that run the length of Cottage Grove Street, creating a natural border between the Madison area to the north and the Garfield Park area.

In the 1970s, the neighborhood around Garfield Park contained three distinct sections: west of Division Avenue to the freeway, north of Burton Street to Cottage Grove Street, and south of Burton Street to 28th Street. The first of these two areas contained low-income housing, while the homes south of Burton Street featured more upper-middle class owners. For many African Americans, the newfound freedom to move south of the tracks into a better neighorhood gave them a chance to escape some of the miseries of inner-city urban blight.[160]

FIGURE 152 **The Garfield Park Lodge, as seen in an early postcard**

But their hopes were met with resistance. As African Americans moved over the tracks and into the all-white neighborhood, many white neighbors grew concerned and began a mass exodus. In some areas, such as Collins or Francis Avenues between Burton and Griggs Streets, the vacating homeowners left before selling their houses. "For Sale" signs appeared faster than the blacks could move into the neighborhood and homes often sold for much less than they were worth.[161] The race riots of 1967 had left a deep scar that many feared would be reopened by blacks moving into the area.

South Field, a football facility located near the north end of the neighborhood, where President Gerald R. Ford was a high school football star, became a victim of the riots. Despite the many memorable football games played there, proximity to the inner-city neighborhoods hit hardest by the riots caused it to be abandoned. The field facilities were torn down and it now serves as a holding basin for water run-off.[162]

FIGURE 153 **A snowy game at South Field in 1950. After the riots, South Field was abandoned, then torn down.**

Another victim was the business district at Burton Heights, which lost over half of its stores after the riots. In an effort that eventually propelled him to City Hall as Mayor, Gerald Helmholdt fought for the businesses in the area, including his grandfather's paint and wallpaper store on South Division Avenue. But even the future mayor's efforts couldn't stop the slide.[163]

White flight was a familiar phenomenon in the city, but the fear that clutched Garfield Park and the speed with which whites left was matched only in the area around Martin Luther King Park. Most of the buying and selling took place north of Burton and west of Division in the lower-income areas, but some whites south of Burton feared problems and moved out as well. Many upper-middle class African Americans filled these vacancies, so the south became integrated as well. Hispanic residents also found the housing a step up from their accommodations along Grandville Avenue, so they began to move into Garfield Park.[164]

The effects of the changes and increased transience in the neighborhood began to show. The exodus left many abandoned homes, low-income renters with absentee landlords, and numerous irresponsible homeowner residents who had never been able to afford housing before.[165] Gangs of teens formed, especially west of Division Avenue, providing an alternative structure to the broken families and conditions of poverty that had begun to develop.

Even the gangs reflected the integration of the neighborhood, observed resident Carol Townsend. Rather than the usual racial divisions between gangs, Garfield Park gangs included diverse ethnic groups in the same gang, and even included women as prominent members. These "progressive" gangs developed as a reaction to the living conditions and the harsh environment, rather than a protection against intruders.[166]

While the southeastern section of the neighborhood integrated fairly well, due to young homeowners who ignored the racial paranoia, the north and west sections took much more effort. The immediate neighborhood around Dickinson School became an area of concern for the residents, who worried about the effects of the integration on their children. As racial tensions and concerns peaked, the brewing crisis called for a special principal to serve at Dickinson and ease the fears of parents, teachers and children. To some critics, Jim Swanlund didn't act or look like a principal, and once he took over, he displayed no love for paperwork or administrative red tape.[167]

In fact, Swanlund's first action as principal of Dickinson was to visit every family who had children at Dickinson. He discussed their fears and his goals as principal, easing many fears and defusing many problems before they occurred. This practice also helped him to get to know every student and their background, and he continued his visits each summer. Swanlund used his cool demeanor to build relationships with the students; quality time and encouragement were the key factors. His intentional relationships with both black and white students became an example of how to deconstruct racism and hate. He seemed to shed color barriers and racial stereotypes more quickly than other whites could flee the neighborhood.[168]

Swanlund spent 10 years at Dickinson, but his mark remains today, not just on the children of Dickinson, but their families as well. The Swanlund

FIGURE 154 **Gerald Helmholdt organized the Burton Heights Business District before becoming Mayor of Grand Rapids.**

FIGURE 155 **Principal Jim Swanlund leads the fun at the "Summer in February" program with Dickinson school kids.**

family remains respected and loved in the neighborhood, even though they left it two decades ago.[169]

Not far from Dickinson Elementary, St. Francis Xavier Catholic Church and School faced the same growing pains. Most of its congregation lived in the neighborhood and many of the children attended St. Francis School. As the surrounding area developed severe drug, gang, and crime problems, parents grew fearful and began to pull their children out of the school, sending them out of the neighborhood to Immaculate Heart of Mary at Burton Street and Plymouth Avenue.[170]

In 1973, frustration with the mounting tensions, decreasing home values, crime, and the increasing "For Sale" signs culminated in a neighborhood meeting. Two concerned residents, Don Jandernoa and Katie Cuncannan, saw the need for organized action. They brought together members of the Burton Heights Ministerial Alliance, business leaders, and other concerned members of the community who overwhelmingly agreed to begin the Garfield Park Neighborhoods Association.[171]

The name of the organization alone displays the wisdom of those who formed it. Their neighborhood was actually several smaller neighborhoods combined, and lumping these together into one entity, GPNA worked to the strengths of each block, managing to unify the entire area despite the economic and geographic differences.[172]

Given the wide area and economic diversity that the neighborhoods had to work with, they needed to locate a central rallying point. They chose Garfield Park. Although once a fine gathering place, the race riots of 1967 cast a spell of fear over the park, and the caretaker's lodge stood vacant in the long, unkempt grass.[173]

Though the city planned to tear down the lodge, the association bought the deteriorating building and began to refurbish it for use as the GPNA office. Neighbors volunteered to trim grass and pick up trash, turning the park into a usable green space again.[174]

GPNA hosted fund raisers and community mixers, such as Easter egg hunts,

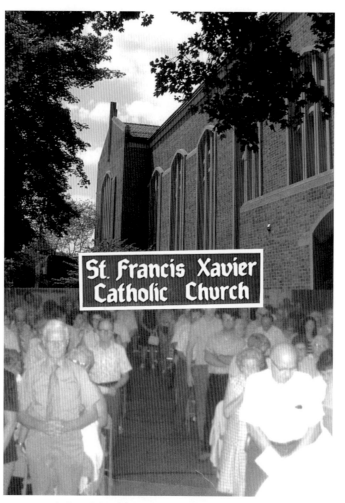

FIGURE 156 **Opening with prayer, the first gathering of the Garfield Park Neighborhoods Association drew hundreds of people to St. Francis Xavier Church on July 31, 1973.**

arts and craft festivals and various concerts in the park. Concerts featured music from bluegrass to pops, in an attempt to meld the diversity in the neighborhood. GPNA co-founder Don Jandernoa even managed to get city funding for the frisbee golf course, an immensely popular addition to the large park.[175]

The first real challenge to GPNA followed closely on the heels of its first major successes. In the fall of 1974, a scant year after its inception, the organization heard rumors that the city planned to widen Eastern Avenue, a major thoroughfare at its eastern boundary. The rumors proved correct: In the interest of handling more traffic, the city planned to remove the oak trees along Eastern to create extra traffic lanes. Residents in Garfield Park detested the destruction of these trees, worried about increased noise pollution and feared for the safety of seniors and children who would have to cross a wider, faster street.[176]

A group of volunteers who charted the traffic during a 24-hour period found that the city had drastically overestimated the count. Led by Jandernoa, 27 enraged members marched to City Hall and presented their case. When the business owners in Alger Heights and Seymour Business District realized that their street parking would disappear, GPNA had all the support needed. The city agreed with the neighbors and gave up the entire project.[177]

The victory gave credibility and visibility to the association. Because the odds had been so much against them, the battle empowered them all the more. The neighbors rallied behind the association, even though the police told them that the area had been written off because of the increasing crime and blight.[178] With extremely diverse involvement from African Americans, whites, and an increasing Hispanic presence in the neighborhood, as well as the all-important CDBG funding obtained in the late 1970s, the neighbors attempted to reverse the damage that had already been done.[179]

Former director Carol Townsend and other GPNA members campaigned to change the view of the neighborhood from within, through newsletters and home visits. Throughout the 1980s, they improved the image with physical labor, organizing

FIGURE 157 **Garfield Park lodge renovation in 1982. GPNA rescued the building from destruction and moved their offices into it in the 1970s.**

against housing blight, crime, and rats that infested the neighborhood. GPNA continued with its initial fervor, drawing upon the immense resources of the neighborhood.[180]

More than any other neighborhood, Garfield Park has gained support from faith-based ministries.[181] A variety of these ministries in addition to 30 churches, most of which feature services to the neighborhoods, have worked to give the community hope and support.[182]

The intersection of Madison Avenue and Brown Street, between St. Francis Xavier and Dickinson School, provides a perfect example of this teamwork. In October of 1997, Arthur Bailey moved his Abundant Life Ministries into the building on the northwest corner. The criminals who cast a dark shadow over the small corner of the neighborhood did not intimidate the massively framed African American man.[183]

Several concerned pastors from the area, mostly from St. Francis Xavier, joined Bailey's effort by walking around and praying for the neighborhood in broad daylight on the particularly bad street corners. The drug dealers tried to intimidate and threaten the pastors at first, but then some began to confide in the pastors.[184]

As an African American himself, Bailey's powerful message carried even more weight with the predominantly black and Latino neighborhood residents. His consistent presence empowered the Garfield Park community to step up and reclaim its neighborhood from those few who kept it in chains.[185]

FIGURE 158 **Arthur Bailey, founder of Abundant Life Ministries**

Bailey's huge presence in the neighborhood caught the attention of other organized forces in the community, namely the police and the Neighborhoods Association. The police department appreciated Bailey's bold and honest, yet peaceful, confrontation of crime.[186] Crime Prevention Organizer Ginger Hallwachs from GPNA organized a massive neighborhood watch program in the immediate area, even partnering with Abundant Life to paint positive signs on the side of the building. Meanwhile, the police department placed police officer and ex-Marine John Keelean as a beat cop in the neighborhood. Together, Keelean, Bailey, and Hallwachs began to shut down the crack houses.[187] A massive raid by the police department in the fall of 1999 was hoped to be the turning point in the battle against crime in the neighborhood.[188]

The Madison-Brown intersection will not be the last battle for the neighbors of Garfield Park. Other strongholds of crime and violence still persist in some pockets. However, the residents of Garfield Park have shown tremendous assertiveness in confronting the problems of racism, crime, drugs and violence to reclaim their neighborhood.

FIGURE 159 **This is one of the many beautiful homes in the Garfield Park neighborhood.**

The South East End

The South East End refers to the southeastern corner of the last ring of the city to develop during the streetcar era. The northwestern corner of the neighborhood also includes older houses from the second ring of the city settled by the Dutch in the 1800s, resulting in a tremendous variety of houses throughout the neighborhood. The South East End is bordered by Franklin and Hall Streets on the north, Giddings and Plymouth Avenues on the east, Burton Street on the south and Eastern Avenue on the west. Two intersections within the neighborhood, one at Hall Street and Fuller Avenue and the other at Burton Street and Sylvan Avenue, were the southeastern corners of the city limits at different times.

On the south side of Franklin Street lay Franklin Park, which was renamed in honor of Martin Luther King, Jr. after his assassination in 1968. For the African Americans who moved into the neighborhood, replacing some of the former Dutch inhabitants, King Park became a cultural icon. As the major green space in the area, it became the place for kids and adults to congregate.

As African American leaders in the 1960s began to break down racial covenants, steering, and redlining practices, the gates that had restrained blacks for so many years burst. They began to push past the old borders of Hall Street to the south,

Originally called Franklin Park, the name was changed to Martin Luther King Park in 1969.

Eastern Avenue to the east, and Franklin Street to the north, settling into all-white neighborhoods. James Jones, whose family was only the second black family to move onto his block on Calvin Avenue near King Park in 1969, jokingly refers to the phenomenon as "black flight."

"Everybody was trying to get out of the ghetto," he said. It was a very natural step for African Americans like his mother to try to buy their first house in a better neighborhood. That's exactly what whites were doing, and it became known as white flight.[189] White flight only made black flight more possible. As more African Americans moved into homes already vacated by white migration to the suburbs, nearby whites grew frightened of the possibility of heightened violence and crime and fled. The "For Sale" signs went up so quickly when a black family moved in, that the African Americans called them "tombstones."[190] Many whites moved out so quickly that their homes sold for incredibly cheap prices, opening up even more opportunities for African American homeowners.[191]

Herschell Turner, an African American resident who moved from Lafayette onto Fisk Street near Fuller Avenue in 1968, notes two problems from this shift. First, a great number of first-time homeowners found themselves held to new standards. Secondly, many who left the neighborhood decided to rent their homes instead of sell.

FIGURE 160 **The swimming pool at Martin Luther King Park is a popular place to beat the summer heat.**

FIGURE 161 **James Jones and his mother, Sophronia Blevins, became the second African American family to move to Calvin Avenue in 1969.**

The sudden increase in amateur homeowners, absentee landlords, and tenants increased the problems in the neighborhood. Those who had fled to the suburbs said "I told you so" within a matter of five years.[192]

Although many whites had left the neighborhood, those who stayed or subsequently moved in, became dedicated neighbors. By the mid-1970s, the migration of whites out of and blacks into the area near Martin Luther King Park began to level off and the diversity has since remained at similar levels.[193]

In May 1974, a group of whites, who had either remained or come into the neighborhood, displayed their commitment to stand by the neighborhood. They formed HEFF, derived from Hall-Eastern-Franklin-Fuller, to address the crime, safety and litter problems in the area bounded by those streets. Early members included Eleanor DeRuiter, David Seiplinga, John Algera, Terry Winberger, and Rev. Virgil Patterson.[194] HEFF hosted a potluck with keynote speaker and then-Mayor Lyman S. Parks to rally neighbors and gain support.[195]

By 1977, this organization had evolved into the South East End Neighborhood Association (SEENA), with new African American leadership in members like Joe Rembert, Fred Thompson, and Harold Hitchcock. By attaining CDBG funding, this group extended the southern border from Hall Street to Burton Street and began work to improve the Boston Square Business District on Kalamazoo Avenue, an area that featured Standard Lumber Company, Boston House Restaurant, and Kingma's Market. SEENA also targeted housing problems and began to build a sense of community by throwing parties and parades in King Park.[196]

According to "leftover hippy" Carl Kelly and wife, Ruth, who both worked at SEENA at different times during the 1980s, the ethnic, economic, and housing diversity of the huge community presented the association with a large number of varied interests and needs.[197]

Just a short distance to the southwest, another crisis brewed that would change the neighborhood. Oakdale Christian Reformed Church had existed in the neighborhood since 1890. In 1972 a sex scandal within the church caused a huge loss of membership. By 1979, the church faced a crucial decision: relocate, die, or reinvigorate itself. The church decided to remain and adapt to the needs of the neighborhood rather than attempt to retain its commuter congregation.

The congregation first hired community-minded Rev. Bill Vanden Bosch. He helped to institute a Wednesday night program with Bible studies for adults and chil-

Herschell Turner

While most young men dream of becoming a professional athlete, Herschell Turner dreamed of becoming an artist. But growing up in Indianapolis, Turner couldn't avoid basketball. He went to play basketball at the University of Nebraska, where he was the first African American to obtain a full athletic scholarship. While flying over the American West to ball games, the beauty of the landscapes reminded him of his boyhood ambition and he found himself wondering about its previous inhabitants. He also pondered if any of the cowboys of the old west were African American. Through research he began to uncover several fascinating African American Western figures.[1]

After college, Turner launched into a semi-pro basketball career that included a season with the Harlem Globetrotters and eventually brought him to Grand Rapids. But he grew frustrated with professional sports and longed to turn to his lifelong ambition.[2]

However, racial unrest and an urban youth ministry called for Turner's leadership and presence. A 10-year stint as director of Baxter Community Center helped the ministry to get started.[3]

After leaving Baxter, Turner focused completely on art, despite the financial difficulty that it caused his family. Turner began to paint portraits of the black cowboys and many other prominent figures in the African American community, such as Sojourner Truth, Malcolm X, and Martin Luther King, Jr.[4]

Today, Turner hopes that his paintings can give a sense of heritage beyond the darkness of slavery to young African Americans. He now uses his art as a vehicle to help individuals in Grand Rapids establish pride and work ethic and to express themselves.

In 1999, Turner was elected a Kent County Commissioner. He was recently inducted into the Black Legends of Basketball. He also continues to work as an artist and for the Kent County Corrections Department. Turner is a firm believer in helping people discover their own pride and self-worth. "Everyone has tremendous abilities, but we need to look within ourselves to find them, rather than keep looking outside for answers," he said.[5]

FIGURE 162 **Herschell Turner drawing at his easel**

A Philadelphia Story
by Charles Honey

I sat on the couch by the picture window that once seemed huge. Forty years before, I'd looked out that window on a snowy night. Philadelphia Avenue. Quiet, white and steep. The street where I played with ants and barreled downhill on my bike. My boyhood home. Perched on the edge of Ottawa Hills, I lived there from 1955 to 1960.

My father, Keith, was city planning director, sweating out the post-war battles of exploding development and urban renewal. My mother, Betty, was active in the PTA and loved Grand Rapids' civic graces, its fine libraries and museums. They raised me along with my older sister, Maureen, and older brother, Mike. We were a family coming into its own, in the most prosperous decade America had ever known.

Now it is a Saturday in 1998 and Robert and Gloria Tolbert sat across from my wife and me, smiling and gracious. This was their home now, had been for 20 years, and they built far more memories here than I will ever know.

My wife Wendy and I moved to the northwest side of Grand Rapids in 1985 but every so often I drove down Philadelphia, just to see. The house at 1231 looked about the same as I remembered it. The trees arched over the street all the way up the steep hill and every autumn the lordly oak still dropped its fat leaves into my old front yard. I found a neighborhood not radically different from the one I had grown up in. The homes of Philadelphia still were not as posh as the brick mini-mansions north of Hall, but they were roomy. It was the kind of street where young white families with one or two cars and two or three kids had gotten a running start in pursuit of the post-war American dream.

But today's Philadelphia families include African Americans like the Tolberts, pursuing their own dreams long after World War II vets like my Dad had retired, and in a city more diverse and troubled than was Wonder Bread-era Grand Rapids.

Two doors up the hill from them lived Barbara McCann, the only person still left on the block from the era when my family lived there. Her house was one of the first on the street. She remembers looking east and seeing farmhouses over by Plymouth Avenue. She fondly recalled shopping at the Hondorp-Veltman market on Hall Street and at Magnan's Drug and the other shops clustered on the corner of Hall and Fuller.

Her neighbors came to include the Tolberts, a friendly family she got to know at block parties and front-yard chats over the years. Robert worked at Smith's Industries and Gloria was a public school teacher. Their sons, Robert Jr. and Derrick, were working on degrees at Michigan State, while 10-year-old Ryan was working on being a boy. He shyly introduced himself to my wife and me.

The Tolberts obligingly let us gawk through their house like tourists. The old screen porch was now closed in and filled with Robert's college belongings. Here was the little breakfast nook where I bawled after spilling my butterscotch pudding. And the tiny bathroom where I trimmed my eyelashes because they were too girly. There was the old milk chute in the wall, where the milkman used to leave sweating glass bottles. It was closed in by siding now, but Ryan stored grasshoppers and other treasures there. It was all familiar; but not, inside and out.

In one corner of the yard was a little maple tree planted by Derrick in fifth grade. This had been a good home for him and his family. Like us, they were a traditional American nuclear family, enjoying the quiet pleasures of a middle-class life. Their sons took piano lessons, like my sister had. Their neighbors kept an eye on the house when they weren't home, and comforted them when they lost a son in 1982.

"When we first moved in here they brought us homemade bread," Gloria recalled. "This is a really nice, friendly neighborhood."

That was how my mother remembered it, too.

Mom had a sense of living amid affluence. Indeed, in 1960 our census tract had the second-highest median income in Grand Rapids. It wasn't monetary wealth to which my mother aspired, but the cultural wealth of a growing city. She would rent fine paintings from the Grand Rapids Public Library and attend concerts at St. Cecilia Music Society. For Sunday dinner, she picked up matzah balls at a Jewish delicatessen on Wealthy Street and made soup with them.

My world was much smaller. About the farthest I would venture was to the Eastown Theater, where Dad would walk with us for matinees. Sometimes I'd walk to the library branch at Hall and Giddings, a favorite haunt of my sister. Mornings I would walk past those fine, north-of-Hall homes to Ottawa Hills Elementary where I remember napping on cool plastic mats next to a goldfish pond in the floor.

Those five years felt long then, especially the interminable Sunday afternoons. But now they're just a brief interlude in my childhood. Today my boyhood in Ottawa Hills comes back to me in a series of memories half-faded. But they are good memories, secure and comforting, the kind of memories Grand Rapids is nice at building.

Philadelphia Avenue is where I begin remembering my life — a life of little pleasures, with a whole family, and in a tree-lined neighborhood that seemed to take good care of me.[1]

FIGURE 163 **Charley, Mike, and Maureen Honey sit outside their Philadelphia Avenue home, 1959.**

FIGURE 164 **Robert and Gloria Tolbert pose with son Ryan outside the same Philadelphia Avenue home.**

dren, a food pantry, summer ministries for kids, and community concert nights in a tent outside the church. The congregation saw the ethnic diversity of the church slowly change to reflect that of the neighborhood, focusing on issues of racial reconciliation. The congregation became more of a walking crowd as well, also reflecting the outreach into the neighborhood. Its decision to stay transformed Oakdale Church into a neighborhood beacon, providing hope, unity and empowerment.[198]

Aside from its growing pains, the entire neighborhood remained fairly stable during the 1970s. By contrast, the 1980s were "a downward spiral," in the words of resident Joe Rembert.[199] The neighborhood lost many key organizers and figures, such as the Kellys, and the association developed problems in dealing with its own diversity. Some inner squabbling resulted from different visions of how to run the organization.[200]

But it was the development of crack cocaine as a street drug that hurt the neighborhood more than anything else. Crack houses popped up throughout the area, bringing more crime with them. This continues to be a problem for SEENA. Through time and contact with the authorities, drug dealers got smarter and learned how to avoid detection. Due to the availability of rental properties and low-income houses, drug dealers can migrate easily into new neighborhoods as other areas in the city are cleaned up.[201]

FIGURE 165 **Carl Kelly and wife Ruth during the early 1980s. They were community organizers in Eastown and Baxter neighborhoods.**

FIGURE 166 **The Wednesday night program at Oakdale Park CRC builds relationships between the church and the community.**

FIGURE 167 **This building on Eastern Avenue at Hall Street dates back to the mid-1800s. For over 50 years it housed the DeVries Funeral Home before becoming Gillespie's Funeral Home in 1989. Today it is a worship center for African immigrants.**

The police department and neighborhood association have done much to clean up the drug problem. However, due to turnover of leaders, redefinition, and various issues within itself, SEENA is in danger of losing CDBG funds. The group would actually like to become independent of the city money.[202]

In 1996, Oakdale Neighbors spun off from the church, not as a competitor to SEENA, but because the church was not equipped to meet community needs. Church members Donna Meyer, Pat Rozema, and Dave Allen developed Oakdale Neighbors to sponsor youth activities, housing issues, and other services.[203]

The church itself has encountered difficulties with its building, as the structure was condemned by the city for roof damage. But the longest-standing member of this community refuses to flee. Since it must rebuild, the church would like to include a community center. Reverend Vanden Bosch suggests that Oakdale could even be considered a tri-cultural church, as many African Americans have been long-time members, and the church is now receiving a lot of Latinos who are moving into the community.[204]

The neighborhood's incredible size, diversity, and age are shown throughout the neighborhood. It stretches from the predominantly African American area around Martin Luther King Park to churches like Oakdale Park CRC and Fuller Avenue CRC, which stand as living reminders of the Dutch who lived there. The Boston Square business district thrives again, featuring quaint businesses like the Boston House Restaurant that inhabits an old stage coach stop built in the late 1800s. Finally, the neighborhood's newest area features the mostly white area around Mulick Park, Immaculate Heart of Mary Catholic Church and School, and Sylvan Christian School and Church at the southeastern tip.

FIGURE 168 & 169 **Over 100 years ago, The Boston House Restaurant on Kalamazoo Avenue was a stage coach stop between Grand Rapids and Lowell. It later became a general store. Today it is a very popular eatery, drawing a diverse patronage.**

Cartoonist Jerry VanAmerongen Remembers

There really wasn't a Mr. Hollingsworth on the 1300 block of Ballard Street when I was growing up. There was a man living down the block who left his house every Saturday morning dressed to play Polo. Compared to the rest of us, he seemed a little quirky at the time.

My memories of growing up on Ballard Street between 1948 and 1956 (we lived down around the corner on Kalamazoo Ave. from '41 to '48), are specific yet scattered. For instance, I remember the horse drawn produce wagon that jingled up our street every week. A big basket scale hung off the rear corner of the canopy. My mom and other moms on the block gathered in the street to make their purchases. There were horse droppings on Ballard Street well after 1948. I remember when the milk man made deliveries to our house. The Buth Dairy truck sat in the drive dripping puddles of water from blocks of ice on the milk cases in back.

There were a lot of kids my age in the neighborhood. We spent a lot of our time playing ball in the vacant lot on the Ballard Street hill. The street dropped sharply into Kalamazoo Ave. Any well hit ball or misguided pass making it to the street, began the long bouncing journey into the traffic of Kalamazoo Ave.

FIGURE 170 **Jerry VanAmerongen grew up on Ballard Street and draws the syndicated cartoon series, The Neighborhood.**

It's that quirky Mr. Hollingsworth.

There were big trees to climb and grape arbors to sneak into. It was a wonderful time to grow up, and a wonderful place to grow up in...the Ballard Street neighborhood in southeast Grand Rapids.

Midtown

Tucked away in a small corner just south of I-196, east of Heritage Hill and north of East Hills, lies the quiet neighborhood of Midtown. Like its southern neighbor, East Hills, it is often forgotten by the shoppers, overshadowed by Heritage Hill, or overlooked by the motorists who speed by on the expressway that separates them from northern neighbor, Highland Park.

Although some of the houses on the western edge near Heritage Hill are large nineteenth-century homes, most of the housing in Midtown is extremely modest. "An abundance of front porches add a very friendly feel to the neighborhood," says Julie Stivers, a 20-year resident. "When you walk down the street, you end up talking to people."[205]

Stivers, who loves Midtown's character, friendliness, and "slight Bohemian edge," started *On-the-Town* magazine in 1982. She said that Midtown lacks a unifying factor that really draws everyone in the neighborhood together and still struggles to find its own identity.[206]

Most contemporary neighborhoods have unified over a political issue. Stivers aptly comments, "It is a fact of life that political activism only happens when something goes wrong." At one time, something did go wrong and Midtown did unify over a political issue.

In 1974, the Baxter Laundry at the corner of Fountain Street and Eastern Avenue went bankrupt, leaving its huge building empty and decaying. The neighbors grew concerned about the eyesore becoming a crime or fire hazard. A group of neighbors went to City Hall to ask that the building be destroyed, but the city waited for the building's owners to tear it down. After a huge fire in the building dropped ashes over the area, Midtown residents organized into a neighborhood group called FUMD, named for their boundary streets Fuller, Union, Michigan and Diamond. The name had a double meaning, as the association harbored strong anger toward the city for hesitating to tear

FIGURE 172 **Julie Stivers is at home on Parkwood Street in Midtown.**

the building down. After the group organized, the city became more cooperative and tore down the Baxter Laundry. Rather than rebuild anything on the spot, they kept it as Midtown Green, a vacant green space for recreation.[207]

The group of volunteers, which incorporated in 1984 but did not receive CDGB funding until the early 1990s, decided to expand its borders. The association decided to stretch east of Fuller Avenue and north to I-196 to include many of the old Polish homes, as no organization represented them yet.[208] The Polish remnant had been cut off from the St. Isidore's neighborhood in the 1960s when the freeway was built.[209]

In its early days, the association met in the house of the leader, but now it works out of the Northeast Complex. Founding members Mary Jane Morris, James R. Jones, and George Pattock immediately began working on housing complaints as well as crime and beautification issues. They cultivated a community garden near Michigan and Dudley, and a neighborhood mural adjacent to the garden.[210]

FIGURE 171 **Midtown Green, former site of the Baxter Laundry building, is now a popular play space.**

FIGURE 173 **The Farmer's Market on East Fulton draws big crowds.**

FIGURE 174 **Martha's Vineyard at Union Avenue and Lyon Street draws customers from all parts of the city to the Midtown neighborhood.**

FIGURE 175 **The East Fulton shopping district, near Diamond Avenue, is an eclectic mix of antique shops, art galleries and restaurants.**

The neighborhood features two very different business districts. The northern district on Michigan Street is geared more toward automobile traffic and fast-food restaurants, while the southern, on East Fulton Street, contains a more eclectic variety of antique shops and art galleries that snare walk-in customers. A small storefront area at Union Avenue and Lyon Street features an exquisite wine store in Martha's Vineyard, and some small art shops.[211]

Current Midtown President Mark Stoddard, who voiced the idea of a neighborhood soccer camp, expresses a mild concern about the lack of a unifying theme for Midtown. They have no school, park, or neighborhood church to rally around, let alone any glorious houses like those of Heritage Hill. He hopes a 2000 neighborhood survey will help nail down something that they can latch onto for identity.[212]

Political issues can unify a neighborhood for only

FIGURE 176 **A sweet house in Midtown**

so long. Midtown doesn't have a lot of problems to either divide it or unify it. The highly effective neighborhood association is still run largely by volunteers.[213] To hear Julie Stivers speak of her neighborhood, you would think it is the best place on earth. "Midtown is friendly, not too gaudy, and above all, it's close to everything," she says.

FIGURE 177 **Jerry Di Trapani has been cutting hair for over fifty years at his barbershop at Fulton Street and Diamond Avenue.**

Madison Square

In 1915, Madison Square, at the intersection of Hall Street and Madison Avenue, was a thriving, bustling area of commerce and traffic that rivaled every shopping area in the city. If someone had told the first Dutch, Greek, or other ethnic inhabitants of Madison Square that the area would later be known as "the killing corner" complete with militant bar traffic, they would have laughed. To bring the story full circle, residents in the 1970s would also laugh if someone told them that outsiders would one day walk down the streets without fear again.

The large area around Madison Square contained a population of African Americans who had begun to edge past their traditional borders. By 1967, the push to the south and east produced a predominantly black neighborhood north of Hall Street, with some blacks spilling over Hall Street, although held back by the invisible boundary of the railroad tracks at Garden Street. Several businesses remained, trying to attract trade from those who drove through the neighborhood on their way to somewhere else.

The riots of 1967 proved to be the dagger in the heart that almost killed the

FIGURE 178 **Madison Square in the 1920s was a thriving business district.**

FIGURE 179 **The United Methodist Community House has been an anchor in the neighborhood for over 95 years.**

neighborhood. Though the violence subsided quickly, the fear and paranoia did not vanish for some time. Paranoia over the recent racial violence quarantined predominantly black areas of the city. Drivers found other routes and retail trade all but stopped, as people from outside feared to venture to the few remaining businesses at Madison Avenue and Hall Street.

The residents were trapped in their own world. The outside world had written them off, housing had deteriorated significantly, crime had begun to take over the neighborhood and a sad, bitter mood fell over the community. The residents who wanted to escape the insurmountable problems couldn't buy houses

elsewhere because of the racist practices of real estate agents, banks, and homeowners. Although these effects lessened with civil rights activism, only wealthier African Americans could choose to fight institutional racism and buy houses elsewhere. With the poverty and unemployment in Madison Square, few could move out.

The problems snowballed throughout the 1970s. No one would invest in what was thought of as a wasteland. Several murders further damaged the community image and Madison Square developed several infamous nicknames such as "killing corner," "hell hole," and "Dodge City." Boarded-up houses

FIGURE 180 **Alda Conley organized the first block club in her area in 1977.**

and businesses lined the streets and vacant lots replaced demolished houses.[214]

"Crime is like a cancer," Alda Conley states emphatically. A Prospect Avenue resident since 1977, she organized her block club to combat the problems of crime, housing, and rodent infestation. Conley's block at Prospect Avenue and Garden Street managed to get a lot done, despite the changes and headaches of the neighborhood.[215]

ACORN, a national community organizing firm, tried to establish a neighborhood organization in the area, but just as in Belknap Lookout, the neighbors grew disenchanted and broke free from ACORN in 1979. The independent association later took the name of Paul I. Phillips to honor the father of the Civil Rights movement in Grand Rapids, who was a key figure in Madison Square. Unfortunately, this organization experienced financial problems and quickly faded into the woodwork.[216]

FIGURE 181 **One of the many homes renovated by the Inner City Christian Federation**

"We had the most severe problem in the city with deteriorated housing."

Etta May

During the early 1980s, Vivian Lewis, and other concerned members of United Methodist Community House on Sheldon Avenue started a new neighborhood organization called South East Community Association (SECA). It drew its borders west of Madison Avenue, while the struggling Paul I. Phillips Association focused on the area east of Madison Avenue. The United Methodist Community House itself had anchored the northwest corner of the neighborhood for about 90 years, featuring day care, youth programs, and senior programs for the community. The Community House, however, sought to bring organized community activism to Madison Square with city funding, and SECA was born. As director of both community development and youth programs, Lewis and others trained youth to become involved in community organizing and block club development.[217]

The organization began to focus on crime, housing, the Madison-Hall business strip, and organizing block clubs such as Alda Conley's. Early director Ezell Brown,

FIGURE 182 **The home shown at left, before renovation**

who raised ten children on Lafayette Avenue, made sure that his neighbors kept up their houses. He brought the same tenacity to the neighborhood organization.[218]

By the 1980s two faith-based, yet extremely different forces had begun targeting the root of the problem in Madison Square. In 1977, Eastern Avenue Christian Reformed Church sponsored a group of men to rehabilitate a house. The project grew into a mission, and in a few years they had incorporated into Inner-City Christian Federation. In 1981, they hired Jonathan Bradford as executive director to carry out ICCF's mandate to revitalize the neighborhood through the rebuilding of homes.[219]

Located in the old fire station on Madison Avenue just south of Franklin Street, ICCF builds beautiful yet modest homes throughout the city, but is mostly focused in the Madison-SECA area. Home ownership, crime prevention, and community development classes, in conjunction with the neighborhood associations, have helped the new owners of these houses become proud members of the community. As the second oldest non-profit housing developer in the state, ICCF has developed a tremendous amount of low-income housing throughout the city. Its ministry to the Madison area has made a significant difference.[220]

FIGURE 183 **Brian Bosgraff, Jonathan Bradford, and Bassie Cummings, executives of ICCF**

Meanwhile, a very different faith-based organization began to take root in the same area. Noah Seifullah, a devout Muslim, became a board member of the Madison Square Housing Co-operative in 1979. Grand Valley State University students had begun the Co-op as a project house on Prospect Avenue, but expansion had plunged the well-intentioned endeavor into severe debt. Seifullah, who became CEO after a few years, developed a vision for expanding the retail offerings of the Square itself.[221]

The Co-op operated from the old location of Kroger's grocery store. Businessmen Frank Thomas and Wilson Tate started Madison Food Town on the southeast corner in 1980. The grocery store became an anchor for the business community.[222] Although it still struggles due to competition from chain supermarkets, the presence of a grocery store helped the residents of Madison Square. It also convinced other businesses that if a grocery store could make it in the Square, they could as well. With Thomas and Tate as the pioneers of resettlement, other businesses followed their lead.[223]

In 1983, the Co-op encountered perhaps the most crucial battle of its existence. President Ronald Reagan sliced the Housing and Urban Development budget. The last chunk of federal money had been designated for a housing project in Nevada. The Co-op sought to use this money for 170 units of housing scattered in the Madison area. Seifullah and local artist Paul Collins convinced Congressman Harold Sawyer that the funds should be used in Madison Square. Sawyer managed to get the direction of the funds changed to Madison Square just 10 minutes before the bill was signed into law. The Congressman then flew in from Alaska and toured the neighborhood with a motorcade before delivering the money to the Co-op.[224]

Despite many critics and naysayers, the Co-op built houses on vacant lots around the neighborhood, mostly on Prospect and Lafayette Avenues. Critics who said that Madison Square could never keep its tenants have been silenced by a 98-percent occupancy rate throughout the years, despite the lack of centralization in the

FIGURE 184 **Madison Food Center was part of a large redevelopment project by Madison Square Housing Co-op.**

housing project. Although rental rates are low, the housing project has generated a constant source of revenue for the Co-op, helping it to escape debt and become independent of government funding.[225]

To top off the early victories, the bar at the northeast corner of the Madison-Hall intersection was replaced by lawyers and offices around 1985. This transition removed the center of neighborhood violence and militancy.[226]

Despite the early victories of ICCF, SECA, and the Madison Square Co-op, the neighborhood suffered a setback in 1986. SECA sponsored a Street Fair of the neighborhood in August of 1986, bringing masses of neighbors out to participate. During the event, 21-year-old Freddie Allen was gunned down in the middle of the crowd. The assailant was later arrested, but the event scarred Madison Square once again in the eyes of outsiders. The

FIGURE 185 **Noah Seifullah, a devout Muslim, brought the vision and energy for a new Madison Square.**

focus became the crime that inhabited the neighborhood rather than the good things taking place. Fear and despair threatened to destroy the spirit of the neighborhood.[227]

Almost immediately, another crushing blow to the housing and crime scene came when crack hit the streets in the late 1980s. "We had the most severe problem in the city with deteriorated housing," states Etta May, then-Vice President of SECA. The already horrible rental relationships became even worse as drug dealers took over run-down or abandoned houses and terrorized the area. Addicts neglected their houses and families.[228]

But the neighbors refused to be intimidated.[229] Pastors Dante Venegas and David Beelen of Madison Square CRC at the corner of Madison Avenue and Garden Street came to Ruth Apol and Etta May at SECA, announcing their intentions to stick with the neighborhood despite the negative events. Strengthened by the church, SECA joined with the near-defunct Paul I. Phillips Association and increased its eastern boundary from Madison Avenue to Eastern Avenue. Its crime prevention work with community police officer Marla Freeman began to clean up the streets and minor gang problems.[230] ICCF also refused to quit. Working out a neighborhood revitalization plan with SECA in 1987, it obtained funding from the state and built houses throughout the neighborhood.[231]

FIGURE 186 **Madison Square Senior Housing**

The forces in Madison Square continue to work. Seifullah and the Co-op convinced the Madison Square branch of the public library to move into a building at the main intersection. It has been a remarkable success despite skepticism. The Co-op also sponsored the development of Madison Area Neighborhood Association (MANA) in 1996.[232] Though there was originally some angst between SECA and MANA over methods of ministering to the neighborhood, most of this has dissipated.[233] ICCF continues to function with remarkable success in the community, helping new homeowners to have pride in their home and community.[234]

FIGURE 187 **Tony Smith and Pastor David Beelen of Madison Square CRC**

Noah Seifullah acknowledges the accomplishments of the neighborhood as a source of African American pride. The black population in Madison Square helped to revitalize the housing, employment opportunities, and businesses in the neighborhood.[235] Other populations are also at work in Madison Square, including an ever-increasing Latino community, ICCF with Jonathan Bradford at the helm, and a racially mixed congregation at Madison Square CRC.

Home Repair Services

A crucial part of the battle against housing problems is interrupting the slide from a few household repairs to an irreparable eyesore. It's like plugging the hole in the water bucket that you are fighting the fire with, said Bob Hengeveld of Home Repair Services on Division Avenue.

Begun as the brainchild of the Catholic Human Development Office, Home Repair Services offers affordable home repair materials, free classes on home maintenance, a volunteer repair crew, and loanable tools.

HRS knows that homeowners often can't afford to keep up their homes. By conducting finance analyses, HRS targets its services to those who care about their homes but can't afford some of the costs. Currently, HRS receives its funding from the city, Kent County, Housing and Urban Development, area churches, and from a full-time private fund-raising campaign.

Over the years, the assistance offered by Home Repair Services has affected hundreds of homes throughout the city. It provides a crucial weapon in the battle against housing decay and for increased home ownership throughout the city.[1]

FIGURE 188 **David Jacobs, Executive Director, and Dick Westra, former Board President of Home Repair Services**

FIGURE 189 **Home Repair Services at 1100 South Division**

FIGURE 190 **Former Police Chief Hegarty, a pioneering advocate for community policing, earned the respect of city residents for his exhaustive work in the community.**

FIGURE 191 **Concerned residents of the city's southeast side attend a meeting held by Police Chief Hegarty.**

Madison Square CRC has lived up to its promises to stand by the neighborhood as well. With a mission for racial reconciliation and social justice, the church has become a bright light to both the neighborhood and the city around it.[236] Its youth programs, run by Laura Carpenter, include children from outside the neighborhood and within.[237] Another ministry has branched out from the church in the last few years. Restorers Inc., led by Renita Reed, rehabilitates houses in the neighborhood with the goal of turning them over to responsible families.[238] "You don't have to go there to know what they're doing," affirms Etta May. "I drive by there and it is always good to see everything that is happening."[239]

Frank Thomas also agrees that Madison Square is a bright spot in the community. He says the same is true for New Hope Church and Messiah Baptist Church, whose REACH program helps to show Black youth the other side of life. At first, the government looked at Madison Square with dollar signs, discouraged about the amount of money it would take to rehabilitate the area from its "killing corner" reputation. But Frank answers, "Money isn't the answer, it's training." People have to learn to take care of their homes, they have to learn to love, they have to learn family values and how to break down racism. "Religion has got to play a big part," he said.[240]

And it has in Madison Square. With the Muslim influence of Seifullah's housing Co-operative, and the Christian influences of ICCF, Madison Square CRC, Messiah Baptist, United Methodist Community House and New Hope, faith-based ministries have played a huge role in resurrecting Madison Square. The Alda Conleys, Gloria Chandlers, Etta Mays, and Tammy Moores of the neighborhood have expressed their love for the community through the neighborhood organizations, despite the changes in the associations.

FIGURE 192 **The new Madison Square Branch of the Grand Rapids Public Library opened in 2001.**

Alger Heights

Mary Beuche calls her neighborhood "the best-kept secret" in the city of Grand Rapids. Proximity to both the central city and 28th Street, yet independent enough to survive on its own, Alger Heights has grown as a successful city within a city. The only neighborhood to build itself during the Depression and World War II, Alger Heights centers around a business district at the intersection of Alger Street and Eastern Avenue, just north of 28th Street. It had escaped most of the urban decay problems experienced by the inner-city neighborhoods.

In the late 1970s, Beuche and several other mothers on Hoyt Street met most weekdays for coffee while their children played together. The concerned mothers began to notice crime edging its way into the neighborhood. Several muggings of senior citizens had occurred near the Old Kent Bank on Eastern Avenue, the northern doorstep of the neighborhood. One assault happened in broad daylight. The mothers decided that any action had to start with them.[241]

They first organized a neighborhood watch by blocks, with advice from the police department. Next, the group worked with Carol Townsend from the Garfield Park Neighborhoods Association and CONA to start the Alger Heights Neighborhood Association. The neighborhood watch program became so effective that it led to the arrest of the purse snatcher who had plagued the Dickinson School area, after just his second attempt in Alger Heights. The watch also helped to curb further violent acts against the residents.[242]

The next battle involved invaders from the suburbs. A group of unruly teens bullied the neighborhood children who played in Alger Park. The parents organized a park watch with the police, and when one of the teens was caught for drug possession the group moved to another area.

The fledgling Neighborhood Association then faced a corporate challenge. A developer sought to turn the northwest corner of 28th Street and Kalamazoo into a huge softball complex with paid memberships and a liquor license. The neighbors feared the neighborhood children would not have access to the park, and the liquor could draw unwanted people from outside the neighborhood. The destruction of a swamp area on Plaster Creek became the final rallying point against the softball complex.[243]

FIGURE 195 **Donna Blackall and Mary Beuche, concerned neighborhood residents on Hoyt Street in Alger Heights in 1982**

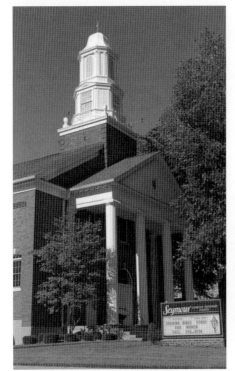

FIGURE 193 **Seymour Christian Reformed Church on Alger Street**

FIGURE 194 **Alger Heights business district at Alger Street and Eastern Avenue**

FIGURE 196 **Seymour Branch of the Grand Rapids Public Library, completed in 2000**

The Alger Heights Neighborhood Association rallied its block clubs against this threat, collecting 2,800 petition signatures in three weeks against the developers. The city sided with the petitioners and restricted the development of the area by an outsider. Alger Heights wasn't satisfied. They raised enough money to create a neighborhood park out of the land, with softball, baseball, and soccer fields, free public

access, no liquor, and a beautiful nature preserve. Mackay/Grand Rapids Jaycees Park now occupies the land, a permanent marker of the Alger Heights' victory.

Aside from these big issues, the neighbors of Alger Heights have tackled small pockets of housing problems, alley clean-ups, the creation of small tree lots and other issues. Beuche believes that the organization has brought out the true neighborhood spirit. It began as a group of women who drank coffee together and carries on as a neighborly source of helpful action.[244]

Today, signs welcome you to Alger Heights at the intersection of Alger Street and Eastern

FIGURE 198 **Stately oak trees are a hallmark of Alger Heights.**

Avenue. Beautiful oak trees line Eastern Avenue, preserved by the efforts of Garfield Park to stop the widening of the street. Alger Heights features neighborhood businesses, Alger Park School, Alger Park, and several thriving neighborhood churches, including Seymour Christian Reformed Church. The construction of the Seymour branch of the Grand Rapids Public Library has also added to the pride of the Alger Heights neighborhood.

FIGURE 197 **Residents proclaim Alger Heights the "best kept secret" in the city.**

East Hills

At the turn of the millennium, the intersection of Cherry Street, Lake Drive and Diamond Avenue was marked by several colorful signs that decorated a dirt parking lot. "Welcome to East Hills, the Center of the Universe," declared one of them. Jammed between two of the most vibrant and visible neighborhoods in the city, the East Hills neighborhood struggles for recognition worthy of its own sense of pride.

Once a small walking neighborhood, East Hills got caught in the downward spiral of white flight to the suburbs, the entrance of absentee landlords and the deterioration of its once-proud business districts on Wealthy Street, Cherry Street, Fulton Street and Lake Drive. Bars filled some of the vacant buildings, while wannabe gangs, like the Wealthy Street Boys, caused further problems.[245]

As crime rates increased dramatically, remaining homeowners like Ruth Gorniewicz of Dwight Avenue became disgusted with the deterioration and violence. Concerned neighbors were walking around in fear. Repeated incidents of violence and drug dealing at the White Rabbit Lounge at Wealthy Street and Fuller Avenue caused the neighbors, led by the East Hills Council of Neighbors (formed in 1978), Eastown, and the South East Economic

FIGURE 199 **Ruth Gorniewicz, long time East Hills resident**

Development (SEED) to petition for the revocation of the bar's liquor license. By 1986, these residents had seen enough. Through the concentrated efforts of the determined residents, the White Rabbit was forced to close[246]

The battle that unified the neighbors of East Hills against the White Rabbit gave power to the neighborhood organization. They hired a crime preven-

FIGURE 200 **The renovated Cherry Hill Market replaced a trouble-plagued party store.**

FIGURE 201 **Hand painted signs proclaim East Hills, "The Center of the Universe," at the intersection of Lake Drive, Cherry Street, and Diamond Avenue.**

tion organizer, conducted fund raisers, began to crack down on crime, and targeted the dilapidated 1100 Wealthy Street block for renovation.[247] The Wealthy Street Business Alliance and SEED managed to change zoning laws, and several new businesses restored the old buildings and moved in. They gave more life and economic vitality to the area, including a miraculous restoration of the Wealthy Street Theatre.[248]

East Hills is actually a conglomeration of six distinct neighborhoods. The two most notable, Cherry Hill and Fairmount Square,[249] have vibrant leadership, active participation, and historic designation status. The other four — Fitch Corners, Congress Park, Diamond Gate, and Orchard Hill — are lesser known, but still developing.[250] The two most active areas, Fairmount Square and Cherry Hill, lie immediately to the west of Orchard Hill.

> "I don't care what color you are — just take care of your property."
>
> Ruth Gorniewicz

Fairmount Square, the most recent district in the city to be declared historic, followed the example of the Cherry Hill District, located just a few blocks to the west. Absentee landlords spelled disaster for Cherry Hill in the 1980s by neglecting many of the beautiful old homes. Some unsupervised homes turned into drug houses. By the mid-1980s, drugs and crime were plentiful, and most of the white homeowners had escaped to the suburbs.[251]

There were some concerned residents in Cherry Hill, however, who would not run. An act of hatred and violence united these people. In 1989 several of them were assaulted by a large group of young people. Two of the victims, Gabrielle Works and her husband, John O'Connor, organized the Cherry Hill Association to fight back.[252]

Immediately the association targeted the decrepit housing issue with a variety of weapons. It managed to sell the vast majority of the absentee landlords' homes at economical prices to would-be homeowners. These new homeowners, thrilled to own a house at such a bargain, fixed up the properties to comply with the historic status.[253]

The results for Cherry Hill have been tremendous, despite a host of naysayers, critics, and seemingly insurmountable odds. Crime has virtually disappeared, and the area received historic designation in 1994.[254] The efforts produced a plethora of economically priced, yet beautiful old homes that disappeared from the market at an astonishing rate.[255]

Directly east of Cherry Hill lies Fairmount Square, a neighborhood dating as far back as the 1880s. These houses originally belonged to white-collar workers rather than lumber barons, said Jim Winter-Troutwine, an architect who resides in Fairmount Square. The housing stock reflects this economic difference, but the district acquired its Historic Designation status in 1999.

FIGURE 202 **John Fetter, Gabrielle Works, and John O'Connor took back Cherry Hill from unaccountable landlords and drug dealers.**

Schoolteacher Dave Huizer, Wealthy Street veteran Carol Moore, and Winter-Troutwine began purchasing and renovating houses that had been inhabited by crack dealers and users. By controlling the properties, their upkeep, and the tenants, concerned neighbors can insure that the housing stock is maintained and that problems are kept to a minimum. Most importantly, the historic designation provides guidelines that prevent landlords from buying properties in the neighborhood and making shoddy repairs. Due in part to the presence and energy of gay and lesbian activists in the neighborhood, Fairmount Square has won significant battles against the infestation of crack cocaine in the neighborhood without displacing a large number of residents.[256]

Despite the independent activism of Cherry Hill and Fairmount Square, the umbrella organization, East Hills Council of Neighbors, continues to support all areas of East Hills.

FIGURE 203 **A home in Fairmount Square on Virginia Street SE**

The struggles of the neighborhood have defined the role of Directors Kathryn Caliendo and Cindy Koning. The earlier years involved the fight against crime and housing blight, but this problem has lessened considerably. Though it continues to wrestle with absentee landlords and irresponsible tenants, the neighborhood organization has turned its efforts to the children of the neighborhood. Building on its proximity to Congress School and Cherry Park, it organized several programs for the children to teach work ethics and other important life lessons. Drawing upon the vast neighborhood resource of artists, art projects to beautify the community and to promote awareness of the neighborhood have included murals, signs, photographs, and the "Fish Project." This latest effort attempts to mimic the Chicago cows urban art project by placing artistically designed fish in every neighborhood around the city.[257]

FIGURE 204 **This mural on Donald Place SE, was painted by artist Donna Munro and neighborhood children.**

A recent influx of Guatemalan immigrants into the neighborhood has added diversity to East Hills. Many live on the streets north of Lake Drive and work at Valley City Laundry on Fulton Street.

In light of all its struggles, East Hills has made tremendous improvement. The community united to fight crime, gangs, housing problems, and blight and restore vitality to the area. Residents refused to flee as their neighborhood decayed, attempting instead to make it a worthwhile place to live. East Hills is proud of its houses, age, beauty, character, and diversity. Resident Ruth Gorniewicz admits, "I don't care what color you are, just take care of your property."[258] Crime has diminished, the gangs have disappeared, home ownership is increasing, and the quaint East Hills neighborhood is beginning to turn some heads.

FIGURE 205 **Organizers Cindy Koning, with infant daughter, and Kathryn "K.C." Caliendo show off their "Fish Project" in front of the East Hills Council of Neighbors building on Eastern Avenue at Cherry Street.**

Rediscovering an Old Jewel

Community policing is not new in Grand Rapids, but prior to Police Chief Harry Dolan, the department only had one such unit. Now the whole department is community based, divided into six teams that cover specific sections of the city. The sections are further subdivided into beats. Officers in patrol cars still respond to calls, but many other officers are now parking their cars, assigned to patrol neighborhoods by foot or bike. In fact, many neighborhoods have a community officer whose primary job is to build relationships with the neighbors.[1]

FIGURE 206 **Grand Rapids Police Chief Harry Dolan with friends**

Community policing isn't a brilliant new idea, but rather, a return to an older style of police work. At some point after World War II, police officers became call-oriented, which sent them to their cars and began to isolate them from personal relationships with the people they served. The recent renaissance towards community policing seeks to establish a relationship between "beat" cops and a neighborhood. As Baxter's Community Officer Tom Opperman put it, "We're rediscovering an old jewel."[2]

Community Officer Dave Nowakowski patrols the area around the Wealthy Theatre. "There is now a change in attitude toward police," he said. "Because I know the community and they know me, people are much more willing to come up and report problems in the neighborhood."[3]

By establishing relationships with the neighborhood, community officers hope to eliminate problem areas and shut down the crime for good. The community officers hope to be a conduit to connect neighbors with each other, helping to foster positive elements of growth and change within a community that will improve it.

Creston

Former Mayor Stanley Davis and his wife, Marjorie, live directly across from two of the oldest landmarks in the Creston area. On the north side of Boltwood Drive stand two elegant and majestic homes, the Comstock House and the Huntley Russell Mansion. Marjorie Davis, a native north-ender, can spout the history of both these houses with pride that rivals any of her neighbors.[259]

It's no small wonder that an area with a strong traditional identity such as Creston's would appeal to Stanley Davis, having grown up a Polish youth on the West Side. His wife, on the other hand, has deeper roots within the area. Her brother, Orville Hoxie, helped start a drug store in the Creston Business District, in a building that still bears the family name.[260]

FIGURE 207, 208 **Huntley Russell Mansion and Comstock House on Boltwood Drive NE**

Although the Comstock and Huntley Russell Mansions are old, the area around them was not settled until much later in Creston's history. To have deeper roots in Creston means going farther south and west in the area bounded by Sweet, Taylor, Plainfield and Leonard Streets. This area contains the oldest houses in the area, settled by a hodge-podge of Irish, Dutch, Polish, English, and Canadian factory workers. The Creston business district, located on Plainfield Avenue between Leonard Street and Knapp Street, has served as the center of this walking neighborhood since the 1860s.

Creston has a history of pulling together as neighbors when necessary. The migration of homeowners farther from the central city is no new phenomenon. But many Creston natives chose only to move farther up the Avenue, expanding the history and tradition of the neighborhood.[261]

The migration has triggered the growth of two additional business districts farther north on Plainfield Avenue. Cheshire Village, which acquired the name almost thirty years ago, lies immediately to the north of Knapp Street in the area formerly known as Fairmount.[262]

The third business district popped up most recently as the farms up to Three Mile Road were parceled out and settled. It testifies to the steady growth and expansion of Creston.

However, the growth has not come without a price. The old housing stock in the original Creston area, now known as Creston Grove, has experienced the typical pattern of housing decay. As older members of the neighborhood moved farther out, they rented their homes to low-income families or individuals. Crime crept into the area as the old houses became inhabited by a transient population unconcerned with the upkeep of the neighborhood.[263]

But those who care about the old neighborhood are fighting for it in a variety of ways. Perhaps the most faithful landmark of the community is the massive St. Alphonsus Catholic Church (known as St. Al's) on Carrier Street, one block north of Leonard Street.

The church has been a harbor of social justice to the neighborhood for years according to many residents, most notably Dominican Sister Roberta Hefferan. She knows the history of St. John's Home, part of the St. Alphonsus parish, better than almost anyone. She wrote her senior thesis for Catholic University on the neighborhood ministry that dates back to the 1880s. Sr. Roberta began to work at St. John's Home in 1963 and later came to St. Al's Food and Clothing Center, an outreach that has coordinated services to the neighborhood for over 25 years.[264] The church also hosts the Catherine's Care Center, a health care service, directed by former Belknap Lookout stalwart Frank Lynn.

FIGURE 209 **Sister Roberta Hefferan waters plants at St. Catherine's Care Center.**

FIGURE 210 **These identical homes on Mathews Court NE, were originally built as temporary lodging for furniture workers.**

Fittingly located just across the street from the church is the Creston Neighborhood Association. CNA is a thriving grass roots neighborhood organization of the 1970s, with the discipline and spirit that few organizations in the city still maintain. The organization enjoyed over 20 years of effective leadership under successive leaders Helen Lehman and Paul Haan, as it fought to increase home ownership, stabilize the business district, reduce crime, and improve education.[265]

CNA has not only maintained a flurry of VISTA volunteers, but somehow attracts former neighborhood workers from various other organizations. Former Alger Heights activist Mary Beuche, who now works as Crime Prevention Organizer for Creston, has seen crime and gang presence decrease drastically throughout her years at Creston.[266]

In addition to St. Al's and CNA, several churches in the neighborhood have remained active in Creston Grove, most notably Plainfield United Methodist and Berean Baptist. Residents agree overwhelmingly that Creston has made huge leaps and bounds, especially in the last five years as businesses and organizations have come together to support the neighborhood.

According to Sr. Roberta, there are still some tough areas that need work, but if the community spirit continues to build, good things will happen in Creston. "We're all in it together," she said. "We've got to depend on one another."[267]

FIGURE 211 **Many north-enders remember Creston High School music teacher Frank B. Goodwin, shown in this 1939 yearbook photo.**

FIGURE 212 **A mural where Lafayette Street and Plainfield Avenue intersect was painted by Creston Neighborhood Association and young people from the neighborhood.**

Rallying Around Kay Pharmacy

Frank and Katherine Koelzer brought work ethics and family tradition to their business when they founded Kay Pharmacy at 2178 Plainfield Avenue NE in 1945. The same spirit remains at the new millennium with their son Jim and grandson Mike, who currently run the independent pharmacy in the Cheshire Village section of Creston.

Jim Koelzer, who lives nearby at Eleanor and Oakwood, recalls a touching moment of neighborhood spirit in 1991, when a Walgreen's chain drug store planned to occupy the lot across the street from Kay. No less than 200 area residents gathered at nearby Second Congregational Church to express their concerns that the larger chain store would force Kay out of business. Walgreen's respected the voice of the neighbors and moved elsewhere.

Today, a Burger King occupies the space that Walgreen's once eyed. The fast-food restaurant proudly displays pictures of the neighborhood throughout its dining room, suggesting that it understands the closeness that has kept Kay Pharmacy in the community for 55 years.

Although the pharmacy has expanded its customer base to the entire city, an estimated 85 percent of its customers come from within three miles of the store. "These people are modest and frugal, but they pay their dues, and we have a loyalty to this neighborhood," Jim Koelzer said.[1]

FIGURE 213 **Interior of Kay Pharmacy, circa 1950s**

Growing Up in the Wonder Years

by Hank Meijer

excerpted from a Grand Rapids Press article, June 19, 1994.

If nostalgia is the sentimental recollection of the past, history is when we begin to put the past into perspective.

The Creston High School Class of 1970 does not feel middle-aged. But we've got enough of a past by now that our common experience is to some degree history — a trail our own kids sometimes ask about. How then do we explain ourselves?

We were born in the midst of war on the Korean peninsula and had a post-riots, pre-Watergate coming of age. In between we witnessed, or participated in, many of the upheavals that buffeted our culture.

We furnished our share of coaches and clerks, a mime and a couple of ministers. We lost classmates to murder and mayhem, although none to the war in Vietnam. We were just a little too young for that.

Graduation is a transition from a way of life called school. For us that began with kindergarten late in the Eisenhower administration, and for me, at least, in Aberdeen School on the Northeast Side of Grand Rapids. Some of us were crossing guards, released from school a few minutes early, the same time the Blessed Sacrament School let out next door. Occasionally there were fights with the Catholic boys as we took up our stations at lonely outposts, giving us an early glimpse of sectarian rivalry in its most pedestrian form.

Growing up in an industrial state, we found factories a logical destination for field trips. Kellogg and Oldsmobile were attractions. There was no Disney World, let alone industrial espionage or nervousness about liability should a child tumble off a catwalk.

In sixth grade some of us played basketball Saturday mornings in the old gym at Creston High, then stopped by Sweetland's on Plainfield for one of their sodas with the scoop of ice cream balanced on the rim of a tall glass. We could still make it home in time for "Fireball XL–5," a TV science fiction series that lives in my mem-

ory as a clunky sort of puppet show. I was nearly home once, when a feeling of nausea washed over me as I realized I forgot to pay for my soda. I raced back up Plainfield filled with terror and shame at the crime I had almost committed.

Sixth grade was also the year Aberdeen School was integrated. I was assigned to welcome our first black student, but felt powerless to prevent the fight that broke out at recess. This was 1963. Our class grew up with the civil rights movement. Nearby was the Auburn Hills neighborhood east of Fuller, a pioneering effort to create a new subdivision of integrated housing.

The summer before high school, riots erupted on Twelfth Street in Detroit and its echoes were heard on South Division. Then came the closing of South High, busing, and the battles at Union High School. We had our fights, too, but I've often thought that Creston fared a little better thanks to those pioneers in Auburn Hills and other Northeast Side neighborhoods who had provided our school with a small

dose of diversity well before the massive changes wrought by busing. The late Paul Phillips lived a few blocks away. Two white friends and I could feel comfortable as the tiny minority at a James Brown concert at Houseman Field.

Native American culture lived in only a few pages of the book on Grand Rapids' history we used. But we learned something of the Indian Mounds, and felt a connection back to the streets we lived on.

Our teachers were predominantly female and mostly very capable. With so few entering other professions or the managerial ranks, teaching talent was deep. Perhaps we were one of the last generations to benefit from a glass ceiling that our own class would help shatter.

Suburban high schools were for the most part smaller institutions somewhere on the edge of things, except for East Grand Rapids, which was our nemesis. Our WZZM Quiz Bowl team was rolling toward a championship when East nipped us over a physics question still disputed by my teammate, Jack Stevens, who went on to MIT. Today these schools see their enrollment eclipsed by the newer institutions in Forest Hills, Kentwood, Rockford and Jenison.

Speaking of our Quiz Bowl team, I remember the show's moderator asking each of us what we thought would be society's biggest challenge in the future. Susan Dahlman cited environmental concerns and I admired her prescience. I said something about race relations and wish now the prediction had been wrong.[1]

The Royce Family – A North End Legacy

While giving birth to her son, Charles, in 1925, Maria Royce expressed her frustration with the jarring noise made by janitors sliding buckets across the floor as they mopped. She suggested that her husband and father place the bucket into a ring with ball bearings, allowing the bucket to move noiselessly. Her Danish father, recruited for his mechanical genius by furniture companies in Grand Rapids, brought his daughter's idea into fruition. Later, the inventors added a mop wringer, and they founded the Royce Rolls Ringer, a family company that eventually became a North End legacy.

> "My mother found some ways to do things that made water running up hill look easy."
>
> Chuck Royce

FIGURE 216 **Maria Royce**

Maria Royce's husband, Frederick, brought his talent of salesmanship to the business, while she kept the books. The company first manufactured mop wringers out of the basements and garages of their houses in East Grand Rapids and Eastown before purchasing an abandoned cabinet factory tucked behind the houses on Knapp Street in the Creston area. The couple traveled extensively, timing their business trips to see concerts and musicians that fueled Maria Royce's lifelong passion for music.

When at home, Royce also worked extensively at St. Cecilia's Music Society promoting concerts and recitals. As a composer and pianist, Maria Royce helped many children, including a number of deaf students, to uncover their musical talents. "My mother had a way of getting everyone involved," said her son, Chuck Royce, who later took over the business with his wife, Stella.

After their marriage in 1954, Chuck and Stella continued to support Maria's legacy to both the family business and St. Cecilia's. In 1955, they moved to their home on Lafayette Avenue NE, in the Creston area where they raised four children. Stella Royce inherited the bookkeeping job from her mother-in-law. Despite her lack of formal training in accounting,

"Miracle Stella" continued the accounting work from the house. Chuck and Stella Royce lived in Creston for 30 years before becoming urban pioneers as the first residents in the Forslund condominiums downtown.

The move downtown has contributed to their participation in the arts. Stella Royce continues to do the company books, while her husband raises funds for St. Cecilia's. The couple has given millions of dollars to support musical organizations such as St. Cecilia's, Opera Grand Rapids, and the Grand Rapids Symphony, where their daughter Maria served as principal harpist for many years. Royce Rolls Ringer still operates out of the factory on Knapp Street, NE.

"My mother found some ways to do things that made water running up hill look easy," Chuck Royce said. Maria Royce's invention led to a family business, and an immeasurable amount of musical heritage in Grand Rapids.[1]

FIGURE 217 **Chuck, Stella, Charles, and Matt Royce, with the Royce Rolls Ringers**

FIGURE 218 **The Herkimer Hotel**

Heartside

The majestic brick structure of the Herkimer Hotel rises like a castle above the surrounding cityscape, a symbol of defiance against the woes of fortune that the neighborhood has battled for five decades. From the turn of the century, when the Herkimer was built, Heartside flourished along with the hotel because of its proximity to Union Station.[268] But when the railroad fell victim to the automobile, many of the railroad dock-workers, hobos, and transient day-workers who lived in the Heartside area lost their jobs.[269] The once-proud spirit of the neighborhood faded and the huge old building began to decay. As crime, homelessness, and ill fortune invaded the neighborhood, the Herkimer adapted. Room prices stayed low at the Herkimer, so those who could afford its cheap rooms stayed for days, months, or even years. These were down-and-out people, mostly men, who felt they had nowhere else to go or to work.[270]

Heartside seemed to welcome such residents from all over the city. Those who had been displaced by the removal of low-income housing along Monroe Avenue and Bridge Street moved to Heartside, living in hotels that had been turned into rooming houses. Throughout the 1960s, 1970s, and 1980s, vacant warehouses, railroad docks, and non-profit agencies housed the homeless, unemployed, drug- and alcohol-addicted, and mentally disturbed. As crime increased, businesses left their buildings vacant and moved to other areas of town.[271]

State mental institutions began releasing residents into the community during the early 1970s, and many of them found solace in Heartside.

But the neighborhood and its citizens have fought back against the woes that have plagued the Heartside. In 1979 the Grand Rapids City Commission identified the area as a historic district. Three years later the area was added to the National

FIGURE 219 **Heartside residents Terry and Ron stand in front of the Herkimer Hotel.**

Register of Historic Places. Tax credits for historic preservation came with this designation, making building renovations possible.[272] These improvements were merely the beginning of a huge chain of dominoes that began to fall into place in Heartside.

During the 1970s, when the number of brothels rivaled the number of apartments in Heartside, a group of people began to show concern. After the completion of the Amway Grand Plaza Hotel, Rev. Dale Sewall of Westminster Presbyterian Church worried about the displacement of lower-income Heartside residents. He organized a group of ministers from Heartside churches to discuss their concerns for the neighborhood. The consensus was that development of Heartside was inevitable. If a housing crisis in the neighborhood was to be avoided, they would have to control large amounts of property for low-income housing. Dwelling Place, Inc. was born in 1980 to serve this purpose.[273]

At first, the goal of Dwelling Place was to buy property in Heartside for low-income housing. As the non-profit corporation acquired and renovated cheap buildings, those who had business investments in the community grew concerned. They felt endangered by the expanding presence of low-income residents who, they feared, would discourage business traffic.[274]

Despite an early series of heated controversies and a major financial crisis in the late 1980s, Dwelling Place has thrived. They currently own and manage more than ten properties that meet a variety of housing needs in the Heartside area.[275]

Between 1993 and 1995, Dwelling Place Inc., bought and renovated the Herkimer, removing the bar. Headed by Dennis Sturtevant, Dwelling Place poured more than $4 million of grant money into the building to restore it to its former glory.[276] Sturtevant approached businessman and philanthropist Peter Wege for financial backing. Wege enthusiastically supported the renovation of the hotel and the apartments where he had spent the first six months of his life.[277] According to building manager

FIGURE 220 **Peter Wege, at age 7 in 1927, poses in a little league baseball uniform. Wege has donated many millions of dollars to the neighborhood where he lived as an infant.**

Sandy Hogue, Dwelling Place is the best thing that ever happened to the hotel and the neighborhood.[278] Since 1980, Dwelling Place Inc., has played an increasingly important role in the neighborhood. "We like to have our nose in pretty much everything that goes on around here," Sturtevant said.[279]

The focus of Dwelling Place has shifted to meet other needs of Heartside residents. By jockeying deals and scrounging funds, the organization works with major development contractors and small businesses to further develop the Heartside in a controlled manner. Casey's Restaurant, for instance, occupies a small section of the Herkimer building, thanks to Dwelling Place.[280]

FIGURE 221 **Sandy Hogue, loyal friend and Herkimer Hotel Manager**

The organization has also taken the leading role in the formation of the Heartside Planning Coalition. This conglomeration of local pastors, residents, businesses, human service agencies, and special interest groups has formed a Neighborhood Revitalization Plan for the continued improvement of the Heartside.[281]

Secondly, both businesses and higher-income residents are becoming more common in the Heartside, without displacing lower-income residents. The inclusivity of diverse residents, as well as the variety of property usage, is a trademark of Heartside. Finally, the influx of restaurants and businesses provides work within the neighborhood for the residents. Dwelling Place no longer has to worry about busing its residents south to 28th Street for their jobs.[282]

FIGURE 222 **Dennis Sturtevant has guided Dwelling Place and a resurgence of the Heartside Neighborhood.**

Several other projects have further changed the face of Heartside. The Main Street Initiative improved Division Avenue through beautification, entry signage, banners, historic building signs, recruiting of new businesses, and street improvements.[283] The Ferguson Project, spearheaded by Larry Bratschie and funded by a coalition including Spectrum Health, area churches, and generous individuals, has relocated lower-income residents to a newer, nicer facility. Finally, the creation of a Heartside Park will bring the area its first park.[284]

Heartside has recently tried to capture the artistic talents of its residents and turn them into an expression of hope and pride. A variety of murals, both old and new decorate building walls, mainly on Division Avenue. In the summer of 1999 the Heartside Arts Market opened, at the corner of Commerce Avenue and Cherry Street, to display and sell works by local residents.[285]

FIGURE 223 **Capitol Lunch, also known as God's Kitchen, serves free lunches to about 300 people each day on South Division Avenue.**

FIGURE 224 **Mel Trotter**

"Everlastingly at It"

Over a hundred years ago, a hopeless alcoholic stumbled into Pacific Garden Mission in Chicago, ready to take his own life. But Melvin Earnest Trotter quickly became a Christian, found hope, and broke his drinking habit. He became a barber and began to volunteer at the mission in his free time, becoming more involved over time.

In 1900, he and a group of men went to Grand Rapids and met in Park Congregational Church with local businessmen who were interested in starting a city mission similar to Pacific Garden. To his surprise, they asked Trotter to become the superintendent. He accepted, beginning the mission on lower Monroe that same year. The mission achieved city-wide notoriety as it preached the Gospel, fed and sheltered the homeless, offered clothing and emergency relief to families, visited jails, and offered hope to the transient inner city that later became Heartside. Mel Trotter was ordained in spectacularly unorthodox fashion in 1912 and served until his death in 1940.[1] Mel Trotter Ministries still serves the neighborhood a century later, offering a home for transients, homeless, and drug and alcohol addicts at 225 Commerce Avenue.[2]

One street east, on Division Avenue, several other ministries have followed Mel Trotter's lead. These include Degagé Ministries, Guiding Light Mission, and God's Kitchen, which serves free lunches daily to a long line of homeless, unemployed, and handicapped.

One of the most active of these urban missions is Heartside Ministries, now located at 54 South Division Avenue. In 1983, Reverend George Beukema started the organization as an outreach to the homeless and transient individuals of the neighborhood.

In 1985, George Heartwell, a mortgage banker turned seminarian, joined Heartside Ministries as an intern. Upon his ordination in 1987, Heartwell joined Heartside Ministries full time. As the ministry thrived, it experimented with different ways to meet the community's needs. Many of these attempts resulted in independent spin-off ministries such as the Heartside Clinic (a medical clinic), In the

FIGURE 225 **Rev. George Heartwell and young Heartside resident**

Image (a clothing bank), and Faith Inc., (employment services). The last of Heartside Ministry's "children" was a recuperation center for hospital patients, a project that involves four major hospitals and funding from Central Reformed Church, Fountain Street Church, and Temple Emanuel.

As a city commissioner for eight years, Heartwell's presence in city politics became extremely important to Heartside when Van Andel Arena was constructed in its north end in 1996. He insured that a certain amount of the arena employees would come from Heartside.[3]

The vision of Mel Trotter Mission, whose early motto was "Everlastingly at It," continues in the other faith-based ministries that have shaped Heartside and ministered to its people.

In the mid- to late-1990s, after the completion of Van Andel Arena, business leaders began investing in the northwestern section of Heartside. While Dwelling Place leads the charge as a non-profit property developer, for-profit businesses have begun, in the last five years, to find a market in the historic, vacant buildings. In 1997, Sam Cummings of Macroe Properties, began to purchase and renovate buildings on Ionia Avenue, just south of Fulton Street, in an attempt to restore life, traffic, and commerce to the area. The area has become known as Old Town, and features new businesses, such as Perceptions, Taps, Gardella's, and the Sierra Room, as well as several loft apartments.[286] Many other developers, such as Rockford Construction, have made equally important contributions to Heartside. The upscale restaurants, night clubs, stores and loft apartments bring a different personality to the area through gentrification.[287]

Ironically, revitalization may spell uncertainty for Heartside. Some fear that the process will lead to the phenomenon known as "psychological displacement." The fear is that lower-income people will feel that they no longer belong in a neighborhood that is increasingly tailored to residents with higher incomes.[288]

FIGURE 226 **Sam Cummings, the first private investor in Heartside, renovated housing and shops on Ionia Avenue.**

FIGURE 227 **The last remaining railroad warehouse was renovated into office space.**

FIGURE 228 **Mural at Heartside Ministry**

FIGURE 229 **On Ionia Avenue, upscale shops and restaurants have changed the street scene.**

Highland Park

"How to Kill a Neighborhood" was the headline of a scathing article by Richard Holm in a 1982 issue of *Grand Rapids Magazine*. In answer to the title of his article, he listed the following six tips:

1. *Slice it in two with a four-lane divided highway.*
2. *Let the ethnic heritage fade and die.*
3. *Don't help your neighbors any more — they've become strangers.*
4. *Loosen up on discipline.*
5. *Break up the clubs, break up the families.*
6. *Take it like a man, and don't make waves.*[289]

From his prose poured a description of some of the understated effects that the construction of I-196 had on the Polish brickyard neighborhood around St. Isidore's, on the East Side of Grand Rapids. Area residents witnessed the destruction of many houses, buildings, and stores to make way for the freeway construction.

The St. Isidore's community had been a strong and concentrated neighborhood at the turn of the century. Every member of the community was taught the same values: hard work, kinship, sharing, and frugality. Eastern Avenue Hall existed not only as a center of social activity, but as a Polish aid group. Nearly everyone in the neighborhood, street after street, was Polish. They all worshiped at the same church, attended the same schools, visited the same social halls, shopped at the same neighborhood Polish grocery stores, and looked after one another. For whatever reason, a significant protest was not made by the Polish community to keep the highway out of their neighborhood. Perhaps, they simply had no idea how it would forever change their neighborhood. After construction, the concrete barrier separated St. Isidore's Church from a large portion of the Polish population. The former walking neighborhood was cut in half. The residents felt disconnected and disheartened. The business center on Michigan Street, with stores like Sacks', that sold almost everything the neighborhood needed, was now inaccessible to many of the former patrons. Over time, many residents moved out of the area.

Now the neighborhood is a mixture of ethnic groups, with little evidence of its Polish roots. Those that remember the old days speak with pride and regret.

A large German population joined the Polish residents within walking distance of Immanuel Lutheran Church. Evelyn Wright is a descendant of that German population. Her family settled in the neighborhood in 1929. Wright and her husband Gerald purchased a house on Harlan Avenue from her father in 1953, when the Polish presence was still strong and Highland Park was a nine-hole golf course. But the golf course had suffered severe neglect throughout World War II and the Depression and rumors of the coming freeway fueled anger and fear in the hearts of the residents.[290]

Until his death a few years ago, renowned local historian Eduard Adam Skendzel lived near the Wrights on Flat Street. As the foremost authority on the history of the Polish population in Grand Rapids, Skendzel wondered why the church never organized to stop the freeway project. Was it simply too big a force to be reckoned with?[291]

The Wrights credit St. Isidore's School with steadying the neighborhood after the freeway opened by providing a neighborhood school that continued to teach the

FIGURE 230   **The I-196 freeway sliced through the St. Isidore parish.**

FIGURE 231 **Gerald and Evelyn Wright in front of their Highland Park home, which has been in their family for over 70 years**

many homeowners moved out from the edges of the neighborhood, many older Polish and German residents remained as reminders of the culture and tradition that once pervaded the entire area. Until two years ago, one icon of the Polish community remained active on Harlan Avenue, just south of the Wrights. The meat market and grocery store of Ted and Olga Janiszewski thrived until his death, when the building became residential.[293]

As more of the old guard left the community, rental properties filled the gap. Property values began to decline as most tenants didn't put enough into their homes or neighborhood. Highland Park experienced mild symptoms of blight. The Park itself suffered neglect as the pool was condemned for structural damage. Concerned neighbors found it difficult to rally the community around anything.

In 1980, however, neighbors grew angry about school traffic that rumbled down Union

traditional values. They are also quick to blame the busing in of students, that began during the 1970s, for dissolving the "grass roots" neighborhood feel of Eastern Elementary, the public school in Highland Park. Busing forced students out of the neighborhood to unfamiliar schools, damaging children's relationships within the neighborhood as well as parents' interactions with the schools outside of the community. This dynamic only amplified the effects of the freeway on breaking up the sense of community of Highland Park.[292]

Despite the changes, the core of the neighborhood remained fairly intact. While

FIGURE 232 **Eduard Adam Skendzel documented the Polish experience in Grand Rapids.**

Avenue to the bus center, causing noise, fumes, cracked plaster, and damaged lawns. Bob and Shirley Karrip organized Highland Park neighbors and worked with the city to change the routes of the buses.[294] By that time, the breech of the freeway was so severe that the association extended its southern border to the freeway, but not farther south to include the severed limb of the Polish neighborhood between Michigan Street and I-196.

As a volunteer organization without funding,

FIGURE 233 **Janiszewski Market on Harlan Avenue NE, was one of the last surviving neighborhood stores.**

the neighborhood association proved to be a one-issue surge. Without a presence in city politics, the neighborhood remained dormant for many years, until a near-tragedy warranted a wake-up call. When a young man robbed an elderly woman in broad daylight, knocking her down and injuring her hip in the process, Gerald and Evelyn Wright grew furious.[295] They rallied Mary Kay Ingram and other concerned residents, met at Eastern School and resurrected the Highland Park Neighborhood Association with Ingram as the director. They began to target crime, housing problems, and deteriorated public areas.

A murder in the park in May of 1999 shocked residents. Highland Park Neighbors realized that the park renovation was crucial to the stability of their neighborhood. In July, homeowners joined forces with city commissioners, a crew from the City Parks and Recreation Department, and Grand Rapids Police Department to clean up the park.[296]

The rejuvenated association then targeted the pool. At first the city told them that no funding could be obtained for a new pool, and offered a water park, but the neighbors persisted. The city eventually granted funds for the pool, which opened during the summer of 2000.

The Wrights hope that an improved park and pool will attract walking residents from nearby. Not only will the added pedestrian traffic bring life to the

> "Could we have ever stopped the freeway?"
>
> Eduard Skendzel

neighborhood, it will help to keep crime off the streets and involve even more neighbors in the affairs of the community.

While the core of the neighborhood has avoided most of the blight problems, the borders still need some work. The Wrights dedicate a significant portion of their time distributing neighborhood flyers in an attempt to inform more residents. Meanwhile, Mary Kay Ingram's volunteer position becomes more time-intensive, as she works with housing and fundraising issues, including raising money for an improved playground at the school.[297]

The Wrights feel strongly about staying in the neighborhood and promoting its stability. While most of the Polish and German influence is gone, those who care about the Highland Park neighborhood refuse to let it slide.

FIGURE 234 **Mary Kay Ingram and her dog walk the neighborhood daily.**

FIGURE 235 **This Highland Park home graced orchards and farmland when built in the mid-1800s.**

FIGURE 236 **Highland Park originally included a golf course.**

FIGURE 237 **Highland Park pool, circa 1953**

FIGURE 238 **A new pool was built by the City in 2000.**

Longtime Neighbors

Bethany Christian Services, a well-established haven for children in need of care, is the result of the early dreams of Marguerite Bonnema and Mary De Boer VandenBosch. The two women met as roommates while attending Reformed Bible Institute and soon realized they shared a lofty goal. Shortly after their 1942 graduation, the women opened their Sigsbee Street apartment to youngsters in need, and worked for area mission organizations.

The first child taken in by the women was an American Indian infant whose life was in danger. Despite the mother's claims, the father did not believe the child was his, and threatened to kill the little girl. Though both women worked at other jobs, they brought the child to their home and cared for her, the first of many children. As the number of children in their care grew, the two women could not leave a baby sitter in charge while they worked. Vanden Bosch continued to work, while Bonnema cared for the children. The two shared their small apartment with the American Indian girl, a blind teenage girl who had outgrown the foster care system, and two young boys.

FIGURE 239 **Bethany Christian Services founders Marguerite Bonnema and Mary DeBoer VandenBosch**

In 1944, the "family" moved into the former Ferris estate on Eastern Avenue. The house was much better equipped to handle them, as it had a playroom for the children, larger bedrooms, several showers, a huge kitchen, and dining room. After incorporation as Bethany Home, the women sought and obtained a license to operate an adoption agency. The outreach of Bethany Home continued to expand. In time the Ferris house was demolished and replaced with five buildings needed to house the ever-expanding agency.

Today, the Bethany Christian Services is an internationally recognized organization, headquartered within the borders of the Highland Park neighborhood in Grand Rapids. Adoption, family counseling, foster care services, and care for pregnant women are some of the

FIGURE 240 **The original Bethany Christian Home on Eastern Avenue**

services offered. The agency that began with a simple outpouring of love for children by two devoted women kept growing to meet their needs. According to Vanden Bosch, "It was the Lord's work. We just made ourselves available."[1]

FIGURE 241 **Bethany Christian Services now reaches beyond the neighborhood to children around the world.**

Conclusion

In the broad scope of history, Grand Rapids is not an old city, even when its roots are traced across millennia to its earliest people, the Mound Builders. With the coming of European influences in the early 19ᵗʰ century, the Odawa who lived along the Grand River were displaced. Tribal villages and gathering places gave way to a new kind of neighborhood, marked by shifting boundaries as waves of immigrants found their way to the Grand River Valley. What we have characterized as walking neighborhoods that defined ethnic enclaves began to change with the coming of modern transportation. First streetcars and trolleys, and finally the automobile and freeway systems, altered the notion of neighborhood and rearranged people's mental maps of how far they were willing or able to go in order to seek goods and services and forge community.

By the 1960s, the resultant phenomenon of urban sprawl saw Grand Rapids, like core cities across the United States losing population and supporting an increasingly fragile infrastructure. Paradoxically, the same period gave rise to a new call for the return to city neighborhoods, where neighbors would know each other and band together to achieve urban revitalization.

Evidence abounds that many have made a conscious decision to actively take part in the creation of a new urban culture sprouting in Grand Rapids today, at the turn of yet another century. Those who have remained or returned to the city bear active witness to the success stories of neighborhood associations, which have battled blight, flight, crime, redlining, and isolation. Both residential and neighborhood commercial areas are drawing renewed investment resulting in significant improvement and vitality. Neighborhoods are becoming walking neighborhoods once again, places where people know and look out for each other. Much has been done; there is much yet to do.

For hundreds of years the face of Grand Rapids and its neighborhoods has been changing. There will always be new stories to tell, shifting landscapes to document. In this book, we have tried to recount a sampling of the aspirations, failures, and victories experienced by the peoples who have called Grand Rapids home. In time our stories will become joined with theirs. We offer this book as an invitation to learn the lessons that the past is teaching, enlightened by the struggles, mistakes, and lasting contributions of those who have gone before. It is also an invitation to engage actively in shaping our present day urban community in such a way that those writing the next chapter may look back and say of us, "They really gave their best to preserve the heart and soul of this community called Grand Rapids."

Section I

The Oldest Neighborhood

1. Dee Brown, *Bury My Heart at Wounded Knee* (New York: Holt, Rinehart, and Winston, 1970), 274.
2. Robert Silverberg, *Moundbuilders of Ancient America* (Greenwich, CN: New York Graphic Society, 1968), 266; Time-Life Books, *Mound Builders & Cliff Dwellers* (Alexandria, VA: Time-Life Books, 1992), 25.
3. Silverberg, 236, 239.
4. Lar Hothem, *Treasures of the Mound Builders: Adena and Hopewell Artifacts of Ohio* (Lancaster, OH: Hothem House Books, 1989), 60; Charles E. Belknap, *The Yesterdays of Grand Rapids* (Grand Rapids: The Dean-Hicks Company, 1922), 42.
5. Albert Baxter, *History of the City of Grand Rapids, Michigan* (New York and Grand Rapids: Munsell & Company, 1891), 15, 17–19; Belknap, 41–44; Charles C. Chapman, *History of Kent County, Michigan* (Chicago: Chas. C. Chapman & Co., 1881), 130.
6. Silverberg, 1–96, 266–267.
7. Ibid., 268–280.
8. Ibid.
9. Belknap, 41–44.
10. Ibid., 41; Baxter, 15.
11. Baxter, 16.
12. "Bones of Contention," *Grand Rapids Magazine* 16 (November 1980): 12–13.
13. Lew Burroughs, interview by Andy Schrier, Norton Indian Mounds, Grand Rapids, 18 November 1999.

The Arrival of the Odawas

14. Brown, 273.
15. Frank Waters, *Book of the Hopi* (New York: Ballantine Books, 1963); David McCutchen, trans., *The Red Record: The Wallum Olum, the Oldest Native North American History* (Garden City Park, NY: Avery Publishing Group, 1993).
16. Baxter, 22.
17. Andrew J. Blackbird, *History of the Ottawa and Chippewa Indians* (Ypsilanti, MI: Ypsilantian Job Printing House, 1887), 90.
18. Baxter, 23, 28.
19. Pamela J. Dobson, ed., *The Tree that Never Dies: Oral History of the Michigan Indians* (Grand Rapids: Grand Rapids Public Library Native American Oral History Project, 1978), 27–29.
20. James A. Clifton, George L. Cornell, and James M. McClurken, *People of the Three Fires: The Ottawa, Potawatomi, and Ojibway of Michigan* (Grand Rapids: West Michigan Printing, 1986), 6.
21. Blackbird, 79.
22. Ibid., 29.
23. Ibid., 13.
24. Ibid., 12.
25. Barbara McCall and Kathi Howes, *The Ottawa* (Vero Beach, FL: Rourke Publications, Inc., 1992), 5–6.
26. Ibid., 5.
27. Clifton, Cornell, and McClurken, 5–6.
28. Joseph H. Cash and Gerald W. Wolff, *The Ottawa People* (Phoenix, AZ: Indian Tribal Series, 1976), 21.
29. Clifton, Cornell, and McClurken, 5.
30. Baxter, 25.
31. Baxter, 45.
32. Charles Richard Tuttle, *History of Grand Rapids with Biographical Sketches* (Grand Rapids: Tuttle & Cooney, 1874), 7–8; Baxter, 25; Chapman, 142–146.
33. Clifton, Cornell, and McClurken, 18–19.
34. Ibid., 19–21.
35. Ibid., 21.
36. Ibid.
37. James M. McClurken, "Strangers in Their Own Land," *Grand River Valley Review* 6, no.1 (July 1985): 5.
38. Ibid., 5; Blackbird, 23.
39. Larry B. Massie, *Potawatomi Tears and Petticoat Pioneers* (Allegan Forest, MI: Priscilla Press, 1992), 22.
40. Ibid., 20.
41. Belknap, 131; Baxter, 26–27; McClurken, 5–9; Chapman, 161–164.
42. Franklin A.M. Everett, *Memorials of the Grand River Valley* (Grand Rapids: Grand Rapids Historical Society, 1984), 279; Chapman, 158; Baxter, 28–29.
43. Isaac McCoy, *History of Baptist Indian Missions: Embracing Remarks on the Former and Present Condition of the Aboriginal Tribes; Their Settlement within the Indian Territory, and their Future Prospects* (New York: H. & S. Raynor, 1840), 249; Baxter, 27–29.
44. Baxter, 27.
45. Isaac McCoy, excerpts from his journal, reprinted in *American Baptist Magazine* 8, no. 3 (March 1828): 16.
46. McCoy, 318.
47. McCoy, *American Baptist Magazine*, 22–23.
48. Ibid., 15.
49. Chapman, 798.
50. McCoy, 329.

51. John W. McGee, *The Catholic Church in the Grand River Valley, 1833–1950* (Lansing, MI: Franklin Dekleine Company, 1950), 57.

52. Gordon L. Olson, *A Grand Rapids Sampler* (Grand Rapids: Grand Rapids Historical Commission, 1992), 16.

53. McCoy, 523.

54. McGee, 44, 56–57, 64–65.

55. McCoy, 428, 575–577.

56. Clifton, Cornell, and McClurken, 28.

57. McCoy, 494–496.

58. Everett, 275.

59. McClurken, 10.

60. Baxter, 48.

61. McGee, 50–51, 53, 77.

62. Frederic Baraga, "A List of the Catholic Indians in the Mission of Grand River," in McGee, 48–49; McGee, 50–52, 56.

63. McGee, 112.

64. McGee, 77.

65. Ibid., 92–93.

66. Ibid., 94.

67. Ibid., 97.

68. McClurken, 12.

69. Ibid., 13.

70. McGee, 94.

71. Ibid., 100–110.

72. Ibid., 98; McClurken, 12.

73. McClurken, 13–15.

74. Ibid., 15–23.

75. Chapman, 154–156; Tuttle, 51–54; Baxter, 32, 90.

76. McGee, 98; Chapman, 147–148; Baxter, 90.

77. McClurken, 23; McGee, 99.

78. Blackbird, 52.

79. Belknap, 24.

80. William J. Etten, ed., *A Citizens' History of Grand Rapids, Michigan with Program of the Campau Centennial September 23 to 26, 1926* (Grand Rapids: A.P. Johnson Co., 1926), 18.

81. Baxter, 124.

82. John Steinbeck, *America and Americans* (New York: Viking Press, 1966), 18.

The First European Settlers

83. Baxter, 8.

84. Etten, 18–19.

85. Everett, 276.

86. Ibid., 36.

87. Baxter, 85.

88. Etten, 51.

89. Belknap, 67, 111; Everett, 21.

90. Belknap, 67.

91. Ibid., 21.

92. Ibid., 112–113.

93. Ibid., 20.

94. Ibid., 81, 95.

95. Baxter, 525–526.

96. Ibid., 188–190.

97. Belknap, 20.

98. Everett, 9.

99. Z. Z. Lydens, *The Story of Grand Rapids* (Grand Rapids: Kregel Publications, 1966), 537.

100. Everett, 9.

101. Belknap, 20.

102. Ibid., 23.

103. Ibid., 20–24.

104. Ibid., 20–21.

105. *Central City Historic Survey*, Grand Rapids, 21 August 1981.

106. Belknap, 93.

107. Ibid., 93–94.

108. *Central City Historic Survey*, 69.

109. Ibid., 69.

110. Baxter, 54.

111. Ibid., 118.

112. Ibid., 59–61.

113. Kenneth A. Bertsch, "Social Stratification in Grand Rapids, Michigan: 1850–1870," (Bachelor of Arts with Honors thesis, Williams College, Williamstown, MA, June 1978): 57.

114. Observations from graphic design work by Aaron Phipps.

115. Baxter, 98–120; Belknap, 167–168.

116. Belknap, 167–168.

117. Ibid.

118. Baxter, 220.

119. Ibid., 221; Belknap, 168–169; Everett, 398, 400.

120. James D. Bratt and Christopher H. Meehan, *Gathered at the River: Grand Rapids, Michigan and its People of Faith* (Grand Rapids: Grand Rapids Area Council for the Humanities and Eerdmans Publishing Co., 1993), 213–278.

121. Baxter, 98–120; Belknap, 155.

122. Application to the National Historic Register by Heritage Hill, filed in the Heritage Hill Vertical File in the Local History Department of the Grand Rapids Public Library.

123. Baxter, 98–120.

124. Ibid.

125. Ibid., 117; *Heritage Hill Historic Homes Tour* (Grand Rapids: The Heritage Hill Association, 1969), 1.

126. *Heritage Hill Historic Homes Tour*, 2.

127. David and Marilyn Hanks, *The Homes of Heritage Hill* (Grand Rapids: The Heritage Hill Association, 1970), 4, 7, 18, 23.

128. Jeffrey D. Kleiman, "The Great Strike: Religion, Labor, and Reform in Grand Rapids, Michigan, 1890–1916," (Ph.D. diss., Michigan State University Dept. of History, Lansing, MI, 1985), 18–19, 28, 55, 183.

129. Ibid., 68.

130. Ibid., 18–19, 83–87, 152, 168, 183.

131. Richard Kurzhals, "The Community on the Bluff: the Belknap-Lookout Neighborhood," *Grand River Valley Review* 5, no. 1, (Winter 1984): 9.

132. Ibid., 8.

133. Ibid., 12.

134. Al Royce, "Citizen Group Battles to Keep an Old Section Desirable," *Grand Rapids Press*, 26 December 1965; Various papers in the Belknap-Lookout Vertical File in the Local History Department of the Grand Rapids Public Library.

135. Kurzhals, 14–15.

Section I – Vignette Notes

The Last of the Mound Builders?

1. William Pidgeon, *Comprising Extensive Explorations, Surveys, and Excavations of the Wonderful and Mysterious Earthen Remains of the Mound Builders in America; the Traditions of the Last Prophet of the Elk Nation Relative to Their Origin and Use; and the Evidences of an Ancient Population More Numerous than the Present Aborigines* (New York: Horace Thayer, 1853); Silverberg, 135–151.

Swallowed by a Great Fish

1. Blackbird, 77–78.

A Great Flood Threatens Mankind

1. Blackbird, 73–78.

Biological Warfare Against the Indians

1. Blackbird, 9–10.

Sweat Lodge

1. Dobson, 79–81; Tuttle, 12–13.

Attack on Baraga

1. McGee, 26.

2. Ibid., 44–45, 37.

3. Ibid., 64.

4. Ibid., 44–45, 58; McCoy, 460–461.

Intoxicated Firefighters

1. Belknap, 176–177.

Grandville Avenue Plowed by Domesticated Beast

1. Belknap, 23.

Chanties in Shantytown

1. Belknap, 134–135.

Steamboats

1. Belknap, 56–61.

Fortune Teller Meets Firefighters

1. Belknap, 177–178.

The First Garbage Collector

1. Belknap, 94–95.

Early Street Problems

1. Observations from graphic design work by Aaron Phipps.

2. Everett, 379.

3. Belknap, 96–97.

The Park on Fulton Street

1. Belknap, 149–156.

Oak Hill Cemetery – Neighbors from the Past

1. Research submitted to the Grand Rapids Council for the Humanities by Dr. Kenneth D. Bratt and Dr. Bert De Vries of Calvin College.

Heritage Hill's "St. Ann"

1. Portrait and Biography file on Anna Bissell in the Local History Department of the Grand Rapids Public Library.

2. Richard Harms, "Bissell House: Healing the Bloody Fifth," *Grand Rapids Magazine* (November 1993): 47.

Braille on Belknap

1. Portrait and Biography file on Roberta Griffiths in the Local History Department of the Grand Rapids Public Library.

Section I – Photo Credits

FIG. 1. Grand Rapids Public Library Local Historical Collection, hereafter referred to as GRPL, 54-20-19.

FIG. 2. GRPL, 54-20-19.

FIG. 3. GRPL, 54-20-19.

FIG. 4. GRPL, 54-20-19.

FIG. 5. Aaron Phipps.

FIG. 6. GRPL, 54-24-34.

FIG. 7. GRPL, 42-1-4.

FIG. 8. GRPL, 42-1-1.

FIG. 9. GRPL, 42-1-4.

FIG. 10. GRPL, 42-1-4.

FIG. 11. GRPL, 42-1-2.

FIG. 12. GRPL, 42-1-2.

FIG. 13. State Historical Society of Wisconsin.

FIG. 14. State Archives of Michigan.

FIG. 15. Courtesy of artist, William Kubiak.

FIG. 16. Courtesy of artist, William Kubiak.

FIG. 17. Courtesy of artist, William Kubiak.

FIG. 18. United States Bureau of Indian Affairs, *Famous Indians* (Washington: U.S. Government Printing Office, 1966), 11.

FIG. 19. Courtesy of artist, William Kubiak.

FIG. 20. Grand Rapids Public Museum, hereafter referred to as GRPM.

FIG. 21. United States Bureau of Indian Affairs, *Famous Indians* (Washington: U.S. Government Printing Office, 1966), 15.

FIG. 22. Courtesy of artist, William Kubiak.

FIG. 23. *The Grand Rapids Press* Archives, hereafter referred to as *GR Press*.

FIG. 24. Aaron Phipps.

FIG. 25. Aaron Phipps.

FIG. 26. Kansas State Historical Society Library. Topeka, KS.

FIG. 27. GRPL, 54-34-58.

FIG. 28. GRPL, 54-6-4.

FIG. 29. John W. McGee, *The Catholic Church in the Grand River Valley, 1833–1950* (Lansing, MI: Franklin Dekleine Company, 1950), 13.

FIG. 30. GRPL, 54-11-14.

FIG. 31. GRPL, 54-10-31.

FIG. 32. GRPL, 54-24-4.

FIG. 33. GRPL, 185-3-16.

FIG. 34. GRPL, 54-26-20.

FIG. 35. GRPL, 54-22-35.

FIG. 36. McGee, 54.

FIG. 37. State Archives of Michigan.

FIG. 38. GRPM.

FIG. 39. Everett, 57B.

FIG. 40. Baxter, 761.

FIG. 41. *GR Press.*

FIG. 42. GRPL, 54-30-50.

FIG. 43. GRPL, 54-6-4.

FIG. 44. GRPL, 18-1-7, photo #73.

FIG. 45. GRPL, 54-6-4.

FIG. 46. GRPL, 54-6-4.

FIG. 47. Everett, 66B.

FIG. 48. GRPL, 18-1-5, photo #46.

FIG. 49. GRPL, 91-1-5, photo #39.

FIG. 50. GRPL, 54-41-13.

FIG. 51. GRPL, 54-32-33.

FIG. 52. Grand Rapids Area Council for the Humanities.

FIG. 53. GRPL, 54-4-11.

FIG. 54. *GR Press.*

FIG. 55. *GR Press.*

FIG. 56. GRPL, 54-19-36.

FIG. 57. GRPL, 54-9-8.

FIG. 58. GRPL, 54-19-36.

FIG. 59. GRPL, 54-19-31.

FIG. 60. GRPL, 18-3-1, photo #215.

FIG. 61. Aaron Phipps.

FIG. 62. GRPL, 18-1-5, photo #48.

FIG. 63. *GR Press.*

FIG. 64. *GR Press.*

FIG. 65. GRPL, 59-1-4.

FIG. 66. GRPL, 54-44-10.

FIG. 67. GRPL, 18-1-4, photo #38.

FIG. 68. GRPL, 43-1-4.

FIG. 69. GRPL, 54-8-10.

FIG. 70. GRPL, 18-2-2, photo #122.

FIG. 71. GRPL, 18-1-8, photo #81.

FIG. 72. GRPL, 54-14-1.

FIG. 73. GRPL, 54-12-9.

FIG. 74. GRPL, 54-44-12.

FIG. 75. GRPL, 54-44-12.

FIG. 76. GRPL, 18-1-7, photo #78.

FIG. 77. GRPL, 54-22-56.

FIG. 78. Everrett, 19B.

FIG. 79. GRPL, 42-2-8.

FIG. 80. Aaron Phipps.

FIG. 81. GRPL, 54-44-19.

FIG. 82. GRPL, 18-1-6, photo #52.

FIG. 83. GRPL, 18-1-1, photo #8.

FIG. 84. GRPL, 18-1-7, photo #70.

FIG. 85. GRPL, 54-14-1.

FIG. 86. GRPL, 54-9-19.

FIG. 87. *GR Press.*

FIG. 88. GRPL, 43-1-6.

FIG. 89. GRPL, 18-1-5, photo #50.

FIG. 90. Aaron Phipps.

FIG. 91. *GR Press.*

FIG. 92. *GR Press.*

FIG. 93. *GR Press.*

FIG. 94. GRPL, 18-2-5, photo #179.

FIG. 95. Aaron Phipps.

FIG. 96. *GR Press.*

FIG. 97. *GR Press.*

FIG. 98. Bert de Vries.

FIG. 99. Bert de Vries.

FIG. 100. Ken Bratt.

FIG. 101. Ken Bratt.

FIG. 102. Ken Bratt.

FIG. 103. Ken Bratt.

FIG. 104. Ken Bratt.

FIG. 105. Bert de Vries.

FIG. 106. *GR Press.*

FIG. 107. Aaron Phipps.

FIG. 108. GRPL, Coll. 224.

FIG. 109. GRPL, 18-1-1, photo #7.

FIG. 110. GRPL, 18-3-2, photo #228.

FIG. 111. GRPL, 18-2-4, photo #169.

FIG. 112. GRPL, 54-2-3.

FIG. 113. GRPL, 54-2-3.

FIG. 114. GRPL, 54-2-3.

FIG. 115. Aaron Phipps.

FIG. 116. Aaron Phipps.

FIG. 117. GRPL, 54-41-15.

FIG. 118. GRPL, 18-3-5, photo #288.

FIG. 119. GRPL, 18-1-7, photo #75; 18-3-1, photo #222.

FIG. 120. GRPL, 18-3-5, photo #287.

FIG. 121. GRPL, 76-1-2.

FIG. 122. GRPL, 84-22-3.

FIG. 123. GRPL, 185-2-68.

FIG. 124. GRPL, 33-12-47.

FIG. 125. GRPL, 54-46-18.

FIG. 126. GRPL, 54-46-18.

FIG. 127. GRPL, 54-27-47.

FIG. 128. GRPL, 33-12-47.

FIG. 129. GRPL, 54-7-9.

FIG. 130. GRPL, 54-12-1.

FIG. 131. GRPL, 54-12-1.

FIG. 132. GRPL, 54-2-3.

FIG. 133. GRPL, 54-50-46.

FIG. 134. GRPL, 54-19-36.

FIG. 135. Grand Rapids City Archives.

Section II

Immigration Fuels Explosive Growth in City

1. *Origins* 13, no. 2 (1995): 21.
2. Bureau of the Census, *Population 1900* (Washington D.C.: U.S. Government Printing Office, 1900), 866.
3. Baxter, 192.

Ethnic Neighborhoods Form

4. Belknap, 44.
5. Baxter, 192.
6. Ibid.
7. David Vanderstel, "Dutch Immigrant Neighborhoods in the City of Grand Rapids 1848–1900," *Origins II*, no. 1 (1983): 22–26.
8. Ibid., 26; Baxter, 192.
9. Vanderstel, 22.
10. Ibid.
11. Baxter, 268–292.
12. Herbert J. Brinks, "Heartside Neighborhood, 1850–2000, 150 Years," (paper submitted to the Grand Rapids Area Council for the Humanities, 1999), 3.
13. *U.S. Census Bureau Decennial Population Statistics, Michigan Schedule, 1850–1900*, (Washington, D.C.: U.S. Government Printing Office).
14. Bratt and Meehan, 50, 232.
15. Brinks, 3.
16. Ibid., 4.
17. Vanderstel, 23–25.
18. Ibid.
19. Ibid.
20. Ibid.
21. *Origins* 13, no. 2 (1995): 31–32.
22. Richard Holm, "How to Kill a Neighborhood," *Grand Rapids Magazine* 19 (August 1982): 42.
23. Vanderstel, 25.
24. Ibid.

25. Ibid., 24.
26. *Origins* 13, no. 2 (1995): 22.
27. Baxter, 191–192.
28. *Central City Historical Survey*, 66–75.
29. Belknap, 81.
30. Dr. Wilhelm W. Seeger, interview by Andy Schrier, Grand Rapids Public Library, 5 December 1999.
31. Seeger, interview; Jim Christiansen, interview by Andy Schrier, Sentinel Pointe, 12 July 1999.
32. *Central City Historic Survey*, 70.
33. Baxter, 204.
34. Ibid., 258.
35. Dr. Wilhelm W. Seeger, "The German Americans in Grand Rapids, Michigan: An Historical Survey," (paper for the 10th Annual Symposium Society for German-American Studies, Cincinnati, OH, April 1986), 6.
36. Ibid.
37. *Central City Historic Survey*, 70.
38. Mateusz Siuchninski, *An Illustrated History of Poland* [trans. by Stanislaw Tarnowski] (Warsaw: Interpress, 1979), 174.
39. Edna K. Wooley, "Mme. Lipczynski," *Grand Rapids Evening Post*, 17 June 1905.
40. Eduard Adam Skendzel, "The Polanders," *Grand River Valley Review* (Spring-Summer 1983): 4–6.
41. Ibid.
42. Holm, 41, 44.
43. Ibid., 42.
44. *Central City Historic Survey*, 71.
45. Ibid., 72.
46. Skendzel.
47. Edward Gillis, *Growing Up Lithuanian in Lithuanian Town* (Grand Rapids: Grand Rapids Historical Commission, 2000), 21.
48. Ibid., 105–106.
49. Ibid., 20–21.
50. Ibid., 21.
51. Ibid.

52. Scott Noto, "Escaping 'La Miseria:' The Story of Grand Rapids' First Italian Residents," *Grand River Valley History* 16 (1999): 12–17.
53. Ibid.
54. Ibid.
55. McGee, 255.
56. Ibid., 255.
57. Ibid., 255.
58. *Central City Historic Survey*, 71.
59. McGee, 431–434.
60. Ibid., 431.
61. *Central City Historic Survey*, 71.
62. Paul Chardoul, ed., *Grand Rapids Greek Heritage* (Grand Rapids: Hellenic Horizons, 1986), 2.
63. Ibid., 1.
64. *Polk's City Street Directory*, Grand Rapids, 1926.
65. Chardoul, 7.
66. Ibid., 4.
67. Ibid., 9.
68. Ibid., 14.
69. Ibid., 18.
70. Randal Jelks, "Livin' For the City: African Americans in Urban Historical Perspective," (Ph.D. diss., Michigan State University, 1999), 151–152.
71. *Central City Historic Survey*, 85.
72. Ibid.
73. Jelks, 175–176.
74. Ibid., 73–74.
75. S. Henri Browne, "The Negro in Grand Rapids," manuscript, 6 April 1913, as quoted in Jelks, 109.
76. Jelks, 152.
77. Ibid.
78. Ibid., 156.
79. Ibid., 167.
80. Bratt and Meehan, 146–151.
81. Various Ahavas Israel yearbooks submitted by Ben Kleiman.
82. "Gifts for Bride Carried in Procession by the Assyrians," *Grand Rapids Press*, 11 February 1905.

83. Lydens, 557.

84. Ibid., 557–558.

85. "Christians in the City Fear the Mohammedans," *Grand Rapids Press*, 2 August 1913.

86. "More Shacks Must Go," *Grand Rapids Press*, 5 November 1908.

87. Lydens, 557.

88. "Syrians to Retaliate," *Grand Rapids Press*, 17 November 1908.

89. "Closing on Sunday," *Grand Rapids Press*, 18 November 1908.

90. "Syrians Organize to Promote Americanism," *Grand Rapids Press*, 22 June 1927.

91. "Hamlet to Voice His Soliloquy In Arabic Language," *Grand Rapids Press*, 18 June 1927.

Section II – Vignette Notes

U.S. "Open Door" Immigration Policy

1. Stephan Thernstrom, ed., *Harvard Encyclopedia of American Ethnic Groups* (Cambridge, MA: Belknap Press of Harvard University, 1980), 476.

Women of Consequence

1. Jo Ellyn Clarey, "A Woman of Letters," *Grand River Valley History* 12 (1995): 19–22.

2. Biography File on Minnie Sheldon Hodges in the Local History Department of the Grand Rapids Public Library.

Frans Van Driele and His Arrival

1. Henry S. Lucas, ed., *Dutch Immigrant Memoirs and Related Writings* (Assen, Netherlands: Van Gorcum, 1955), 336.

Piggeries in Grand Rapids

1. Richard Harms, "Grand Rapids and its Piggeries," *Grand Rapids Magazine* (August 1996): 45; Lydens, 201.

The Immigrant Experience

1. Oscar Handlin, *The Uprooted* (Boston: Little, Brown, 1973), 8,9.

A Snapshot of Dutch Life, 1892

1. Hank Meijer, "Vandenberg Manuscript," (publication forthcoming).

John Ter Braak: The Wooden Shoe Man

1. "The Wooden Shoes," *Grand Rapids Evening Press*, 4 November 1893.

Rebelling against Dutch Life, 1913

1. David DeJong, *With A Dutch Accent* (New York: Harper & Brothers, 1944), 260–261.

A Chosen Isolation

1. Henry Ipple, "The Brickyard, A Dutch Neighborhood in Grand Rapids," *Origins XII*, no. 1 (1994): 2–8.

The Schnitz

1. Karl Siebert, interview by Andy Schrier, The Schnitzelbank, Grand Rapids, 18 November 1999.

Positive Effects of Beer

1. Baxter, 203.

Queen of the Poles

1. "Poland to Confer Coveted Emblem on Woman Patriot in Ceremony Here Tonight," *Grand Rapids Herald*, 25 August 1927.

2. Eduard Adam Skendzel, "Mme. Lipczynski – Queen of the Poles," *Grand River Valley History* 10, no. 2 (Spring 1992) McGee, 235.

St. Isidore's Neighborhood – The Brickyard

1. Skendzel, "The Polanders," 3.

The Widdicomb Factory Family

1. Christian G. Carron, *Grand Rapids Furniture: The Story of America's Furniture City* (Traverse City, MI: Village Press, 1998), 54.

So How Big Was Furniture in Grand Rapids?

1. Kleiman, 107–109.

2. Ibid., 108–111.

3. Ibid., 66–69.

4. Olson, *Sampler*, 95–102.

5. Kleiman, 41–53.

6. Ibid., 83–87, 113, 116.

7. Ibid., 22–28, 55, 68, 164, 183; *Polk's City Street Directory*, Grand Rapids, 1912.

8. Kleiman, 36–37, 41, 45, 115, 167.

9. Ibid., 106.

10. Ibid., 97.

11. Ibid., 112, 125–128.

12. Ibid., 136–138, 164.

13. Ibid., 148–149, 152–153.

14. Ibid., 160.

15. Ibid., 161–164.

Polish Name Changes

1. Edward Symanski, "Polish Settlers in Grand Rapids, MI," *Polish American Studies* 21 (1964): 91–106.

Snake Tonic Memories in Lithuania Town

1. Gillis, 70–71.

The West Side Ladies Literary Club

1. West Side Ladies Literary Club Scrapbook

Hattie Beverly

1. Biography File on Hattie Beverly in the Local History Department of the Grand Rapids Public Library.

Julius Houseman

1. Baxter, 682.

2. "Death of Julius Houseman," *Grand Rapids Evening Leader*, 9 February 1891.

A Jewish Childhood in Grand Rapids

1. Max Apple, *Roommates* (New York: Warner Books, 1994), 10.

Immigration Restrictions

1. Warren C. Vander Hill, *Settling the Great Lakes Frontier: Immigration to Michigan, 1837–1924* (Lansing, MI: Michigan Historical Commission, 1970), 82.
2. David Bender, *Immigration Policy* (San Diego, CA: Greenhaven Press, 1995), 13.
3. Ibid.

Section II – Photo Credits

FIG. 1. GRPL, Coll. 291, photo #130.
FIG. 2. GRPL, Pheonix Furniture Co. Catalog Collection.
FIG. 3. GRPL, Berkey and Gay Furniture Co. Catalog Collection.
FIG. 4. GRPL, 54–42–5.
FIG. 5. Everett, 547.
FIG. 6. GRPL, 66–1–1.
FIG. 7. GRPL, 54–34–13.
FIG. 8. Everett, 73B.
FIG. 9. GRPL, 54–45–2.
FIG. 10. GRPL, 185–2–59.
FIG. 11. GRPL, Coll. 277.
FIG. 12. Archives, Calvin College.
FIG. 13. Archives, Calvin College.
FIG. 14. GRPL, 54–44–23.
FIG. 15. Archives, Calvin College.
FIG. 16. GRPL, 54–5–31.
FIG. 17. Archives, Calvin College.
FIG. 18. Archives, Calvin College.
FIG. 19. GRPL, 54–48–17.
FIG. 20. GRPL, 141–10–18.
FIG. 21. GRPL, 54–4–31.
FIG. 22. Archives, Calvin College.
FIG. 23. GRPL, Coll. 291, photo #175.
FIG. 24. Archives, Calvin College.
FIG. 25. Courtesy of M.Christine Byron and Thomas R. Wilson.
FIG. 26. GRPL, 78–3–67.
FIG. 27. GRPL, 78–3–67.

FIG. 28. GRPL, 54–10–8.
FIG. 29. GRPL, 54–9–18.
FIG. 30. GRPL, 54–13–16.
FIG. 31. GRPL, 54–10–20.
FIG. 32. GRPL, 147–1–14.
FIG. 33. GRPL, 18–1–4, photo #34.
FIG. 34. GRPL, 54–17–11.
FIG. 35. GRPL, 54–17–11.
FIG. 36. GRPL, 33–10–16.
FIG. 37. GRPL, 54–12–1.
FIG. 38. GRPL, 54–17–11.
FIG. 39. GRPL, 54–19–28.
FIG. 40. GRPL, 18–1–2, photo #12.
FIG. 41. Courtesy of M. Christine Byron and Thomas R. Wilson.
FIG. 42. Grand Rapids City Archives.
FIG. 43. GRPL, 54–17–7.
FIG. 44. GRPL, 54–17–7.
FIG. 45. GRPL, 78–3–44.
FIG. 46. GRPL, 54–17–7.
FIG. 47. Photo by James Budzynski, published in Skendzel, "The Polanders."
FIG. 48. Philip Jung, *The First 100 Years, Basilica of St. Adalbert, 1881–1981* (Grand Rapids, 1981), 21.
FIG. 49. GRPL, Coll. 234, Emily Latzek Jennings Family Photograph Collection.
FIG. 50. GRPL, 43–1–3.
FIG. 51. GRPL, Coll. 125.
FIG. 52. GRPL, 43–2–2.
FIG. 53. GRPL, 54–48–2.
FIG. 54. GRPL, 54–48–2.
FIG. 55. GRPL, 54–41–14.
FIG. 56. GRPL, 54–26–11.
FIG. 57. GRPL, *The Tragic Fall of the First Baptist Church* (Grand Rapids: Baptist Testimony Publishers, Inc., 1956), 23
FIG. 58. GRPL, 43–2–2.
FIG. 59. GRPL, 43–2–1.
FIG. 60. GRPL, Coll. 291, photo #69.

FIG. 61. GRPL, Coll. 291, photo #78.
FIG. 62. GRPL, Coll. 291, photo #156.
FIG. 63. Grand Rapids City Archives.
FIG. 64. GRPL, Coll. 291, photo #125.
FIG. 65. GRPL, Coll. 291, photo #103.
FIG. 66. GRPL, Coll. 291, photo #192.
FIG. 67. GRPL, Coll. 291, photo #21.
FIG. 68. Archives of the Diocese of Grand Rapids.
FIG. 69. Courtesy of the DiTrapani family.
FIG. 70. GRPL, 54–13–20.
FIG. 71. GRPL, 43–2–2.
FIG. 72. GRPL, 43–1–3
FIG. 73. *St. Alphonsus Church 1888–1988* (Grand Rapids: 1988), 5.
FIG. 74. GRPL, 54–43–11.
FIG. 75. Bethlehem Lutheran Church.
FIG. 76. GRPL, Coll. 277.
FIG. 77. GRPL, Coll. 277.
FIG. 78. GRPL, Coll. 277.
FIG. 79. GRPL, Coll. 277.
FIG. 80. GRPL, Coll. 277.
FIG. 81. GRPL, 113–3–3.
FIG. 82. GRPL, 113–3–26.
FIG. 83. GRPL, 113–3–32.
FIG. 84. GRPL, 113–3–40.
FIG. 85. GRPL, Coll. 125.
FIG. 86. GRPL, 113–3–14.
FIG. 87. GRPL, 113–3–38.
FIG. 88. GRPL, 113–3–38.
FIG. 89. GRPL, 113–3–7.
FIG. 90. GRPL, 113–3–20.
FIG. 91. *GR Press*
FIG. 92. Dedication: Congregation Ahavas Israel (Grand Rapids: 1971), 11.
FIG. 93. GRPL, 54–28–60.
FIG. 94. Photo by K. Krueger Jones, published in Max Apple, *I Love Gootie: My Grandmother's Story* (New York: Warner Books, 1998).
FIG. 95. GRPL, 43–1–3.

FIG. 96. GRPL, Coll. 291, photo #183.

FIG. 97. GRPL, Susanna Wieland Collection, (unprocessed).

FIG. 98. GRPL, Susanna Wieland Collection, (unprocessed).

FIG. 99. GRPL, Susanna Wieland Collection, (unprocessed).

FIG. 100. GRPL, 185-3-59.

FIG. 101. Grand Rapids Area Council for the Humanities.

FIG. 102. Courtesy of Randal Jelks.

Section III

Streetcars Launch Era of Opportunity

1. Lydens, 123.
2. Lewis Gordon Stuart, "History of the Grand Rapids Street Railway Down to Purchase by the Commonwealth Power Company in 1910," (paper presented as a gift to the Local History Department of the Grand Rapids Public Library, 23 December 1926), 9.
3. "Desperate Violence," *Grand Rapids Telegram-Herald*, 20 May 1891; "Refused to Arbitrate: The Street Car Company Will not Yield a Point," *Grand Rapids Telegram-Herald*, 20 May 1891.
4. "Bullet and Bludgeon: A Dastardly Dynamite Plot Foiled by the Police," *Grand Rapids Telegram-Herald*, 11 June 1891.
5. "They Were Entrapped," *Grand Rapids Telegram-Herald*, 12 June 1891; "Got Them on the List," *Grand Rapids Telegram-Herald*, 13 June 1891; "Bought the Dynamite: Important Confessions by Two of the Rioters," *Grand Rapids Telegram-Herald*, 14 June 1891.
6. Gordon L. Olson, interview by Michelle Gunderson and Andy Schrier, Grand Rapids Public Library, 23 February 2000.
7. Stuart, 1.
8. Ibid.
9. Ibid., 2.
10. Ibid.
11. Ibid., 4.
12. Lynn G. Mapes, "The Streetcar Era," *Grand Rapids Magazine* (March 1975): 48.
13. Stuart, 10; Stephen R. Ford, "A History of North Park," (unpublished paper submitted to the Grand Rapids Area Council for the Humanities, 1999).
14. Stuart, 8-9.
15. Mapes, 47; Stuart, 11.
16. *Insurance Maps of Grand Rapids, Michigan* (New York: Sanborn Map Company, 1912); City of Grand Rapids Annexation Map.
17. Gerald Elliott, *Grand Rapids, Renaissance on the Grand* (Tulsa, OK: Continental Heritage Press, 1982), 82.
18. Stuart, 11.
19. Ibid.
20. *Trolley Topics* (published by the Grand Rapids Railway Company, 5 August 1905 – October 1926).
21. *The White Printing Company's Street and Railway Service Directory of Grand Rapids, Michigan* (Grand Rapids: White Printing Co., 1912); Ford; Grand Rapids Railway Company Records, Collection in the Local History Department of the Grand Rapids Public Library, 1908-1950.
22. *Insurance Maps of Grand Rapids.*
23. *Trolley Topics.*
24. Mapes, 51.
25. *Trolley Topics.*
26. Lydens, 137-138.
27. *Trolley Topics.*
28. Portrait and Biography File on Louis J. De Lamarter in the Local History Department of the Grand Rapids Public Library.
29. Ibid.
30. "City Sees Passing of Trolley Cars," *Grand Rapids Press*, 26 August 1935.

Autos Push the Boundaries

31. Lydens, 139.
32. City of Grand Rapids Annexation Map.
33. Richard DeVos, telephone interview by Linda Samuelson and Andy Schrier, Grand Rapids, 29 March 2000.
34. Morrow, interview.
35. Olson, *Sampler*, 155-157.
36. *Central City Historic Survey*, 92; Richard Kurzhals, "The Community on the Bluff: The Belknap-Lookout Neighborhood," *Grand River Valley Review* 5, no. 1. (Winter 1984): 14-15.
37. "The Story of Alger Heights," *Grand Rapids Herald*, 5 March 1950.
38. Kurzhals, 7, 20; Olson, *Sampler*, 181.
39. Gordon L. Olson, *Grand Rapids, A City Renewed* (Grand Rapids: Grand Rapids Historical Commission, 1996), 17.
40. Ibid., 8.
41. Ibid., 17.
42. Charles Press, "When One-Third of a City Moves to the Suburbs," (East Lansing, MI: Institute for Community Development and Services, 1959): 2.
43. Bratt and Meehan, 158.
44. Olson, *City Renewed*, 18.
45. Gordon L. Olson, interview by Nate Bradford, Grand Rapids Public Library, 27 December 1999.
46. Olson, *City Renewed*, 34.
47. Olson, Bradford interview.
48. Olson, *City Renewed*, 34.
49. Jack Smalligan, "Suburban Growth in Grand Rapids," (paper presented to Calvin College History Department, Grand Rapids, 1981), 6.
50. Olson, *City Renewed*, 34-35.
51. Elliott, 144.

52. Theodore Rottman, *Metropolitan Community Subsystems as Reference Groups in a Suburban Annexation Ballot Decision* (Ann Arbor, MI: University Microfilms, 1965), 245, as quoted in Smalligan, Table 4 of the Appendix.

53. Olson, *City Renewed*, 36.

54. Olson, *Sampler*, 179.

55. Olson, *City Renewed*, 28.

56. Ibid.

57. Olson, *Sampler*, 187.

58. Ibid., 189.

59. Russell Lynes, "'The Treatment' in Grand Rapids," *Harper's Magazine* (January 1962): 22.

60. Olson, *City Renewed*, 42.

61. Ibid., 43.

62. Ibid., 47.

63. Holm, 41–47.

64. Olson, *City Renewed*, 30.

65. Ibid., 18–21.

66. Ibid., 23.

67. Olson, *Sampler*, 186.

68. Elliott, 146.

69. Olson, *City Renewed*, 41–42.

70. Ibid., 43.

Section III – Vignette Notes

Creston

1. Kleiman.

2. Richard Harms, "The Bissell House," 47.

3. Adrian Koene, "Unique and Complete," (paper presented to Calvin College History Department, Grand Rapids).

4. Ibid.

5. *Insurance Maps of Grand Rapids.*

6. "The Creston Grove Neighborhood," *Creston Grove Home Ownership Seminar*, (Grand Rapids: Creston Neighborhood Association, 1998), 22–23.

7. "Given Hard Raps, at Creston Banquet," *Grand Rapids Press*, 14 December 1906.

8. Ibid.

9. Ralph Koll, "Memories: Sy's Story," (unpublished, 1994); *Insurance Maps of Grand Rapids.*

10. Wilma Ingham, Emma Jean Forsetlund-Clawson, Bob Taylor, and Dorine Powell, group interview by Andy Schrier, Leisure Village, Belmont, MI, 3 February 2000.

11. Jim Koelzer, interview by Andy Schrier, Kay Pharmacy, Grand Rapids, 24 January 2000.

North Park

1. Stephen R. Ford, "A History of North Park" (unpublished paper submitted to the Grand Rapids Area Council for the Humanities, 1999).

Eastown

1. *Central City Historic Survey*, 60.

2. Ibid., 125.

3. William L. Bennett, *Memories of East Grand Rapids 1834–1982* (East Grand Rapids: William Bennett 1983), 3–4.

4. *Central City Historic Survey*, 125.

5. Linda Easley, Thomas Edison, and Michael Williams, *Eastown: A report on how Aquinas College helped its local community reverse neighborhood transition and deterioration* (Battle Creek, MI: The W.K. Kellogg Foundation, 1978), 7.

Can You Find the Golden Egg?

1. *Trolley Topics* 3 (5 May, 1906 – 8 September 1906).

The Loss of Neighborhood Grocery Stores

1. *Origins* 8, no. 1 (1990): 46–49.

Burton Heights

1. Margo Lopez, "Burton Heights," (unpublished paper presented to the Burton Heights Business Association, 1994), 25.

2. Ibid., 6, 7, 10.

3. Ibid., 30.

4. Ibid., 27–29.

West Side

1. *Central City Historic Survey*, 74.

2. Ibid., 78.

Mother and Daughter Keep Women Forever Young

1. Richard Harms, "Forever Young," *Grand Rapids Magazine* (March 1997): 17.

Ottawa Hills

1. "Would Have City Take Golf Links," *Grand Rapids Press*, 2 October 1915; "Old Golf Links Being Platted," *Grand Rapids Press*, 9 September 1922.

2. J. H. Weller, "History of Ottawa Hills," (Ottawa Hills Neighborhood Association Video Script, 1998.)

3. Weller.

4. Weller.

Fulton Heights

1. DeVos, interview.

2. Ibid.

3. Research by Grand Valley State University student and Fulton Heights resident Mark Wiggert.

4. DeVos, interview.

Stanley Davis and the Polish West Side

1. Stanley Davis, interview by Charles Honey, Grand Rapids, 1998.

Alger Heights

1. "The Story of Alger Heights," *Grand Rapids Herald*, 5 March 1950.

Section III – Photo Credits

FIG. 1.   *GR Press.*

FIG. 2.   GRPL, 76-2-59.

FIG. 3.   GRPL, 54-43-2.

FIG. 4.   GRPL, 33-12-45.

FIG. 5.   Baxter, 418.

FIG. 6.   GRPL, Coll. 125 - H016279.

FIG. 7.   GRPL, 43-1-1.

FIG. 8.   GRPL, 54-17-1.

FIG. 9. GRPL, 33–11–2.

FIG. 10. GRPL, 54–16–9.

FIG. 11. GRPL, 76–2–61.

FIG. 12. GRPL, 46–21c-29.

FIG. 13. GRPL, 18–1–5.

FIG. 14. GRPL, 18–2–6.

FIG. 15. GRPL, 18–1–5.

FIG. 16. GRPL, 54–23–25.

FIG. 17. GRPL, 54–32–4.

FIG. 18. GRPL, 54–34–20.

FIG. 19. GRPL, 54–54–1.

FIG. 20. GRPL, 43–1–4.

FIG. 21. GRPL, 54–20–16.

FIG. 22. GRPL, 43–2–3.

FIG. 23. GRPL, 54–20–16.

FIG. 24. GRPL, 54–20–16.

FIG. 25. GRPL, Coll. 35.

FIG. 26. GRPL, Coll. 35.

FIG. 27. GRPL, Coll. 35.

FIG. 28. GRPL, 54–44–21.

FIG. 29. GRPL, 54–42–17.

FIG. 30. GRPL, 99–1–3.

FIG. 31. GRPL, 46–21c-45.

FIG. 32. GRPL, 54–50–45.

FIG. 33. GRPL, Coll. 125 – E2045.

FIG. 34. GRPL, 54–42–10.

FIG. 35. GRPL, 54–42–10.

FIG. 36. GRPL, 43–2–1.

FIG. 37. GRPL, 43–1–7.

FIG. 38. GRPL, 43–2–3.

FIG. 39. GRPL, 43–2–3.

FIG. 40. GRPL, 46–22B-6.

FIG. 41. GRPL, 67–1–1.

FIG. 42. GRPL, Coll. 125 - 02476s.

FIG. 43. GRPL, 57–27–16.

FIG. 44. GRPL, Coll. 125 – H008618A.

FIG. 45. GRPL, 43–2–3.

FIG. 46. GRPL, 43–2–3.

FIG. 47. GRPL, 67–1–3.

FIG. 48. GRPL, 67–2–10.

FIG. 49. GRPL, 67–2–9.

FIG. 50. GRPL, 43–2–1.

FIG. 51. GRPL, 67–2–1.

FIG. 52. GRPL, 54–5–28.

FIG. 53. GRPL, 54–45–23.

FIG. 54. GRPL, 33–10–21.

FIG. 55. GRPL, 66–1–4.

FIG. 56. GRPL, Coll. 125 – H008678A.

FIG. 57. GRPL, Coll. 264.

FIG. 58. GRPL, 252–2.

FIG. 59. GRPL, 78–3–30.

FIG. 60. GRPL, 252–2.

FIG. 61. GRPL, Coll. 125 –H008651A.

FIG. 62. Courtesy of the City of Grand Rapids.

FIG. 63. GRPL, 54–46–16.

FIG. 64. Courtesy of Richard DeVos.

FIG. 65. Grand Rapids Area Council for the Humanities.

FIG. 66. GRPL, 138–5–37.

FIG. 67. GRPL, Coll.125 – H006536B.

FIG. 68. Courtesy of Albert Dilley.

FIG. 69. GRPL, Coll. 125 – H00199C.

FIG. 70. GRPL, 46–22b-1.

FIG. 71. Courtesy of Robert and Bernice Lalley.

FIG. 72. GRPL, 54–12–2.

FIG. 73. GRPL, 54–12–2.

FIG. 74. GRPL, 54–12–2.

FIG. 75. *GR Press.*

FIG. 76. GRPL, 118–3–16.

FIG. 77. GRPL, 118–3–30.

FIG. 78. GRPL, 118–3–29.

FIG. 79. City of Grand Rapids Parks and Recreation Department.

FIG. 80. Courtesy of Frey Foundation and John Berry.

FIG. 81. GRPL, 54–10–25.

FIG. 82. GRPL, 54–10–25.

FIG. 83. GRPL, 54–10–25.

FIG. 84. GRPL, 54–10–25.

FIG. 85. GRPL, 46–18B-53.

FIG. 86. GRPL, 185–3–60.

FIG. 87. GRPL, 78–4–41.

FIG. 88. GRPL, 138–6–19.

FIG. 89. GRPL, 138–6–19.

Postcard Section

Courtesy of M. Christine Byron and Thomas R. Wilson.

Section IV

Idealism and Strife of the Sixties and Seventies

1. Michael Harrington, *The Other America* (New York: Macmillan, 1962).

2. Ibid.

3. Karl E. and Alma F. Tauber, *Negroes in Cities: Residential Segregation and Neighborhood Change* (Chicago: Aldine Publishing, 1965), 32–33.

4. Whitney Young Jr., "Author Says Segregation in GR Tops that of Detroit," *Grand Rapids Press*, 19 October 1965.

5. "Report to the City Commission," (The City's Study Committee on Human Relations, 1954), 7.

6. "A Study of Housing in Selected Areas of Grand Rapids," (Grand Rapids Urban League, 1952).

7. Lee Weber, interview by Nate Bradford, Grand Rapids, 12 August 1999; Carol Townsend, interview by Nate Bradford, Grand Rapids, 14 July 1999.

8. "Report to the City Commission," 13.

9. "Crisis in Black and White," *Grand Rapids Press*, 31 August 1969; Robert Alt, "Negro Housing: A Giant Problem for GR," *Grand Rapids Press*, 10 September 1967.

10. "South's Racial Problem Hits Grand Rapids, Says Phillips," *Grand Rapids Press*, 27 September 1967.

11. Robert Alt, "Whites Pressure House-Hunting Negroes to Stay in the Ghetto," *Grand Rapids Press*, 12 September 1967.

12. Jelks, 153.

13. "Anti-Bias Unit Forms," *Grand Rapids Press*, 6 June 1955; "Lauds Local Concord," *Grand Rapids Press*, 17 November 1955; Olson, *City Renewed*, 48.

14. "Cities Race Prejudice," *Grand Rapids Press*, 15 September 1958; "Seven Clergymen Here Allege Discrimination in Housing," *Grand Rapids Press*, 23 January 1962; "Open Housing Here? It's Just a Bad Joke," *Grand Rapids Press*, 1 October 1967.

15. Robert Alt, "Riot Cause Inquiry Concludes in Frustration," *Grand Rapids Press*, 7 September 1967.

16. Olson, *Sampler*, 191.

17. "State of Emergency Declared in City," *Grand Rapids Press*, 28 July 1968.

18. "City Rioting Brought Under Control," *Grand Rapids Press*, 26 July 1967.

19. Olson, *City Renewed*, 52.

20. Ibid.

21. "City Declares Emergency, Imposes Curfew After Gangs Threaten Riot," *Grand Rapids Press*, 25 July 1967.

22. "Nonviolent Black Power Backed Here," *Grand Rapids Press*, 8 August 1968.

23. Robert Alt, "Grand Rapids Awakes to Inner City Ills, but Slowly," *Grand Rapids Press*, 6 May 1968.

24. Robert Alt, "A Third of GR Churches Shun Open Housing, Sociologist Says," *Grand Rapids Press*, 16 September 1967; Floyd Allbaugh, "Open Housing Code Pushed," *Grand Rapids Press*, 25 October 1967.

25. Floyd Allbaugh, "City Hailed for Adopting Fair Housing Code," *Grand Rapids Press*, 3 January 1968.

26. Weller.

27. Tom Limmer, "City Groups Played Major Role in New Law on Redlining," *Grand Rapids Press*, 8 November 1977.

28. Report by the Committee of 100 for 100 Days of Progress, 1968.

29. Joseph Zainea, interview by Nate Bradford, Grand Rapids, 23 July 1999.

30. Mike Lloyd, "City's Finance Move Opens Way for Model Cities Project," *Grand Rapids Press*, 30 September 1969.

31. Ibid.

32. Zainea, interview.

33. Brian Malone, "Model Neighborhood Group Meets Contract Deadline," *Grand Rapids Press*, 30 March 1974.

34. Victor Vasquez and Connie Bohatch, interview by Nate Bradford, Grand Rapids, 2 July 1999.

35. Ibid.

36. Ibid.

37. Ibid.

38. John Peterson, interview by Andy Schrier, Grand Rapids Public Library, 9 December 1999.

39. Anita Post, "The History of The Neighborhood Alliance of Grand Rapids, Inc. and The Council of Neighborhood Associations," (paper presented to Calvin College History Department, Grand Rapids, 1979), 12.

40. Vasquez and Bohatch, interview.

41. Mark Stoddard, interview by Andy Schrier, Grand Rapids City Attorney's Office, 15 February 2000.

Neighborhood Profiles

42. Frederick Buechner, *The Sacred Journey* (San Francisco: Harper & Row, 1982).

43. Marian Hall, interview by Andy Schrier, Grand Rapids, 11 February 2000.

44. Al Royce, "Citizen Group Battles to Keep an Old Section Desirable," *Grand Rapids Press*, 26 December 1965.

45. Steve Ladd, interview by Andy Schrier, Grand Rapids, 11 February 2000.

46. Frank Lynn, interview by Andy Schrier, Grand Rapids, 21 January 2000.

47. Ibid.

48. Corinne Carey, telephone interview by Andy Schrier, Grand Rapids, 31 March 2000.

49. Lynn, interview; Belknap Lookout Vertical File in the Local History Department of the Grand Rapids Public Library.

50. Lynn, interview.

51. Ibid.

52. Ibid.; Steve and Carol Faas, interview by Andy Schrier, Clancy Street Ministries, Grand Rapids, 1 February 2000.

53. Faas, interview; Officer Kelly Bowers, interview by Andy Schrier, Grand Rapids Police Dept., 8 February 2000.

54. Dorothy Munson, interview by Andy Schrier, Spectrum Health, Grand Rapids, 2 February 2000.

55. Ibid.

56. Lynn, interview.

57. Bowers, interview.

58. Munson, interview; Lynn, interview; Faas, interview.

59. Munson, interview.

60. Ibid.

61. Jennifer Harrison, interview by Andy Schrier, Belknap Commons, Grand Rapids, 9 February 2000.

62. Munson, interview; Faas, interview; Harrison, interview; Ed Ohman, telephone interview by Andy Schrier, Grand Rapids, 7 February 2000.

63. Ken and Lois Blake, interview by Andy Schrier, His Place, Grand Rapids, 24 February 2000.

64. Faas, interview.

65. Bowers, interview.

66. Ladd, interview.

67. Ibid.; Bowers, interview.

68. Ladd, interview.

69. Ibid.

70. Ibid.; Bowers, interview; Faas, interview.

71. Blake, interview.

72. Ibid.; Ladd, interview; Lynn, interview.

73. Blake, interview.

74. Ohman, interview.

75. Hall, interview.

76. Pat Shellenbarger, "Permanent Fixtures," *Grand Rapids Press*, 14 May 1998.

77. Linda DeJong, "Heritage Hill," *Heritage Herald* (January/February 1998): 8.

78. Tom Truesdale, "The Early Years," *Heritage Herald* (March/April 1998): 8.

79. Mayor John Logie, interview by Andy Schrier, Old Kent Building, Grand Rapids, 6 December 1999.

80. Shellenbarger, "Permanent Fixtures."

81. DeJong, "Heritage Hill," 8.

82. Truesdale, "The Early Years," 9.

83. Ibid.

84. Shellenbarger, "Permanent Fixtures."

85. Truesdale, "The Early Years," 10.

86. Logie, interview.

87. Shellenbarger, "Permanent Fixtures."

88. Truesdale, "The Early Years," 10.

89. Shellenbarger, "Permanent Fixtures."

90. Jack Hoppus, interview by Andy Schrier, Grand Rapids, 14 December 1999.

91. Ed Golder, "Top of the Hill," *Grand Rapids Press*, 25 January 1998.

92. Ibid.

93. Logie, interview.

94. Golder, "Top of the Hill."

95. Chuck Assenco, interview by Andy Schrier, Grand Rapids, 15 December 1999; Callie Simmons, interview by Andy Schrier, Grand Rapids, 25 January 2000.

96. Barb Lester, "Drug Watch: How to Close the Drug House Down the Block," (pamphlet produced by the Heritage Hill Association), 4.

97. Assenco, interview.

98. Lydens, 508–510.

99. Lisa Johnson, "Rezoning for Part of Wealthy Street Pleases Neighborhood Groups," *Grand Rapids Press*, 28 January 1987; Carol Moore, interview by Nate Bradford and Andy Schrier, Wealthy Street Theatre, Grand Rapids, 6 January 2000.

100. Carl and Ruth Kelly, interview by Nate Bradford and Andy Schrier, Grand Rapids, 24 January 2000.

101. Herschell Turner, interview by Andy Schrier, Grand Rapids, 29 February 2000.

102. Ibid.; Paul Chaffee, "Job Done, 'Nice Guy' Turner is Moving On," *Grand Rapids Press*, 15 January 1977.

103. Miguel Navarro, interview by Andy Schrier, El Matador Tortilla Factory, Grand Rapids, 15 December 1999.

104. "A Special Bond," *Grand Rapids Press*, 28 July 1986; George P. Graff, *The People of Michigan* (Grand Rapids: Michigan Dept. of Education, 1974), 119.

105. James Van Brunt Sr., interview by Andy Schrier, Grand Rapids, 22 November 1999.

106. "We are a Mosaic," *Grand Rapids Press*, 27 July 1986.

107. Virginia Moralez, R.N., interview by Andy Schrier, Clinica Santa Maria, Grand Rapids, 10 January 2000.

108. June Whitehead, interview by Andy Schrier, Hall Elementary School, Grand Rapids, 12 January 2000; Mary Angelo, interview by Andy Schrier, Grand Rapids, 4 April 2000; Moralez, interview.

109. Moralez, interview.

110. Ibid.

111. Sr. Joan Pichette, interview by Andy Schrier, Grandville Avenue Library, Grand Rapids, 26 January 2000.

112. Ibid.

113. Angelo, interview.

114. Ibid.

115. Ibid.

116. Ibid.

117. Mayda Bahamonde-Gunnel and Debora Romero-Utley, interview by Andy Schrier, Franklin Elementary School, Grand Rapids, 1 February 2000.

118. Easley et al., 8.

119. Susan Posternack, "Street Fight," *The Paper*, 10–16 June 1999.

120. Easley et al., 8.

121. George Harper, interview by Nate Bradford, Grand Rapids, 10 January 2000.

122. Irene Wiersma, interview by Nate Bradford, Grand Rapids, 18 January 2000.

123. Ibid.

124. Dan West, interview by Nate Bradford, Grand Rapids, 13 January 2000.

125. Donna Hasleiet, "Bill Blickley and the Neighbors in a 'beautiful working thing,'" *Grand Rapids Press*, 4 July 1971.

126. William and LaVerne Blickley, interview by Nate Bradford, Grand Rapids, 18 January 2000.

127. Easley et al., 1–2.

128. Ibid., 13–19.

129. Mary Alice Williams, interview by Andy Schrier, Grand Rapids, 5 April 2000.

130. Ibid.

131. Ibid.

132. Easley et al., 22–23.

133. Ibid., 23.

134. Ibid., 15.

135. Ibid., 20.

136. Ibid., 22.

137. Morrow, interview.

138. Ibid.

139. Rev. Dick Ter Maat, interview by Andy Schrier, Otherway Ministries, Grand Rapids, 14 January 2000.

140. Ibid.

141. Ibid.

142. Ibid.

143. Ibid.

144. Ibid.

145. Ibid.

146. Ed Glynn, interview by Andy Schrier, Grand Rapids, 25 February 2000.

147. Morrow, interview.

148. Ed Salvin, interview by Andy Schrier, Grand Rapids, 21 January 2000; Joe Bulgarella, interview by Andy Schrier, Bulgarella Insurance Co., Grand Rapids, 6 January 2000; Ter Maat, interview.

149. Ibid.

150. Salvin, interview.

151. Ibid.; Bulgarella, interview; Ter Maat, interview.

152. Ter Maat, interview.

153. Salvin, interview

154. Al Calderon, interview by Andy Schrier, Grand Rapids, 23 February 2000.

155. John Szczytko, interview by Andy Schrier, West Grand Neighborhood Organization, Grand Rapids, 22 February 2000; "Neighborhood Watch Newsletter," (West Grand Neighborhood Organization, July 1999–January 2000).

156. Szczytko, interview.

157. Ibid.

158. Morrow, interview.

159. Ibid.

160. Carol Townsend, interview by Andy Schrier, Grand Rapids, 28 January 2000.

161. Roy Howard Beck, "Garfield Park Area Fights White Flight," *Grand Rapids Press*, 29 August 1973; "Integration Working in Garfield Park Neighborhoods," *Grand Rapids Press*, 1 December 1976; Don Jandernoa, telephone interview by Andy Schrier, Grand Rapids, 1 February 2000; Willie and Charles Wells, interview by Andy Schrier, Grand Rapids, 28 January 2000.

162. Jandernoa, interview.

163. Ted Roelofs, "At the Helm," *Grand Rapids Press*, 27 September 1987.

164. Townsend, Schrier interview.

165. Wells, interview; Townsend, interview; Jandernoa interview.

166. Townsend, Schrier interview.

167. Jim Swanlund, interview by Andy Schrier, Grand Rapids, 17 December 1999.

168. Ibid.; Townsend, Schrier interview; Wells, interview.

169. Wells, interview.

170. Townsend, Schrier interview.

171. Ibid.; Jandernoa, interview.

172. Townsend, Schrier interview.

173. Ibid.; Jandernoa, interview.

174. Townsend, Schrier interview; Jandernoa, interview.

175. Jandernoa, interview.

176. Ibid.

177. Ibid.

178. Roy Howard Beck, "Association Tries to Stabilize Garfield," *Grand Rapids Press*, 30 August 1973.

179. Jandernoa, interview.

180. Townsend, Schrier interview.

181. Ken Baldwin, interview by Andy Schrier, St. Francis Xavier Catholic Church, Grand Rapids, 15 February 2000.

182. Ted Roelofs, "A Group of Grand Rapidians is Taking its Neighborhoods Back Block by Block," *Grand Rapids Press*, 14 February 1999.

183. Gary W. Morrison, "Church Emphasizes Community Service," *Grand Rapids Press*, 23 October 1997; Baldwin, interview.

184. Baldwin, interview.

185. Ibid.

186. Gary W. Morrison, "Center Nurtures 'Abundant Life,'" *Grand Rapids Press*, 18 June 1998; Arthur Bailey, interview by Andy Schrier, Abundant Life Ministries, Grand Rapids, 18 February 2000.

187. Roelofs, "Group of Grand Rapidians."

188. Baldwin, interview; Bailey, interview.

189. James Jones, interview by Andy Schrier, Oakdale Park Christian Reformed Church, Grand Rapids, 15 February 2000.

190. Turner, interview.

191. Jones, interview.

192. Turner, interview.

193. Jones, interview.

194. "Southeast Area Neighborhood Body Organizes," *Grand Rapids Press*, 31 May 1974.

195. "Neighborhood Group Plans Parent Potluck," *Grand Rapids Press*, 6 November 1974.

196. Joe Rembert, interview by Andy Schrier, South East End Neighborhood Association, Grand Rapids, 22 February 2000.

197. Kelly, interview.

198. Rev. Bill Vanden Bosch, interview by Andy Schrier, Oakdale Park Christian Reformed Church, Grand Rapids, 28 February 2000.

199. Rembert, interview.

200. Kelly, interview; Rembert, interview.

201. Kelly, interview.

202. Peggy Watson, interview by Andy Schrier, South East End Neighborhood Association, Grand Rapids, 22 February 2000; Rembert, interview.

203. Vanden Bosch, interview.

204. Ibid.

205. Julie Stivers, interview by Andy Schrier, Grand Rapids, 17 February 2000.

206. Ibid.

207. Stoddard, interview.

208. Ibid.; Brian Malone, "Baxter Laundry Spawns Bigger Goals," *Grand Rapids Press*, 21 March 1975.

209. Holm, "How to Kill a Neighborhood."

210. Stoddard, interview; Malone, "Baxter Laundry."

211. Stivers, interview; Stoddard, interview.

212. Stoddard, interview.

213. Ibid.

214. Jim Mencarelli, "The Struggle of Madison Square," *Grand Rapids Press*, 27 September 1981.

215. Aida Conley, interview by Andy Schrier, Grand Rapids, 24 February 2000.

216. Tammy Moore, telephone interview by Andy Schrier, Grand Rapids, 17 February 2000; Etta May, interview by Andy Schrier, True Light Baptist Church, Grand Rapids, 15 March 2000.

217. Vivian Lewis, telephone interview by Andy Schrier, Grand Rapids, 14 April 2000.

218. May, interview.

219. Jonathan Bradford, interview by Andy Schrier, Inner City Christian Federation, Grand Rapids, 7 January 2000.

220. Ibid.; Frank Thomas, interview by Andy Schrier, Madison Food Town, Grand Rapids, 9 February 2000.

221. Noah Seifullah, interview by Andy Schrier, Grand Rapids Public Library, 16 February 2000.

222. John Sinkevics, "City Oks $100,000 Loan For Madison Square Grocery," *Grand Rapids Press*, 18 August 1982.

223. Thomas, interview.

224. Ed Hoogterp, "Promise of HUD Money Gives Life to Madison Square Housing," *Grand Rapids Press*, 2 October 1982; Seifullah, interview.

225. Seifullah, interview.

226. Thomas, interview; Mencarelli, "Struggle of Madison Square."

227. Denise L. Smith, "Man is Fatally Shot in Midst of Madison Street Fairgoers," *Grand Rapids Press*, 24 August 1986; Theresa D. McClellan, "'Nice Guy's Neighbors Can't Explain Motive Behind Slaying at Street Fair," *Grand Rapids Press*, 25 August 1986.

228. May, interview.

229. Seifullah, interview.

230. Conley, interview.

231. May, interview.

232. Seifullah, interview.

233. May, interview.

234. Ibid.

235. Seifullah, interview.

236. May, interview; Conley, interview; Thomas, interview.

237. Laura Carpenter, interview by Nate Bradford, Madison Square Christian Reformed Church, Grand Rapids, 15 February 2000.

238. Renira Reed, interview by Andy Schrier, Restorers, Inc., Grand Rapids, 13 June 2000.

239. May, interview.

240. Thomas, interview.

241. Tom Fitzgerald, "Residents in Alger Heights Close Ranks Against Crime," *Grand Rapids Press*, 15 December 1982.

242. Mary Beuche, interview by Andy Schrier, Creston Neighborhood Association, Grand Rapids, 20 January 2000.

243. Ibid.

244. Ibid.

245. Ruth Gorniewicz, interview by Andy Schrier, Grand Rapids, 17 November 1999; Lisa Johnson, "Neighbors Want Commission to Lift Rabbit Lounge's License," *Grand Rapids Press*, 1 July 1986; Chris Meehan, "Parents Press Quest For Clues To Son's Killing," *Grand Rapids Press*, 29 July 1990.

246. Tracy L. Sypert, "Commission Hears Impassioned Plea for Bar Closing," *Grand Rapids Press*, 2 July 1986.

247. Jim Mencarelli, "SE Side Group Beefs Up Fund to Fight Crime," *Grand Rapids Press*, 19 April 1988; Gail Peterson, "Q & A: War against Racism Must Start at Home," *Grand Rapids Press*, 18 January 1988.

248. Lisa Johnson, "Zoning Change is Sought for 3 City Neighborhoods," *Grand Rapids Press*, 8 July 1991.

249. Rebecca Smith-Hoffman, telephone interview by Andy Schrier, Grand Rapids, 29 November 1999.

250. Kathryn Caliendo and Cindy Koning, interview by Andy Schrier, East Hills Council of Neighbors Office, Grand Rapids, 21 December 1999.

251. Tammy Bergstrom, "Dealing Homes to Take Out Crime," *Grand Rapids Magazine* (January 1994).

252. Richard Louv, "Neighbors Unite in Creative Effort for Better Future," *San Diego Union Tribune*, 1 July 1992.

253. Theresa D. McClellan, "Home Rules: Cherry Hills Neighbors Eye Historic Status," *Grand Rapids Press*, 12 June 1994.

254. Dan Bollman, "Network News," *Michigan Historic Preservation* (Fall 1994).

255. "How to Own Your Own Home Just When You Thought You Couldn't," (Cherry Hill Association Bulletin).

256. Jim Winter-Troutwine, interview by Andy Schrier, Grand Rapids, 25 March 2000.

257. Caliendo and Koning, interview.

258. Gorniewicz, interview.

259. Stanley and Marjorie Davis, interview by Nate Bradford and Andy Schrier, Grand Rapids, 25 October 1999.

260. Orville Hoxie, telephone interview by Andy Schrier, Grand Rapids, 13 January 2000.

261. Ingham, Forsetlund-Clawson, Taylor, and Powell, interview.

262. Koelzer, interview.

263. Paul Haan, interview by Andy Schrier, Grand Rapids, 23 December 1999; Rose Doering, interview by Andy Schrier, Grand Rapids, 29 January 2000.

264. Sr. Roberta Hefferan, interview by Andy Schrier, St. Alphonsus, Grand Rapids, 1 May 2000.

265. Haan, interview.

266. Beuche, interview.

267. Hefferan, interview.

268. Ted Roelofs, "The Herkimer: 1887–1987, A Landmark on South Division is Home to Forgotten People," *Grand Rapids Press*, 22 November 1987.

269. Brinks, 12.

270. Roelofs, "Herkimer."

271. Brinks, 12.

272. Ibid., 12–13.

273. Dennis Sturtevant, interview by Andy Schrier, Dwelling Place, Inc., Grand Rapids, 30 November 1999.

274. Ibid.

275. "Planning Hope in the Heart of the City," (pamphlet published by Dwelling Place and the United Way, Grand Rapids).

276. Ed Golder, "Dwelling Place Trying to Buy Herkimer Hotel," *Grand Rapids Press*, 6 December 1992.

277. Peter Wege, interview by Linda Samuelson and Andy Schrier, Grand Rapids, 8 June 2000.

278. Sandy Hogue, interview by Andy Schrier, Grand Rapids, 25 November 1999.

279. Sturtevant, interview.

280. Ibid.

281. Dennis Sturtevant, "Heartside Neighborhood Revitalization Plan," (Heartside Planning Coalition, July 1996).

282. Ibid.

283. "Heartside Main Street Initiative," (flyer submitted to the Grand Rapids Area Council for the Humanities by Dennis Sturtevant).

284. Sturtevant, interview.

285. "Arts Market Drawing up Attention for Heartside," *Grand Rapids Press*, 26 August 1999; Gary Morrison, "Artists Decorate Wall at Heartside Ministry," *Grand Rapids Press*, 24 June 1999.

286. Sam Cummings, interview by Andy Schrier, Grand Rapids, 29 November 1999.

287. Brinks, 15.

288. Sturtevant, interview.

289. Holm, "How to Kill Neighborhood."

290. Gerald and Evelyn Wright, interview by Andy Schrier, Grand Rapids, 7 April 2000.

291. Holm, "How to Kill Neighborhood."

292. Wright, interview.

293. Ibid.

294. Rita M. Rouse, "Rumbling School Busses Drive Residents to Threaten More Pressure," *Grand Rapids Press*, 29 July 1981.

295. Wright, interview.

296. Ibid.; Doug Guthrie, "Suspect Arrested in Highland Park Slaying," *Grand Rapids Press*, 17 June 1999; Margarita Bauza, "Slain Teen's Supporters Raise Money for Park," *Grand Rapids Press*, 16 August 1999.

297. Wright, interview.

Section IV - Vignette Notes

A Fighting Family

1. Mary Lu Sulentich, "A Conversation with Helen Jackson Claytor," *Grand River Valley History* 12 (1995): 17.

2. Ibid., 18.

3. Maris Brancheau, "Quiet Change," *The Paper*, 11- 17 February 1999.

4. Dave Murray, "Madison Ave. Health Clinic Dedicated," *Grand Rapids Press*, 21 June 2000.

Paul I. Phillips

1. Biographical Folder, Paul Phillips Collection, located in the Local History Department of the Grand Rapids Public Library.

2. "It's Up to the Negro Now: Phillips Says Door is Open, But He Must Walk Through it Himself," *Grand Rapids Press*, 14 November 1969; "Urban League Will Match Negro Skills to Jobs Here," *Grand Rapids Press*, 4 March 1964.

3. Paul I. Phillips, "Brief Account of Our 25 Years of Stewardship," Paul Phillips Collection, 1971, 3-4.

4. Ibid.

5. Ibid., 5.

Roger Wilkins

1. Roger Wilkins, *A Man's Life: An Autobiography* (New York: Simon and Schuster, 1982), 40.

A Neighborhood that Broke the Color Barrier

1. Pat Shellenbarger, "A Neighborhood that Broke the Color Barrier," *Grand Rapids Press*, 5 February 1995.

Race

1. Wilkins, 41.

Clancy Street Ministries

1. Faas, interview.

Michigan Street: This Was My World

1. Bonnie Barber Hamlin, (text submitted to the Grand Rapids Area Council for the Humanities, July 2001).

Chuck Assenco

1. Assenco, interview.

Back to the Future at Fountain School

1. Teacher Mark Dykstra's 4th grade class, Fountain School, 1997.

Wealthy Theatre

1. Moore, interview.

2. Ibid.

3. Wealthy Theatre Historic Designation Study Committee Final Report.

4. Ibid.

5. Carol Moore, "Wealthy Street Business District Building Occupant Survey," 1988.

6. Tracy L. Sypert, "Biermeister Renovation Project to Benefit Wealthy Street Area," *Grand Rapids Press*, 4 November 1988.

7. Peterson, interview.

8. Assenco, interview.

9. Assenco, interview; Moore, interview.

10. "Renewed Wealthy Theatre Opens, Hosts Events Today," *Grand Rapids Press*, 11 September 1999.

11. Moore, interview.

12. Sypert, "Biermeister Renovation."

13. Moore, interview.

The Navarros

1. Navarro, interview.

The Black Hills

1. Jerry and Judy Rose, interview by Andy Schrier, Grand Rapids, November 1999.

Peter C. Cook: Firmly Rooted in Grandville Avenue

1. Peter Cook, interview by Lane Den Boer and Linda Sameulson, Grand Rapids, 15 August 1999.

Grand Rapids Indians at the Millennium

1. Levi Rickert, (text submitted to the Grand Rapids Area Council for the Humanities, 1999).

Ter Maat at Otherway Ministries

1. Ter Maat, interview.

Herschell Turner

1. Turner, interview.
2. "For GR Man, Playing with the Trotters was Time of Awakening," *Grand Rapids Press*, 31 January 1996.
3. Chaffee, "Job Done."
4. Charles Honey, "Frontiers to Pride," *Grand Rapids Press*, 16 March 1994.
5. Turner, interview.

A Philadelphia Story

1. Charles Honey, (text submitted to the Grand Rapids Area Council for the Humanities, 1999).

Home Repair Services

1. Bob Hengeveld, interview by Andy Schrier, Home Repair Services, Grand Rapids, 14 February 2000.

Rediscovering an Old Jewel

1. Captain Mark Herald, interview by Nate Bradford, Grand Rapids Police Department, 16 June 1999.
2. Officer Tom Opperman, interview by Nate Bradford and Andy Schrier, Grand Rapids, 6 January 2000.
3. Officer Dave Nowakowski, interview by Nate Bradford and Andy Schrier, Grand Rapids, 6 January 2000.

Rallying Around Kay Pharmacy

1. Koelzer, interview; Mary Radigan, "Pharmacy Mixes Rx for Success," *Grand Rapids Press*, 25 June 1995.

Growing Up in the Wonder Years

1. Hank Meijer, "Growing Up in Grand Rapids Graduation Season Invites Nostalgia on the Home Front," *Grand Rapids Press*, 19 June 1994.

The Royce Family – A North End Legacy

1. Charles and Stella Royce, interview by Linda Samuelson and Andy Schrier, Grand Rapids, 2 June 2000.

"Everlastingly at It"

1. Bratt and Meehan, 124.
2. "Serving 75 Years," *Mel Trotter Mission Messenger* (1975); Melvin Trotter, *These Forty Years* (Grand Rapids: Zondervan Publishing, 1940), 14.
3. George Heartwell, interview by Andy Schrier, Aquinas College, Grand Rapids, 14 April 2000.

Longtime Neighbors

1. Lillian Grissen, *For Such a Time as This: Twenty Six Women of Vision and Faith Tell Their Stories* (Grand Rapids: Eerdmans Publishing, 1991).

Section IV– Photo Credits

FIG. 1.   Grand Rapids City Archives.
FIG. 2.   GRPL, 113–3–18.
FIG. 3.   GRPL, 113–3–18.
FIG. 4.   Grand Rapids Area Council for the Humanities.
FIG. 5.   Gift of Ron Carowitz, GRPL, Coll. 54–17–7.5.
FIG. 6.   GRPL, 113–3–30.
FIG. 7.   GRPL, Coll. 125–H002035.
FIG. 8.   GRPL, Coll. 125–H002037.
FIG. 9.   GRPL, Coll. 125–H008925.
FIG. 10. Roger Wilkins, *A Man's Life: An Autobiography* (Woodbridge, CT: Ox Bow Press, 1991), front cover photo.
FIG. 11. GRPL, 54–27–27.
FIG. 12. *GR Press.*
FIG. 13. *GR Press.*
FIG. 14. *GR Press.*
FIG. 15. Grand Rapids City Archives.
FIG. 16. *GR Press.*
FIG. 17. *GR Press.*
FIG. 18. Grand Rapids Area Council for the Humanities.
FIG. 19. Grand Rapids Area Council for the Humanities.
FIG. 20. Grand Rapids Area Council for the Humanities.
FIG. 21. Grand Rapids Area Council for the Humanities.
FIG. 22. Grand Rapids City Archives.
FIG. 23. Grand Rapids City Archives.
FIG. 24. Garfield Park Neighborhood Association.
FIG. 25. *GR Press.*
FIG. 26. Grand Rapids City Archives.
FIG. 27. Grand Rapids City Archives.
FIG. 28. GRPL, 212–2–7.
FIG. 29. Eastown Community Association.
FIG. 30. Grand Rapids Planning Department.
FIG. 31. *GR Press.*
FIG. 32. Inner City Christian Federation.
FIG. 33. Grand Rapids Area Council for the Humanities.
FIG. 34. City of Grand Rapids Community Development.
FIG. 35. GRPL, 141–10–16.
FIG. 36. Grand Rapids Area Council for the Humanities.
FIG. 37. Grand Rapids Area Council for the Humanities.
FIG. 38. Grand Rapids Area Council for the Humanities.
FIG. 39. Grand Rapids Area Council for the Humanities.
FIG. 40. Butterworth Good Neighbors Program.
FIG. 41. Grand Rapids Area Council for the Humanities.
FIG. 42. Grand Rapids Area Council for the Humanities.
FIG. 43. Grand Rapids Area Council for the Humanities.
FIG. 44. Grand Rapids Area Council for the Humanities.
FIG. 45. GRPL, Coll. 286.
FIG. 46. GRPL, Coll. 286.
FIG. 47. GRPL, Coll. 286.
FIG. 48. G. R. City Assessor's Office.
FIG. 49. G. R. City Assessor's Office.
FIG. 50. GRPL, Coll. 286.
FIG. 51. GRPL, Coll. 286.
FIG. 52. GRPL, Coll. 286.

FIG. 53. GRPL, Coll. 286.

FIG. 54. *GR Press.*

FIG. 55. *GR Press.*

FIG. 56. GRPL, 54–19–12.

FIG. 57. Courtesy of M. Christine Byron and Thomas R. Wilson.

FIG. 58. GRPL, 54–6–1.

FIG. 59. Grand Rapids Area Council for the Humanities.

FIG. 60. Courtesy of Chuck Assenco.

FIG. 61. Courtesy of Chuck Assenco.

FIG. 62. Courtesy of Chuck Assenco.

FIG. 63. *GR Press.*

FIG. 64. Grand Rapids Area Council for the Humanities.

FIG. 65. *GR Press.*

FIG. 66. Grand Rapids Area Council for the Humanities, Fountain School students.

FIG. 67. Grand Rapids Area Council for the Humanities, Fountain School students.

FIG. 68. Grand Rapids Area Council for the Humanities, Fountain School students.

FIG. 69. Grand Rapids Area Council for the Humanities, Fountain School students.

FIG. 70. Grand Rapids Area Council for the Humanities, Fountain School students.

FIG. 70. Grand Rapids Area Council for the Humanities, Fountain School students.

FIG. 72. Grand Rapids Area Council for the Humanities, Fountain School students.

FIG. 73. Grand Rapids Area Council for the Humanities, Fountain School students.

FIG. 74. Grand Rapids Area Council for the Humanities, Fountain School students.

FIG. 75. Grand Rapids Area Council for the Humanities, Fountain School students.

FIG. 76. Grand Rapids Area Council for the Humanities, Fountain School students.

FIG. 77. Grand Rapids Area Council for the Humanities, Fountain School students.

FIG. 78. Grand Rapids Area Council for the Humanities, Fountain School students.

FIG. 79. Grand Rapids Area Council for the Humanities, Fountain School students.

FIG. 80. Grand Rapids Area Council for the Humanities, Fountain School students.

FIG. 81. Grand Rapids Area Council for the Humanities, Fountain School students.

FIG. 82. Courtesy of Beverly Farrow.

FIG. 83. GRPL, 165–2–4.

FIG. 84. Grand Rapids Area Council for the Humanities.

FIG. 85. Baxter Community Center.

FIG. 86. Baxter Community Center.

FIG. 87. GRPL, Coll. 125 – P112701B.

FIG. 88. Baxter Community Center.

FIG. 89. Grand Rapids Area Council for the Humanities.

FIG. 90. *GR Press.*

FIG. 91. *GR Press.*

FIG. 92. GRPL, Coll. 125 – E204549.

FIG. 93. Grand Rapids Area Council for the Humanities.

FIG. 94. Grand Rapids Area Council for the Humanities.

FIG. 95. Grand Rapids Area Council for the Humanities.

FIG. 96. Grand Rapids Area Council for the Humanities.

FIG. 97. Grand Rapids Area Council for the Humanities.

FIG. 98. Grand Rapids Area Council for the Humanities.

FIG. 99. Grand Rapids Area Council for the Humanities.

FIG. 100. Grand Rapids Area Council for the Humanities.

FIG. 101. Grand Rapids Area Council for the Humanities.

FIG. 102. Grand Rapids Area Council for the Humanities.

FIG. 103. Grand Rapids Area Council for the Humanities.

FIG. 104. Grand Rapids City Assessor.

FIG. 105. Grand Rapids City Assessor.

FIG. 106. Grand Rapids Area Council for the Humanities.

FIG. 107. Homework House.

FIG. 108. Grand Rapids Area Council for the Humanities.

FIG. 109. Courtesy of Judy and Jerry Rose.

FIG. 110. Courtesy of Judy and Jerry Rose.

FIG. 111. Courtesy of Judy and Jerry Rose.

FIG. 112. Courtesy of Judy and Jerry Rose.

FIG. 113. Grand Rapids Area Council for the Humanities.

FIG. 114. Courtesy of Peter Cook.

FIG. 115. Courtesy of Peter Cook.

FIG. 116. Courtesy of Peter Cook.

FIG. 117. Courtesy of Peter Cook.

FIG. 118. Courtesy of Peter Cook.

FIG. 119. Courtesy of Peter Cook.

FIG. 120. Courtesy of Peter Cook.

FIG. 121. Grand Rapids Area Council for the Humanities.

FIG. 122. *GR Press.*

FIG. 123. Grand Rapids Area Council for the Humanities.

FIG. 124. Grand Rapids Area Council for the Humanities.

FIG. 125. Grand Rapids Area Council for the Humanities.

FIG. 126. *GR Press.*

FIG. 127. Aquinas College Archives.

FIG. 128. Courtesy of Frances Geib.

FIG. 129. Grand Rapids Area Council for the Humanities.

FIG. 130. Eastown Community Association.

FIG. 131. Courtesy of Robert Verhey.

FIG. 132. Grand Rapids Area Council for the Humanities.

FIG. 133. Eastown Community Association.

FIG. 134. Grand Rapids Area Council for the Humanities.

FIG. 135. Grand Rapids Area Council for the Humanities.

FIG. 136. Grand Rapids Area Council for the Humanities.

FIG. 137. GRPL, Coll. 212–1–4.

FIG. 138. *GR Press.*

FIG. 139. Grand Rapids Area Council for the Humanities.

FIG. 140. Grand Rapids Area Council for the Humanities.

FIG. 141. Grand Rapids Area Council for the Humanities.

FIG. 142. Grand Rapids Area Council for the Humanities.

FIG. 143. Otherway Ministries.

FIG. 144. Otherway Ministries.

FIG. 145. Union High School Yearbook, 1970.

FIG. 146. South West Area Neighbors.

FIG. 147. Grand Rapids Area Council for the Humanities.

FIG. 148. Grand Rapids Area Council for the Humanities.

FIG. 149. Grand Rapids Area Council for the Humanities.

FIG. 150. Grand Rapids Area Council for the Humanities.

FIG. 151. Grand Rapids Area Council for the Humanities.

FIG. 152. Courtesy of M. Christine Byron and Thomas R. Wilson.

FIG. 153. GRPL, Coll. 125 – 034921.

FIG. 154. *GR Press.*

FIG. 155. *GR Press.*

FIG. 156. Grand Rapids Area Council for the Humanities (top), Garfield Park Neighborhood Association (bottom).

FIG. 157. Grand Rapids City Archives.

FIG. 158. *GR Press.*

FIG. 159. Grand Rapids Area Council for the Humanities.

FIG. 160. Grand Rapids Area Council for the Humanities.

FIG. 161. Grand Rapids Area Council for the Humanities.

FIG. 162. *GR Press.*

FIG. 163. Courtesy of Charles Honey.

FIG. 164. Courtesy of Charles Honey.

FIG. 165. Eastown Neighborhood Association.

FIG. 166. Oakdale Park Christian Reformed Church.

FIG. 167. Grand Rapids Area Council for the Humanities.

FIG. 168. Courtesy of Boston House Restaurant.

FIG. 169. Courtesy of Boston House Restaurant.

FIG. 170. Courtesy of Jerry VanAmerongen.

FIG. 171. Grand Rapids Area Council for the Humanities.

FIG. 172. Grand Rapids Area Council for the Humanities.

FIG. 173. Grand Rapids Area Council for the Humanities.

FIG. 174. Grand Rapids Area Council for the Humanities.

FIG. 175. Grand Rapids Area Council for the Humanities.

FIG. 176. Grand Rapids Area Council for the Humanities.

FIG. 177. Courtesy of Jerry Di Trapani.

FIG. 178. GRPL, 138–4–7.

FIG. 179. Grand Rapids Area Council for the Humanities.

FIG. 180. Grand Rapids Area Council for the Humanities.

FIG. 181. Grand Rapids Area Council for the Humanities.

FIG. 182. Inner City Christian Federation.

FIG. 183. Gemini Publications.

FIG. 184. Grand Rapids Area Council for the Humanities.

FIG. 185. *GR Press.*

FIG. 186. Grand Rapids Area Council for the Humanities.

FIG. 187. Madison Square Christian Reformed Church.

FIG. 188. Home Repair Services.

FIG. 189. Home Repair Services.

FIG. 190. Courtesy of William Hegarty.

FIG. 191. Courtesy of William Hegarty.

FIG. 192. Grand Rapids Area Council for the Humanities.

FIG. 193. Grand Rapids Area Council for the Humanities.

FIG. 194. Grand Rapids Area Council for the Humanities.

FIG. 195. Grand Rapids Area Council for the Humanities.

FIG. 196. Grand Rapids Area Council for the Humanities.

FIG. 197. Grand Rapids Area Council for the Humanities.

FIG. 198. Grand Rapids Area Council for the Humanities.

FIG. 199. Grand Rapids Area Council for the Humanities.

FIG. 200. Grand Rapids Area Council for the Humanities.

FIG. 201. Grand Rapids Area Council for the Humanities.

FIG. 202. Grand Rapids Area Council for the Humanities.

FIG. 203. Grand Rapids Area Council for the Humanities.

FIG. 204. Grand Rapids Area Council for the Humanities.

FIG. 205. Grand Rapids Area Council for the Humanities.

FIG. 206. Grand Rapids Area Council for the Humanities.

FIG. 207. Grand Rapids Area Council for the Humanities.

FIG. 208. Grand Rapids Area Council for the Humanities.

FIG. 209. Grand Rapids Area Council for the Humanities.

FIG. 210. Grand Rapids Area Council for the Humanities.

FIG. 211. Creston High School Yearbook, 1939.

FIG. 212. Grand Rapids Area Council for the Humanities.

FIG. 213. Courtesy of the Koelzer family.

FIG. 214. Courtesy Hank Meijer.

FIG. 215. Courtesy of the Meijer family.

FIG. 216. Courtesy of the Royce family.

FIG. 217. Courtesy of the Royce family.

FIG. 218. Grand Rapids Area Council for the Humanities.

FIG. 219. *GR Press.*

FIG. 220. Courtesy of Peter Wege.

FIG. 221. Grand Rapids Area Council for the Humanities.

FIG. 222. *GR Press.*

FIG. 223. Grand Rapids Area Council for the Humanities.

FIG. 224. GRPL, 54–36–23.

FIG. 225. Heartside Ministries.

FIG. 226. Grand Rapids Area Council for the Humanities.

FIG. 227. Grand Rapids Area Council for the Humanities.

FIG. 228. Grand Rapids Area Council for the Humanities.

FIG. 229. Grand Rapids Area Council for the Humanities.

FIG. 230. Grand Rapids Area Council for the Humanities.

FIG. 231. Grand Rapids Area Council for the Humanities.

FIG. 232. Eduard Skendzel, *The Sacred Heart Story* (Grand Rapids, MI: Eduard Skendzel, 1981), dust jacket photo.

FIG. 233. Grand Rapids City Assessor's Office.

FIG. 234. Grand Rapids Area Council for the Humanities.

FIG. 235. Grand Rapids Area Council for the Humanities.

FIG. 236. GRPL, 78–2–23.

FIG. 237. Grand Rapids City Archives.

FIG. 238. Grand Rapids Area Council for the Humanities.

FIG. 239. Bethany Christian Services.

FIG. 240. Bethany Christian Services.

FIG. 241. Grand Rapids Area Council for the Humanities.

Every effort has been made to contact copyright holders. The project director would be pleased to hear from any copyright holders not acknowledged above.

Index

Numbers in italic refer to photos.

Grand Rapids, Mich., Michigan Soldiers Home.

Grand Rapids, Mich., Ramona Theatre, Reed's Lake.

CANAL STREET, GRAND RAPIDS, MICH.   PEARL STREET,   MONROE STREET, GRAND RAPIDS, MICH.

MONUMENT PARK, GRAND RAPIDS, MICH.   MONROE AND S. DIVISION STS., GRAND RAPIDS, MICH.